Friedrich Nietzsche and Weimar Classicism

Studies in German Literature, Linguistics, and Culture

Edited by James Hardin
(*South Carolina*)

Friedrich Nietzsche and Weimar Classicism

Paul Bishop and R. H. Stephenson

CAMDEN HOUSE

First published 2005
by Camden House

Camden House is an imprint of Boydell & Brewer Inc.
668 Mt. Hope Avenue, Rochester, NY 14620, USA
www.camden-house.com
and of Boydell & Brewer Limited
PO Box 9, Woodbridge, Suffolk IP12 3DF, UK
www.boydellandbrewer.com

ISBN: 1–57113–280–5

Library of Congress Cataloging-in-Publication Data

Bishop, Paul, 1967–
    Friedrich Nietzsche and Weimar Classicism / Paul Bishop and R. H.
Stephenson
        p. cm. — (Studies in German literature, linguistics, and culture)
    Includes bibliographical references and index.
    ISBN 1–57113–280–5 (hardcover: alk. paper)
    1. Nietzsche, Friedrich Wilhelm, 1844–1900. 2. Aesthetics,
Modern—19th century. 3. German literature—18th century—History
and criticism. 4. Classicism—Germany—Weimar (Thuringia)—
History—18th century. 5. Schiller, Friedrich, 1759–1805. 6. Goethe,
Johann Wolfgang von, 1749–1832. I. Stephenson, R. H. (Roger H.).
II. Title. III. Series: Studies in German literature, linguistics, and
culture (Unnumbered)

B3318.A4B54 2004
193—dc22

2004019956

A catalogue record for this title is available from the British Library.

This publication is printed on acid-free paper.
Printed in the United States of America.

Contents

Es war nur Schein, allein der Schein war groß.

[It was only semblance, but the semblance was great.]

— Goethe, *Faust* Part Two

*Wirklich den Pessimismus ü b e r w i n d e n —; ein Goethischer
Blick voll Liebe und gutem Willen als Resultat.*

[Truly to *overcome* pessimism —; a Goethean glance full of love
and good will as the result.]

— Nietzsche, Nachlass, Autumn 1887

*[Goethe] hat das Spiel des Werdens als "wahrer Schein" durchschaut,
als einen Schein, der das Wesen nicht verhüllt, sondern offenbart.*

[Goethe penetrated the play of becoming as "true illusion," as an
illusion that does not conceal but rather reveals being.]

— Ernst Cassirer, *Freiheit und Form*

Acknowledgments

THIS BOOK HAS BEEN WRITTEN as part of the Arts and Humanities Research Board funded Large Research Project "Conceptions of Cultural Studies in Cassirer's Philosophy of Symbolic Forms," on which both authors are engaged. We are grateful to the AHRB for funding this project, and for providing a framework for our common research interests. Much of the book emerged from intensive discussions arising from our teaching at various levels, both undergraduate and postgraduate, in the Department of German Language and Literature at the University of Glasgow. And so some co-taught classes, such as those on the M. Phil. course "Modern German Thought" delivered in the context of the AHRB Cassirer Project, have given rise to a co-authored book, in which each of us became involved in all the various aspects of its development. In other ways, too, the Cassirer Project, on which our colleagues John Krois (Humboldt Universität, Berlin) and Graham Whitaker (Glasgow University Library) are also engaged, has helped crystallize for us some of the central affinities between Weimar Classicism and Nietzsche's philosophy, and helped clarify the relevance of both for the "postmodern" age.

Earlier versions of chapters 1 and 3, which have been revised and rewritten for this volume, appeared in the following journals: "Nietzsche and Weimar Aesthetics," *German Life and Letters* 52 (1999): 412–29; and "Zarathustras Evangelium des Schönen: Nietzsche und die klassische Weimarer Ästhetik," *Sprachkunst: Beiträge zur Literaturwissenschaft* 32 (2001): 1–26. We are grateful to the publishers of these journals, Blackwell and the Österreichische Akademie der Wissenschaften, for permission to draw on this material.

Our thanks go to Meta Jamison for her technical assistance with the production of the preliminary as well as the final version of the manuscript; and to Sue Innes for her precise and helpful copyediting.

For financial assistance in the production of this book, the authors would like to thank Noël Peacock, Associate Dean (for Research) and Convenor of the Faculty Research Committee of the Faculty of Arts and Divinity of the University of Glasgow.

P. B.; R. S.

A Note on Editions, Abbreviations, and Translations

THE FOLLOWING EDITIONS OF Nietzsche's works and correspondence have been used:

Friedrich Nietzsche, *Sämtliche Werke: Kritische Studienausgabe*, ed. Giorgio Colli and Mazzino Montinari, 15 vols. (Berlin and New York/Munich: Walter de Gruyter/Deutscher Taschenbuch Verlag, 1967–77 and 1988). Cited as KSA followed by volume and page reference.

Friedrich Nietzsche, *Sämtliche Briefe: Kritische Studienausgabe*, ed. Giorgio Colli and Mazzino Montinari, 8 vols. (Berlin and New York/Munich: Walter der Gruyter/Deutscher Taschenbuch Verlag, 1975–84). Cited as KSB followed by volume and page reference.

To refer to individual works by Nietzsche, the following abbreviations are used:

PTZ = *Die Philosophie im tragischen Zeitalter der Griechen* (Philosophy in the Tragic Age of the Greeks)

GT = *Die Geburt der Tragödie* (The Birth of Tragedy)

UB = *Unzeitgemässe Betrachtungen* (Untimely Meditations)

MA = *Menschliches, Allzumenschliches* (Human, All Too Human)

M = *Morgenröthe* (Daybreak)

FW = *Die fröhliche Wissenschaft* (The Gay Science)

Z = *Also sprach Zarathustra* (Thus Spoke Zarathustra)

JGB = *Jenseits von Gut und Böse* (Beyond Good and Evil)

GM = *Zur Genealogie der Moral* (On the Genealogy of Morals)

GD = *Götzen-Dämmerung* (Twilight of the Idols)

EH = *Ecce Homo* (Ecce Homo)

AC = *Der Anti-Christ* (The Antichrist)

WM = *Der Wille zur Macht* (The Will to Power)

The following translations of Nietzsche's works have been consulted as a basis for our own translations (listed in chronological order of first publication):

The Birth of Tragedy, from *Basic Writings of Nietzsche,* ed. and trans. Walter Kaufmann (New York: The Modern Library, 1968), 1–144; *Untimely Meditations,* trans. R. J. Hollingdale (Cambridge: Cambridge UP, 1983); *Human, All Too Human,* trans. R. J. Hollingdale (Cambridge: Cambridge UP, 1986); *Daybreak,* trans. R. J. Hollingdale (Cambridge: Cambridge UP, 1982); *The Gay Science,* trans. Walter Kaufmann (New York: Vintage Books, 1974); *Thus Spoke Zarathustra,* in *The Portable Nietzsche,* ed. and trans. Walter Kaufmann (New York: Viking Penguin, 1954), 103–439, and *Thus Spoke Zarathustra,* trans. R. J. Hollingdale (Harmondsworth: Penguin, 1961); *Beyond Good and Evil,* from *Basic Writings of Nietzsche,* 179–435; *On the Genealogy of Morals,* from *Basic Writings of Nietzsche,* 437–599; *Twilight of the Idols,* from *The Portable Nietzsche,* 463–563; *Ecce Homo,* from *Basic Writings of Nietzsche,* 655–791; *The Antichrist,* from *The Portable Nietzsche,* 565–656; *Dithyrambs of Dionysus,* trans. R. J. Hollingdale (London: Anvil Press Poetry, 1984); *The Will to Power,* ed. Walter Kaufmann, trans. Walter Kaufmann and R. J. Hollingdale (New York: Vintage Books, 1968).

To refer to works by Goethe, Schiller, and Schelling, the following editions and abbreviations have been used:

Johann Wolfgang Goethe, *Werke,* ed. Erich Trunz, 14 vols. (Hamburg: Christian Wegner, 1948–60; Munich: Beck, 1981); *Hamburger Ausgabe.* Cited as HA.

Johann Wolfgang Goethe, *Werke: Weimarer Ausgabe,* edited by Johann Ludwig Gustav von Loeper, Erich Schmidt, and Paul Raabe, im Auftrage der Großherzogin Sophie von Sachsen; 4 parts, 133 vols. in 143 (Weimar: Hermann Böhlau, 1887–1919); *Weimarer Ausgabe.* Cited as WA.

Friedrich Schiller, *Werke: Nationalausgabe,* edited by Julius Peterson and Gerhard Fricke, im Auftrag des Goethe- und Schiller Archivs, des Schiller-Nationalmuseums und der Deutschen Akademie, 43 vols. (Weimar: Hermann Böhlaus Nachfolger, 1943–); *Nationalausgabe.* Cited as NA.

Friedrich Wilhelm Joseph Schelling, *Sämmtliche Werke,* ed. Karl Friedrich August Schelling, 14 vols. (Stuttgart: Cotta, 1856–61). Cited as SW.

References to Goethe's *Faust* are given by line number; the following translations have been consulted:

Johann Wolfgang von Goethe, *Faust: Part One,* trans. David Luke (Oxford and New York: Oxford UP, 1987) and *Faust: Part Two,* trans. David Luke (Oxford and New York: Oxford UP, 1994).

Johann Wolfgang von Goethe, *Faust: A Tragedy,* ed. Cyrus Hamlin, trans. Walter Arndt, Norton Critical Edition (2nd ed., New York and London: W. W. Norton, 2001).

The following work has been used as a basis for the translations of Schiller's *Ueber die ästhetische Erziehung:*

Friedrich Schiller, *On the Aesthetic Education of Man in a Series of Letters,* ed. and trans. Elizabeth M. Wilkinson and L. A. Willoughby, with introduction, commentary, and glossary of terms (2nd ed., Oxford: Clarendon P, 1982).

Introduction

Meine allgemeine Aufgabe: zu zeigen, wie Leben Philosophie und Kunst ein tieferes und verwandtschaftliches Verhältniss zu einander haben können, ohne dass die Philosophie flach ist und das Leben des Philosophen lügenhaft wird.

[My general task is to show how life, philosophy, and art can have a deeper and familial relationship to each other, without philosophy being shallow and the life of the philosopher becoming untruthful.]

Nietzsche, 6[17]; KSA 8:104

ACCORDING TO FRIEDRICH NIETZSCHE, the meaning of an object may be revealed by tracing its origin, which is uncovered by genealogy. Certainly, there has been no lack of studies placing him, genealogically, in relation to Immanuel Kant, Friedrich Wilhelm Joseph Schelling, Arthur Schopenhauer, Richard Wagner, and so forth, and this with good reason. In this book, we shall argue that the missing *perspective,* to use one of Nietzsche's favorite terms, is that of Weimar Classicism. When this perspective, the *Kulturkampf* or "cultural struggle" waged by Goethe and Schiller, is overlooked, the framework, and hence the structure, of Nietzsche's thinking is distorted to the point of unintelligibility. Once restored, however, this perspective opens up afresh the coherence and purposiveness in Nietzsche's philosophical aesthetics.

Friedrich Nietzsche's education at Schulpforta, where he studied from 1858 to 1864, gave him access to the world of the ancient classics, as well as to the Weimar classicists of the previous generation, Johann Wolfgang Goethe and Friedrich Schiller. In his biography of Nietzsche, Curt Paul Janz reminds us that "die Jugend, die hier aufwuchs [. . .], ging auf in der Welt von Hellas und Rom und in der Welt Goethes und Schillers" ("the young men who grew up here . . . did so in the world of ancient Greece and Rome, and in the world of Goethe and Schiller.")[1] In *Die Geburt der Tragödie* (*The Birth of Tragedy,* 1872), Nietzsche makes constant allusion to Schiller in general and to his concept of "aesthetic semblance" in particular, as well as to Goethe. So when Nietzsche, who had devoured Schiller's aesthetic writings when he was still at school, speaks of the world as being justified "only as an aesthetic phenomenon" (*nur als aesthetisches Phänomen*), he is thinking of Schiller's concept of the aesthetic as a fusion of physical and intellectual experience (*GT* Versuch §5; KSA 1:17; cf. *GT* §5 and §24; KSA 1:47 and 152). Similarly, Nietzsche's immensely influential "polaristic thinking" (that is, thinking in terms of polar opposites), in which each term (such as the Apollonian and the Dionysian) is affirmative and exists in its own right, rather than as a negation of the other, is inherited via Goethe. More specifically, Nietzsche draws from Weimar Classicism the distinction between *Schein des Scheins* (*falscher/logischer Schein*) and *Schein des Seins* (*wahrer/aufrichtiger Schein*); a mode of argumentation usefully called "binary synthesis";[2] and the notion of transformation (*Verwandlung, Veredlung, Verklärung*) through the aesthetic. Later, Nietzsche regretted using Kantian and Schopenhauerian terminology in *Die Geburt der Tragödie;* but he let stand the alignment of his concept of the Apollonian with Schiller's idea of the naïve. And in all his later works, the aesthetic — in the precise Schillerian sense — remains a central, positive concept.

In particular, the British Germanists Elizabeth M. Wilkinson (1909–2001) and L. A. Willoughby (1885–1977) argued, in a series of books, articles, and commentaries, that it was possible to discern and elucidate a common set of ideas and concepts in such writers as Goethe and Schiller, whom they understood as participating in what they called a "perennial aesthetic."[3] Because Nietzsche not only read Goethe and Schiller but, as becomes clear from *Die Geburt der Tragödie* and *Also sprach Zarathustra*, deployed aspects of their texts to support his own aesthetic arguments, it is not only possible but fruitful to regard Nietzsche, too, as participating in this perennial aesthetic. In answer, then, to their question, "whatever happened to Weimar Classicism?" one answer is that it reemerged in the philosophy of Friedrich Nietzsche.[4]

The conception of aesthetic experience as a conciliation of the sensuous Dionysian and the formal Apollonian, borrowed from Weimar Classicism and placed at the heart of *Die Geburt der Tragödie* and *Zarathustra*, leads Nietzsche to set up the *artist* — not the philosopher, not the scholar, nor the soldier or warrior — as the model of human being. Artists, as opposed to philosophers, love their senses (compare *FW* §372; KSA 3:624), employ "die Falschheit mit gutem Gewissen" ("falseness with a good conscience"; *FW* §361; KSA 3:608), and have "den *guten* Willen zum Scheine" ("the *good* will to semblance"; *FW* §107; KSA 3:464). Nietzsche wrote that for him "Schein ist [. . .] das Wirkende und Lebende selber" (*FW* §54; KSA 3:417; "semblance is the very thing that is effective and is alive"). In *Menschliches, Allzumenschliches* (*Human, All Too Human*) Nietzsche talks of "die unschuldigen Listen der Seelenverführung" ("the innocent subterfuges for seducing the soul") that artists must needs understand, "denn in ihrer Welt, in der es auf Schein abgesehen ist, brauchen auch die Mittel des Scheins nicht nothwendig ächt zu sein" (*MA* II §154; KSA 2:442; "for in their world, in which what is aimed at is semblance, even the methods by which semblance is produced do not necessarily have to be genuine"). Of course, Nietzsche is not to be read as recommending untruth: he is simply recasting Schiller's concept of "frank illusion" as definitive of art and the aesthetic.

In this book, we take as our starting point the view, contested in some circles or, rather, simply denied, that Nietzsche's work, *Also sprach Zarathustra*, has a single, coherent message.[5] This study identifies that message with what Goethe, referring to the aesthetic doctrines of Oeser, called "das Evangelium des Schönen" ("the gospel of beauty").[6] In addition, it seeks to relate the central theme of *Zarathustra* with Nietzsche's major preoccupation in his earlier writings, namely, aesthetics. Moreover, Nietzsche's use of themes, ideas, and even formulations borrowed from Schiller's aesthetic writings in general and Goethe's *Faust* in particular are shown to provide a link between *Die Geburt der Tragödie* and *Also sprach Zarathustra* (composed in four parts between 1882 and 1884). A hitherto unappreciated unity of plot, style, and argument is thereby revealed in Nietzsche's *Zarathustra* and, indeed, his philosophical *oeuvre* as a whole. A rare example of a recognition of the tradition to which Nietzsche was so indebted can be found in the work of Peter Sloterdijk, who notes in his study of *Die Geburt der Tragödie: Der Denker auf der Bühne* (*Thinker on Stage*, 1986):

> *The whole man must move at once* — diesen Satz Addisons, den Lichtenberg einmal zustimmend in seine Notizbücher eintrug, hätte auch Nietzsche als seine Devise wählen können; der Mensch muß sich als ganzer in seine Äußerungen legen.
>
> ["The whole man must move at once": Nietzsche could have chosen this adage from Addison, which Lichtenberg had once recorded approvingly in his notebook, as his own motto. Man must express himself as a whole self.][7]

Ten years after Sloterdijk, a British Germanist examined at length the relationship between Schiller and Nietzsche, only to be taken to task by one reviewer for his reliance on the scholarship of Wilkinson and Willoughby.[8] Nevertheless, the same reviewer drew explicit attention to "the theory of 'Schein,' to which Nietzsche emphatically alludes in the opening chapter of *Die Geburt der Tragödie* and which is central to his concept of the Apollinine [*sic*]"; a theory which the work of Wilkinson and Willoughby, and their students, has done much to elucidate.[9]

In autumn 1883, whilst he was writing *Zarathustra*, Nietzsche quoted a passage from his earlier work and saw in it the key theme of his subsequent philosophy: "'sie [the theory of 'Schein'] *rettet* die Kunst — und durch die Kunst rettet sie sich das Leben.' **Grundgedanke**. *Mein weiteres Leben ist die Consequenz*" (KSA 10,16[11]: 501; cf. *GT* §7; KSA 1:57; "'it *rescues* art — and through art it saves life.' **Fundamental thought**. *The rest of my life is the* *consequence*"). Furthermore, Zarathustra faces up to "die höchste und wahrhaftig ernst zu nennende Aufgabe der Kunst" ("the highest and, indeed, the truly serious, task of art"), precisely as that is set out in *Die Geburt der Tragödie:* "das Auge vom Blick in's Grauen der Nacht zu erlösen und das Subject durch den heilenden Balsam des Scheins aus dem Krampfe der Willensregungen zu retten" (*GT* §19; KSA 1:126; "to save the eye from gazing into the horrors of night and to deliver the subject by the healing balm of semblance from the spasms of the agitations of the will"): Nietzsche turns to art to find what Faust looks to nature for, when he asks Mephistopheles: "Hat die Natur und hat ein edler Geist / Nicht irgendeinen Balsam aufgefunden?" (*Faust* Part One, lines 2345–46; "Has nature and a noble mind / Not found some soothing balm?") *Zarathustra* certainly stares long and hard into the dark night of nihilism;[10] what has often been ignored, however, is the vitalizing balsam of the aesthetic doctrine it offers. For in *Zarathustra,* the solution to the problem, posed in *Die Geburt der Tragödie,* of the aesthetic justification of the world is worked out at length.

> Wachet und horcht, ihr Einsamen! Von der Zukunft her kommen Winde mit heimlichem Flügelschlagen; und an feine Ohren ergeht gute Botschaft.
>
> Ihr Einsamen von heute, ihr Ausscheidenden, ihr sollt einst ein Volk sein: aus euch, die ihr euch selber auswähltet, soll ein auserwähltes Volk erwachsen; — und aus ihm der Übermensch.
>
> Wahrlich, eine Stätte der Genesung soll noch die Erde werden! Und schon liegt ein neuer Geruch um sie, ein Heil bringender, — und eine neue Hoffnung! (*Z* I 22 §2; KSA 4:100–101)

> [Wake and listen, you solitary ones! From the future there come winds with secret wing-beats; and good tidings go out to delicate ears.
>
> You solitary ones of today, you who have withdrawn, you shall one day be a people: from you, who have chosen yourselves, shall a chosen people spring; — and from them, the Superman.
>
> Truly, the earth shall yet become a site of healing! And already a new fragrance surrounds it, one which brings salvation, — and a new hope!]

What is Weimar Classicism?

Already we have used the (much disputed) expression "Weimar Classicism": what do we mean by it? What do we mean by "classicism," and to what extent are we justified in applying the term to the collaborative *Kulturkampf* undertaken by Goethe and Schiller in the years from 1794 to Schiller's death in 1805, and continued thereafter by Goethe until his own death in 1832?

The recent revival of interest in classicism is by no means restricted to the "new classicism" in architecture that Charles Jencks and Paolo Portoghesi have called for as a new, postmodern renaissance of the abiding presence of the past.[11] Classicism, in the traditional sense of a canon of qualities and ideals turned to account over and over again in all the plastic arts for well over two thousand years, although thought to be dead only some thirty or forty years ago, is apparently "alive and well but, as always, living in interesting times."[12] And in other areas, too, there has been a considerable quickening of interest,[13] emboldening a growing self-confidence amongst enthusiasts, characterized in the comment that classicism is "as inevitable as a phenomenon of nature."[14] However that may be, this recent return to classicism does seem to have some affinity with Jean Baudrillard's injunction that we should "pass over to the side of the object."[15] For, as Adrian Stokes put it, over fifty years ago, in his study of Cézanne:

> [Classicism] springs from a precise love and a passionate identification with what is other, insisting on an order there, strong, enduring and final *as being an other being,* untainted by the overt gesture, without the summary treatment, without the *arrière pensée* of "thinking makes it so."[16]

At least this is certainly what Goethe had in mind when, late in life, he recommended Greek poetry as the kind that one may come to terms with "as if it were a reality."[17] Seeing it as "our duty" to turn as far as possible ideas into reality, and to resist the destructive action of a corrosive kind of imagination that would seek to undo "the reality we thereby achieve,"[18] Goethe notes that his younger contemporaries are "shy of the real," "upon which everything imaginary is based and everything ideational must come to rest."[19] If objectivity and objectification may be taken as the hallmarks of the notoriously evasive term "classicism," then Goethe seems to be unambiguously endorsing core classical values.

And yet, in recent debates amongst *Germanisten* in Germany itself the very identity of Weimar Classicism has been called into question. By contrast, in *A Reassessment of Weimar Classicism,* published in 1996 for an English-speaking audience, the editor could state that "so much has been written about this canonical period in German literature that surely nothing can be added to change the accepted view of this era."[20] And a distinguished English Germanist has felt able to sum up the aim of Goethe and Schiller's classical program aphoristically as the reconciliation of "particular and general, sense and reason, experience and necessary truth, man's particularities and his generic character."[21] Perhaps suspecting that this widely accepted view comes perilously close to identifying the Weimar program with the traditional topos of the poet's office in general — "he diffuses a tone and spirit of unity, that blends and (as it were) *fuses* each to each," as Coleridge has it —[22] the German debate since the late sixties has been marked by deep-seated suspicion of the ideological investment, initially on the part of nationalistically-minded nineteenth-century literary historians, that the *Klassik-Legende* represents.[23] One of the fruits of this debate has been the careful historical work it has stimulated, in particular in setting German culture of the late eighteenth, early nineteenth centuries in a somewhat wider context than the traditionally narrow, national one, both historically and geographically (especially with reference to the European Enlightenment).[24] This (sometimes quite explicitly) historicist approach[25] has thrown into doubt the accepted periodization of so-called "German Classicism" (1750?–1832?); and of the narrower notion of "Weimar Classicism" (1794–1805? or 1780–1810? or 1789–1815?).[26] It has also led, because of the identification of overlapping issues and shared concerns on each side, to a fashionable tendency to blur, or even ignore, the traditional demarcations of *Klassik* and *Romantik*.[27]

Undoubtedly, the intellectual and artistic achievement of Goethe and Schiller is illuminated in the perspective of the movements of events and ideas amidst which they lived and worked. But it is surely an exaggeration to claim that the function of the Weimar classical aesthetic "is intelligible only if one takes into account the contemporary historical context in which it arose."[28] Other contexts — not least, the logical — can be equally, if not more, enlightening, as can a lengthening of the historical perspective, to take in developments in poetics and aesthetics before and since the period in question. Concentration on the immediate social and historical context can unduly restrict understanding to the localized and parochial, and may, as can be the case with, for instance, *Rezeptionsästhetik,* privilege, even canonize, a quite untypical, ill-informed, first reaction on the part of a writer's contemporaries, or on the part of succeeding generations of readers.[29]

The wider significance of Weimar Classicism has been accurately identified by Paul de Man (1919–83) in *The Rhetoric of Romanticism,* when he writes that "the Schillerian aesthetic categories, whether we know it or not, are still the taken-for-granted premises of our own pedagogical, historical, and political ideologies."[30] For, while it is true that the ideas of the German Romantics have enjoyed a renewed currency in international intellectual circles in the last thirty years or so,[31] a version of Goethe's and Schiller's cultural theory has, for much longer, been deeply influential in German, British, and American secondary and tertiary education, in particular through the reforming zeal of Wilhelm von Humboldt (1767–1835).[32] And there seems to be something insistently important at stake in the tension that de Man, along with many others (including Friedrich Schlegel, Schiller, and Goethe), detects between the classical and the Romantic tendencies in late eighteenth- and early nineteenth-century Germany. Goethe and Schiller's critique of dilettantism, for example, is obviously aimed at the Romantic school.[33] The remarkable conceptual consistency, after Schiller's death in 1805, of Goethe's own outwardly unsystematic writings on art and culture (which traced, in respect of a rich variety of cultural phenomena, the ramifications of the theory he and Schiller had worked on together) clearly owes a great deal of its precision to the way in which he keeps his Romantic contemporaries firmly in his critical sights.[34] The Winckelmann essay of 1805, for instance, represents a defiant stand against the rising tide of Romanticism;[35] and there is no mistaking the bitterness of Goethe's words about the "irresponsible regressiveness," as he put it, of the Romantics in his announcement of the last of the annual art exhibitions that he and a small circle of supporters had set up in order to promote classical values — an initiative that failed.[36] Indeed, his journal *Kunst und Altertum* (*Art and Antiquity*), begun in 1816, which some of his younger contemporaries expected to undergo a late conversion to Romantic art, had, in fact, as one of its central aims, the continuation of the critique of Romanticism.[37] As Goethe wrote to Schiller on 18 March 1801: "Wir stehen gegen die neuere Kunst wie Julian gegen das Christenthum" ("We stand in the same relation to the recent developments in art as [the Emperor] Julian stood in relation to Christianity)."[38] In order to avoid regressing to the undifferentiated identification of, say, the Schlegels with Schiller and Goethe, such as characterized the *colportage* of German ideas by Madame de Staël (1766–1817) and by Henry Crabb Robinson (1775–1867), we clearly need to be in a position to distinguish one intellectual tendency from the other.

Exactly what divides them, however, has proved not at all easy to pinpoint. After all, what is sometimes regarded as the quintessential quality of Romantic sensibility, "the Romantic keynote, the longing (*Sehnsucht*) for the lost object," is the very constituent of that "sentimental" outlook that Schiller set up in opposition to the "naïve," and with the merits of which he so clearly identified.[39] For that matter, Goethe, too, is as aware as Jacques Lacan (1901–81) that the structure of human feeling is essentially "Romantic," in this sense: that desire (*das Wollen*) — "der Gott der neuern Zeit" ("the god of modern times"), as he calls it in a late essay on Shakespeare — is never fulfilled, but is always seeking an unattainable satisfaction.[40] Far from excluding his own sensibility from what he regards as an ineluctable fact of human experience, Goethe insists that "sehnsuchtsvolle Phantasie" ("everyearning imagination") is an essential ingredient of all art.[41] And, evoking the "serious play" that he and Schiller, as well as Nietzsche, see at the heart of aesthetic experience, he notes resignedly in a sympathetic review of Ludwig Tieck in 1826:

> Da der Mensch doch einmal die Sehnsucht nicht los werden soll, so ist es heilsam, wenn sie sich einem bestimmten Objekte hin richtet, wenn sie sich bestrebt, ein abgeschiedenes großes Vergangene ernst und harmlos in der Gegenwart wieder darzustellen.[42]

[Since a human being cannot ever get rid of longing, it is salutary if it is directed toward a particular object, if it strives to re-present seriously and harmlessly in the present something great that happened in the past.]

Nor does it seem possible to differentiate "Weimar Romanticism," as it has been called recently,[43] from Weimar Classicism by simply invoking irony, whether "Romantic" or not. Such blatantly open-ended works as *Wilhelm Meister, West-östlicher Divan,* and *Faust* abound in playful, disruptive ironies;[44] moreover Goethe, like Schiller in his review of Bürger's poetry, is insistent that ironic distance is essential to aesthetic effect, citing Laurence Sterne (1713–68) and Oliver Goldsmith (1728–74), as well as some Spanish romances, as exemplary instances of "diese hohe Lebensansicht" ("this exalted outlook on life").[45] Indeed, the pervasive tone of Goethe's essays, letters, and conversations after 1800 is one of ironic skepticism. And it is certainly not plausible to argue for a distinctively anti-theoretical stance on the part of either Goethe or Schiller. Schiller, who took his reader on a bracing, abstract, indeed transcendental, route through Letters 11 and 12 of his *Aesthetic Letters,* was quick to discern, as one of the points of affinity between them, Goethe's "philosophischer Instinkt" ("inborn intellectual tendency"), as if to forestall the ever-repeated attempts to drive a wedge between the two of them.[46] Indeed, for someone who, in the middle of battle, takes the trouble to think up "allerlei Hypothesen" ("all kinds of hypotheses") to explain a rogue cannonball;[47] who insists that, when theorizing, one go to the very limit of one's powers of abstraction;[48] who argues "daß wir schon bei jedem aufmerksamen Blick in die Welt theoretisieren" ("that with every attentive glance into the world, we already theorize") and that such theorizing needs to be conducted "mit Ironie" ("with irony");[49] and who emphasizes that literary criticism, like artistic practice itself, needs the context of a coherent (Schillerian) aesthetic theory to be fully developed[50] — is it not remarkable that such a writer can be so routinely presented and caricatured as an arch-empiricist, and therefore dismissed?[51]

The thoroughgoing difference between the outlook of Weimar Classicism and that of the German Romantics may, to some extent at least, be clarified with reference to Goethe's relation with Schelling. Looking back on his interest in Schelling, Goethe notes in the unsent draft of a letter to Boisserée on 2 March 1828 that, while he appreciated Schelling's respect for nature, he could neither grasp nor share "die Art und Weise wie er zu Werke ging" ("the way he went about his task"). In his *Darstellung meines Systems der Philosophie* (*Presentation of my System of Philosophy*) of 1801, Schelling had claimed to be collaborating with Goethe in opposing the "confused night" of Newtonian physics. But for all his (to Goethe, no doubt flattering) talk of aesthetic unity, or "*Poesie,*" representing Nature, the term that Schelling used, *intellektuelle Anschauung* ("intellectual perception" or "intuition"), turned out to be a contradiction in terms, at least when considered retrospectively from his lectures on the philosophy of art of 1802/3.[52]

In his *Erster Entwurf eines Systems der Naturphilosophie (First Outline of a System of Philosophy of Nature,* 1799) Schelling assigns to art, indeed to aesthetic productivity in general, the unique capacity to manifest "der letzte Grund der Harmonie zwischen Subjektivem und Objektivem" (SW 3:610; "the ultimate foundation, that of harmony between subject and object"), thus linking the conscious with the unconscious (SW 3:616), the realm of Freedom with that of Nature (SW 3:612–13). And since "die ästhetische Anschauung eben ist die objektiv gewordene intellektuelle" ("aesthetic perception is intellectual perception become objective"), art recreates the absolutely identical state of being that can be thought of as obtaining before the emergence of the separated, and alienated, ego (SW 3:625). Goethe could be forgiven for seeing in all this a humble recognition of the superiority of art to philosophy, of the aesthetic to the abstractly intellectual (SW 3:627–28); but it cannot have been long before it dawned on him that, notwithstanding beguiling verbal similarities, there was in fact a thorough-going difference between his own and Schelling's view of nature. For while in the *Erster Entwurf* of 1799 art is, ostensibly at least, accorded the status of revealing the absolute identity, in the *Kunstphilosophie (Philosophy of Art)* of 1802/3 it is now philosophy that really comprehends it. Although Schelling still speaks of art and philosophy as being on a par (SW 5:369), it is quite clear that philosophy has the higher calling in that it is "die unmittelbare Darstellung des Göttlichen" ("the immediate representation of the Divine"), whereas art is relegated to being "nur Darstellung der Indifferenz [des Idealen und Realen]" (SW 5:381; "only the representation of the lack of difference between the Ideal and the Real"). Where Jürgen Habermas, referring to the conflict between absolutist and historicist-genetic modes of thought in Schelling's philosophy, speaks of a "disunity" (*Zwiespaltigkeit*), Goethe talks quite bluntly (in conversation with Kanzler Friedrich von Müller on 21 September 1820) of Schelling's "forked tongue" (*Zweizüngigkeit*), clearly indicating his rejection of Schelling's attempts at uniting opposites into conciliatory synthesis by means of mere verbal identities. Goethe is insistent that aesthetic consciousness, although it embraces intellect, is not essentially intellectual: "Abstraktion" ("abstraction"), he holds, entails a "Reduktion auf Begriffe" ("reduction to concepts");[53] nor is it simply a matter of imagination, unless it be imagination in its aesthetic, productive modality;[54] and nor, most important of all, is aesthetic perception in any way transcendent or religious. It is rather, Goethe claimed, what Spinoza had in mind when he spoke of that "third kind of knowledge," that coordinates "confused" empirical knowledge with "distinct" intellectual knowledge to yield "intuitive" knowledge of individual objects.[55] In Goethe's own terms, aesthetic knowledge arises when, however fleetingly, our sense-impressions are coordinated with our conceptual thought, rather than subordinated to purposive thinking, as is the common case. It is this that marks Weimar Classicism's divergence from its Romantic contemporaries' identification of intellectual play with aesthetic play, of *Poesie* with (allegorical) rhetoric, of the sublime with the beautiful — a distinction on which Goethe emphatically insists.[56] Paul de Man is, therefore, quite right to point out that "what gives the [Weimar] aesthetic its power [. . .] is its intimate link with knowledge"; but Goethe and Schiller would not accept his characterization of their aesthetic thinking as an "ideology."[57] For them, as for its founder Alexander Gottlieb Baumgarten (1714–62), aesthetics was the science of such knowledge as can be gained by the mind in collaboration with our physiology.[58] For them, as for our cultural tradition, classicism is, therefore, a way of perceiving this world in its rich and varied particularity;[59] nothing could be more alien to their aesthetic outlook than, say, Jean-François Lyotard's Romantic nostalgia for a sublime transcendent. For the Weimar Classicists, aesthetic and mystical experience are quite distinct.[60]

That is not to say that the knowledge gained from aesthetic mindfulness of the individual object — of the *Urphänomen* that so fascinated Walter Benjamin (1892–1940) — could, in their view, be expressed in discursive language any more easily than the mystic's vision. As Goethe told Hegel,[61] the whole difficulty arises from trying to express in discursive language the quality inhering in the self-regulating relations between things, in which the combination of two rhythms will instantaneously create a third, subsuming one of the operative polarities.[62] Indeed, while it may be an exaggeration to claim that Goethe's classical solidarity "was a direct result of his early studies in alchemy," this assertion contains a kernel of truth.[63] For one of Goethe's fundamental contributions to his collaboration with Schiller consisted in the subtle modes of thought and of rhetorical presentation that he had developed over many years since he first became fascinated with hermeticism and "mystisch-kabbalistische Chemie" ("mystical cabalistic chemistry"),[64] and which he went on to apply in his scientific work. Of particular relevance here is the adoption and adaptation by Goethe, and later by Schiller, of that variation of the principle of *coniunctio oppositorum* known as "binary synthesis."[65] William James offered an illuminating analysis of just this kind of synthesis in a discussion of mystical modes of experience:

> The keynote [. . .] is invariably a reconciliation. It is as if the opposites of the world [. . .] were melted into unity. Not only do they, as contrasted species, belong to one and the same genus, but *one of the species, the nobler and better one, is itself the genus and so soaks up and absorbs its opposite into itself.*[66]

The most significant element for Goethe in this hermetic-mystical tradition seems to have been that the feminine principle was restored to a position of equality with the masculine principle — or Nature with Spirit — and that woman was again coequal with man.[67] For what he had in mind by "developing more consistently" (*konsequenter ausbilden*) his hermetic heritage (HA 9:414) becomes manifest in the poem "Zueignung" of 1794, first intended as a prologue to "Die Geheimnisse," itself an articulation of mystical doctrine. Working in a tradition stretching back at least as far as Apuleius's invocation of the Goddess Isis, and with intertextual reference to Dante's encounter with Beatrice in *Purgatory* (Canto 30, line 32) — "una donna m'apparve" — Goethe's speaker encounters his mother-image as mountain-goddess. She offers him a veil, an age-old symbol associated with Ishtar's descent into the underworld, "der Dichtung Schleier aus der Hand der Wahrheit" ("the veil of poetry from the hand of truth"; HA 1:152). Goethe's use of this ancient theological symbol in the context of aesthetics has led to its being called "the symbol of symbols."[68] And rightly so, for what Goethe meant by "the veil of poetry" is the network of sensuous, "sound-look," relations, drawn as it were across the discursive surface of the text, some meaningless and obscuring, others meaningful and heightening what is revealed. In other words, what Goethe could not accept literally as revelation of mystical intuition, he understands symbolically, in the sense of an aesthetic conjunction of the artist's medium — here, language — with the felt life of the psyche. The upshot of this particular "chymical marriage" is *Gestalt*, the living form of art, which gives tongue to what is otherwise left inarticulate — the voice of the Goddess, "the god-like woman," evoked by Schiller in his *Aesthetic Letters* as the epitome of *aesthetic* experience (Letter 15, §9).

Goethe and Schiller's identification of the Feminine with the imagination in its aesthetic modality is made quite explicit throughout their work. Of particular significance in the present context is the fact that Goethe, when he reflected on how Mother Nature was to be described in language, drew on these same aesthetic principles. In Nature, he states in the preface to his *Morphologie* of 1817, we find "nirgend ein Bestehendes, nirgend ein Ruhendes, ein Abgeschlossenes" ("nowhere anything stable, at rest, or detached"); rather, we find "daß alles in einer steten Bewegung schwanke" (HA 13:55; "that everything is in constant flux.") And later, in an essay of 1823 entitled *Probleme*, he noted that the simultaneity of oppositional forces at work in Nature cannot be expressed in discursive language (HA 13:35–36). He suggests that an "artificial-cum-artistic mode of discourse" (*einen künstlichen Vortrag*) be introduced, matching the ebb and flow and subtle interconnectedness of Nature's workings. In the language of contemporary modern French feminist theory, we may speak of this recommended aesthetic style as *l'écriture féminine* or *parler femme*, marked as it is by fluidity and dislocation, elasticity and spontaneity, and going beyond syntactical correctness.[69] The liquid, primordial feminine matrix in which the Goddess traditionally has her being is precisely what is reflected in Luce Irigaray's call for a specifically feminine style, for "its privileging of the tactile, the simultaneous, the fluid, the proximate — a disruptive excess."[70] Clearly, when Goethe ended his *Faust* with the famous lines, "Das Ewig-Weibliche / Zieht uns hinan" ("The Eternal Feminine / Draws us on"), he had far more in mind than any glorification-as-humiliation, as Theodor W. Adorno has it, of the Woman-as-(subordinate)-Muse.[71] Rather, he was evoking here the long classical tradition stretching from paganism to Christianity of a gentle, tender, nurturing, aesthetic Goddess.

Above all, what Weimar Classicism has in common with *parler femme* is what Goethe's Werther famously denounced as the inadequacy of the "Either-Or," and what Irigaray has deplored as phallocentric "either . . . or" stabilities.[72] Just as Schiller argues that the "naïve" and the "sentimental" are aspects of a fundamental unity ("das Naïve ist das Sentimentalische," in Peter Szondi's memorable formulation),[73] so what appear to the discursive mind to be opposites are re-presented by Goethe as stages in a process of successive reciprocal subordination. Whatever else this is, it is not the dialectic associated with Hegel culminating in a Third Thing; nor is it the identity-philosophy of Schelling, for what the mind distinguishes remains, conceptually at least, distinct; and nor again is it the deconstructive irony of Friedrich Schlegel, inducing an ever more frenzied vertigo.[74] Although, as Goethe freely admits, employment of this figure of thought lends a paradoxical tone to his discourse (and Schiller's),[75] such linguistic play is necessary since "keine Worte zart und subtil genug sind" ("no words are delicate or subtle enough") to convey the workings of the inner life,[76] particularly of that mode of (aesthetic) thinking that, for Goethe, defines the artist.[77] So in contrast to that "romantic confusion" championed by Friedrich Schlegel, and extolled as genial "mixing and melting" (*bald mischen, bald verschmelzen*) in his 116th Fragment,[78] Goethe seeks to hold together quite diverse elements in a unity that yet keeps intact their distinct identities. Examples of these "paradoxical" yokings of opposites into a unit that is composed of distinct entities in varying proportions abound in his and Schiller's work. When Goethe says "die Erfahrung [ist] nur die Hälfte der Erfahrung," for instance, understanding this maxim requires the reader to give the second occurrence of "experience" a heightened meaning, in which the antithesis ("idea," "theory") is incorporated, whereas in the case of the first occurrence, it is absent.[79] This same "double-coding" is quite explicitly at work in his exposition of what he argues is Shakespeare's thought-process in his dramas:

Weil aber Sollen und Wollen im Menschen nicht radikal getrennt werden kann, so müssen überall beide Ansichten zugleich, wenn schon die eine vorwaltend und die andere untergeordnet, gefunden werden.

[Because obligation and desire in the human being cannot be absolutely separated, both aspects must coexist at the same time everywhere, even if one may be predominant and the other subordinated.]

In Shakespeare, he claims, this simultaneity is presented, at moments of crisis, as "an unrealizable desire raised to the level of a compelling obligation" (*daß ein unzulängliches Wollen* [. . .] *zum unerläßlichen Sollen erhöht wird*).[80] Here conceptual distinctness is preserved, while the undivided reality it clarifies is kept steadily in focus. Such ironic skepticism with regard to the gulf between linguistic and natural reality could hardly be more unlike "ideology."

The totality that Schiller quite uncompromisingly aimed at in his *Aesthetic Letters* — "so muß es bei uns stehen, diese Totalität in unsrer Natur, welche die Kunst zerstört hat, durch eine höhere Kunst wieder herzustellen" (Letter 6, §15; "it must be open to us to restore by means of a higher art the totality of our nature that civilization itself has destroyed") — is not, then, the totality on which Lyotard has urged us to wage war, and which some contemporary cultural theory routinely attacks.[81] Wholeness for Weimar Classicism is not the abstract universality promoted by the Romantics, and systematically codified by Hegel. Whatever term may be used, "totality" for Goethe and Schiller, and so it was understood by Nietzsche, means the imperfect but unique integrity of some particular: an individual action, or poem, or natural object, or event, or social practice, or person. It is, in a word, *realism,* as Georg Lukács rightly senses: respect for actual (aesthetic) entities, for *res.* The kind of work of art they promoted, says Goethe, need not be complete down to the last detail:

Eine solche Arbeit braucht nicht im höchsten Grade ausgeführt und vollendet zu sein; wenn sie gut gesehen, gedacht und fertig ist, so ist sie für den Liebhaber oft reizender als ein größeres ausgeführtes Werk.[82]

[Such a work does not need to be executed to the highest degree and be perfected; if it is well-observed, thought-through and ready, then it is often more attractive for the amateur than a larger, fully executed work.]

In an early piece of art criticism, Goethe writes that "wer allgemein sein will, wird nichts" ("he who wants to be general, ends up being nothing").[83] The movement of Weimar Classical thought is away from the general and toward the particular, away from what Erich Heller called the characteristic "scene of Romantic art [. . .] the play with abstractions [. . .] and with disembodied forms and patterns."[84] The human mind, Goethe argues, while enjoying the elevation of high abstraction, longs for the particular, without losing a universal perspective.[85] According to classical theory, then, it is the office of the artist to provide this stereoscopic perspective by "epitomizing" human significance in a particular form.[86] Significant entities that engage our aesthetic interest are, then, like the people we fall in love with, not exemplifications of a general proposition, but symbols on to which we project, by isomorphy, our felt-thought.[87] It is, of course, the business of reflection to subject aesthetic perceptions to intellection; but not to displace them with the resultant conceptual entities — a reifying tendency which, in Goethe's view, Romanticism and Newtonian science had in common.

The overriding concern in the cultural theorizing of Goethe and Schiller is to make conceptual room for a reasoned account of our aesthetic experience of human life and the universe we live in — "die Welt als ästhetisches Phänomen" ("the world as an aesthetic phenomenon"), in Nietzsche's famous phrase — alongside, though not in competition with, the empirical-scientific and the romantic-religious worldviews. Conflict with these other, in our Western culture more prevalent, modes of consciousness arose, not from any inherent antagonism towards them on the part of the Weimar Classicists and Nietzsche, but rather from the tendency of both outlooks to encroach illegitimately on the proper province of aesthetic consciousness. The concerted challenge of Weimar Classicism to the hegemony of either the scientific or the religious culture that has alternately dominated Western civilization goes some way, perhaps, to explaining Metternich's spreading the word in the Russian and Prussian courts that Weimar was a hot-bed of revolutionary sentiment.[88] Thus Adorno's appeal in his *Minima Moralia* for respect for individual existence may be seen as a continuation of this inherently ethical tradition, of the call to resist what Adorno characterizes as "die erledigende Gebärde, mit welcher Hegel [. . .] stets wieder das Individuelle traktiert" ("the dismissive gesture which Hegel constantly accords the individual entity"), the same Hegel whom he accuses of opting "mit überlegener Kälte [. . .] für die Liquidation des Besonderen" ("with serene indifference for liquidation of the particular").[89] Indeed Adorno avers that "nur dort vermag Erkenntnis zu erweitern, wo sie beim Einzelnen so verharrt, daß über der Insistenz seine Isoliertheit zerfällt" ("knowledge can only widen horizons by abiding so insistently with the particular that its isolation is dispelled"), and he refers explicitly to Nietzsche (*FW* §228; KSA 3:511) when presenting his case for what he calls "the morality of thought":

> Die Moral des Denkens besteht darin, weder stur noch souverän, weder blind noch leer, weder atomistisch noch konsequent zu verfahren. Die Doppelschlächtigkeit der Methode, welche der Hegelschen Phänomenologie unter vernünftigen Leuten den Ruf abgründiger

Schwierigkeit eingetragen hat, nämlich die Forderung, gleichzeitig die Phänomene als solche sprechen zu lassen — das "reine Zusehen" — und doch in jedem Augenblick ihre Beziehung auf das Bewußtsein als Subjekt, die Reflexion präsent zu halten, drückt diese Moral am genauesten und in aller Tiefe des Widerspruchs aus.[90]

[The morality of thought lies in a procedure that is neither entrenched nor detached, neither blind nor empty, neither atomistic nor consequential. The double-edged method that has earned Hegel's *Phenomenology* the reputation among reasonable people of unfathomable difficulty, that is, its simultaneous demands that phenomena be allowed to speak as such — in a pure "looking-on" — and yet that their relation to consciousness as the subject, reflection, be at every moment maintained, expresses this morality most directly and in all its depths of contradiction.]

What Adorno says here of Hegel at his best applies *a fortiori* to Weimar Classicism. When Goethe, for whom was what was ultimately at stake was the issue of barbarism or culture,[91] famously defined classicism as healthy,[92] he meant by this, succinctly restating Schiller's central thesis, wholesome sensitivity to the particulars of (sensuous) beauty.[93] In a sense, we are dealing here with a secularized version of the distinction made by St. Augustine (354–430) between use (*uti*) and enjoyment (*frui*).[94] In his treatise *On Christian Doctrine,* Augustine defined enjoyment of a thing in terms of "resting with satisfaction in it for its own sake," whereas its use consisted in its employment "to obtain what one desires."[95] For Augustine, however, God alone was to be enjoyed;[96] following His death, however, as proclaimed by Nietzsche, it becomes not only legitimate, it becomes the new commandment, to enjoy the objects of the world for their own sake. Augustine wrote:

The beauty of the country through which we must pass, and the very pleasure of the motion, charm our hearts, and turning these things which we ought to use into objects of enjoyment, we become unwilling to hasten the end of our journey; and becoming engrossed in a factitious delight, our thoughts are diverted from that home whose delights would make us truly happy.[97]

For the outlook of Weimar Classicism, however, as for Nietzsche, we have already reached the goal of our journey, and our home is the earth — "*bleibt der Erde treu!*" ("*remain true to the earth!*"), as Zarathustra urges us (*Z* Vorrede §3; KSA 4:15). Christianity, morality, the argument for the existence of God from design, the belief in Providence — "das ist nunmehr *vorbei*" ("that's all over now"), says Nietzsche, and we are free to enjoy the objects of the world for their own sake, to see the world *as an aesthetic phe-*

nomenon.[98] By the same token, the same respect of, and love for, the particular is nowhere more powerfully expressed than by Nietzsche's Zarathustra, who counsels his disciples, his "friends," who are like children, to be yet more like them:

> [Die Kinder] spielten am Meere, — da kam die Welle und riss ihnen ihr Spielwerk in die Tiefe: nun weinen sie.
> Aber die selbe Welle soll ihnen neue Spielwerke bringen und neue bunte Muscheln vor sie hin ausschütten!
> So werden sie getröstet sein; und gleich ihnen sollt auch ihr, meine Freunde, eure Tröstungen haben — und neue bunte Muscheln! —
> (Z II 5; KSA 4:123)

> [The children were playing by the sea, — then the wave came and swept their playthings into the deep: now they are crying,
> But the same wave shall bring them new playthings and shower new, colorful sea-shells before them!
> Thus they will be consoled; and, like them, you too, my friends, shall have your consolations — and new, colorful sea-shells!"]

Notes

[1] Curt Paul Janz, *Friedrich Nietzsche: Biographie,* 3 vols. (Munich and Vienna: Carl Hanser Verlag, 1978), 1:67.

[2] For further discussion of this mode of argumentation, see Elizabeth M. Wilkinson and L. A. Willoughby, introduction to Friedrich Schiller, *On the Aesthetic Education of Man in a Series of Letters* (2nd ed., Oxford: Clarendon P, 1982), lxxxv–lxxxix, and "Appendix III: Visual Aids" (348–50).

[3] For a thorough analysis of the modern phase of this tradition, see Carsten Zelle, *Die doppelte Ästhetik der Moderne: Revisionen des Schönen von Boileau bis Nietzsche* (Stuttgart: Metzler, 1995). Despite a tendency to conflate the beautiful with the sublime, Zelle offers a stimulating reconstruction of Schiller's aesthetic theory.

[4] See Elizabeth M. Wilkinson and L. A. Willoughby, "Missing Links or Whatever Happened to Weimar Classicism?" in Hinrich Siefken and Alan Robinson, eds., *Erfahrung und Überlieferung: Festschrift for C. Magill* (Cardiff: Trivium Special Publications, 1974), 57–74.

[5] A recent study of *Also sprach Zarathustra* refers to, and rejects, "the traditional but increasingly disputed view" — which it associates with Arthur Danto and J. Stern — "that Nietzsche's fiction is a disorganized and disconnected set of aphorisms and sermons" (Robert Gooding-Williams, *Zarathustra's Dionysian Modernism* (Stanford, CA: Stanford UP, 2001), 316; compare Arthur Danto, *Nietzsche as Philosopher* (New York: Columbia UP, 1980), and J. Stern, *A Study of Nietzsche* (Cambridge: Cambridge UP, 1979).

[6] See Goethe, *Dichtung und Wahrheit,* part 2, bk. 8 (HA 9:314). Similarly, Nietzsche spoke of "die Kunst als die eigentliche Aufgabe des Lebens, die Kunst als dessen *metaphysische* Tätigkeit" ("art as the real task of life, as life's *metaphysical* activity") as an "Artisten-Evangelium" ("artists' gospel"; *WM* §853; KSA 13, 17[3] §4:522; compare *GT,* Vorwort an Richard Wagner; KSA 1:24).

[7] Peter Sloterdijk, *Der Denker auf der Bühne: Nietzsches Materialismus* (Frankfurt am Main: Suhrkamp, 1986), 30; *Thinker on Stage: Nietzsche's Materialism,* trans. Jamie Owen Daniel (Minneapolis: U of Minnesota P, 1989), 12. Sloterdijk's attribution of this remark to Joseph Addison (1672–1719) may well be due to the influence of Hugo von Hofmannsthal. Wilkinson and Willoughby attribute the remark to Sir Richard Steele (1672–1729) who, with Addison, edited *The Spectator* from 1711 to 1712, and cite the sixth issue of 7 March 1711 as its source, noting: "It would be a fascinating exercise in the comparative morphology of ideas to trace the life-history of this model" (Elizabeth M. Wilkinson and L. A. Willoughby, "'The Whole Man' in Schiller's Theory of Culture and Society: On the Virtue of a Plurality of Models" [1969], in *Models of Wholeness: Some Attitudes to Language, Arts and Life in the Age of Goethe,* ed. Jeremy Adler, Martin Swales, and Ann Weaver (Oxford, Bern, Berlin: Peter Lang, 2002), 233–68; here, 241).

[8] Nicholas Martin, *Nietzsche and Schiller: Untimely Aesthetics* (Oxford: Oxford UP, 1996); reviewed by David Pugh in *The Modern Language Review* 93 (1998): 1167–69.

[9] Pugh, Review of *Nietzsche and Schiller,* 1168. See Elizabeth M. Wilkinson, "Schiller's Concept of *Schein* in the Light of Recent Aesthetics," *The German Quarterly* 28 (1955): 219–27; Marie-Luise Waldeck, "Shadows, Reflexions, Mirror-Images and Virtual 'Objects' in 'Die Künstler' and their Relation to Schiller's Concept of 'Schein,'" *The Modern Language Review* 58 (1963): 33–37; and Marie-Luise Waldeck, "Further Thoughts on the Genesis of a Key Concept in Schiller's Aesthetic Thinking," *Forum for Modern Language Studies* 12 (1976): 304–13. For a discussion of the concept of "Schein" from a different perspective, see Karl Heinz Bohrer, "Ästhetik und Historismus: Nietzsches Begriff des 'Scheins,'" in *Plötzlichkeit: Zum Augenblick des ästhetischen Scheins* (Frankfurt am Main: Suhrkamp, 1981), 111–38; Peter Bürger, "Zum Problem des ästhetischen Scheins in der idealistischen Ästhetik," Franz Koppe, "Mimetischer Schein, imaginärer Schein, schöner Schein — und was davon bleibt," and Karlheinz Stierle, "Bemerkungen zur Geschichte des schönen Scheins," in Willi Oelmüller, ed., *Ästhetischer Schein* (Paderborn, Munich, Vienna, Zurich: Ferdinand Schöningh, 1982), 34–50, 126–30, and 208–32; and, most recently, Birgit Recki, "'Artisten-Metaphysik' und ästhetisches Ethos: Friedrich Nietzsche über Ästhetik und Ethik," in Andrea Kern and Ruth Sonderegger, eds., *Falsche Gegensätze: Zeitgenössische Positionen zur philosophischen Ästhetik* (Frankfurt am Main: Suhrkamp, 2002), 262–85.

[10] For a recent discussion of nihilism before and in Nietzsche, see Michael Allen Gillespie, *Nihilism before Nietzsche* (Chicago and London: U of Chicago P, 1995), especially "Dionysus and the Triumph of Nihilism," 203–54.

[11] Charles Jencks, *Postmodernism* (New York: Academy Editions, 1987), especially 329–35; Paolo Portoghesi, *Postmodern* (New York: Rizzoli, 1983), especially 10–13.

[12] Michael Greenhalgh, *What is Classicism?* (New York: Martin's P, 1990), 8, 61.

[13] See, for instance, Frederick Turner, *Natural Classicism: Essays on Literature and Science* (New York: Paragon House, 1985).

[14] See Robert A. M. Stern, *Modern Classicism* (London: Thames and Hudson, 1988), 8.

[15] Jean Baudrillard, "Toward a Principle of Evil," in *Selected Writings*, ed. Mark Poster, (Cambridge: Polity P, 1988), 198–206; here, 206.

[16] Adrian Stokes, *Inside Out: An Essay in the Psychology and Aesthetic Appeal of Space* (Harmondsworth: Pelican, 1947), 174.

[17] See "Moderne Guelfen und Ghibellinen" (1827): "Jene Dichtkunst, welche dahin strebt, daß der Einbildungskraft Gehalt, Gestalt und Form dargebracht werde, so daß sie sich daran als einem Wirklichen beschäftigen und erbauen könne" (WA 1.42/ii:266; "That poetic art that strives to present to the faculty of imagination import, form, and structure with the result that imagination can concern, and edify, itself with it as if it were a reality").

[18] See his review of "*Universalhistorische Übersicht der Geschichte der alten Welt und ihrer Cultur von Schlosser. Frankfurt 1826*," in his "Kurze Anzeigen" of 1826: "Bleibt es doch unsere Pflicht, selbst die Idee, insofern es möglich ist, zu verwirklichen; warum sollten wir das erlangte Wirkliche einer auflösenden, vernichtenden Einbildungskraft dahin geben?" (WA 1.41/ii:210; "If it remains precisely our duty to realize, as far as possible, what is ideal, why should we surrender the reality we have thereby achieved to a dissolving, destructive faculty of imagination?")

[19] Writing to Karl August on 31 January 1826, Goethe spoke of "eine Scheu vor dem Wirklichen, worauf denn doch alles Imaginative sich gründen und alles Ideelle sich niederlassen muß" (WA 4.40:275; "a fear of reality, on which nevertheless everything imaginary and everything ideal must be based").

[20] Gerhart Hoffmeister, ed., *A Reassessment of Weimar Classicism* (Lewiston, NY, Queenston, ON, and Lampeter, Wales: Edwin Mellen P, 1996), vii.

[21] T. J. Reed, *The Classical Centre: Goethe and Weimar 1775–1832* (London: Croom Helm, 1980), 75.

[22] Samuel Taylor Coleridge, *Biographia Literaria,* ed. John Shawcross, 2 vols. (Oxford: Clarendon P, 1907), 2:12.

[23] For an illuminating historical account of this debate, from the perspective of German political reunification, see Klaus L. Berghahn, "Das Andere der Klassik: Von der 'Klassiker-Legende' zur jüngsten Klassik-Diskussion," *Goethe-Yearbook* 6 (1992): 1–27. The German identification with the myth of Greece was, of course, already part of the search for national identity in the eighteenth century. See H. B. Nisbet, ed., *German Aesthetic and Literary Criticism: Wickelmann, Lessing, Hamann, Herder, Schiller, Goethe* (Cambridge: Cambridge UP, 1985), 6.

[24] See, for example, Hans-Joachim Simm, ed., *Literarische Klassik* (Frankfurt am Main: Suhrkamp, 1988).

[25] See, for instance, Wilhelm Vosskamp, ed., *Klassik im Vergleich: Normativität und Historizität europäischer Klassiken* (Stuttgart and Weimar: Metzler, 1993), especially 1–5, 9–11, 160–70.

[26] Compare Dieter Borchmeyer, *Weimarer Klassik: Portrait einer Epoche* (Weinheim: Beltz Athenäum, 1994), 9–12, 39–40.

[27] See Jochen Hörisch, "'Ein höherer Grad von Folter': Die Weimarer Klassik im Lichte früh romantischer Kritik," in Simm, ed., *Literarische Klassik,* 410–20.

[28] Wilhelm Vosskamp, "Klassik als Epoche: Zur Typologie und Funktion der Weimarer Klassik," in Simm, ed., *Literarische Klassik,* 248–77: "Die Funktion der klassischen 'Ausgleichs-Ästhetik' [. . .] wird nur verständlich, wenn man den zeitgeschichtlichen Kontext bedenkt, in dem sie entsteht" (256).

[29] Compare John M. Ellis, *The Theory of Literary Criticism: A Logical Analysis* (Berkeley, CA: California UP, 1974), 134–37 and 148.

[30] Paul de Man, *The Rhetoric of Romanticism* (New York: Columbia UP, 1984), 266.

[31] See Andrew Bowie, *Schelling and Modern European Philosophy: An Introduction* (London: Routledge, 1993).

[32] For an informative account of von Humboldt's highly influential, but somewhat distorting, work in this area, see Borchmeyer, *Weimarer Klassik,* 299–313.

[33] Borchmeyer, *Weimarer Klassik,* 58.

[34] For a demonstration of the continuity of development in Goethe's ideas on art (and their connection with his scientific thinking), see Hans-Rudolf Vaget, *Dilettantismus und Meisterschaft: Zum Problem des Dilettantismus bei Goethe: Praxis, Theorie, Zeitkritik* (Munich: Winkler, 1971).

[35] Nisbet, *German Aesthetic and Literary Criticism,* 3.

[36] "Letzte Kunstausstellung 1805" (HA 12:129).

[37] See Karl-Heinz Hahn, "Goethes Zeitschrift 'Über Kunst und Altertum,'" *Goethe-Jahrbuch* 92 (1975): 128–39.

[38] For an elegant and accurate account of the early Romantics' critique of Goethe and Schiller, see Victor Lange, *The Classical Age of German Literature 1740–1815* (London: Edward Arnold, 1982), 165–72.

[39] Borchmeyer, *Weimarer Klassik,* 32.

[40] "Shakespeare und kein Ende" (1815/1826, HA 12:293). For a discussion of some of the significant parallels and differences between (German) classicism and Lacanian thought, see Paul Bishop, "An Herderian Perspective on Lacanian Psychoanalysis," *History of European Ideas* 26(2000): 1–18.

[41] *Zur Farbenlehre,* "Betrachtungen über Farbenlehre und Farbenbehandlung der Alten" (HA 14:41).

[42] "Ludwig Tiecks Dramaturgische Blätter" (1826, WA 1.40:179). For further discussion of Goethe's acute awareness of the mismatch between feeling and discursive language, see R. H. Stephenson, *Goethe's Conception of Knowledge and Science* (Edinburgh: Edinburgh UP, 1995), 66–68.

[43] Borchmeyer, *Weimarer Klassik,* 358.

[44] See Ehrhard Bahr, *Die Ironie im Spätwerk Goethes: "Diese sehr ernsten Scherze":
Studien zum West-östlichen Divan, zu den Wanderjahren und zu Faust II* (Berlin:
Erich Schmidt Verlag, 1972).

[45] See Goethe's letter to Friedrich Zelter of 25 December 1829. See, too, "Spanische
Romanzen, übersetzt von Beauregard Pandin" (1823; WA 1.41/ii:69–72).

[46] See Schiller's letter to Goethe of 23 August 1794 (NA 27:24–27).

[47] *Campagne in Frankreich* (HA 10:241).

[48] "'Irrthümer und Wahrheiten' von Wilhelm Schütz" (1827; WA 1.42/ii:64–69).

[49] *Zur Farbenlehre*, "Vorwort" (1810, HA 13:317). For Goethe's deliberately ironic
employment of those "depth-models" that Frederic Jameson has identified as having
been repudiated in contemporary theory, see Stephenson, *Goethe's Conception of
Knowledge and Science*, 65–69; compare Frederic Jameson, *Postmodernism or the Cultural Logic of Late Capitalism* (London: Duke UP, 1991), 58–71.

[50] In his review of Manzoni's *Adelchi* (1822; WA 1.42/i:170–79); compare with
"Einleitung in die Propyläen" (1798; HA 12:53).

[51] For a discussion of the intellectual sophistication of Goethe's epistemological
stance, see Herman Meyer, *Zarte Empire: Studien zur Literaturgeschichte* (Stuttgart:
Metzler, 1963); and for a perspective on Goethe through the prism of postmodernism, see Carl Paschek, *Das Goethe-Bild der Postmoderne 1975–1999 in Büchern und
elektronischen Medien: Begleitschrift zur Ausstellung der Stadt- und Universitätsbibliothek zum Goethe-Jubiläum 1999*, Frankfurter Bibliotheksschriften, vol. 7 (Frankfurt
am Main: Vittorio Klostermann, 1999).

[52] For further discussion of the notion of "intellectual intuition," see Paul Bishop,
Synchronicity and Intellectual Intuition in Kant, Swedenborg, and Jung (Lewiston,
NY, Queenston, ON, and Lampeter, Wales: Edwin Mellen P, 2000), especially 199–
260.

[53] "Der Sammler und die Seinigen" (1798, HA 12:92).

[54] See Stephenson, *Goethe's Conception of Knowledge and Science*, 51–54. Compare
Goethe's saying that "Einbildungskraft wird nur durch Kunst, besonders durch
Poesie geregelt" (*Maximen und Reflexionen*, ed. Hecker, 507; HA 12:506; "imagination is only regulated by art, particularly by poetry"). By contrast, the following
statement of Schelling's is typical of his "identity-philosophy," and wholly alien to
Goethe's temper of mind: "Dieselben Ineinsbildungen des Allgemeinen und Besonderen, die an sich betrachtet, Ideen, d.h. Bilder des Göttlichen sind, sind real betrachtet *Götter*" (SW 5:390; "The same instantiations of the general and the
particular, which are, considered in themselves, ideas, i.e., images of the divine, are,
when considered as real, *gods*").

[55] Benedict de Spinoza, *Ethics*, part two ("On the Nature and Origin of the Mind"),
proposition 40, note 2, in *On the Improvement of the Understanding/The Eth-
ics/Correspondence*, trans. R. H. M. Elwes, 113 (New York: Dover, 1955).

[56] In, for example, his posthumously published essay on Dante (1833; HA 12:340).
Contrast with Friedrich Schlegel's statement: "Alle Schönheit ist Allegorie. Das
Höchste kann man eben weil es unaussprechlich ist, nur allegorisch sagen" (*Kritische
Friedrich Schlegel Ausgabe*, ed. Ernst Behler et al., 19 vols. (Munich, Paderborn, and

Vienna: Schöningh, 1961–1971), 2:324; "All beauty is allegory. One can only express the highest, precisely because it is inexpressible, allegorically").

[57] De Man, *The Rhetoric of Romanticism,* 264–65.

[58] See David Simpson, ed., *German Aesthetic and Literary Criticism: Kant, Fichte, Schelling, Schopenhauer, Hegel* (Cambridge: Cambridge UP, 1984), 3.

[59] See Greenhalgh, *What is Classicism?,* 8.

[60] For Goethe's insistence on the discontinuity between the aesthetic and the religious, see Stephenson, *Goethe's Conception of Knowledge and Science,* 87–89.

[61] See Goethe's letter to Hegel of 7 October 1820 (WA 4.33:294–95).

[62] *Zur Farbenlehre,* "Vorwort" (HA 13:316).

[63] Ronald Gray, *Goethe the Alchemist: A Study of Alchemical Symbolism in Goethe's Literary and Scientific Works* (London: Cambridge UP, 1952), 182.

[64] *Dichtung und Wahrheit,* part two, bk. 10 (HA 9:414).

[65] See J. E. Cirlot, *A Dictionary of Symbols,* trans. Jack Sage (London: Routledge and Kegan Paul, 1967), 26, 145–47.

[66] William James, *The Varieties of Religious Experience: A Study in Human Nature* (1903; rcpr. Glasgow: Collins, 1960), 374. Although James wrote that this "dark saying" was "something like what the Hegelian philosophy means," and ultimately assigned such synthesis a mystical status ("to me the living sense of its reality only comes in the artificial mystic state of mind"), his description applies more accurately to Schillerian, "binary" synthesis, and is not necessarily mystical.

[67] See Alice Raphael, *Goethe and the Philosopher's Stone* (London: Routledge and Kegan Paul, 1965), 31–32.

[68] William Larrett, "Der Dichtung Schleier: From Theology With Love to Aesthetics," in *Tradition and Creation: Essays in Honour of Elizabeth Mary Wilkinson,* ed. C. Magill et al. (Leeds: W. S. Maney & Son, 1978), 89–100; here, 99. See, too, Wilhelm Emrich, *Die Symbolik von Faust II: Sinn und Vorformen* (Königstein: Athenäum, 1981), 51; and Emil Staiger, *Goethe,* 3 vols. (Zürich: Atlantis, 1970), 2:484.

[69] For further discussion, see Patricia D. Zecevic, *The Speaking Divine Woman: López de Úbeda's "La pícara Justina" and Goethe's "Wilhelm Meister"* (Oxford: Peter Lang, 2001); and R. H. Stephenson and Patricia D. Zecevic, "Goethe and the Divine Feminine in the Light of the Spanish Kabbalah," *Quaderni di Lingue e Litterature Straniere* 12 (2003): 299–334.

[70] Luce Irigaray, *Speculum of the Other Woman,* trans. Gillian C. Gill (Ithaca: Cornell UP, 1985), 78.

[71] "Die Glorifizierung des weiblichen Charakters schließt die Demütigung aller ein, die ihn tragen" (Theodor W. Adorno, *Minima Moralia: Reflexionen aus dem beschädigten Leben* [1951; repr. Frankfurt am Main: Suhrkamp, 1989], 121; "Glorification of the feminine character implies the humiliation of all who bear it": *Minima Moralia: Reflections from Damaged Life,* trans. E. F. N. Jephcott (London: Verso, 1974), 96).

[72] HA 6:43; Luce Irigaray, *je, tu, nous: Toward a Culture of Difference,* trans. Alison Martin (New York: Routledge, 1993), 42–43.

[73] Cited in Rainer Nägele, "Modernism and Postmodernism: The Margins of Articulation," *Studies in Twentieth-Century Literature* 5 (1980): 5–25.

[74] The phrase is Paul de Man's, in his "The Rhetoric of Temporality," in Charles S. Singleton, ed., *Interpretation: Theory and Practice* (Baltimore: Johns Hopkins UP, 1969), 173–209; here, 198.

[75] "Über Laokoon" (1798; HA 12:57).

[76] "Über Wahrheit und Wahrscheinlichkeit der Kunstwerke: Ein Gespräch" (1798; HA 12:68).

[77] Compare "Kunst und Altertum am Rhein und Main" (1816; HA 12:160), where Goethe emphasizes the thought-process involved in art, speaking of "der denkende Künstler" ("the thinking artist"), in the same way as in the title of his essay "Rembrandt der Denker" ("Rembrandt the Thinker," 1831; WA 1.49:303–5).

[78] Schlegel, *Kritische Ausgabe,* 2:182–83.

[79] *Maximen und Reflexionen,* 1072 (HA 12:490); compare Wilkinson and Willoughby, introduction to Friedrich Schiller, *On the Aesthetic Education of Man in a Series of Letters,* ed. and trans. Elizabeth M. Wilkinson and L. A. Willoughby (2nd ed., Oxford: Clarendon P, 1982), lxxxv–vi and 350.

[80] "Shakespeare und kein Ende" (HA 12:292 and 294).

[81] Jean-François Lyotard, "Answering the Question: What is Postmodernism?," in Ihab Habib Hassan and Sally Hassan, eds., *Innovation/Renovation: New Perspectives on the Humanities* (Madison, WI: U of Wisconsin P, 1983), 329–41; here, 341.

[82] *Maximen und Reflexionen,* 455 (HA 12:489).

[83] "Nach Falconet und über Falconet" (1775; HA 12:27).

[84] Erich Heller, *The Artist's Journey into the Interior and Other Essays* (New York: Random House, 1968), 129–30.

[85] "Der Sammler und die Seinigen" (1799; HA 12:84).

[86] "Shakespeare und kein Ende" (HA 12:297).

[87] *Maximen und Reflexionen,* 289 (HA 12:471).

[88] Borchmeyer, *Weimarer Klassik,* 462.

[89] Adorno, *Minima Moralia,* 9–10; trans. Jephcott, 16–17.

[90] Adorno, *Minima Moralia,* 90–91; trans. Jephcott, 74.

[91] See his conversation with Eckermann of 14 March 1830.

[92] See his conversation with Eckermann of 2 April 1829. Goethe is participating, under a metaphor, in that emergence of new norms of "health" and "sickness" in the late eighteenth- and early nineteenth-century world of discourse (see Clifford Siskin, *Historicity of Romantic Discourse* [New York and London: Oxford UP, 1988], especially 186) and which Nietzsche likewise foregrounds (see Malcolm Pasley, "Nietzsche's Use of Medical Terms," in Malcolm Pasley, ed., *Nietzsche: Imagery and Thought,* 123–58 [London: Methuen, 1978]).

[93] "Ruysdael als Dichter" (1816; HA 12:142), where Goethe speaks of Ruysdael's "Gesundheit [des] äußeren und inneren Sinnes."

[94] See M. H. Abrams, "Kant and the Theology of Art," *Notre Dame English Journal* 3, no. 3 (Summer, 1981): 75–106; and Darian Leader, *Stealing the Mona Lisa: What Art Stops us from Seeing* (London: Faber and Faber, 2002), 48 and 169. Tellingly, Augustine wrote of his conversion: "Late have I loved you, O Beauty so ancient and so new; late have I loved you! For behold you were within me, and I outside; and I sought you outside and in my ugliness fell upon those lovely things that you have made. You were with me and I was not with you" (*Confessions,* trans. R. S. Pine-Coffin [Harmondsworth, UK: Penguin, 1961], bk. 10, §27).

[95] St. Augustine, *On Christian Doctrine,* bk. 1, ch. 4, §4. The first three books were written in 397, and a fourth was added in 426.

[96] *On Christian Doctrine,* bk. 1, ch. 22, §21.

[97] *On Christian Doctrine,* bk. 1, ch. 4, §4. See also *City of God,* bk. 22, ch. 24. Inspired by the fall of Rome to the barbarian chief Alaric in 410, Augustine composed *De civitate Dei* between 413 and 426.

[98] FW §357; KSA 3:600. For further discussion of Nietzsche's break with the Platonism of Christianity, see Laurence Lampert, *Nietzsche and Modern Times: A Study of Bacon, Descartes, and Nietzsche* (New Haven and London: Yale UP, 1993), especially 128 and 352.

1: *Die Geburt der Tragödie* and Weimar Classicism

Was wäre die Welt ohne des Leibes Liebesleben?

[What would the world be without the love-life of the body?]
 — Goethe, "Was ist der Himmel, was ist die Welt?"; WA 1.4:164

Denn was wäre die Welt ohne Kunst?

[For what would the world be without art?]
 — Goethe, *Tag- und Jahreshefte 1805;* WA 1.35:198

IN HIS "VERSUCH EINER SELBSTKRITIK" ("Attempt at a Self-Criticism," 1886), written fifteen years after *Die Geburt der Tragödie (The Birth of Tragedy)* was conceived with the thunder of the Battle of Wörth in the background (§1; KSA 1:11), Nietzsche highlighted — but recognized as problematic — the phrase which, in all, occurred three times in his book, namely, "dass nur als ästhetisches Phänomen das Dasein der Welt *gerechtfertigt* ist" (Versuch §5; KSA 1:17; "that the existence of the world is *justified* only as an aesthetic phenomenon"; compare GT §5 and §24; KSA 1:47 and 152).[1] Nietzsche explained the phrase as follows in a passage containing two important words, *Augenblick* and *Schein,* which point to two key themes of *Die Geburt der Tragödie* derived from Goethe[2] and Schiller:[3]

> Die Welt, in jedem Augenblicke die *erreichte* Erlösung Gottes, als die ewig wechselnde, ewig neue Vision des Leidendsten, Gegensätzlichsten, Widerspruchreichsten, der nur im *Scheine* sich zu erlösen weiss [. . .]. (*GT* Versuch §5; KSA 1:17)
>
> [The world — at every moment the *attained* salvation of God, as the eternally changing, eternally new vision of the most deeply suffering, conflicted, and contradictory being, who can find salvation only in *semblance* . . .]

In fact, Nietzsche's "Versuch einer Selbstkritik" underlines the book's importance as a work dedicated to aesthetics. Nietzsche calls the central problem of the work "ein Problem mit Hörnern" ("a problem with horns"; §2; KSA 1:13). While his "Versuch" says he would now call it "das *Problem der Wissenschaft* selbst" ("*the problem of science itself*"), the phrase also echoes Schiller's letter of 26 October 1795 to Wilhelm von Humboldt (1767–

1835), where he confessed his close affinity to the Greeks: "Ja ich bilde mir in gewissen Augenblicken ein, daß ich eine größere Affinitaet zu den Griechen haben muß, als viele andre, weil ich sie, ohne einen unmittelbaren Zugang zu ihnen, doch noch immer in meinen Kreis ziehen und mit meinen Fühlhörnern erfassen kann" (NA 28:84; "Yes, I imagine in certain moments that I must have a greater affinity to the Greeks than many others because I can, without any direct access to them, draw them into my circle and grasp them with my feelers"). Moreover, Nietzsche's "Versuch einer Selbstkritik" repeated the phrase, used in the first edition in the *Vorwort an Richard Wagner* ("Preface to Richard Wagner"), about art — and not morality — constituting "die höchste Aufgabe und die eigentlich metaphysische Thätigkeit dieses Lebens" (Vorwort; KSA 1:24; "the highest task and the truly metaphysical activity of this life"; compare Versuch §5; KSA 1:17). In a note from his *Nachgelassene Fragmente,* Nietzsche added that the book was written against Wagner, as well as against Schopenhauer and "die moralische Deutung des Daseins, — ich stellte **darüber die aesthetische,** *ohne die moralische zu leugnen* oder zu ändern" (12[220]; KSA 9:615; "the moral interpretation of existence — I placed **the aesthetic** above it, *without denying the moral* or changing it"). Furthermore, Nietzsche recognized that his book was opposed to Christianity: "Es giebt zu der rein ästhetischen Welt-auslegung und Welt-Rechtfertigung, wie sie in diesem Buche gelehrt wird, keinen grösseren Gegensatz als die christliche Lehre, welche *nur* moralisch ist und sein will" (Versuch §5; KSA 1:18; "Nothing is be more opposed to the purely aesthetic interpretation and justification of the world which is taught in this book than the Christian teaching, which is, and wants to be, *only* moral").[4] For Nietzsche, by contrast, life itself is based on semblance: "Alles Leben ruht auf Schein, Kunst, Täuschung, Optik, Nothwendigkeit des Perspektivischen und des Irrthums" (Versuch §5; KSA 1:18; "All life is based on semblance, art, deception, points of view, and the necessity of perspectives and error").[5] Furthermore, Nietzsche claimed, his book articulated "eine grundsätzliche Gegenlehre und Gegenwerthung des Lebens, eine rein artistische, eine *antichristliche*" ("a fundamental counter-doctrine and valuation of life, one which is purely artistic, *anti-Christian*"), which he baptized with the name of the Greek god — "die *dionysische*" ("*Dionysian*"; Versuch §5; KSA 1:19).[6] Significantly, Nietzsche closed his "Versuch einer Selbstkritik" with a long quotation from *Zarathustra,* in which Zarathustra exhorts the Higher Men to engage in Dionysian dance and laughter (Versuch §7; KSA 1:22; compare *Z* IV 13 §§17–18, 20; KSA 4:366–68).

As a classicist, Nietzsche had been preoccupied with the study of ancient Greece for a long time.[7] In particular, he had studied the use of rhetoric in classical texts. In *Die Philosophie im tragischen Zeitalter der Griechen* (*Philosophy in the Tragic Age of the Greeks,* 1872–73), Nietzsche wondered how philosophy had begun in ancient Greece, and argued that Greek philosophy had its roots, not in sorrow and distress, but rather in strength and happiness:

> Dagegen haben die Griechen es verstanden, zur rechten Zeit anzufangen, und diese Lehre, wann man zu philosophiren anfangen müsse, geben sie so deutlich, wie kein anderes Volk. Nicht nämlich erst in der Trübsal: was wohl Einige vermeinen, die die Philosophie aus der Verdrießlichkeit ableiten. Sondern im Glück, in einer reifen Mannbarkeit, mitten heraus aus der feurigen Heiterkeit des tapferen und siegreichen Mannesalters. (*PTZ* §1; KSA 1:805)

> [In contrast the Greeks knew the right time to begin, and this doctrine about when one should begin to philosophize is taught by them more clearly than by any other people. Namely, not only when in depression: which some, who derive philosophy from moroseness, think is the case. Rather, in happiness, in sexual maturity, right in the middle of the fiery cheerfulness of bold and victorious manhood.]

In particular, Nietzsche argued in his section on Heraclitus,[8] such strength and confidence derived from a view of the world which he proceeded to define as the *aesthetic:*

> Ein Werden und Vergehen, ein Bauen und Zerstören, ohne jede moralische Zurechnung, in ewig gleicher Unschuld, hat in dieser Welt allein das Spiel des Künstlers und des Kindes. [. . .] So schaut nur der ästhetische Mensch die Welt an, der an dem Künstler und an dem Entstehen des Kunstwerks erfahren hat, wie der Streit der Vielheit doch in sich Gesetz und Recht tragen kann, wie der Künstler beschaulich über und wirkend in dem Kunstwerk steht, wie Nothwendigkeit und Spiel, Widerstreit und Harmonie sich zur Zeugung des Kunstwerkes paaren müssen. (*PTZ* §7; KSA 1:830–31)[9]

> [A becoming and a passing away, building and destruction, without any moral responsibility, in an innocence that remains forever — in this world only the play of the artist and the child has these . . . Only the aesthetic person sees the world in this way, who has learned from the artist and from the creation of a work of art how the strife of multiplicity can bear within itself rule and law, how the artist stands, in contemplation above, and at work in, the work of art, how necessity and play, conflict and harmony, must be combined for the procreation of the work of art.]

In *Die Geburt der Tragödie,* Nietzsche takes up the same themes; but, although the book is ostensibly about the historical ancient Greeks and was taken by many contemporaries to be a defense of Wagner, it can also be understood — and with greater significance — as an investigation of the views developed by Goethe and Schiller, which may be conveniently referred to as the aesthetics of Weimar classicism.

Die Geburt der Tragödie contains many direct references as well as passing allusions to Goethe and Schiller.[10] More important, it draws directly on key notions from Weimar aesthetics in its ostensible discussion of Greek tragedy. For example, Nietzsche alludes to and quotes from Schiller's poem "An die Freude" ("Ode to Joy,"1786; *GT* §1; KSA 1:29), quotes from Schiller's letter to Goethe of 18 March 1796 (*GT* §5; KSA 1:43), refers to Schiller's notion of the naïve (*GT* §3; KSA 1:37) and of the idyll (*GT* §19; KSA 1:125) as they are set out in *Ueber naive und sentimentalische Dichtung* (*On the Naïve and the Sentimental in Literature*, 1795–96), and also refers more generally to the "Bildungskampf" ("cultural struggle") of Goethe, Schiller and Winckelmann, describing it as "most noble" (*GT* §20; KSA 1:129). In section 7, Nietzsche refers to Schiller's essay "Ueber den Gebrauch des Chors in der Tragödie" (*GT* §7; KSA 1:54–55; "On the Use of the Chorus in Tragedy," 1803), and in section 22, albeit dismissively, to his lecture "Was kann eine gute stehende Schaubühne eigentlich wirken?" (*GT* §22; KSA 1:144; "What Difference Can a Good Theatrical Stage Actually Make?," 1784). Although Nietzsche concentrates on Schiller's argument that the chorus acts as a living wall to exclude the real world and preserve the ideal world of poetic freedom,[11] the main emphasis of the essay of 1803 is on aesthetic pleasure. For Schiller art is, above all, conducive to happiness:

> Aber indem man das Theater ernsthafter behandelt, will man das Vergnügen des Zuschauers nicht aufheben, sondern veredeln. Es soll ein Spiel bleiben, aber ein poetisches. Alle Kunst ist der Freude gewidmet, und es gibt keine höhere und keine ernsthaftere Aufgabe, als die Menschen zu beglücken. Die rechte Kunst ist nur diese, welche den höchsten Genuß verschafft. Der höchste Genuß aber ist die Freiheit des Gemüts in dem lebendigen Spiel aller seiner Kräfte. (NA 10:8)

> [But by treating the theatre more seriously, one does not want to abolish, but to ennoble, the pleasure of the spectator. It should remain play, but poetic play. All art is dedicated to joy, and there is no higher and more serious task than of making people happy. The only real art is the art that creates the highest enjoyment. The highest enjoyment, however, is the freedom of the inner life of feeling in the living play of all its powers.]

Although Nietzsche alludes to the later title of Schiller's lecture "Die Schaubühne als moralische Anstalt betrachtet" (1802; The Theatrical Stage viewed as a Moral Institution) in describing "die Tendenz, das Theater als Veranstaltung zur moralischen Volksbildung zu verwenden" ("the tendency to use the theater as an institution for the moral education of the people") in highly negative terms — "welche Entfremdung der eigentlichen Kunst-absichten hier und da geradezu zu einem Cultus der Tendenz führen musste" ("an alienation from the true aims of art that sometimes inevitably resulted in an outright cult of tendentiousness") — he does not, it should be noted, condemn Schiller directly, remarking merely that this tendency was taken seriously "zu Schillers Zeit" ("in Schiller's time"; *GT* §22; KSA 1:143–44). Nor, for that matter, would Nietzsche have disagreed with Schiller's description of the task of Beauty in "Die Schaubühne als eine moralische Anstalt betrachtet":

> Unsre Natur [. . .] verlangte einen mittleren Zustand, der beide widersprechende Enden vereinigte, die harte Spannung zu sanfter Harmonie herabstimmte, und den wechselsweisen Uebergang eines Zustandes in den andern erleichterte. Diesen Nutzen leistet überhaupt nun der ästhetische Sinn, oder das Gefühl für das Schöne. (NA 20:90)

> [Our nature . . . demanded a middle condition, which unified both contradictory ends, toned down hard tension to soft harmony, and permitted the reciprocal transition of the one condition into the other. This task is achieved only by the aesthetic sense, or by the feeling for what is beautiful.]

Yet Schiller plays an even more substantial role in *Die Geburt der Tragödie*, for in his discussion of Apollo and Dionysus Nietzsche takes over central concepts from *Ueber die ästhetische Erziehung des Menschen in einer Reihe von Briefen* (*On the Aesthetic Education of Humankind in a Series of Letters*, 1795), a work that, as we know from Nietzsche's autobiographical writings, he had read while at school.[12] In the first of these *Aesthetic Letters*, Schiller admitted that his work was based on Kantian principles (Letter 1, §3). In a similar way, the figure of Kant lurks in the background of *Die Geburt der Tragödie*, not just because of the Schillerian terminology but, on two occasions in particular, more directly. In section 18, Nietzsche congratulates Kant, together with Schopenhauer, for having broken the optimism of scientific logic — thereby inaugurating a new tragic culture![13] And, in section 21, Nietzsche criticizes contemporary aestheticians for being ignorant of the distinction between the phenomenon (*Erscheinung*) and the noumenon (*Ding an sich;* *GT* §21; KSA 1:139), a Kantian ontology, central to Weimar Classicism's theoretical formulations, found earlier on in his work (*GT* §8; KSA 1:58–59). But implicitly, Nietzsche is also arguing that contemporary aestheticians have ignored the importance of aesthetic (Schillerian) *Schein*.

Both the vocabulary and the imagery of Weimar aesthetics turn out to be central to Nietzsche's discussion of Apollo and Dionysus. The status of these figures in *Die Geburt der Tragödie* is highly complex. In section 1, Nietzsche presents Apollo and Dionysus in three different ways. First, they represent gods; more specifically, they are "Kunstgottheiten" ("art deities"). Second, they represent creative human drives or *Triebe*. On this level, they correspond to Schiller's two basic drives, the *Formtrieb* and the *Stofftrieb*. Finally, they represent corresponding physiological states, namely *Traum* (dream) and *Rausch* (frenzy). Nietzsche's discussion of Apollo in particular is saturated with Schillerian terminology.[14]

At the core of Schiller's thinking on aesthetics lies the concept of *schöner Schein*. Schiller's concept draws here on the Kantian view of the individual human as the citizen of two realms: the phenomenal and the noumenal. In "Ueber Anmuth und Würde" ("On Grace and Dignity," 1793), Schiller argued that Beauty belongs to both these realms: "Die Schönheit ist [. . .] als die Bürgerin zwoer Welten anzusehen, deren einer sie durch *Geburt*, der andern durch *Adoption* angehört; sie empfängt ihre Existenz in der sinnlichen Natur, und *erlangt* in der Vernunftwelt das Bürgerrecht" (NA 20:260; "Beauty is to be considered the citizen of two worlds, to one of which it belongs by *birth*, to the other by *adoption;* it receives its existence in sensuous nature, and reaches in the world of reason its civil rights"). What unites these two realms, according to Schiller, is aesthetic judgment: "Der Geschmack, als ein Beurtheilungsvermögen des Schönen, [tritt] zwischen Geist und Sinnlichkeit in die Mitte [. . .], und [verbindet] diese beyden, einander verschmähenden Naturen, zu einer glücklichen Eintracht" (NA 20:260; "Taste, as a means of judging the beautiful, steps in between the mind and sensuousness . . . and combines both of these mutually antipathetic natures into a happy concord"). Humankind's destiny, its *Bestimmung*, as a member of two realms finds its highest expression in love which, for Schiller, is closely united with the aesthetic. Only by means of Beauty, Schiller argues in his *Aesthetic Letters*, can lust become love, for a person can overcome the "gemeinen Charakter" ("crude character") imposed by physical need upon sexual desire, which she or he "durch Sittlichkeit auslöscht und durch Schönheit veredelt" (Letter 3, §2; "obliterates by means of morality, and ennobles by means of beauty"). Just as Juno Ludovisi, that great eighteenth-century cultural icon of the aesthetic, demands "unsre Anbetung" ("our veneration"), so the god-like woman, says Schiller, kindles "unsre Liebe" ("our love," Letter 15, §9). Indeed, for Schiller, the appreciation of the Beauty of the beloved represents a high moment of aesthetic achievement:

> Eine schönere Notwendigkeit kettet jetzt die Geschlechter zusammen, und der Herzen Anteil hilft das Bündnis bewahren, das die Begierde nur launisch und wandelbar knüpft. [. . .] Die Begierde erweitert und erhebt sich zur Liebe, so wie die Menschheit in ihrem Gegenstand aufgeht [. . .]. Das Bedürfnis zu gefallen unterwirft den Mächtigen des Geschmackes zartem Gericht; die Lust kann er rauben, aber die Liebe muss eine Gabe sein. (Letter 27, §7)

[Now compulsion of a lovelier kind binds the sexes together, and a communion of the hearts helps sustain a connection but intermittently established by the fickle caprice of desire. . . . Desire widens, and is exalted into love, once humanity has dawned in its object . . . The need to please subjects the all-conquering male to the gentle tribunal of taste; lust he can steal, but love must come as a gift.]

Famously, Schiller used the image of the loving couple to symbolize the relationship between the poet and language: "Laß die Sprache dir seyn, was der Körper den Liebenden" (NA 1:302; "Let language be for you what the body is for lovers"). And in "Ueber Anmuth und Würde," Schiller described love as "das *absolut Große* selbst, was in der Anmuth und Schönheit sich nachgeahmt und in der Sittlichkeit sich befriedigt findet, es ist der Gesetzgeber selbst, der *Gott* in uns, der mit seinem eigenen Bilde in der Sinnenwelt spielt" (NA 20:303; "*absolute greatness* itself, what is imitated in grace and beauty and finds its satisfaction in morality, it is the legislator itself, the *god* in us, which plays with its own image in the sensuous world"). Because Beauty, as Schiller wrote in his *Aesthetic Letters,* unites both sensuous and spiritual aspects of humankind, the aesthetic becomes an important path to psycho-physiological unity: "Durch die Schönheit wird der sinnliche Mensch zur Form und zum Denken geleitet; durch die Schönheit wird der geistige Mensch zur Materie zurückgeführt und der Sinnenwelt wiedergegeben" (Letter 18, §1; "By means of Beauty the sensuous human is led to form and thought; by means of Beauty the spiritual human is brought back to matter and restored to the world of sense").

In the *Kallias-Briefe,* written to Christian Gottfried Körner in 1793, Schiller outlined his ideas for a treatise on Beauty that never appeared but whose central tenets were integrated into the *Aesthetic Letters.* In his letter of 8 February, Schiller argued that an object is beautiful only when it appears to be free, thus defining Beauty as freedom in appearance: "Schönheit also ist nichts anders als Freiheit in der Erscheinung" (NA 26:183; "Thus Beauty is nothing other than freedom in appearance"). For Schiller, the whole question of Beauty is "den Faden [. . .], der uns durch das ganze Labyrinth der Ästhetik führt" (Letter 18, §3; "the thread that will guide us through the whole labyrinth of aesthetics"). The essence of Beauty lies in its appearance, its semblance. And in Weimar aesthetics the image of the veil came to symbolize the transforming effect of the aesthetic moment.[15]

In his *Aesthetic Letters,* Schiller made a distinction between two basic drives: the *Stofftrieb* (or "sensuous drive"), and the *Formtrieb* (or "formal drive"; Letter 12). The reciprocal coordination of these two drives resulted in what he called the *Spieltrieb* (or "ludic drive"; Letter 14, §§3–6). Out of the ludic drive, Schiller argued, there arises the aesthetic. Or, as Nietzsche noted in his *Nachlass:* "Schönheit tritt ein, wenn die einzelnen Triebe einmal parallel laufen, aber nicht gegen einander" (7[182]; KSA 7:157; "Beauty descends when the individual drives run in parallel, but not against each other"). In his *Kritik der Urteilskraft* (*Critique of Judgment*, 1790), Kant had defined the aesthetic judgment as "der Zustand eines *freien Spiels* der Erkenntnisvermögen" ("the state of *free play* of the cognitive faculties").[16] The importance of play, as an aesthetic phenomenon, lies at the heart of what Schiller thought aesthetics could do to civilize humankind: "Der Mensch spielt nur, wo er in voller Bedeutung des Worts Mensch ist, und *er ist nur da ganz Mensch, wo er spielt*" (Letter 15, §9; "The human being only plays when he or she is in the fullest sense of the word a human being, and *a human being is only fully one when he or she plays*").[17] Finally, Schiller was unambiguous in his praise for ancient Greece: "Eine wohltätige Gottheit reisse den Säugling bei Zeiten von seiner Mutter Brust, nähre ihn mit der Milch eines bessern Alters und lasse ihn unter fernem griechischen Himmel zur Mündigkeit reifen" (Letter 9, §4; "Let some beneficent deity snatch the suckling betimes from his mother's breast, nourish him with the milk of a better age, and suffer him to come to maturity under a distant Grecian sky").

In *Die Geburt der Tragödie*, Apollo is repeatedly identified with *schöner Schein:* "[Apollo], der seiner Wurzel nach der 'Scheinende,' die Lichtgottheit ist, beherrscht auch den schönen Schein der inneren Phantasie-Welt" (*GT* §1; KSA 1:27; "Apollo who, as the etymological root of his name indicates, is the 'shining one,' the deity of light, also rules over the beautiful semblance of the inner world of fantasy"). The Apollonian dream, Nietzsche says in section 4, is "der Traum als der *Schein des Scheins*" (KSA 1:39; "the dream as the *mere semblance of mere semblance*"). In other words, the Apollonian in its aesthetic modality is merely the representation ([*schöner*] *Schein*) of the phenomenal world (*Erscheinung*). According to Nietzsche, however, Apollonian *Schein*, the object's merely phenomenal modality (its mere appearance), constitutes only one half of the poetic experience: "Der schöne Schein der Traumwelten, in deren Erzeugung jeder Mensch voller Künstler ist, ist die Voraussetzung aller bildenden Kunst, ja auch [. . .] einer wichtigen Hälfte der Poesie" (*GT* §1; KSA 1:26; "The beautiful semblance of the dream worlds, in the creation of which every individual is truly an artist, is the prerequisite of all plastic art, and also . . . an important part of poetry").[18] Like Goethe and Schiller, Nietzsche also uses the image of the veil to symbolize aesthetic semblance. Indeed, in his *Nachlass* of summer 1872 to the beginning of 1873, Nietzsche wrote: "Jede Art von *Kultur* beginnt damit, daß eine Menge von Dingen *verschleiert* werden" (19[50]; KSA 7:435; "Every kind of *culture* begins when a number of things are *veiled*"). In section 2, he identifies the Apollonian consciousness — in both its full aesthetic and its merely phenomenal modalities — with a veil, covering up a Dionysian reality: "Dass sein apollinisches Bewusstsein nur wie ein Schleier diese dionysische Welt vor ihm verdecke" (*GT* §2; KSA 1:34; "only his

Apollonian consciousness, like a veil, hid this Dionysian world from him"). And in section 8, he speaks of the Apollonian dream as a transforming veil:

> Dies ist der apollinische Traumeszustand, in dem die Welt des Tages sich verschleiert und eine neue Welt, deutlicher, verständlicher, ergreifender als jene und doch schattengleicher, in fortwährendem Wechsel sich unserem Auge neu gebiert. (*GT* §8; KSA 1:64)

> [This is the Apollonian state of dreams, in which the world of the day becomes veiled, and a new world, clearer, more comprehensible, more moving than the other and yet more shadowy, is born before our eyes in a constant rhythm of change.]

Most famously, quoting from *Die Welt als Wille und Vorstellung* (*The World as Will and Representation*), he associates Apollo with Schopenhauer's image of the human being caught up in the veil of Maya.[19] And he continues, using Schopenhauer's terminology, as follows:

> Ja es wäre von Apollo zu sagen, dass in ihm das unerschütterte Vertrauen auf jenes principium und das ruhige Dasitzen des in ihm Befangenen seinen erhabensten Ausdruck bekommen habe, und man möchte selbst Apollo als das herrliche Götterbild des principii individuationis bezeichnen, aus dessen Gebärden und Blicken die ganze Lust und Weisheit des "Scheines," sammt seiner Schönheit, zu uns spräche. (*GT* §1; KSA 1:28)[20]

> [Indeed, one could say of Apollo that, in him, the unshaken trust in this *principium* and the calm repose of the individual receive their most sublime expression; and we might describe Apollo himself as the glorious divine image of the *principium individuationis,* from whose gestures and glances all the joy and wisdom of "semblance," together with its beauty, speak to us.]

By contrast, Dionysus is said to represent the destruction of this veil, leaving it as if in tatters and revealing — beneath the phenomenal world of appearance (that is, *Erscheinung*) — the fundamental noumenal unity of Being.

> Unter dem Zauber des Dionysischen schließt sich nicht nur der Bund zwischen Mensch und Mensch wieder zusammen: auch die entfremdete, feindliche oder unterjochte Natur feiert wieder ihr Versöhnungsfest mit ihrem verlorenen Sohne, dem Menschen. [. . .] Jetzt, bei dem Evangelium der Weltenharmonie, fühlt sich Jeder mit seinem Nächsten nicht nur vereinigt, versöhnt, verschmolzen, sondern eins, als ob der Schleier der Maja zerrissen wäre und nur noch in Fetzen vor dem geheimnissvollen Ur-Einen herumflattere. (*GT* §1; KSA 1:29–30)

[Under the spell of the Dionysian not only is the union between individual human beings reaffirmed, but nature, which has become alienated, hostile, or subjugated, celebrates once more her reconciliation with her prodigal son, humankind . . . Now, with the gospel of universal harmony, all feel themselves not only united, reconciled, and fused with their neighbors, but as one with them, as if the veil of *maya* had been torn aside and were now merely fluttering in tatters before the mysterious primal unity.]

Yet it is important to realize that, for Nietzsche, the essence of tragedy, as of all art, lies in the *union* of these two drives. Central to our argument here is that Nietzsche's comments on the Apollonian — sculpture during a particular historical period of Greek civilization — and on the Dionysian — the music deriving from the ceremony of the mystery cult — as an aid to cyclic periodization should not be confused with his logical analysis of their function in the aesthetic.[21] Taken separately, neither Apollo nor Dionysus — neither the form drive (that is, the Apollonian phenomenal form) nor the material drive (that is, the Dionysian passion) — constitutes the aesthetic moment proper of the ludic drive (in other words, the Apollonian aesthetic form that *contains* the Dionysian), which arises out of a reciprocal coordination of the two: "'Schein,' sammt seiner Schönheit" ("'semblance,' together with its beauty").

In other words, it is important to distinguish between Nietzsche's various uses of the word *Schein*. First, there is "Schein" as the phenomenon of ordinary perception (or, in other words, "Er[*schein*]ung"). Second, there is "Schein des Scheins," the "realistic" semblance achieved by what Schiller called "falscher" or "logischer Schein." And third, there is "Schein des Seins," or the aesthetic proper — the "as if" (*als ob*) of aesthetic semblance (*Schein* or *der Dichtung Schleier*), Schiller's "schöner" (or "wahrer") "Schein," in which Being is not repressed but revealed. It is certainly true that Nietzsche does not distinguish in explicit terms between "Schein des Scheins" ("logischer"/"falscher Schein") and "schöner Schein," and there are two reasons for this. First, by the time Nietzsche came to write *Die Geburt der Tragödie,* the expression "schöner Schein" had acquired, in addition to its full connotations in the context of the aesthetic of Weimar classicism, the trivial meaning of "keeping up appearances" (a sense of which, however, Schiller was also aware [NA 2:91]). And second, Nietzsche, as part of his characteristically rhetorical style, obliges *the reader* to make this distinction, in order to be able to construe an argument which, otherwise, appears contradictory. In this respect, Nietzsche's argument deploys a mode of argumentation, "binary synthesis," which is found in Weimar classical aesthetics. This "proto-Hegelian" mode of argumentation is clearly already at work in Schiller's *Aesthetic Letters.*[22]

In binary synthesis, the name of one element in a pair of antitheses is also applied to the synthesis, which thus represents both a richer concept, but one that tends towards one of the original antitheses in an ascending hierarchy.[23] Such is the case in Nietzsche's claim that in tragedy, as in all art, Apollo and Dionysus are united. In the first section of *Die Geburt der Tragödie,* Nietzsche speaks of the unified appearance ("mit einander gepaart erscheinen") of Apollo and Dionysus as the birth of Attic tragedy (*GT* §1; KSA 1:25). Later on, Nietzsche makes it clear that the fully articulated union of Apollo and Dionysus represents the highest goal, not just of tragedy, but of art as a whole. In this passage, it looks as if Apollo is going to lose out to Dionysus —

> Das Drama [. . .] erreicht als Ganzes eine Wirkung, die *jenseits aller apollinischen Kunstwirkungen* liegt. In der Gesammtwirkung der Tragödie erlangt das Dionysische wieder das Uebergewicht; sie schliesst mit einem Klange, der niemals von dem Reiche der apollinischen Kunst her tönen könnte. Und damit erweist sich die apollinische Täuschung als das, was sie ist, als die während der Dauer der Tragödie anhaltende Umschleierung der eigentlichen dionysischen Wirkung: die doch so mächtig ist, am Schluss das apollinische Drama selbst in eine Sphäre zu drängen, wo es mit dionysischer Weisheit zu reden beginnt und wo es sich selbst und seine apollinische Sichtbarkeit verneint.

> [The drama . . . attains as a whole an effect that transcends *all Apollonian artistic effects.* In the total effect of tragedy the Dionysian regains its predominance; tragedy closes with a sound that could never come from the realm of Apollonian art. And thus the Apollonian deception reveals itself for what it really is — the veiling during the performance of the tragedy of the real Dionysian effect, which is so powerful that it ends up forcing the Apollonian drama itself into a sphere where it begins to speak with Dionysian wisdom and where it denies itself and its Apollonian visibility.]

— but, in the end, both are combined:

> So wäre wirklich das schwierige Verhältniss des Apollinischen und des Dionysischen in der Tragödie durch einen Bruderbund beider Gottheiten zu symbolisiren: Dionysus redet die Sprache des Apollo, Apollo aber schliesslich die Sprache des Dionysus: womit das höchste Ziel der Tragödie und der Kunst überhaupt erreicht ist. (*GT* §21; KSA 1:139–40)

> [Thus the complex relation of the Apollonian and the Dionysian in tragedy may really be symbolized by a fraternal union of the two deities: Dionysus speaks the language of Apollo, but Apollo, finally, the language of Dionysus; whereby the highest goal of tragedy and of all art is attained.]

By using Apollo and Dionysus as quantitative concepts to express a difference of mere rhetorical style, the chiasmus of this final sentence in section 21
suggests that the succession of Apollo and Dionysus is itself overcome. From
art in which the Apollonian is predominant (in other words, the merely rep-
resentational), a higher art (Nietzsche calls its import "tragic") develops. To
put it another way, while *mere* (purely Apollonian) semblance is rejected, the
union of the Apollonian with the Dionysian is regarded by Nietzsche as *essential* for the truly aesthetic experience[24] — "das höchste Ziel [. . .] der
Kunst überhaupt" ("the highest goal of all art").[25] Or, in terms of Weimar
aesthetics,[26] the *Gehalt* ("import") of art is raw, Dionysian feeling that has
been given expression by the fusion of the Apollonian form with Dionysian
inwardness in a given medium (one of the meanings of *Stoff* in Goethe and
Schiller) to yield an aesthetic *Gestalt*.[27] Moreover, if we are to believe
Nietzsche's note in his *Nachlass* from the end of 1870 to April 1871, the full
satisfaction of Being lies in achieved — that is to say, aesthetic — *Schein:*
"*Das Sein befriedigt sich im vollkommenen Schein*" (7[157]; KSA 7:200; "*Being satisfies itself in achieved semblance*"). Thus "mere" Apollonian semblance or "Schein des Scheins" is *aufgehoben* ("sublated") in aesthetic
semblance or "schöner Schein" (in other words, "Schein des Seins"). And
so, for Nietzsche, art — and the aesthetic justification of life — is Apollonian
"schöner Schein" that contains Dionysian wisdom.[28] In Nietzsche's later
writings a similar and related example of binary synthesis structures his argument. For the Dionysian — as, for example, applied to Goethe in the famous passage in *Götzen-Dämmerung* — consists of the union of the
Apollonian and the Dionysian in the sense that they are used in *Die Geburt
der Tragödie*.[29]

Nietzsche's use of Goethe in *Die Geburt der Tragödie* is an equally important part of his strategy to weave key concepts of Weimar aesthetics into a
bewildering combination of references to ancient Greek drama and
Schopenhauerian philosophy, while pursuing an argument that is quasi-
Hegelian in its dialectical thrust. For Goethe, like Schiller, is overtly mentioned on numerous occasions. Nietzsche refers to a stanza from the poem
"Prometheus" (1774; *GT* §9; KSA 1:67),[30] to the later of his two poems entitled "Grabschrift" (1814; *GT* §11; KSA 1:78), to his project to write a play
called *Nausikaa* (*GT* §12; KSA 1:83), to his conversation about Napoleon
with Eckermann of 11 March 1828 (*GT* §18; KSA 1:116–17), to the poem
"Generalbeichte" (1802; *GT* §18; KSA 1:119), to *Iphigenia* (1779; *GT* §20;
KSA 1:131), and to Goethe's letter to Schiller of 9 December 1797 (*GT*
§22; KSA 1:142). More important, Nietzsche makes sustained reference
throughout to *Faust*. Taken together, these allusions and quotations alert
the sensitive reader to the tradition in which Nietzsche is working.

In his presentation of the Dionysian, Nietzsche's reference to
"Hexentrank" ("witches' brew"; *GT* §2; KSA 1:32) recalls the *Hexenküche*

scene of *Faust I* (lines 2365–67). The next reference, to "Zaubertrank im Leibe" ("magic potion in the body"; *GT* §3; KSA 1:35), alludes to Faust's vision, having drunk the magic potion, of Gretchen; Mephistopheles tells him: "Du siehst, mit diesem Trank im Leibe, / Bald Helenen in jedem Weibe" (lines 2603–4; "With that elixir coursing through you, / Soon any women will be Helen to you"). In his very next line, Nietzsche follows the sense of Mephisto's words, mentioning Helen.[31] The phrase he quotes, "in süßer Sinnlichkeit schwebend" ("floating in sweet sensuality"), comes, however, not from *Faust,* but from *Wilhelm Meisters Lehrjahre* (Bk. 4, ch. 14), where Wilhelm, in conversation with Aurelie, says of Shakespeare's character Ophelia: "Ihr ganzes Wesen schwebt in reifer, süßer Sinnlichkeit" ("Her whole being is pervaded by ripe, sweet sensuality").[32] In section 3 of *Geburt der Tragödie,* the phrase "der olympische Zauberberg" (KSA 1:35; "the Olympian magic mountain") recalls the words of the "Irrlicht" ("Will-o'-the Wisp") in the *Walpurgisnacht* scene of Part One, "der Berg ist heute zaubertoll" ("The whole mountain's magic-mad tonight"; line 3868), where Faust has his second vision of Gretchen; later, Nietzsche uses the phrase "den hellenischen Zauberberg" ("the Hellenic magic mountain") directly in connection with the (failed) attempts of Goethe and Schiller to initiate a classical aesthetic revival in the Germany, and Europe, of their time by breaking down the bewitched door to the magic mountain (*GT* §20; KSA 1:131). The phrase "wie Rosen aus dornigem Gebüsch hervorbrechen" ("just as roses burst from thorny bushes"), also in section 3 (KSA 1:36), echoes the line "es steht ein Kreuz mit Rosen dicht umschlungen" ("a cross, dense roses embrace it") from Goethe's fragmentary epic poem "Die Geheimnisse" (HA 2:271–84; see also 3[62]; KSA 7:77; "The Mysteries," 1789).

    In section 8, Nietzsche compares "die apollinischen Erscheinungen" ("the Apollonian appearances") to the vision of the world conjured up by the *Erdgeist* in the opening *Nacht* scene of *Faust* Part One (505–7), adding that in a work of tragedy this Dionysian world is transformed (KSA 1:64). The phrase "die Werdelust des Künstlers" ("the artist's delight in what becomes") in section 9 (KSA 1:68) echoes the hymn sung by the boys' choir on Easter Morning (789), as well as alluding to the more general Goethean motif of Becoming. Nietzsche concludes his discussion of the concepts of blasphemy and sin in this chapter with a quotation from the *Hexenchor* (3982–85; KSA 1:70). And section 9 itself concludes (KSA 1:71) with a reformulation of the aesthetic justification of the world and an echo (in this context, highly ironic) of Faust's exclamation — "Das ist deine Welt! das heißt eine Welt!" (409; "That is your world! Do you call that a world?") — when he reflects on the emptiness and sterility of his life at the beginning of the play. Then again, in section 13 (KSA 1:90), Nietzsche quotes five lines of the ambiguous lament of the *Geisterchor* when Faust curses the everyday world of life and love (1606–11). Whereas in Goethe's play the "Halbgott" ("demigod") is Faust himself, the term applies in Nietzsche's context to Socrates. Section 18 quotes Faust's lines in the *Klassische Walpurgnisnacht* of Part Two: "Und sollt' ich nicht, sehnsüchtigster Gewalt, / In's Leben ziehn die einzigste Gestalt?" (7438–39; "And shall I not, by passion's power, draw / Back into life that unique form I saw?"). These words refer, of course, to Helen (as well as, in the economy of Goethe's drama, repeating the rhyme on "Gewalt" and "Gestalt" earlier in Part One [1251–52] when Mephistopheles first appeared). In *Die Geburt der Tragödie,* Nietzsche places these words in the mouth of "der tragische Mensch dieser Kultur" ("the tragic individual of such a culture") who, just as Faust desires Helen, desires tragedy as "eine neue Kunst, die Kunst des metaphysischen Trostes" (KSA 1:119; "a new art, the art of metaphysical comfort").[33] Nietzsche repeated this passage in his "Versuch einer Selbstkritik," as part of his satirical attack on Romanticism (Versuch §7; KSA 1:21). In section 18, the quotation is followed by an allusion to Mephistopheles' encounter later in the *Klassische Walpurgnisnacht* with the seductive Lamiae, whom Mephisto embraces and then rejects, a humorous (and merely physical) counterpoint to the aesthetic attraction for Faust of Helen. In Nietzsche's context, the episode symbolizes the waning self-confidence of Socratic culture as opposed to the Faustian determination to regain the aesthetic.

Yet it is not until section 18 that the significance of this dense network of allusions to *Faust* becomes clear. The figure of Faust represents the modern individual who, like Socrates, is committed to science and yet, also like Socrates, is aware of its limits:[34]

> Wie unverständlich müsste einem ächten Griechen der an sich verständliche moderne Culturmensch *Faust* erscheinen, der durch alle Facultäten unbefriedigt stürmende, aus Wissenstrieb der Magie und dem Teufel ergebene Faust, den wir nur zur Vergleichung neben Sokrates zu stellen haben, um zu erkennen, dass der moderne Mensch die Grenzen jener sokratischen Erkenntnisslust zu ahnen beginnt und aus dem weiten wüsten Wissensmeere nach einer Küste verlangt. (*GT* §18; KSA 1:116)

> [How unintelligible must *Faust,* the modern cultured human, who is in himself intelligible, have appeared to a true Greek — Faust, storming unsatisfied through all the faculties, devoted to magic and the devil because of his desire for knowledge; Faust, whom we have only to place next to Socrates for the purpose of comparison, to see that the modern human is beginning to divine the limits of this Socratic desire for knowledge and yearns for a coast in the wide, waste ocean of knowledge.]

Faust's problem, as it is presented in the opening scenes of Goethe's play, is precisely the problem of knowledge. His predicament is like that of the human being of science, as portrayed in section 15 of *Die Geburt der Tragödie*. Faust wants to find out "was die Welt / Im Innersten zusammenhält" (383–84; "the inmost force / That binds the very universe"), yet he recognizes "daß wir nichts wissen können!" ("there is nothing we can know!"; 364). Similarly, the human being of science realizes "zu seinem Schrecken" ("to his horror") that logic runs up against its own boundaries and "endlich sich in den Schwanz beisst" (*GT* §15; KSA 1:101; "finally bites itself in the tail").[35]

Among its abundance of synchronic and diachronic reference, the plot of Goethe's play contains one clear narrative thread: the wager Faust makes with Mephistopheles.[36] Despairing of life and of the transience of Beauty (a despair caught in his ironic challenge to Mephistopheles: "Zeig' mir die Frucht die fault, eh' man sie bricht, / Und Bäume die sich täglich neu begrünen" (1686–87; "Show me the fruit that rots before it's plucked / And trees that change their foliage every day"), Faust strikes a famous bargain with the Devil. According to the agreement, in a much-quoted passage, if Faust desires that a moment (*Augenblick*) last forever, Mephistopheles will have won the wager — and, in terms of the religious symbolism of the play, can claim Faust's soul (1699–1706). The wager structures the whole of Goethe's massive drama; moreover, the substance of the wager as well as the details of the terms according to which it is undertaken are also a recurrent motif both in *Die Geburt der Tragödie* and, as we shall see, in *Also sprach Zarathustra*.

Faust desires Helen; the modern individual desires tragedy. How can they both reach their goal? In Goethe's play, Mephistopheles explains to Faust how he might fulfill the Emperor's demand to be presented with Helen and Paris, by telling him about the Mothers. "Denn wer den Schatz, das Schöne, heben will, / Bedarf der höchsten Kunst, Magie der Weisen" (6315–16; "For who would raise that treasure, beauty's prize, / Needs wisdom of the magi, highest art"). What the Mothers represent is controversial.[37] There is evidence, however, to suggest, at least, that the Mothers represent the realm of the aesthetic. Their realm is characterized by *Schein* (6285, 6431); by transformation ("Gestaltung, Umgestaltung, / Des ewigen Sinnes ewige Unterhaltung" [6287–88; "Formation, Transformation, / The eternal mind's eternal Recreation"]); and by suspension of temporal-spatial categories ("Um sie kein Ort noch weniger eine Zeit" [6214; "No space, no place around them, time still less"]). In his *Aesthetic Letters* Schiller wrote that, in the aesthetic state, the individual is "Null" ("Nothing"; Letter 21 §4); yet, at the same time, this condition is also "ein Zustand der *höchsten Realität*" (Letter 22 §1; "a state of *supreme reality*"). Likewise, Faust tells Mephistopheles: "Du sendest mich in's Leere, / Damit ich dort so Kunst als Kraft vermehre [. . .] Nur immer zu! wir wollen es ergründen, / In deinem Nichts hoff' ich das All zu finden" (6251–52, 6256;

"I / Am sent into your void to magnify / My art and strength there . . . But I am game! Let me explore that scope, / Within your Naught to find the All, I hope"). And Faust's words suggest that he is beginning to understand that the only way to convey eternity in the moment is through the aesthetic: "Was einmal war, in allem Glanz und Schein, /Es regt sich dort; denn es will ewig sein" (6431–32; "What once has been, what once shone gloriously, / Still stirs there, seeking evermore to be").

In *Die Geburt der Tragödie* the shadowy presence of the Mothers can also be felt, for they are alluded to on no less than three occasions (once for each of them). In tragedy, Nietzsche writes, Dionysus opens up the way to the Mothers:

> Apollo steht vor mir, als der verklärende Genius des *principii individuationis*, durch den allein die Erlösung im Scheine wahrhaft zu erlangen ist: während unter dem mystischen Jubelruf des Dionysus der Bann der Individuation zersprengt wird und der Weg zu den Müttern des Sein's, zu dem innersten Kern der Dinge offen liegt. (*GT* §16; KSA 1:103)

> [Apollo stands before me as the transfiguring genius of the *principium individuationis* through which alone redemption in semblance is truly to be obtained; while by the mystical triumphant cry of Dionysus the spell of individuation is broken and the way lies open to the Mothers of Being, to the innermost heart of things.]

But exactly how many Mothers are there? If they are outside space and time, it is hard to tell. In his second reference, Nietzsche speaks of just one primal Mother:

> In der dionysischen Kunst und in deren tragischer Symbolik redet uns dieselbe Natur mit ihrer wahren, unverstellten Stimme an: "Seid wie ich bin! Unter dem unaufhörlichen Wechsel der Erscheinungen die ewig schöpferische, ewig zum Dasein zwingende, an diesem Erscheinungswechsel sich ewig befriedigende Urmutter!" (*GT* §16; KSA 1:108)

> [In Dionysian art and its tragic symbolism the same nature cries to us with her true, undissembled voice: "Be as I am! Amid the ceaseless flux of phenomenal appearance, the eternally creative primal mother, eternally compelling into existence, eternally satisfying myself in this change of phenomena!"]

Significantly, in both Goethe's and Nietzsche's texts the Mothers have sexual as well as aesthetic undertones. Corresponding to the phallic connotation of the magic key which swells and expands in Faust's hand, Nietzsche's primal Mother is eternally "pleasuring herself," just as Zarathustra talks of sensual delight as a great simulacrum for higher happiness and highest hope:

"Wollust: das grosse Gleichniss-Glück für höheres Glück und höchste Hoffnung" (*Z* III 10 §2; KSA 4:237; "Sex: the happiness that is the great symbol of higher happiness and the highest hope"). Finally, the Mothers appear again in section 20, as a kind of triad of tragic sirens, beckoning the personified figure of Tragedy:

> Die Tragödie sitzt inmitten dieses Ueberflusses an Leben, Leid und Lust, in erhabener Entzückung, sie horcht einem fernen schwermüthigen Gesange — er erzählt von den Müttern des Seins, deren Namen lauten: Wahn, Wille, Wehe. (*GT* §20; KSA 1:132)

> [Tragedy sits in the midst of this excess of life, suffering, and pleasure, in sublime ecstasy, she listens to a distant melancholy song — it tells of the mothers of being whose names are: Illusion, Will, Woe.]

Having called up the figure of Helen from the (aesthetic) shadows in act 1 of Part Two, Faust, by mistaking a mere schema for reality, then loses her; he meets her again in the classical splendor of act 3, but she eventually disappears again when she descends to the underworld, leaving behind her (aesthetic) veil. So within the economy of the drama, Faust's salvation must wait until his ascension to *das Ewig-Weibliche* ("the Eternal Feminine") in the *Bergschluchten* (Mountain Gorges) scene in act 5. In the meantime, however, there is the matter of the wager to be resolved. Haunted in his palace by Want, Debt, Need and, most terrifying of all, Anxiety (*Sorge*), who penetrates his stronghold, the blind and aged Faust realizes, and comes eventually to accept, the limitations of knowledge. Echoing his earlier words when he castigated himself as a fool (compare line 358), and providing a summation of the *erkennen/begreifen* complex in the drama, Faust cries:

> Der Erdenkreis ist mir genug bekannt,
> Nach drüben ist die Aussicht uns verrannt;
> Thor! wer dorthin die Augen blinzelnd richtet,
> Sich über Wolken seinesgleichen dichtet;
> Er stehe fest und sehe hier sich um;
> Dem Tüchtigen ist diese Welt nicht stumm.
> Was braucht er in die Ewigkeit zu schweifen;
> Was er erkennt, läßt sich ergreifen.
>
> (11443–48)

> [I've seen enough of this terrestrial sphere.
> There is no view to the Beyond from here:
> A fool will seek it, peer with mortal eyes
> And dream of human life above the skies!
> Let him stand fast in this world, and look around
> With courage: here is so much to be found!

Why must he wander into timelessness?
What his mind grasps, he may possess.]

Faust comes to term with the limits of knowledge and experience when he concludes: "Das ist der Weisheit letzter Schluß: / Nur der verdient sich Freiheit wie das Leben, / Der täglich sie erobern muß" (11574–76; "This is the final word of wisdom:/ The only way to earn freedom, like life / Is to have to conquer them both every single day"). While the Lemuren dig his grave, Faust seems to speak the words for which Mephistopheles has been waiting: "Zum Augenblicke dürft' ich sagen: / Verweile doch, du bist so schön!" (11581–82; "Then to the moment I might say: / Beautiful moment, do not pass away!"). Anticipating his highest (aesthetic) happiness, Faust cries: "Im Vorgefühl von solchem hohen Glück / Genieß' ich jetzt den höchsten Augenblick" (11585–86; "And in anticipation of such bliss / What moment could give me greater joy than this?"). Mephistopheles and the chorus add the elements of detail, echoing Faust's words sealing the pact in Part One:

Mephistopheles

[. . .] Die Zeit wird Herr, der Greis liegt hier im Sand.
Die Uhr steht still —

Chor

                Steht still! Sie schweigt wie Mitternacht.
Der Zeiger fällt.

Mephistopheles

                Er fällt, es ist vollbracht.
                        (11592–94)

[*Mephistopheles*

. . . Time winds; the old man lies here in the sand.
The clock has stopped —

Chorus

            — Has stopped! Like midnight it is silent.
The clock-hands fall.

Mephistopheles

            They fall. It is finished.]

As the pomp, splendor, and beauty of the *Bergschluchten* scene serve to demonstrate however, Faust is saved. For he has learned to love the Beauty of the moment and to understand his as an aesthetic experience. Whereas in Part One he cried: "Zwei Seelen wohnen, ach! in meiner Brust" (1112; "In me there are two souls, alas!"), at the end of the whole drama he has become "Geeinte Zwienatur" (11962; "Unified double nature").[38] In other works, too, Goethe celebrates the transformation of the moment through the aesthetic. For example, the poem entitled "Das Göttliche" ("The God-like," 1783) says of the human individual: "Er kann dem Augenblick / Dauer verleihen" ("He can give lasting / Life to the moment").[39] And the later poem "Vermächtnis" ("Testament," 1829) concludes the fifth stanza with the following lines: "Dann ist Vergangenheit beständig, / Das Künftige voraus lebendig, / Der Augenblick ist Ewigkeit" ("Then the past is stable, / The future alive in anticipation, / The moment is eternity").[40]

Nietzsche's text contains important hints that the substance of Faust's wager is at stake in *Die Geburt der Tragödie,* too. In section 17 the happiness of the theoretical individual is said to reside in the ability to say to life: "'Ich will dich: du bist werth erkannt zu werden'" (KSA 1:115; "'I desire you; you are worth knowing'"). The Alexandrian individual seeking knowledge is, according to Nietzsche, full of Apollonian *Heiterkeit:* but, although desiring to know life, he or she has not yet come, as Faust does, to love it — despite such knowledge. For the theoretical individual, unlike Faust, does not understand the limits of knowledge; and, unlike Faust, has not learned to love life in its full aesthetic mode and to entertain a wish for the moment to last forever. Yet there is a more positive echo of Faust's last words in section 21 when, thanks to music, the tragic spectator is overcome by an anticipation of highest — aesthetic — pleasure:

> Insbesondere überkommt durch [die Musik] den tragischen Zuschauer gerade jenes sichere Vorgefühl einer höchsten Lust, zu der der Weg durch Untergang und Verneinung führt, so dass er zu hören meint, als ob der innerste Abgrund der Dinge zu ihm vernehmlich spräche. (*GT* §21/KGW 1:134–35)

> [In particular it is through music that the tragic spectators are overcome by an assured premonition of the highest pleasure, to which the path of destruction and negation leads, so that they feel as if the innermost abyss of things were speaking perceptibly to them.]

A similar phrase to "eine höchste Lust" ("the highest pleasure") occurs in section 24, when Nietzsche explains the fact that Greek art represents "die Exemplifikation jener Weisheit des Silen, oder, aesthetisch ausgedrückt, das Hässliche und Disharmonische" ("the exemplification of this wisdom of Silenus, or, to put it aesthetically, that which is ugly and disharmonic") in terms of "eine höhere Lust" ("a higher pleasure"; KSA 1:151). Furthermore, in that section Nietzsche explains how art offers "ein metaphysisches Supplement der Naturwirklichkeit. [. . .], zu deren Ueberwindung neben sie gestellt" ("a metaphysical supplement of the reality of nature, placed beside it in order to overcome it"), using the image of the clock hands of life. Here, again, the *Schein* of the phenomenal world is "overcome" in the *Verklärung* or enhancement of full aesthetic *Schein:*

> Der tragische Mythus, sofern er überhaupt zur Kunst gehört, nimmt auch vollen Antheil an dieser metaphysischen Verklärungsabsicht der Kunst überhaupt: was verklärt er aber, wenn er die Erscheinungswelt unter dem Bilde des leidenden Helden vorführt? Die "Realität" dieser Erscheinungswelt am wenigsten, denn er sagt uns gerade: "Seht hin! Seht genau hin! Dies ist euer Leben! Dies ist der Stundenzeiger an eurer Daseinsuhr!" (*GT* §24; KSA 1:151)

> [The tragic myth, too, inasmuch as it belongs to art at all, participates fully in this metaphysical intention of art to transfigure: but what does it transfigure when it presents the world of appearance in the image of the suffering hero? Least of all the "reality" of this world of appearance, for it says to us: "Look at this! Look closely! This is your life, this is the hand on the clock of your existence."]

The story of Faust, as told by Goethe, is, at least in part, the story of what constitutes the aesthetic experience. It does this by itself being a complex work of art, rich in literary allusion and intellectual-historical topoi. By the same token, *Die Geburt der Tragödie* is (as Nietzsche's "Versuch einer Selbstkritik" makes clear) not simply a work of philological analysis, but also a story, and one that tries to show the necessity of regaining the possibility of tragedy. Here, tragedy has two distinct senses: the despair felt at the mind's incapacity to overcome the gulf as it conceives it between *Schein* and *Sein,* but also the art form that, in its aesthetic mode, reconciles these apparent opposites. Thus tragedy, as far as Nietzsche is concerned, also acts as a cipher for the aesthetic, as a close reading of his presentation of "das höchste Ziel der Tragödie und der Kunst überhaupt" (*GT* §21; KSA 1:140; "the highest goal of tragedy and of all art") in terms of Apollo and Dionysus, and his remarks about "die metaphysische Verklärungsabsicht der Kunst" (*GT* §24; KSA 1:151; "the metaphysical intention of art to transfigure"), suggest.

For in section 17 Nietzsche expresses his hope that, through this fuller understanding of the aesthetic, art will be renewed:

> Jenes Ringen des Geistes der Musik nach bildlicher und mythischer Offenbarung [. . .] bricht plötzlich [. . .] ab [. . .]: während die aus diesem Ringen geborne dionysische Weltbetrachtung in den Mysterien weiterlebt und in den wunderbarsten Metamorphosen und Entartungen nicht aufhört, ernstere Naturen an sich zu ziehen. Ob sie

nicht aus ihrer mystischen Tiefe einst wieder als Kunst emporsteigen wird? (*GT* §17; KSA 1:110–11)

[That striving of music toward visual and mythical objectification . . . suddenly breaks off . . . While the Dionysian world view born of this striving lives on in the mysteries and, in its strangest metamorphoses and degeneracies, does not cease to attract more serious natures. Will it not rise once again out of its mystical depths as art?]

Die Geburt der Tragödie suggests that in order to regain the aesthetic two things are necessary. First, on Nietzsche's account, myth is the prerequisite to the survival of culture: "Ohne Mythus aber geht jede Cultur ihrer gesunden schöpferischen Naturkraft verlustig: erst ein mit Mythen umstellter Horizont schliesst eine ganze Culturbewegung zur Einheit ab" (*GT* §23; KSA 1:145; "Without myth, however, every culture loses the healthy, natural power of its creativity: only a horizon defined by myths rounds off a whole cultural movement"). According to Nietzsche, the myth that sustained the Greek worldview is dead. Later, in the parable of the madman and the lamp, Nietzsche will proclaim that the myth that sustained the Christian worldview — God — is dead. Yet the decay of myth is, as Nietzsche realized, inevitable: "Denn es ist das Loos jedes Mythus, allmählich in die Enge einer angeblich historischen Wirklichkeit hineinzukriechen und von irgend einer späteren Zeit als einmaliges Factum mit historischen Ansprüchen behandelt zu werden" (*GT* §10; KSA 1:74; "For it is the fate of every myth to creep gradually into the narrow limits of some alleged historical reality, and to be treated by some later generation as a unique fact with historical claims"). But he also argued that in the past myth had come to its highest expression in tragedy: "Durch die Tragödie kommt der Mythus zu seinem tiefsten Inhalt, seiner ausdrucksvollsten Form" (*GT* §10; KSA 1:74; "Through tragedy the myth attains its most profound content, its most expressive form").

Second, modern humankind needs the spirit of music out of which tragedy is reborn.[41] Greek tragedy had been born out of music, the accompaniment to the Dionysian mystery rites. In particular, Nietzsche attached great significance to the dithyramb, one of the most important forms of song performed by the chorus in Greek drama. In its oldest form, found in the celebrated Greek iambic and elegiac poet, Archilochos, it is associated with the cult of Dionysus.[42] Early on in *Die Geburt der Tragödie* Nietzsche described the transformation of humankind under the effect of the Dionysian dithyramb in strikingly Goethean terms:

Im dionysischen Dithyrambus wird der Mensch zur höchsten Steigerung aller seiner symbolischen Fähigkeiten gereizt; etwas Nieempfundenes drängt sich zur Aeusserung, die Vernichtung des Schleiers der Maja, das Einssein als Genius der Gattung, ja der Natur. Jetzt soll sich das Wesen der Natur symbolisch ausdrücken; eine neue

Welt der Symbole ist nöthig, einmal die ganze leibliche Symbolik, nicht nur die Symbolik des Mundes, des Gesichts, des Wortes, sondern die volle, alle Glieder rhythmisch bewegende Tanzgebärde. Sodann wachsen die anderen symbolischen Kräfte, die der Musik, in Rhythmik, Dynamik und Harmonie, plötzlich ungestüm. (*GT* §2; KSA 1:33–34)

[In the Dionysian dithyramb human beings are incited to the greatest exaltation of all their symbolic faculties; something never before consciously felt struggles for utterance, the annihilation of the veil of *maya*, oneness as the soul of the race and of nature itself. Now the essence of nature is to be expressed symbolically; we need a new world of symbols, at once the entire symbolism of the body is called into play, not the mere symbolism of the lips, face, and speech but the entire pantomime of dancing, forcing every member into rhythmic movement. Then the other symbolic powers suddenly arise, particularly those of music, in rhythm, dynamics, and harmony.]

Significantly, Nietzsche writes here "etwas Nieempfundenes," not "Niegefühltes." *Empfindung* suggests feeling raised to consciousness ("zur Steigerung [. . .] gereizt") whereas, logically, the *Gefühl* was always present, if unconsciously. Similarly, Weimar Classicism insisted that *Gehalt* became conscious, and transformed (or *verwandelt),* only in *Gestalt* — and thus truly felt (*empfunden*).

Furthermore, Nietzsche presented Archilochos, in contrast to the epic (Apollonian) Homer, as the first Dionysian artist (*GT* §5; KSA 1:42–43). Yet the lyric output of Archilochos, as the antecedent of tragedy, is said to contain Apollonian elements, too:

Wenn Archilochus, der erste Lyriker der Griechen, seine rasende Liebe und zugleich seine Verachtung den Töchtern des Lykambes kundgiebt, so ist es nicht seine Leidenschaft, die vor uns in orgiastischem Taumel tanzt: wir sehen Dionysus und die Mänaden, wir sehen den berauschten Schwärmer Archilochus zum Schlafe niedergesunken — wie ihn uns Euripides in den Bacchen beschreibt, den Schlaf auf hoher Alpentrift, in der Mittagssonne —: und jetzt tritt Apollo an ihn heran und berührt ihn mit dem Lorbeer. Die dionysisch-musikalische Verzauberung des Schläfers sprüht jetzt gleichsam Bilderfunken um sich, lyrische Gedichte, die in ihrer höchsten Entfaltung Tragödien und dramatische Dithyramben heissen. (*GT* §5; KSA 1:44)[43]

[When Archilochos, the first lyricist of the Greeks, proclaims his mad love and at the same time his contempt to the daughters of Lycambes, it is not his passion alone that dances before us in orgiastic frenzy; we see Dionysus and the Maenads, we see the drunken reveler Archilochos sunk down in sleep — as Euripides describes it in the *Bacchae,* the sleep on the high mountain pasture, in the midday sun —: and now Apollo approaches him and touches him with the laurel. The Dionysian-musical enchantment of the sleeper seems to emit image-sparks, lyrical poems, which in their highest development are called tragedies and dramatic dithyrambs.]

What is more, Nietzsche's fundamental thesis about the origin of tragedy argues that the tragic chorus arose, not as a result of political representation (as Hegel had argued) nor as a kind of ideal spectator (as A. W. Schlegel had claimed), but from the musical dithyramb. The distinctive characteristic of the dithyramb, Nietzsche wrote, was its *transformative* function, and that is why he described it, using another of Goethe's key terms, as part of "das *dramatische* Urphänomen" ("the *dramatic* primal phenomenon"; *GT* §8; KSA 1:61).[44]

Against the quasi-historical background of his treatise, however, Nietzsche also presents a symbolic cultural history, whose main purpose is to show the disappearance of the tragedy of Sophocles and Aeschylus (for which Nietzsche is full of praise [*GT* §9; KSA 1:64–71]) and its replacement by the tragedy of Euripides, characterized by an excess of theoretical knowledge and "schöner Schein" in its debased sense of an illusion of reality (or "logischer"/"falscher Schein"). For Nietzsche the central villain of this piece is Socrates, who represents "den Typus des *theoretischen Menschen*" ("the type of the *theoretical human being*"; *GT* §15; KSA 1:98) and destroys the cultural achievement of the Greeks. Socrates is condemned by Nietzsche for being "das Urbild des theoretischen Optimisten, der in dem bezeichneten Glauben an die Ergründlichkeit der Natur der Dinge dem Wissen und der Erkenntniss die Kraft einer Universalmedizin beilegt und im Irrthum das Uebel an sich begreift" (*GT* §15; KSA 1:100; "the primal image of the theoretical optimist who, having faith that the nature of things can be fathomed, ascribes to knowledge and insight the power of a cure-all, while understanding error as evil itself"). Yet Nietzsche, ever the dialectician, sees in the figure of Socrates a contradictory element that promises better things to come. In the dialectic of *Die Geburt der Tragödie,* knowledge extends itself ever more, destroying art, until it starts to destroy itself; at this stage of tragic sensibility ("das Tragische"), art becomes necessary once more and tragedy-as-art is reborn: "Wenn [der edle und begabte Mensch] hier zu seinem Schrecken sieht, wie die Logik sich an diesen Grenzen um sich selbst ringelt und endlich sich in den Schwanz beisst — da bricht die neue Form der Erkenntniss durch, *die tragische Erkenntniss,* die, um nur ertragen zu werden, als Schutz und Heilmittel die Kunst braucht" (*GT* §15; KSA 1:101; "When the noble and gifted individual sees to his or her horror how logic coils up at these boundaries and finally bites itself in the tail — suddenly the new form of insight breaks through, *tragic insight* which, merely to be endured, needs art as a protection and remedy").[45] For tragedy was born "aus dem Geiste der Musik" ("out of the spirit of music") — Nietzsche's contention in the subtitle of the first edition of his book and the substance of its central sections — and Socrates, too, played music (in the Greek sense of not just music but also poetry):

> Hier nun klopfen wir, bewegten Gemüthes, an die Pforten der Gegenwart und Zukunft: wird jenes "Umschlagen" zu immer neuen Configurationen des Genius und gerade des *musiktreibenden Sokrates* führen? [. . .] Wenn die alte Tragödie durch den dialektischen Trieb zum Wissen und zum Optimismus der Wissenschaft aus ihrem Gleise gedrängt wurde, so wäre aus dieser Thatsache auf einen ewigen Kampf zwischen *der theoretischen* und *der tragischen Weltbetrachtung* zu schliessen; und erst nachdem der Geist der Wissenschaft bis an seine Grenze geführt ist, und sein Anspruch auf universale Gültigkeit durch den Nachweis jener Grenzen vernichtet ist, dürfte auf eine Wiedergeburt der Tragödie zu hoffen sein: für welche Culturform wir das Symbol *des musiktreibenden Sokrates,* in dem früher erörterten Sinne, hinzustellen hätten. (*GT* §§15 and 17; KSA 1:102 and 111)

> [Here we knock, deeply moved, at the gates of the present and the future: will this "turning" lead to ever-new configurations of genius and specifically of the *Socrates who plays music*? . . . If ancient tragedy was diverted from its course by the dialectical drive to knowledge and to the optimism of science, this fact might lead us to believe that there is an eternal conflict between *the theoretical* and *the tragic world view;* and only after the spirit of science has been pursued to its limits, and its claim to universal validity destroyed by the evidence of these limits, may we hope for a rebirth of tragedy — a form of culture for which we should have to use the symbol of *the music-playing Socrates* in the sense used above.]

According to legend, when Socrates was in prison he repeatedly dreamed that a voice said to him "Sokrates, treibe Musik!" ("Socrates, make music"), until he sat down and wrote a poem to Apollo. Nietzsche asks "ob denn zwischen dem Sokratismus und der Kunst *nothwendig* nur ein antipodisches Verhältniss bestehe und ob die Geburt eines 'künstlerischen Sokrates' überhaupt etwas in sich Widerspruchsvolles sei" ("whether there is *necessarily* only an oppositional relation between Socratism and art, or whether the birth of an 'artistic Socrates' is altogether a contradiction in terms"). Or to put it another way, could it be that science and art both participate in a logic of supplementarity: "Vielleicht ist die Kunst sogar ein nothwendiges Correlativum und Supplement der Wissenschaft?" (*GT* §14; KSA 1:96; "Is art perhaps even a necessary correlative or, and supplement for, science?"). As M. S. Silk and J. P. Stern have pointed out, in *Die Geburt der Tragödie* the figure of Socrates playing music comes to stand as a cipher for a specific kind of art: "The paradox, Socratic *mousikē,* points to a mode of artistic discourse for which *The Birth of Tragedy* is the original, perhaps imperfect, prototype":

> Nietzsche's Socrates practises *Musik,* which in the context is not "music," but *mousikē* in its wider Greek sense of "poetry" or "art." The "Socrates who practises *mousikē*" has nothing directly to do with the Nietzsche who esteems and composes music, but once again with the Nietzsche who devises a new kind of conceptual art in *The Birth of Tragedy* itself.[46]

This demand for a "new kind of conceptual art" is, as we shall see, answered in *Also sprach Zarathustra.*[47]

The style of this new art is to be based on ancient principles. In particular, the dithyramb (as Nietzsche conceived it) comes to set the predominant tone. In *Ecce Homo,* Nietzsche went so far as to claim: "Das ganze Bild des *dithyrambischen* Künstlers ist das Bild des *präexistenten* Dichters des Zarathustra" (*EH GT* §4; KSA 6:314; "The entire picture of the dithyrambic artist is a picture of the pre-existent poet of *Zarathustra*"). And he made clear that, in important respects, *Die Geburt der Tragödie* anticipated his later work:

> Auf Seite 71 wird der *Stil* des Zarathustra mit einschneidender Sicherheit beschrieben und vorweggenommen; und niemals wird man einen grossartigeren Ausdruck für das *Ereigniss* Zarathustra, den Akt einer ungeheuren Reinigung und Weihung der Menschheit, finden, als er in den Seiten 43 bis 46 gefunden ist. (*EH GT* §4; KSA 6:315)

> [At the beginning of section 9 the *style* of *Zarathustra* is described with incisive certainty and anticipated; and one will find no more magnificent expression for the *event* of *Zarathustra,* the act of a tremendous purification and consecration of humanity, than is found in section 6.]

In the final chapter of *Die Geburt der Tragödie* Nietzsche claims that music and myth are inseparable. They are so, he continues, because they embody, albeit on different levels of consciousness, the aesthetic justification of the world, saving every "moment" and enabling us to move to the next:

> Musik und tragischer Mythus sind in gleicher Weise Ausdruck der dionysischen Befähigung eines Volkes und von einander untrennbar. [. . .] Beide spielen mit dem Stachel der Unlust [. . . und] rechtfertigen durch dieses Spiel die Existenz selbst der "schlechtesten Welt." Hier zeigt sich das Dionysische, an dem Apollinischen gemessen, als die ewige und ursprüngliche Kunstgewalt, die überhaupt die ganze Welt der Erscheinung in's Dasein ruft: in deren Mitte ein neuer Verklärungsschein nöthig wird, um die belebte Welt der Individuation im Leben festzuhalten. Könnten wir uns eine Menschwerdung der

Dissonanz denken —und was ist sonst der Mensch? — so würde diese Dissonanz, um leben zu können, eine herrliche Illusion brauchen, die ihr einen Schönheitsschleier über ihr eignes Wesen decke. Dies ist die wahre Kunstabsicht des Apollo: in dessen Namen wir alle jene zahllosen Illusionen des schönen Scheins zusammenfassen, die in jedem Augenblick das Dasein überhaupt lebenswerth machen und zum Erleben des nächsten Augenblicks drängen. (*GT* §25; KSA 1:154–55)

[Music and tragic myth are equally expressions of the Dionysian capacity of a people, and they are inseparable. . . . Both play with the sting of displeasure . . . and by means of this play they justify the existence of even the "worst world." Here the Dionysian shows itself to be, compared to the Apollonian, the eternal and original artistic power, which first calls the whole world of phenomena into existence — in the midst of which a new transfiguring semblance becomes necessary in order to keep the animate world of individuation alive. If we could imagine an incarnation of dissonance — and what else is the human being? — then this dissonance, to be able to live, would need a splendid illusion, which would cover dissonance with a veil of beauty. This is the true artistic aim of Apollo, under whose name we summarize all those countless illusions of beautiful semblance, which at every moment make life worth living at all and urge us on to experience the next moment.]

From *Die Geburt der Tragödie* it emerged that a new myth and a new music are needed. Both requirements were met, ten years later, by *Also sprach Zarathustra*, which was designed by Nietzsche to implement the program that, implicitly, and under the guise of Wagner worship, he had sketched in his book on Greek tragedy.

Historically speaking, the figure of Zarathustra is of mythic, or at least legendary, status; Nietzsche equips him with such trappings of mythical symbolism as the eagle and the snake.[48] To embody his myth, Nietzsche chose to write a tragedy — of sorts. And, as a tragedy, *Zarathustra* contains strong echoes of *Faust,* the paradigmatic tragedy in German culture. In *Zarathustra,* the central import of Faust is preserved and re-presented, so that it arises, just as myth does according to Nietzsche, "wie ein verwundeter Held, und der ganze Ueberschuss von Kraft, sammt der weisheitsvollen Ruhe des Sterbenden, brennt in seinem Auge mit letztem, mächtigem Leuchten" (*GT* §10; KSA 1:74; "like a wounded hero, and its whole excess of strength, together with the wisdom-laden calm of the dying, burns in its eyes with a last, powerful gleam").

Inasmuch as it is "the music of the future," *Zarathustra* — the genesis of which is examined in the next chapter — strives towards that condition by a sophisticated use of rhetoric, an imaginative deployment of imagery, and an intricate use of *Leitmotiv,* sufficiently elaborate for it to be taken as a parody of Wagner's operas.[49] Yet this music draws on and in some cases parodies eighteenth-century sources and forms, too. As Nietzsche wrote in *Menschliches, Allzumenschliches* (*Human, All Too Human*): "Von *Goethe* aus führt mancher Weg in diese Dichtung der Zukunft" (*MA* II §99; KSA 2:420; "Many a path to this poetry of the future starts out from *Goethe*"). On the evidence of *Die Geburt der Tragödie,* this "art of the future" is a further projection of that perennial aesthetic Nietzsche discerned in Weimar Classicism and to which he gave a new and revitalizing formulation.

Notes

¹ For a useful perspective on the development of previous discussions of and commentaries on *Die Geburt der Tragödie,* see Jerry S. Clegg, "Nietzsche's Gods in *The Birth of Tragedy,*" *Journal of the History of Ideas* 10 (1972): 431–38; Hans Reiss, "Nietzsche's 'Geburt der Tragödie': Eine kritische Würdigung," *Zeitschrift für deutsche Philologie* 92 (1973): 481–511; Benjamin Bennett, "Nietzsche's Idea of Myth: The Birth of Tragedy from the Spirit of Eighteenth-Century Aesthetics," *Publications of the Modern Languages Association* 94 (1979): 420–33; M. S. Silk and J. P. Stern, *Nietzsche on Tragedy* (Cambridge: Cambridge UP, 1981); Friedhelm Decher, "Nietzsches Metaphysik in der 'Geburt der Tragödie' im Verhältnis zur Philosophie Schopenhauers," *Nietzsche-Studien* 14 (1985): 110–25; Michael Sprinker, "Poetics and Music: Hopkins and Nietzsche," *Comparative Literature* 37 (1985): 334–56; Marshall Carl Bradley, "Nietzsche's Critique of Pure Reason: With a Nietzschean Critique of Parsifal," *Neophilologus* 72 (1988): 394–403; Margot Fleischer, "Dionysos als Ding an sich: Der Anfang von Nietzsches Philosophie in der ästhetischen Metaphysik der 'Geburt der Tragödie,'" *Nietzsche-Studien* 17 (1988): 74–90; Robert Rethy, "The Tragic Affirmation of the 'Birth of Tragedy,'" *Nietzsche-Studien* 17 (1988): 1–44; Henry Staten, "*The Birth of Tragedy* Reconstructed," *Studies in Romanticism* 29 (1990): 9–37; Horst Turk, "Nietzsches 'Geburt der Tragödie' und die Rettung des Apollinischen," in Gerhard Buhr and Friedrich A. Kittler, eds., *Das Subjekt der Dichtung: Festschrift für Gerhard Kaiser* (Würzburg: Königshausen & Neumann, 1990), 17–29; and, particularly useful, Barbara von Reibnitz, *Ein Kommentar zu Friedrich Nietzsche, »Die Geburt der Tragödie aus dem Geiste der Musik« (Kap.1–12)* (Stuttgart and Weimar: Metzler, 1992). The most recent major publication is James I. Porter, *The Invention of Dionysus: An Essay on "The Birth of Tragedy"* (Stanford, CA: Stanford UP, 2000).

² For previous discussions of Nietzsche's relation to Goethe, see Heinz Nicolai, "Die Entwicklung von Nietzsches Goethebild," *Germanisch-Romanische Monatsschrift* 21 (1933): 337–60; A. E. J. Knight, "Nietzsche and Goethe," *Publications of the English Goethe Society* (NS) 10 (1934): 63–78; Fritz Kraus, "Auf dem Wege zum Übermenschen: Friedrich Nietzsches Verhältnis zu Goethe," *Goethe-Kalender* 32 (1939): 131–74; Erich Heller, "Nietzsche and Goethe," in *The Importance of Nietzsche* (Chicago and London: U of Chicago P, 1988), 18–38; Karl Schlechta, "The German 'Classicist' Goethe as Reflected in Nietzsche's Works," in James C. O'Flaherty, Timothy F. Sellner, and Robert M. Helm, eds., *Studies in Nietzsche and*

the Classical Tradition (Chapel Hill, NC: U of North Carolina P, 1976), 144–55; and Eckhard Heftrich, "Nietzsches Goethe," *Nietzsche-Studien* 16 (1987): 1–20.

[3] For previous discussions of Nietzsche and Schiller, see Herbert Cysarz, "Schiller und Nietzsche," *Jahrbuch des Freien Deutschen Hochstifts* 1927: 121–50; Helmut Rehder, "The Reluctant Disciple: Nietzsche and Schiller," in O'Flaherty, Sellner, and Helm, eds., *Studies in Nietzsche and the Classical Tradition*, 156–64; Adrian Del Caro, "Ethical Aesthetic: Schiller and Nietzsche as Critics of the Eighteenth Century," *The Germanic Review* 55 (1980): 55–63; Renato Saviene, *Il Bello: Il Dionisiaco: Schiller: Nietzsche* (Florence: Olschki, 1995); and, most recently, Nicholas Martin, *Nietzsche and Schiller: Untimely Aesthetics* (Oxford: Clarendon P, 1996).

[4] Above all, it is the metaphysics of Christianity — as "Platonismus für's 'Volk'" ("Platonism for 'the people'"; *JGB* Vorrede; KSA 5:12) and "eine Metaphysik des Henkers" ("a metaphysics of the hangman"; *GD* Die vier grossen Irrthümer §7; KSA 6:96) — that Nietzsche opposes. In his *Nachlass*, Nietzsche speculated about "eine artistische Weltbetrachtung" ("an artistic view of the world") being "eine antimetaphysische Weltbetrachtung — ja, aber eine artistische" (*WM* §1048/2[186]; KSA 12:160; "an anti-metaphysical view of the world — yes, but an artistic one"); and, elsewhere in his *Nachlass*, Nietzsche concluded: "Man muß das 'Kreuz' empfinden wie Goethe" (*WM* §175/10[181]; KSA 12:565; "One must feel about the 'cross' as Goethe did"). In his *Nachlass* from the end of 1870 to April 1871, Nietzsche described his own project in terms of "inverted Platonism": "Meine Philosophie *umgedrehter Platonismus:* je weiter ab vom wahrhaft Seienden, um so reiner schöner besser ist es. Das Leben im Schein als Ziel" (7[156]; KSA 7:199; "My philosophy, inverted Platonism: the further away from what truly is, the purer, the more beautiful, the better it is. Life in semblance as the goal").

[5] In "Das Bewusstsein vom Scheine" ("The Consciousness of Semblance"), Nietzsche developed this thought: "Schein ist für mich das Wirkende und Lebende selber, das soweit in seiner Selbstverspottung geht, mich fühlen zu lassen, dass hier Schein und Irrlicht und Geistertanz und nichts Mehr ist [. . .]" (*FW* §54; KSA 3:417; "Semblance is for me the very thing that is effective and alive, which goes so far in its self-mockery that it makes me feel that this is semblance and will-o'-the-wisp and a dance of spirits and nothing more").

[6] Nietzsche refers to this expression in his encomium of Goethe in *Götzen-Dämmerung* (*Twilight of the Idols*): "*Goethe* — kein deutsches Ereigniss, sondern ein europäisches [. . .]. Was er wollte, das war *Totalität;* er bekämpfte das Auseinander von Vernunft, Sinnlichkeit, Gefühl, Wille (— in abschreckendster Scholastik durch *Kant* gepredigt, den Antipoden Goethe's), er disciplinirte sich zur Ganzheit, er *schuf* sich . . . [. . .] Ein solcher *freigewordner* Geist steht mit einem freudigen und vertrauenden Fatalismus mitten im All, im *Glauben,* dass nur das Einzelne verwerflich ist, dass im Ganzen sich Alles erlöst und bejaht — *er verneint nicht mehr* . . . Aber ein solcher Glaube ist der höchste aller möglichen Glauben: ich habe ihn auf den Namen des *Dionysos* getauft. —" (*GD* Streifzüge eines Unzeitgemässen §49; KSA 6:151–52; "*Goethe* — not a German event, but a European one . . . What he wanted was *totality;* he strove against the separation of reason, senses, feeling, and will (preached with the most terrible scholasticism by *Kant,* the antipode of Goethe), he disciplined himself to wholeness, he *created* himself . . . Such a spirit who has *become free* stands in

the midst of the cosmos with a joyous and trusting fatalism, in the *faith* that only the particular can be dismissed, and that in the whole all is redeemed and affirmed — *he does not negate any more*. . . . But such a faith is the highest of all possible faiths: I have baptized it with the name of *Dionysos*").

[7] For further discussion of Nietzsche as a classicist, see Karl Schlechta, *Der junge Nietzsche und das klassische Altertum* (Mainz: Kupferberg, 1948); Hugh Lloyd-Jones, "Nietzsche and the Study of the Ancient World," in O'Flaherty, Sellner, and Helm, eds., *Studies in Nietzsche and the Classical Tradition*, 1–15; and Paul Bishop, ed., *Nietzsche and Antiquity: His Reaction and Response to the Classical Tradition* (Rochester, NY and Woodbridge, UK: Camden House, 2004).

[8] See Diels-Kranz, fragment no. 22 (B 52): αἰὼν παῖς ἔστι παίζων, πεσσεύ· παιδὸς ἡ βασιλήη. "(Das ewige Leben ist ein Kind, spielend wie ein Kind, die Brettsteine setzend; die Herrschaft gehört einem Kind"; cited from *Die Vorsokratiker*, ed. Jaap Mansfeld, 2 vols. [Stuttgart: Reclam, 1983], 1:281; "eternal life is a child, is at play like a child with board-checkers; mastery belongs to a child"). Here, this fragment is combined with the symbolic use of the child to represent aesthetic play, following Schiller's maxim that the human being is only fully human when at play (see below). Nietzsche refers explicitly to this pre-Socratic fragment in the *Nachlass* fragments known as *Der Wille zur Macht* (*The Will to Power*): "'Das Spiel,' das Unnützliche, als Ideal des mit Kraft Überhäuften, als 'kindlich.' Die 'Kindlichkeit' Gottes, παῖς παίζων" (*WM* §797/2[130]; KSA 12:129; "'Play,' what is useless, as the ideal of someone who is overfull of strength, as 'childlike.' The 'childlikeness' of God, *pais paizon* [a child at play]").

[9] Compare with the following passage from *Die Geburt der Tragödie:* "Jenes Streben in's Unendliche, der Flügelschlag der Sehnsucht, bei der höchsten Lust an der deutlich percipirten Wirklichkeit, erinnern daran, dass wir in beiden Zuständen [= Tragödie, Musik] ein dionysisches Phänomen zu erkennen haben, das uns immer von Neuem wieder das spielende Aufbauen und Zertrümmern der Individualwelt als den Ausfluss einer Urlust offenbart, in einer ähnlichen Weise, wie wenn von Heraklit dem Dunklen die weltbildende Kraft einem Kinde verglichen wird, das spielend Steine hin und her setzt und Sandhaufen aufbaut und wieder einwirft" (GT §24; KSA 1:153; "That striving into the infinite, the wing-beat of desire that accompanies the highest delight in clearly perceived reality, reminds us that in both states we must recognize a Dionysian phenomenon, which time and again reveals to us the playful construction and destruction of the individual world as the overflow of a primal pleasure. Thus the dark Heraclitus compares the world-building force to a child who playfully places stones here and there, building sandhills only to knock them over again"). Both passages anticipate the famous later fragment from 1885 that begins: "Und wißt ihr auch, was mir 'die Welt' ist?" (*WM* §1067/38[12]; KSA 11:610; "And do you know what 'the world' is to me?").

[10] "There are more references, implicit and direct, to Goethe's *Faust* in Nietzsche's book than to any other modern work, partly because it is with *Faust* that the hunt for 'reality' enters German and European literature. This is the dominant theme of Goethe's dramatic poem" (M. S. Silk and J. P. Stern, *Nietzsche on Tragedy*, 354).

[11] "Eine unendlich werthvollere Einsicht über die Bedeutung des Chors hatte bereits Schiller in der berühmten Vorrede zur Braut von Messina verrathen, der den Chor als eine lebendige Mauer betrachtete, die die Tragödie um sich herum zieht, um sich von der wirklichen Welt rein abzuschliessen und sich ihren idealen Boden und ihre poetische Freiheit zu bewahren" (*GT* §7; KSA 1:54; "An infinitely more valuable insight into the significance of the chorus had already been displayed by Schiller in the famous Preface to his *Bride of Messina,* which regards the chorus as a living wall that tragedy constructs around itself in order to close itself off from the world of reality and to preserve its ideal domain and its poetic freedom").

[12] See the notes entitled "Autobiographisches aus dem Jahre 1856 bis 1869": "Meine literarische Tätigkeit . . . 1862" (Friedrich Nietzsche, *Werke in drei Bänden,* ed. Karl Schlechta [Munich: Hanser, 1966], 1:101). Nietzsche's continuing reception of Weimar Classicism can be also be followed through his *Nachlass;* see, for example, his sequence of notes on Goethe and Schiller in Summer and Autumn 1873 (29[78–80], 28[83–84], 29[110–12], 29[116–17], 29[124–31], 29[134], 19[186–87]; KSA 7:664–65, 666, 681–82, 683–85, 687–90, 691, 707). For further discussion of Nietzsche's relation to German classicism, see Matthias Politycki, *Der frühe Nietzsche und die deutsche Klassik: Studien zu Problemen literarischer Wertung* (Straubing, Munich: Dornau, 1981). For further discussion of Nietzsche's aesthetic theory in general, see Bernd Bräutigam, *Reflexion des Schönen — schöne Reflexion: Überlegungen zur Prosa ästhetischer Theorie — Hamann, Nietzsche, Adorno* (Bonn: Bouvier, 1975); Julian Young, *Nietzsche's Philosophy of the Arts* (Cambridge: Cambridge UP, 1992); and Theo Meyer, *Nietzsche und die Kunst* (Tübingen, Basel: Francke, 1993). Nietzsche's derogatory caricature of Schiller as "der Moral-Trompeter von Säckingen" (*GD* Streifzüge eines Unzeitgemässen §1; KSA 6:111; "the Moral-Trumpeter of Säckingen") is directed not against his aesthetics but against his perceived emphasis on morality, as is his criticism in a note in the *Nachlass* for winter 1880–1881 of "jenen falschen 'Classicismus,' der einen innerlichen Haß gegen die natürliche Nacktheit und schreckliche Schönheit der Dinge hatte" (9[7]; KSA 9:410–11; "that false 'classicism' that had an inner hatred of natural nudity and the terrible beauty of things").

[13] "Der ungeheuren Tapferkeit und Weisheit *Kant's* und *Schopenhauer's* ist der schwerste Sieg gelungen, der Sieg über den im Wesen der Logik verborgen liegenden Optimismus, der wiederum der Untergrund unserer Cultur ist" (*GT* §18; KSA 1:118; "The extraordinary courage and wisdom of *Kant* and *Schopenhauer* have succeeded in gaining the most difficult victory, the victory over the optimism concealed in the essence of logic, an optimism that in turn is the basis of our culture"). The validity of Nietzsche's judgment concerning optimism may be gauged from the following comment on our contemporary society: "The American identity can be summarised in a single polling question: we are the only country in the world where a majority has consistently believed — with the exception of a few years in the late 1970s — that next year will be better. Such optimism must seem obnoxious to the rest of the world"; it certainly would have to Nietzsche (Joe Klein, "Neither here nor there," *The Guardian,* 3 July 2002, G2, 2–4 [3]).

[14] As Elizabeth M. Wilkinson and L. A. Willoughby suggestively noted, "Nietzsche made no secret of the fact that his own doctrine of the Apollonian principle in art was

rooted in the concept of *schöner Schein*" (introduction to Friedrich Schiller, *On the Aesthetic Education of Man in a Series of Letters* [2nd ed., Oxford: Clarendon P, 1982], cxl). Citations from Schiller's *Aesthetic Letters* use the translation by Wilkinson and Willoughby, adapted where appropriate.

[15] For example, see Goethe's poem "Amor als Landschaftsmaler" ("Amor as a Landscape Painter," 1787/1788; HA 1:235–37; Johann Wolfgang von Goethe, *Selected Poems,* ed. Christopher Middleton, Goethe Edition, vol. 1 [Boston: Suhrkamp/Insel, 1983), 98–101]; and his letter to Schiller of 5 May 1798 (in the context of a discussion of revising *Faust*): "Einige tragische Szenen waren in Prosa geschrieben, sie sind durch ihre Natürlichkeit und Stärke [. . .] ganz unerträglich. Ich suche sie deswegen gegenwärtig in Reime zu bringen, da denn die Idee wie durch einen Flor durchscheint, die unmittelbare Wirkung des ungeheuern Stoffes aber gedämpft wird" (WA 4.13:137; "Some tragic scenes were written in prose; they are because of their naturalness and strength . . . quite unbearable. For this reason I am presently trying to transform them into verse, for then the idea shines through as if through gauze, but the immediate effect of the tremendous material is muted"). For further discussion of aesthetic semblance as a veil, see Wilhelm Emrich, *Die Symbolik von Faust II: Sinn und Vorformen* (3rd ed., Frankfurt am Main and Bonn: Athenäum, 1964), 44–55; William Larrett, "Der *Dichtung Schleier:* From Theology with Love to Aesthetics," in C. P. Magill, Brian A. Rowley and Christopher J. Smith, eds., *Tradition and Creation: Essays in Honour of Elizabeth Mary Wilkinson* (Leeds: W. S. Maney and Son, 1978), 89–100; R. H. Stephenson, *Goethe's Wisdom Literature* (Bern, Frankfurt am Main and New York: Peter Lang, 1983), 157–63; Pierre Hadot, *Zur Idee der Naturgeheimnisse: Beim Betrachten des Widmungsblattes in den Humboldtschen 'Ideen zu einer Geographie der Pflanzen'* (Wiesbaden: Steiner; Mainz: Akademie der Wissenschaften und der Literatur, 1982), 1–33; and E. H. Gombrich, "The Symbol of the Veil: Psychological Reflections on Schiller's Poetry," in Peregrine Horden, ed., *Freud and the Humanities* (London: Duckworth, 1985), 75–109. Nietzsche uses the image of the veil in *Also sprach Zarathustra* on two occasions (*Z* II 10 and 14; KSA 4:141 and 154) and in a fragment from the *Nachlass* of summer 1883 he wrote: "Als ich den Übermenschen geschaffen hatte, ordnete ich um ihn den großen Schleier des Werdens und ließ die Sonne über ihm stehen im Mittage" (12[17]; KSA 10:403; "When I had created the superman, I arranged around him the great veil of Becoming and made the sun stand above him at midday").

[16] See Kant, *Kritik der Urteilskraft,* §9; Immanuel Kant, *The Critique of Judgement,* trans. James Creed Meredith (Oxford: Clarendon P, 1952), 58; compare §26: "Die ästhetische Urteilskraft in Beurteilung des Schönen [bezieht] die Einbildungskraft in ihrem freien Spiele auf den *Verstand* [. . .], um mit dessen *Begriffen* überhaupt (ohne Bestimmung derselben) zusammenzustimmen" (104; "The aesthetic judgment in its estimate of the beautiful refers the imagination in its free play to the *understanding,* to bring out its agreement with the *concepts* of the latter in general (apart from their determination)").

[17] Nietzsche cites this passage in his *Nachlass* for winter 1869/1870 to spring 1870 (3[49]; KSA 7:74). For further discussion of Nietzsche's use of the metaphor of play and its eighteenth-century sources, see Ernst Behler, "Nietzsche und die romantische Metapher von der Kunst als Spiel," in Michael S. Batts, Anthony W. Riley, and Heinz

Wetzel, *Echoes and Influences of German Romanticism: Essays in Honour of Hans Eichner* (New York, Bern, Frankfurt am Main: Peter Lang, 1987), 11–28.

[18] The distinction between plastic and verbal art goes back, within the history of German aesthetics, to Lessing's treatise *Laokoon oder Über die Grenzen der Malerei und Poesie* (*Laocoön or on the Limits of Painting and Poetry*, 1766), arguing against Horace's principle of *ut pictura poesis* ("as is painting so is poetry") in *De arte poetica*. For further discussion, see Edward Allen McCormick's introduction to his translation in Gottfried Ephraim Lessing, *Laocoön: An Essay on the Limits of Painting and Poetry* (1962; repr. Baltimore and London: Johns Hopkins UP, 1984), ix–xxx. In section 16 and elsewhere, Nietzsche distinguishes between plastic art (associated with Apollo) and music (associated with Dionysos); but, as the conclusion to section 21 shows, he was ultimately concerned with the aesthetic experience in general. Equally, it was important for Nietzsche to choose a particular vehicle for his aesthetic message.

[19] Schopenhauer, *Die Welt als Wille und Vorstellung* (1:1819; third ed., 2 vols, 1859), §63. Arthur Schopenhauer, *Werke in fünf Bänden,* ed. Ludger Lütkehaus (Zurich: Haffmanns Verlag, 1988–99), 1: 456–57.

[20] Schopenhauer uses the term *principium individuationis* to refer to the phenomenal world of appearance. Here, as part of his polemic against Schopenhauer, Nietzsche here elides the epistemological and aesthetic sense of "appearance" and "semblance" (*Erscheinung* and *schöner Schein*).

[21] As Silk and Stern have argued, Nietzsche presents five successive historical phases in Greek culture: 1. the pre-Hellenic (Dionysian) age with its dark mythology and the austere wisdom of Silenus (second millenium B.C.E.); 2. the world of Homeric *naïveté* (Apollonian; tenth to eighth centuries B.C.E.); 3. the early lyric age (Dionysian) with influx of Dionysos-worship (seventh century B.C.E.); 4. the Dorian reassertion of the Apollonian (seventh to sixth centuries B.C.E.), undermined by concomitant trivialization of Apollonian religion and mythology; 5. The tragic age: Attic tragedy as union of Apollonian and Dionysian (late sixth and fifth centuries B.C.E.); and 6. The Socratic-Alexandrian age (*Nietzsche on Tragedy*, 66 and 185).

[22] In his *Nachlass* Nietzsche noted: "Die Denkweise *Hegels* ist von der *Goetheschen* nicht sehr entfernt" (*WM* §95/9[178]; KSA 12:443; "*Hegel's* way of thinking is not far different from *Goethe's*"). For further discussion of the relation of Nietzsche to Hegel, see Joseph Juszezak, *L'Anthropologie de Hegel à travers la pensée moderne: Marx, Nietzsche, A. Kojève, E. Weil* (Paris: Editions Anthropos, 1977); Siegfried Blasche, "'Hegelianismen im Umfeld von Nietzsches 'Geburt der Tragödie,'" *Nietzsche-Studien* 15 (1986): 59–71; and Stephen Houlgate, *Hegel, Nietzsche and the Criticism of Metaphysics* (Cambridge: Cambridge UP, 1986).

[23] See the discussion by Wilkinson and Willoughby in the introduction to their edition of Schiller's *On the Aesthetic Education of Man,* lxxxvi.

[24] What Kant calls "die ästhetische Idee" ("the aesthetic idea") (*Kritik der Urteilskraft,* §49).

[25] Nietzsche's notes in his *Nachlass* from the period of summer 1872 to the beginning of 1873 provide confirmation of this reading of *Die Geburt der Tragödie*. There he defined the tragic as follows: "Man muß selbst die *Illusion wollen* — darin liegt das Tragische" (19[35]; KSA 7:428; "One must oneself *want the illusion* — therein

lies the tragic"). In the opening paragraph of *Die Geburt der Tragödie,* Nietzsche spoke of the union of Apollo and Dionysus in Attic tragedy as resulting from "einen metaphysischen Wunderakt des hellenischen 'Willens'" ("a metaphysical miracle of the Hellenic 'will'"; *GT* §1; KSA 1:25), and in his *Nachlass* notes Nietzsche expanded on this notion as follows: "In allen griechischen Trieben zeigt sich eine *bändigende Einheit:* nennen wir sie den hellenischen *Willen.* Jeder diese Triebe versucht allein in's Unendliche zu existiren. Die alten Philosophen versuchen aus ihnen die Welt zu construiren. Die *Kultur* eines Volkes offenbart sich in der *einheitlichen Bändigung* der *Triebe dieses Volkes:* die Philosophie bändigt den Erkenntnißtrieb, die Kunst den Formentrieb und die Ekstasis, die ἀγάπη den ἔρως usw. Die Erkenntniß *isolirt:* die älteren Philosophen stellen isolirt dar, was die griechische Kunst zusammen erscheinen läßt" (19[41]; KSA 7:432; "There shows itself in all Greek drives a *unity holding them in check:* let us call it the Hellenic *will.* Each of these drives tries to exist alone into infinity. Out of them the old philosophers try to construe the world. The *culture* of a people reveals itself in the *unified control of the drives of this people:* philosophy holds in check the cognitive drive, art the form-drive and ecstasy, the *agape* the *eros* etc. Knowledge *isolates:* the older philosophers represent as isolated what Greek art shows as being together"). On this account, aesthetics supersedes philosophy. This conclusion is explicitly stated in another note: "Mit anderen Worten: es entscheidet nicht der reine *Erkenntnißtrieb,* sondern der *aesthetische:* die wenig erwiesene Philosophie des Heraklit hat einen größeren Kunstwerth als alle Sätze des Aristoteles" (19[76]; KSA 7:444; "In other words: it is not the pure *cognitive drive* that decides, but the *aesthetic drive:* the little proved philosophy of Heraclitus has a greater artistic value than all the principles of Aristotle").

[26] For a helpful explanation of these key concepts of Weimar Classicism — *Stoff, Gestalt,* and *Gehalt* — see Elizabeth M. Wilkinson, "'Form' and 'Content' in the Aesthetics of German Classicism," in Paul Böckmann, ed., *Stil- und Formprobleme in der Literatur* [*Vorträge des VII. Kongresses der Internationalen Vereinigung für moderne Sprachen und Literaturen in Heidelberg, August 1957*] (Heidelberg: C. Winter, 1959), 18–27.

[27] The (apparent) problem that arises here is that *Stoff* means "medium" as well as "material," "content." The latter is (phenomenologically) Apollonian, and the former Dionysian. The *Stofftrieb* aims at Dionysian, "felt" experience of the bodiliness of the external world, the *Formtrieb* at those abstractions from the world that we call "forms," and that Schiller and Goethe, from the artist's perspective, called *Stoff.* The *Spieltrieb* aims at the conciliation of the Apollonian and the Dionysian in (aesthetic) *Gestalt.*

[28] Dionysian truth is, in part at least, the Wisdom of Silenus. According to legend, the companion of Dionysos told King Midas: the best thing is not have been born, the next best thing is to die early (*GT* §3; KSA 1:35). The reaction to which this wisdom speaks is horror of life. In one of his fragments from the *Nachlass* from the period of summer 1872 to the beginning of 1873, Nietzsche writes: "Das Erschrecken ist der Menschheit bestes Theil" (19[80]; KSA 7:447; "Terror is the best part of humankind"), alluding to *Faust II:* "Das Schaudern ist der Menschheit bestes Theil" (line 6272; "To shudder is the best part of humanity"), words uttered by Faust before Mephistopheles reveals to him the secret of the Mothers. The horror is one side of

the Dionysian coin, the other of which is vitality and passion. And, transformed through the aesthetic (see above), horror of life becomes love of life: "Weh spricht: Vergeh! / Doch alle Lust will Ewigkeit —" (*Z* III 15 §3; KGW 4:286; "Woe implores: Go! / But all joy wants eternity").

[29] See Walter Kaufmann, *Nietzsche: Philosopher, Psychologist, Antichrist* (Princeton, NJ: Princeton UP, 1968), 129.

[30] Compare with Goethe's remarks on Prometheus in *Dichtung und Wahrheit* (part 3, bk. 15): "Das gemeine Menschenschicksal, an welchem wir alle zu tragen haben, muß denjenigen am schwersten aufliegen, deren Geisteskräfte sich früher und breiter entwickeln [. . .] so ist es doch immer das Final, daß der Mensch auf sich zurückgewiesen wird. [. . .] [Mein productives Talent] verließ mich seit einigen Jahren keinen Augenblick; was ich wachend am Tage gewahr wurde, bildete sich sogar öfters nachts in regelmäßige Träume, und wie ich die Augen auftat, erschien mir entweder ein wunderliches neues Ganze, oder der Teil eines schon Vorhandenen. [. . .]. Wie ich nun über diese Naturgabe nachdachte und fand, daß sie mir ganz eigen angehöre und durch nichts Fremdes weder begünstigt noch gehindert werden könne, so mochte ich gern hierauf mein ganzes Dasein in Gedanken gründen. Diese Vorstellung verwandelte sich in ein Bild, die alte mythologische Figur des *Prometheus* fiel mir auf, der, abgesondert von den Göttern, von seiner Werkstätte aus eine Welt bevölkerte" (HA 10:47–48; Johann Wolfgang von Goethe, *From My Life: Poetry and Truth: Parts One to Three,* ed. Thomas P. Saine and Jeffrey L. Sammons, trans. Robert R. Heitner, Goethe Edition, vol. 4 [New York: Suhrkamp Publishers, 1987], 4:468–69 "The common fate of human beings, which all of us have to bear, cannot but fall most heavily on the shoulders of him whose intellectual powers develop earliest and most broadly . . . but in the final analysis a human being is always thrust back on himself . . . For several years my productive talent had not abandoned me for a moment; what I perceived while awake in the daytime often developed into regular dreams at night, and when I opened my eyes I would see either a curious new whole or a part of something already begun . . . As I reflected on this natural gift and saw that it was my very own possession, which no outside influence could either facilitate or hinder, I was glad to make it, conceptually, the basis for my whole existence. The idea transformed itself into an image: I was struck by the old mythological figure of Prometheus, who was separated from the gods and populated the world for himself out of his own workshop" [translation adapted]).

[31] See Nietzsche's commentary on Helen in his *Nachlass* from the end of 1870 to April 1871, in answer to the question "Was ist das *Schöne?*" ("What is the beautiful?"): "— eine Lustempfindung, die uns die eigentlichen Absichten, die der Wille in einer Erscheinung hat, verbirgt. Wodurch wird nun die Lustempfindung erregt? Objektiv: das *Schöne* ist ein Lächeln der Natur, ein Überschuß von Kraft und Lustgefühl des Daseins: man denke an die Pflanze. Es ist der Jungfrauenleib der Sphinx. Der Zweck des Schönen ist das zum Dasein Verführen. Was ist nun eigentlich jenes Lächeln, jenes Verführerische? Negativ: das Verbergen der Noth, das Wegstreichen aller Falten und der heitre Seelenblick des Dinges. 'Sieht Helena in jedem Weibe' die Gier zum Dasein verbirgt das Unschöne. [. . .] Mit diesem Traum, dieser Ahnung im Kopfe sieht Faust 'Helena' in jedem Weibe. Wir erfahren also, daß der Individualwille auch träumen kann, ahnen kann, Vorstellungen und Phantasie-

bilder hat. Der Zweck der Natur in diesem schönen Lächeln seiner Erscheinungen ist die Verführung anderer Individuen zum Dasein. [. . .] Die *Schöpfungen der Kunst sind das höchste Lustziel des Willens*" (7[27]; KSA 7:143–45; "— a sensation of pleasure, which hides from us the real intentions which the will has in an appearance: think of the plant. How is this sensation of pleasure aroused? Objectively: the *beautiful* is a smile of nature, a surplus of power and the feeling of pleasure of existence. It is the virgin body of the sphinx. The purpose of the beautiful is to seduce into existence. What actually is that smile, that seductiveness? Negatively: the concealment of distress, the sweeping away of all wrinkles and the cheerful glance of the soul of the object. 'Sees Helen in every woman,' the greed for existence conceals what is ugly . . . With this dream, with this premonition in his head Faust sees 'Helen' in every woman. Thus we experience that the individual will can also dream, have premonitions, has an imagination and fantasy images. The purpose of nature in this beautiful smile of its appearances is the seduction of other individuals to existence . . . The *creations of art are the highest goal of pleasure of the will*"). In another note, Nietzsche speculated *à propos* of the Franco-Prussian War: "Ich könnte mir einbilden, man habe deutscher Seite den Krieg geführt, um die Venus aus dem Louvre zu befreien, als eine zweite Helena. Dies wäre die pneumatische Auslegung dieses Krieges. Die schöne antike Starrheit des Daseins durch diesen Krieg inaugurirt — es beginnt die Zeit des Ernstes — wir glauben daß es auch die der *Kunst* sein wird" (7[88]; KSA 7:158; "I could imagine that on the German side the war was fought to liberate the Venus [the famous Venus of Milo] from the Louvre, as a second Helena. This would be the spiritual interpretation of this war. The beautiful ancient rigidity of existence is inaugurated by means of this war — there begins the time of earnestness — we believe that it will also become the time of *art*").

[32] HA 7:247; Johann Wolfgang von Goethe, *Wilhelm Meister's Apprenticeship*, ed. and trans. Eric A. Blackall with Victor Lange, Goethe Edition, vol. 9 (New York: Suhrkamp, 1989), 146.

[33] An abstract concept is again personified as a woman in Zarathustra's aphorism: "Muthig, unbekümmert, spöttisch, gewaltthätig — so will uns die Weisheit: sie ist ein Weib und liebt immer nur einen Kriegsmann" (*Z* I §7; KSA 4:49; "Brave, unconcerned, mocking, violent — thus wisdom wants us: she is a woman and only ever loves a warrior"; compare *GM* III §1; KSA 5:339).

[34] For further discussion, see Richard Kühnemund, "Faust and Zarathustra in our Time," *The Germanic Review* 15 (1940): 116–36; and James M. van der Laan, "Die Faustfigur bei Goethe und Nietzsche im Hinblick auf die Postmoderne," *Euphorion* 88 (1994): 458–67. For further analyses of the cultural significance of the figure of Faust, see Hans Schwerte, *Faust und das Faustische: Ein Kapitel deutscher Ideologie* (Stuttgart: Klett, 1962); and Marshall Berman, *All That Is Solid Melts Into Air: The Experience of Modernity* (New York: Viking Penguin, 1988).

[35] "In Nietzsche's view, scientific progress undermines and negates the defining assumption of the Socratic spirit: namely, that scientific reason is the measure of the real. When scientific progress reaches the point where the hunger for knowledge turns into despair at the prospect of fully understanding reality, it reveals the possibility, as well as the need, for a new art and a new form of life. Nietzsche believes that science initiates a cultural movement beyond science" (Robert Gooding-Williams,

Zarathustra's Dionysian-Modernism (Stanford, CA: Stanford UP, 2001), 6–7). Compare with Nietzsche's remark in *Zur Genealogie der Moral* (*On the Genealogy of Morals*): "Von dem Augenblick an, wo der Glaube an den Gott des asketischen Ideals verneint ist, *giebt es auch ein neues Problem:* das vom *Werthe* der Wahrheit" (*GM* III §24; KSA 5:401; "From the moment that faith is denied in the God of the ascetic ideal, *a new problem arises:* that of the *value* of truth").

[36] For a diachronic reading of the play, see R. H. Stephenson, "The Diachronic Solidity of Goethe's *Faust*," in Paul Bishop, ed., *A Companion to Goethe's "Faust": Parts I and II* (Rochester, NY and Woodbridge, UK: Camden House, 2001), 243–79.

[37] For further discussion of the Mothers, see Arthur Frederking, "Fausts Gang zu den Müttern," *Euphorion* 18 (1911): 422–40; Georg Moritz Wahl, "Zum Schlüssel in der Mütterszene," *Euphorion* 21 (1914): 294–97; Robert Petsch, "Fausts Gang zu den Müttern," in *Gehalt und Form: Abhandlungen zur Literaturwissenschaft und zur allgemeinen Geistesgeschichte* (Dortmund: Ruhfus, 1925), 446–59; Franz Koch, "Fausts Gang zu den Müttern," in *Geist und Leben* (Hamburg: Hanseatische Verlagsanstalt, 1939), 62–80; Carl Enders, *Faust-Studien: Müttermythos und Homunkulus-Allegorie in Goethes Faust* (Bonn: Bouvier, 1948); Friedrich Bruns, "Die Mütter in Goethes 'Faust': Versuch einer Deutung," *Monatshefte* 43 (1951): 364–89; Stuart Atkins, "The Mothers, the Phorcides and the Cabiri in Goethes Faust," *Monatshefte* 45 (1953): 289–96; Johannes Nabholz, "A Note on the Mothers in Goethe's *Faust*," *Symposium* 15 (1961): 198–203; Albert Fuchs, "Die 'Mütter': Eine Mephistopheles-Phantasmagorie: Ein Triumph und eine Niederlage — Eine Niederlage und ein Triumph," in *Goethe-Studien* (Berlin: Walter de Gruyter, 1968), 64–81; Harold Jantz, *The Mothers in Faust: The Myth of Time and Creativity* (Baltimore: John Hopkins P, 1969); and, more recently, John R. Williams, "The Problem of the Mothers," in Bishop, ed., *A Companion to Goethe's "Faust,"* 122–43.

[38] Like the subject of the poem "Gingo Biloba" in the *West-östlicher Divan* (*West-Eastern Divan*), the phrase "geeinte Zwienatur" is a formulation of the mode of argumentation, binary synthesis, that Nietzsche derived from Weimar Classicism. For further discussion, see Ilse Graham, "Geeinte Zwienatur: On the Structure of Goethe's Urfaust," in Magill, Rowley, and Smith, eds., *Tradition and Creation,* 131–45.

[39] HA 1:148; Goethe, *Selected Poems,* 81 (trans. Vernon Watkins).

[40] HA 1:370; Goethe, *Selected Poems,* 269 (trans. Christopher Middleton, translation adapted). For Goethe's celebration of the Moment elsewhere in his works, see *Dichtung und Wahrheit* (part 3, bk. 14): "Ein Gefühl aber, das bei mir gewaltig überhand nahm, und sich nicht wundersam genug äußern konnte, war die Empfindung der Vergangenheit und Gegenwart in Eins: eine Anschauung, die etwas Gespenstermäßiges in die Gegenwart brachte. Sie ist in vielen meiner größern und kleinern Arbeiten ausgedrückt, und wirkt im Gedicht immer wohltätig, ob sie gleich im Augenblick, wo sie sich unmittelbar am Leben und im Leben selbst ausdrückte, jedermann seltsam, unerklärlich, vielleicht unerfreulich scheinen mußte" (HA 10:32; "Yet one feeling did get a powerful grip on me and became inexpressibly fascinating: it was the sensation of past and present being one, a perception that introduced a spectral quality into the present. Many of my longer and shorter works express this, and its effect on poems is always salutary, even though the sensation, at the moment

when it was aroused directly by life, or in life itself, no doubt seemed strange, inexplicable, and even unpleasant to everyone"; *From My Life: Poetry and Truth,* 457). On 27 October 1787, during his second visit to Rome, Goethe wrote to Herder: "Auch habe ich dieses Jahr unter fremden Menschen achtgegeben und gefunden, daß alle wirklich kluge Menschen mehr oder weniger, zärter oder gröber, darauf kommen und bestehen: daß der Moment alles ist, und daß nur der Vorzug eines vernünftigen Menschen darin bestehe: sich so zu betragen, daß sein Leben, insofern es von ihm abhängt, die möglichste Masse von vernünftigen, glücklichen Momenten enthalte" (HA 11:419; "I have also found, living among strangers during the past year, that all really intelligent persons, to a greater or lesser extent, in a subtler or cruder way, come to and abide by the conclusion that the moment is everything, and that a rational person's advantage consists only in his conducting himself in such a manner that his life, insofar as it is under his control, will contain the largest possible number of rational, happy moments"; Johann Wolfgang von Goethe, *Italian Journey,* ed. Thomas P. Saine and Jeffrey L. Sammons, trans. Robert R. Heitner, Goethe Edition, vol. 6 [New York: Suhrkamp, 1989], 336). And on Ash Wednesday 1788, it occurred to Goethe, "daß die lebhaftesten und höchsten Vergnügen [. . .] nur einen Augenblick uns erscheinen, uns rühren und kaum eine Spur in der Seele zurücklassen, daß Freiheit und Gleichheit nur in dem Taumel des Wahnsinns genossen werden können, und daß die größte Lust nur dann am höchsten reizt, wenn sie sich ganz nahe an die Gefahr drängt und lüstern ängstlich-süße Empfindungen in ihrer Nähe genießet" (HA 11:515; "that the most intense and extreme pleasures . . . appear to us only for a moment, stir us, and scarcely leave a mark on our mind; that freedom and equality can be enjoyed only in the frenzy of madness; and that, in order to spur us to the highest pitch of excitement, the greatest delights must come into very close proximity with danger and let us wantonly savor, in their vicinity, feelings of pleasure mixed with fear"; Goethe, *Italian Journey,* 414). From the same period, the following fragment is also preserved: "Und soll ich dir gesteh[en] wie ich den[ke] / Die goldne Zeit / Sie war wohl nie wenn sie jetzt nicht ist / Und war sie je so kann sie wieder [ja auch] seyn" (WA 1.32:461; "And should I confess to you how I imagine / The golden age / There never was one if there is not also one now / And if there was one then it can be again"). And in his public response to the archaeologist Friedrich Karl Ludwig Sickler, who had discovered an ancient grave illustrated with bas-reliefs at Cumae, "Der Tänzerin Grab" ("A Grave Near Cumae," 1812), Goethe noted of one relief that "die schöne Beweglichkeit der Übergänge, die wir an solchen Künstlerinnen bewundern, ist hier für einen Moment fixirt, so daß wir das Vergangene, Gegenwärtige und Zukünftige zugleich erblicken und schon dadurch in einen überirdischen Zustand versetzt werden" (WA 1.48:144; "The beautiful fluidity of movement that we admire in such artists is here fixed for the moment, so that we simultaneously see previous, present and subsequent movements, and are already transported into a different world"; Johann Wolfgang von Goethe, *Essays on Art and Literature,* ed. John Gearey, trans. Ellen von Nardroff and Ernst H. von Nardroff, Goethe's Collected Works, 3 [New York: Suhrkamp, 1986], 29–35; here, 30). Later, in a letter to Wilhelm von Humboldt of 1 September 1816, Goethe, in his discussion of Humboldt's translation of Aeschylus's *Agamemnon,* drew a link between the achievement of the aesthetic and a proximity to the divine *nunc stans* (eternal now): "Vergangenheit, Gegenwart und Zukunft sind so glücklich in eins geschlungen, daß man selbst zum Seher, das heißt: Gott ähnlich wird. Und das ist doch am Ende der Triumph aller Poesie im Größten und im Kleinsten" (WA 4.27:157; "Past, present, and future are so fortuitously combined into one, that readers themselves become like a seer, that is to say, a god. And in the end that is the triumph of all poetry in its greatest and smallest aspects").

[41] Nietzsche talks of "die engste Verwandtschaft zwischen Musik und Mythus" (*GT* §24; KSA 1:153; "the closest relationship between music and myth"). Both music and myth are born of the Dionysian, but both require Apollonian form. According to Nietzsche, Apollonian form characterizes the Dionysian Greek, its absence the Dionysian barbarian (*GT* §2; KSA 1:31).

[42] "Car je sais entonner le beau chant du seigneur Dionysos, le dithyrambe, quand le vin a frappé mon esprit de sa foudre" (Archiloque, *Fragments,* ed. François Lasserre, trans. André Bonnard [Paris: Les Belles lettres, 1958], no. 96, 31; "And I know how to lead off / The sprightly dance / Of the Lord Dionysos, the dithyramb. / I do it thunderstruck / With wine": *Archilochos, Sappho, Alkman: Three Lyric Poets of the Late Greek Bronze Age,* trans. Guy Davenport [Berkeley, Los Angeles, London: U of California P, 1980], no. 249, 69).

[43] Similarly, in "Mittags" ("At Noon"), Zarathustra, like the dithyrambic artist, Archilochos, falls asleep at midday — the hour of Pan — to experience Apollonian dreams of Dionysian content (Z IV 10; KSA 4:342–45). However, according to Lampert, "the Images of 'At Midday' are uniformly Dionysian and draw frequently on images employed in the previous parts to depict Dionysian perfection" (*Nietzsche's Teaching: An Interpretation of "Thus Spoke Zarathustra"* [New Haven and London: Yale UP, 1986], 299).

[44] "Dieser Prozess des Tragödienchors ist das *dramatische* Urphänomen: sich selbst vor sich verwandelt zu sehen und jetzt zu handeln, als ob man wirklich in einen andern Leib, in einen andern Charakter eingegangen wäre. [. . .] Der Dithyramb ist deshalb wesentlich von jedem anderen Chorgesange unterschieden. [. . .] Alle andere Chorlyrik der Hellenen ist nur eine ungeheure Steigerung des apollinischen Einzelsängers; während im Dithyramb eine Gemeinde von unbewussten Schauspielern vor uns steht, die sich selbst unter einander als verwandelt ansehen" (*GT* §8; KSA 1:61; "This process of the tragic chorus is the *dramatic* primal phenomenon: to see oneself transformed before one's own eyes and to begin to act as if one had actually entered into another body, another character. . . . The dithyramb is thus essentially different from all other choral odes. . . . All the other choral lyric poetry of the Hellenes is merely a tremendous intensification of the Apollonian solo singer, while in the dithyramb we confront a community of unconscious actors who consider themselves and one another transformed" .

[45] Nietzsche's argument anticipates the structure of *Zur Genealogie der Moral,* where nihilism is said to eat away at values, transforming Good and Bad into Good and Evil, until, in the form of Christianity, it undermines itself. "Das Alles bedeutet, wagen wir es, dies zu begreifen, einen *Willen zum Nichts,* einen Widerwillen gegen das Leben, eine Auflehnung gegen die grundsätzlichsten Voraussetzungen des Lebens, aber es ist und bleibt ein *Wille!* . . . Und, um es noch zum Schluss zu sagen, was ich Anfangs sagte: lieber will noch der Mensch *das Nichts* wollen, als *nicht* wollen. . . ." (*GM* III §28; KSA 5:412; "All this means — let us dare to grasp it — a

will to nothingness, an aversion to life, a rebellion against the most fundamental pre-suppositions of life; but it is and remains a *will!* . . . And, to repeat in conclusion what I said at the beginning: humankind would rather will *nothingness* than *not* will").

[46] Silk and Stern, *Nietzsche on Tragedy,* 194.

[47] "Nietzsche's constant philosophico-polemical concern [is] to present the Greek poets, their creations and their public alike to our impoverished 'reality' in terms of these comparatives. Only thus are the Greeks able to offer us the exemplary spectacle of their 'richer' existence. The aerial roots of this argument are in Hölderlin's *Hyperion,* its flowering is to be in Wagner's mythopoeia. This is what Wagner will be called on to contribute to German culture, and this too, after the rejection of Wagner, will be Zarathustra's message" (Silk and Stern, *Nietzsche on Tragedy,* 354–55).

[48] For further discussion of these mythological symbols, see David Thatcher, "Eagle and Serpent in *Zarathustra,*" *Nietzsche-Studien* 6 (1977): 240–60.

[49] For further discussion, see Roger Hollinrake, *Nietzsche, Wagner, and the Philosophy of Pessimism* (London: George Allen and Unwin, 1982).

2: The Formative Influence of Weimar Classicism in the Genesis of *Zarathustra*

Und wer weiß, ob nicht auch der ganze Mensch wieder nur ein
Wurf nach einem höhern Ziele ist?

[And who knows whether even the whole individual is not just
another gamble for a yet higher goal?]

— Goethe, conversation with J. D. Falk, 14 June 1809;
WA *Gespräche* 2:263

Himmel! Was bin ich einsam!

IN APRIL 1869 NIETZSCHE, just twenty-four years old, began his appointment as extraordinary professor of classical philology at Basel University. On 28 May he gave his inaugural lecture, a discussion of the identity of Homer, which made a favorable impression on his audience, or at least so he told his university friend, Erwin Rohde (1845–98), and his mother, Franziska Nietzsche (1826–97), in his letters to them of 29 May and mid-June: "Gestern hielt ich vor ganz gefüllter Aula meine Antrittsrede, und zwar 'über die Persönlichkeit Homers,' mit einer Menge von philosophisch-aesthetischen Gesichtspunkten, die einen lebhaften Eindruck hervorgebracht zu haben scheinen" (KSB 3:13; "Yesterday I gave in front of a full auditorium my Inaugural Lecture, 'On the Personality of Homer,' with lots of philosophical-aesthetic points of view, which seem to have provoked a lively reaction"); "Durch diese Antrittsrede sind die Leute hier von Verschiedenem überzeugt worden, und mit ihr war meine Stellung, wie ich deutlich erkenne, gesichert" (KSB 3:15; "Because of this inaugural lecture the people here have been convinced about a number of things, and with it my position, as I can clearly see, has been secured"). Nietzsche's academic colleagues at the University included the philologists Jacob Mähly (1828–1902) and Hermann Usener (1834–1905), the ethnologist Johann Jakob Bachofen (1815–87), the geologist Ludwig Rütimeyer (1825–95), and the Greek specialist Wilhelm Vischer-Bilfinger (1808–74), as well as the historian Jacob Burckhardt (1818–97), the theologian Franz Overbeck (1837–1905), and the philosopher Heinrich Romundt (1845–1919). To begin with, all seemed to be well. Writing just a few months later to Rohde in mid-July 1869, however, Nietzsche sounded a note of caution:

An meinen "Collegen" mache ich eine seltsame Erfahrung: ich fühle mich unter ihnen, wie ich mich ehedem unter Studenten fühlte: im Ganzen ohne jedes Bedürfniß mich mit ihnen näher abzugeben, aber auch ohne allen Neid: ja genau genommen, fühle ich einen kleinen Gran von Verachtung gegen sie in mir, mit dem sich ja ein sehr höflicher und gefälliger Verkehr ganz gut verträgt. (KSB 3:28)

[With my "colleagues" I am having a strange experience: I feel among them as I used to feel among students: entirely without any need to get to know them more closely, but also without any envy at all: in fact, strictly speaking, I feel in me a small grain of contempt for them, with which indeed very polite and obliging intercourse is quite compatible.]

Ten years later, in 1879, Nietzsche took early retirement, on grounds of ill health. In April of that year, he was complaining, in postcards to Franz Overbeck, who was to remain one of his closest friends, of "die *Basileophobie,* eine wahre Angst und Scheu vor dem schlechten Wasser, der schlechten Luft, dem ganzen gedrückten Wesen dieser unseligen Brütestätte meiner Leiden" (KSB 5:402; "Basel-phobia, a real anxiety about and aversion towards the bad water, the bad air, the entire depressed nature of this unholy breeding-ground of my sufferings"), and that "man stimmt überein, dass Basel eine schlechte drückende, zu Kopfleiden disponirende Luft habe" (KSB 5:405–6; "everyone agrees that Basel has a bad, oppressive air that makes one disposed to headaches"). Not only did he write *Ceterum censeo Basileam esse dereliquendam* ("furthermore I am of the opinion that Basel should be forsaken"), but he also concluded: *Academia derelinquenda est* ("academia is to be forsaken"). In a postcard to his mother and his sister, Elisabeth Nietzsche (1846–1935), he wrote: "Ach das schändliche schädliche Basel, wo ich meine Gesundheit verloren habe und mein Leben verlieren werde!" (KSB 5:407; "Oh, disgraceful, harmful Basel, where I have lost my health and will lose my life!"). In a postcard to his friend, the philosopher Paul Rée (1849–1901) of 23 April 1879, Nietzsche complained: "*Mein* Zustand ist eine Thierqüalerei und Vorhölle, ich kann's nicht leugnen. *Wahrscheinlich* hört es mit meiner akademischen Thätigkeit auf, *vielleicht* mit der Thätigkeit überhaupt" (KSB 5:410; "I am in torment and in hellish limbo, I can't deny it. My academic activity will probably cease, indeed perhaps all my activity"). Nietzsche sent his letter of resignation to the President of the University, Carl Burckhardt, on 2 May 1879. In the days following the acceptance of his resignation by the Regierungsrat and the Erziehungsrat of the Canton of Basel, Nietzsche wrote in postcards to such acquaintances as Paul Widemann (1851–1928) and Marie Baumgartner (1831–97): "Ich habe meine Professur niedergelegt und gehe in die Höhen — fast zur Verzweiflung gebracht und kaum noch hoffend. [. . .] Ich habe *schwer* gelitten, alles ist zum Äußersten gekommen, die Professur ist niedergelegt" (KSB 5:412–13; "I have resigned my professorship and am going up into the mountains — almost brought to the point of despair and with hardly any hope . . . I have suffered *seriously,* everything has gone to the last extreme, the professorship has been resigned").[1]

For the next ten years, Nietzsche lived in various places in Europe, mainly in Italy and Switzerland, moving from hotel to hotel and from *Pension* to *Pension* on a regular basis. During the years 1881 to 1884, Nietzsche began, and completed, work on what turned out to be the four sections of *Also sprach Zarathustra* (*Thus Spoke Zarathustra*). This chapter provides an overview of the compositional framework to the genesis of this central text, referring to his autobiographical text, *Ecce Homo* (1888, published posthumously), his correspondence, and his *Nachlass,* to examine the circumstances under which the text was written, some of the reasons for its structure and style, and the multifarious points at which characteristic doctrines of Goethe and Schiller are woven into the emergent whole of the text.

Ecce Homo

In his controversial "autobiography," *Ecce Homo,* Nietzsche gives us a partial account of the composition of *Zarathustra.*[2] This account, however, subordinates the composition of the work to two key concepts — the idea of the eternal recurrence, and the notion of inspiration. As a result, Nietzsche's account, whilst factually accurate, gives a simplified picture of the complex origin of the text.

The section on *Zarathustra* opens with a characteristically bold gesture for the late Nietzsche: "Ich erzähle nunmehr die Geschichte des Zarathustra" (*EH Z* §1; KSA 6:335; "I shall now relate the history of *Zarathustra*"). According to Nietzsche, "die Grundconception dieses Werks" ("the fundamental conception of this work"), the idea of the eternal recurrence — "die höchste Formel der Bejahung, die überhaupt erreicht werden kann" ("this highest formula of affirmation that is at all attainable") — came to him in August 1881. "Er ist auf ein Blatt hingeworfen" ("It was scrawled on a sheet"), Nietzsche adds, "mit der Unterschrift: '6000 Fuss jenseits von Mensch und Zeit'" ("with the notation underneath: '6000 feet beyond Humanity and Time'").[3] He adds the detail that he was walking through the woods along the lake of Silvaplana, and stopped at a pyramid-shaped rock not far from Surlej, a small town in the Engadine.[4]

Reconstructing his life from his notebooks and letters, we know that Nietzsche was indeed in Switzerland at this time, staying in Sils-Maria. He stayed from 4 July to 1 October 1882. It was not his first visit to the Engadine; he had visited Sankt Moritz in 1879, but could not stand the town this time, and the prices for rooms were too high, so, on the advice of a fellow traveler from the region, he took the coach to Sils-Maria.[5] Shortly after his arrival, he wrote to his sister, echoing Goethe's Werther: "Ich habe es noch nie so ruhig gehabt, und die Wege, Wälder, Seen, Wiesen sind wie für mich gemacht; und die Preise sind nicht außer allem Verhältniß zu meinen Mitteln. [. . .] Der Ort heißt Sils-Maria; bitte, haltet den Namen vor meinen Freunden und Bekannten geheim, ich wünsche keine Besuche" (7 July 1881; KSB 6:99; "I have never found anywhere as quiet, and the paths, woods, lakes, meadows are as if made for me; and the prices are not entirely unrelated to my means . . . The place is called Sils-Maria; please, keep the name secret from my friends and acquaintances, I don't want any visits").[6] In the elevated atmosphere, both topographically and psychologically speaking, Nietzsche — who had just completed and seen to publication his recent book, *Morgenröthe* (*Dawn*) — found his mood (or at least, so he told his family) considerably improved:[7]

> Nie gab es einen Menschen, auf den das Wort "niedergedrückt" weniger gepaßt hätte. Meine Freunde, die mehr von meiner Lebensaufgabe und deren unaufhaltsamer Förderung errathen, meinen, ich sei wenn nicht der *Glücklichste* so jedenfalls der *Muthigste* der Menschen. Ich habe Schwereres auf mir als meine Gesundheit und werde damit fertig, auch dies zu tragen. Mein Aussehen ist übrigens vortrefflich, meine Muskulatur in Folge meines beständigen Marschirens fast die eines Soldaten, Magen und Unterleib in Ordnung. Mein Nervensystem ist, in Anbetracht der ungeheuren Thätigkeit die es zu leisten hat, prachtvoll und der Gegenstand meiner Verwunderung, sehr fein und sehr stark: selbst die langen schweren Leiden, ein unzweckmäßiger Beruf und die fehlerhafteste Behandlung haben ihm nicht wesentlich geschadet, ja im letzten Jahre ist es stärker geworden, und, Dank ihm, habe ich eines der muthigsten und erhabensten und besonnensten Bücher hervorgebracht, welche jemals aus menschlichem Gehirne und Herzen geboren sind. (KSB 6:102–3)

> [Never has there been a human being for whom the word "depressed" would have been less appropriate. My friends, who know more about my life's task and who can guess its inexorable demands, are of the opinion that I am, if not the *happiest,* then at any rate the *bravest* of all men. I have something heavier weighing on me than my health and am able to cope with bearing this as well. My appearance is, incidentally, excellent, my muscular system, as a result of my constant walking, is almost that of a soldier, stomach and abdomen in working order. My nervous system is, considering the immense activity which it has to perform, splendid and the object of my amazement, very fine and very strong: even the long, difficult illnesses, an unsuitable career, and the most imperfect treatment have not damaged it substantially, in fact in the last year it has become stronger, and, thanks to it, I have produced

one of the most courageous and most sublime and most well thought-out books ever born from the human brain and heart.]

His "life's task" — the phrase Nietzsche used to refer to his philosophical project — was, very soon, about to take on a new contour in terms of its expression and urgency. Finally, he urged his sister only to write "good things" to him — including, among those "good things" to be sent, perhaps, a sausage: "Schreibt mir *gute* Dinge hier hinauf, wo ich über der Zukunft der Menschheit brüte, und lassen wir alles das kleine persönliche Leiden und Sorgen bei Seite. Auch eine äußerst delikate Wurst würde zu den *guten* Dingen gehören" (KSB 6:104; "Write *good* things to me up here, where I am pondering the future of humanity, and let's put all petty personal sorrows and problems on one side. An extremely tasty sausage would also belong to the *good* things").[8]

In this new environment, Nietzsche turned to fresh intellectual tasks, including, as he told Franz Overbeck on 30 July 1881, reading the works of Spinoza with an admiration reminiscent of Goethe's for the Dutch philosopher:[9]

> Ich bin ganz erstaunt, ganz entzückt! Ich habe einen *Vorgänger* und was für einen! Ich kannte Spinoza fast nicht: daß mich *jetzt* nach ihm verlangte, war eine "Instinkthandlung." Nicht nur, daß seine Gesamttendenz gleich der meinen ist — die Erkenntniß zum *mächtigsten Affekt* zu machen — in fünf Hauptpunkten seiner Lehre finde ich mich wieder, dieser abnormste und einsamste Denker ist mir gerade in *diesen* Dingen am nächsten: er leugnet die Willensfreiheit —; die Zwecke —; die sittliche Weltordnung —; das Unegoistische —; das Böse —; wenn freilich auch die Verschiedenheiten ungeheuer sind, so liegen diese mehr in dem Unterschiede der Zeit, der Cultur, der Wissenschaft. In summa: meine Einsamkeit, die mir, wie auf ganz hohen Bergen, oft, oft Athemnoth machte und das Blut hervorströmen ließ, ist wenigstens jetzt eine Zweisamkeit. — Wunderlich! (KSB 6:111)[10]

> [I am completely astonished, completely delighted! I have a *predecessor,* and what a predecessor! I hardly knew Spinoza at all: that I longed for him *now* was an "act of instinct." Not only is his general tendency the same as mine — to turn knowledge into the *most powerful emotion* — in five main points of his doctrine I find myself again, this most exceptional and most solitary thinker is close to me precisely in *these* things: he denies the freedom of the will; purposiveness; the moral order of the world; unselfishness; evil; even if the differences are of course immense, these lie more in the differences in time, culture, and the advance of knowledge. In summa: my solitude, which, just as on very high mountains, often, often made my breathing difficult and my blood gush forth, is now at least a "duo-tude." — Remarkable!]

Nietzsche's interest at this time in Spinoza is reflected in his notebook, where he excerpts Spinoza and comments on him.[11] In this letter, Nietzsche speaks of his "Einsamkeit" becoming a "Zweisamkeit," anticipating his later use of the phrase "wurde Eins zu Zwei" ("one became two"); but the encounter with Spinoza was no prototype for his encounter with Zarathustra. For Nietzsche would soon turn against Spinoza, describing him in his next book, *Die fröhliche Wissenschaft* (*The Gay Science*), as one of the "philosophical vampires" of the Western tradition: "Fühlt ihr nicht an solchen Gestalten, wie noch der Spinoza's, etwas tief Änigmatisches und Unheimliches? [. . .] denn, man vergebe mir, das was von Spinoza *übrig blieb*, amor intellectualis dei, ist ein Geklapper, nichts mehr! was ist amor, was deus, wenn ihnen jeder Tropfen Blut fehlt? . . ." (*FW* §372; KSA 3:624; "Looking at these figures, even Spinoza, don't you have a sense of something profoundly enigmatic and uncanny? . . . for, forgive me, what was left of Spinoza, *amor intellectualis dei*, is mere chatter and no more than that: What is *amor*, what *deus*, if there is not a drop of blood in them?").

Even more swiftly than his view of Spinoza, Nietzsche's sense of his own good fortune changed, as it so often did. In a letter, dated 14 August 1881, to the man who was arguably his closest friend, the musician Heinrich Köselitz (1854–1918), whom he dubbed Peter Gast, — that is, around the time when, according to his own testimony, he experienced the thought of the eternal recurrence — he wrote of the "intensity of his feeling":

> Ach, Freund, mitunter läuft mir die Ahnung durch den Kopf, daß ich eigentlich ein höchst gefährliches Leben lebe, denn ich gehöre zu den Maschinen, welche *zerspringen* können! Die Intensitäten meines Gefühls machen mich schaudern und lachen — schon ein Paarmal konnte ich das Zimmer nicht verlassen, aus dem lächerlichen Grunde, daß meine Augen entzündet waren — wodurch? Ich hatte jedesmal den Tag vorher auf meinen Wanderungen zuviel geweint, und zwar nicht sentimentale Thränen, sondern Thränen des Jauchzens; wobei ich sang und Unsinn redete, erfüllt von einem neuen Blick, den ich vor allen Menschen voraus habe. (KSB 6:112)

> [Ah, my friend, sometimes the intimation comes to me that I am in fact leading an extremely dangerous life, for I am one of those machines which can *explode*! The intensities of my feeling make me shudder and laugh — a few times already I could not leave the room, for the ridiculous reason that my eyes were inflamed — from what? Each time, the previous day I had cried too much on my walks, and these were not sentimental tears, but tears of jubilation while I was singing and talking nonsense, filled with a new vision that I have in advance of all other human beings.]

In other words, Nietzsche was in precisely the same kind of highly emotional state that he recalls being provoked in him by the idea of eternal recurrence; and two years later, in his letter to Heinrich Köselitz of 3 September 1883, he would refer to the Engadine as "die Geburtsstätte meines Zarathustra" ("the birth-place of my Zarathustra"), and mention the same note as he did in *Ecce Homo* about the idea of the eternal recurrence: "Ich fand eben noch die erste Skizze der in ihm verbundenen Gedanken; darunter steht 'Anfang August 1881 in Sils-Maria, 6000 Fuss über dem Meere und viel höher über allen menschlichen Dingen'" (KSB 6:444; "I have just found the first sketch of the thoughts that are bound up with it; underneath it reads: 'Beginning of August 1881 in Sils-Maria, 6000 feet above the sea and much higher above all human things'").

The note to which Nietzsche is referring both in *Ecce Homo* and in his correspondence can be found in the published edition of the *Nachlass*, as fragment 11 [141] from the period Spring to Autumn 1881 (KSA 9:494). This lengthy note, entitled "*Die Wiederkunft des Gleichen*. Entwurf" ("*The Recurrence of the Same*. Sketch"), includes a paragraph with the phrase, "the new weight," that would provide the title for the section about the eternal recurrence in *Die fröhliche Wissenschaft:*

> Das neue *Schwergewicht: die ewige Wiederkehr des Gleichen*. Unendliche Wichtigkeit unseres Wissen's, Irren's, unsrer Gewohnheiten, Lebensweisen für alles Kommende. Was machen wir mit dem *Reste* unseres Lebens — wir, die wir den grössten Theil desselben in der wesentlichsten Unwissenheit verbracht haben? Wir *lehren die Lehre* — es ist das stärkste Mittel, sie uns selber *einzuverleiben*. Unsre Art Seligkeit, als Lehrer der grössten Lehre.
>
> Anfang August 1881 in Sils-Maria,
> 6000 Fuss über dem Meere und viel höher über allen
> menschlichen Dingen! —

> [The new *weight: the eternal recurrence of the same*. The infinite importance of our knowledge, error, our habits, ways of living for everything to come. What do we do with the *rest* of our life — we, who have spent the greatest part of the same in a state of essential ignorance? We *teach the teaching* — it is the strongest means of *incorporating* it into ourselves. Our kind of bliss, as teachers of the greatest teaching.
>
> Beginning of August 1881 in Sils-Maria,
> 6000 feet above the sea and much higher above all
> human things! —]

From around the same time we have the earliest evidence for a new project, which would turn into *Also sprach Zarathustra*. This evidence is the following three sketches in his notebook for Spring-Autumn 1881, beginning with fragment 11[195]:

Mittag und Ewigkeit
Fingerzeige zu einem neuen Leben

Zarathustra, geboren am See Urmi, verliess im dreissigsten Jahre seine Heimat, gieng in die Provinz Aria und verfasste in den zehn Jahren seiner Einsamkeit im Gebirge den Zend-Avesta.

(KSA 9:519)[12]

[Midday and Eternity
A pointer to a new life

Zarathustra, born on Lake Urmi, left his homeland in his thirtieth year, went to the province of Aria and in the ten years of his solitude in the mountains wrote the Zend-Avesta.]

Why did Nietzsche choose the figure of Zarathustra (or, as he is more usually called in English, Zoroaster)? Historically speaking, Zoroaster was a Persian prophet of the sixth century B.C.E., from an area now part of Afghanistan and Uzbekistan. The ancient religious text, the Avesta, contains verses in which Zoroaster proclaims the doctrine of Good and Evil, and converses with the god Ahura Mazda. In *Ecce Homo* Nietzsche would gloss his decision to use the figure of the Persian prophet in the following terms: "Zarathustra hat zuerst im Kampf des Guten und des Bösen das eigentliche Rad im Getriebe der Dinge gesehn, — die Übersetzung der Moral in's Metaphysische, als Kraft, Ursache, Zweck an sich, ist *sein* Werk" ("Zoroaster was the first to discover in the fight of good and evil the very wheel in the machinery of things: the transposition of morality into the metaphysical, as a force, cause, and end in itself, is *his* work"). Nietzsche saw his own work in terms of a reversal of this "achievement": "Zarathustra *schuf* diesen verhängnissvollsten Irrthum, die Moral: folglich muss er auch der Erste sein, der ihn *erkennt* [. . .] Die Selbstüberwindung der Moral aus Wahrhaftigkeit, die Selbstüberwindung des Moralisten in seinen Gegensatz — in *mich* — das bedeutet in meinem Munde der Name Zarathustra" (*EH* Warum ich ein Schicksal bin §3; KSA 6:367; "Zoroaster created this most calamitous error, morality; consequently, he must also be the first to recognize it . . . The self-overcoming of morality out of truthfulness, the self-overcoming of the moralist into his opposite — into *me* — that is what the name of Zarathustra means in my mouth").

In his notebooks from the period September 1870 to January 1871, Nietzsche excerpted briefly several passages from the nineteenth-century Orientalist Max Müller (1823–1900), one of which mentions "Zoroaster";[13] in "Die Philosophie im tragischen Zeitalter der Griechen" (*Philosophy in the Tragic Age of the Greeks*, 1873), Nietzsche discussed the morphological proximity of ancient oriental and Greek ideas, or "Zoroaster neben Heraklit" ("Zoroaster next to Heraclitus"), while disputing the idea of any historical link (KSA 1:806). In a later note from early 1874, Nietzsche summarized the values of the "Perser" ("Persians") as "gut schiessen, gut reiten, nicht borgen und nicht lügen" (32[82]; KSA 7:785; "shoot well, ride well, do not borrow and do not lie"), thus anticipating the lines in "Von tausend und Einem Ziele" ("On a Thousand and One Goals") where Zarathustra says: "'Wahrheit reden und gut mit Bogen und Pfeil verkehren' — so dünkte es jenem Volke zugleich lieb und schwer, aus dem mein Name kommt" (*Z* I 15; KSA 4:75; compare KSA 14:553; "'To speak the truth and to handle well bow and arrow' — that seemed both dear and difficult to the people who gave me my name").

Nietzsche's source of information about the historical figure of Zoroaster was probably *Die Symbolik und Mythologie der alten Völker, besonders der Griechen,* published in 4 volumes (1810–12; second ed., 1819–21) by Georg Friedrich Creuzer (1771–1858), which he had consulted as early as 1871 during his work on *Die Geburt der Tragödie*.[14] However, the original Zoroastrian texts were appearing in translation in the 1850s and 1860s, when Nietzsche was a student in Bonn, and he may well have been alerted to the tenets of Zoroastrianism by the contemporary discussion surrounding them.[15] As another source for the figure of Zarathustra, the editors of the Kritische Gesamtausgabe, Giorgio Colli and Mazzino Montinari, have suggested Ralph Waldo Emerson who, in one of his *Essays,* refers to Zoroaster in a passage marked in Nietzsche's edition (KSA 14:279).[16] In a letter to Köselitz dated 23 April 1883, Nietzsche noted the etymological origin of the name (mentioned by Creuzer), but disclaimed all knowledge of this at the time of composition: "Heute lernte ich zufällig, *was* "Zarathustra" bedeutet: nämlich "Gold-Stern." Dieser Zufall machte mich glücklich. Man könnte meinen, die ganze Conception meines Büchleins habe in dieser Etymologie ihre Wurzel: aber ich wußte bis heute nichts davon" (KSB 6:366; "Today I learned by chance *what* 'Zarathustra' means: namely, 'Gold-Star.' This chance made me happy. One might think that the whole conception of my little book has its root in this etymology: but until today I knew nothing about it").[17]

Furthermore, as the next fragment from the *Nachlass* of 1881, 11[196], makes clear, during this period Nietzsche not only took the decision to use the name "Zarathustra," but developed the imagery and literary style of the work:

> Die Sonne der Erkenntniß steht wieder einmal im Mittag: und geringelt liegt die Schlange der Ewigkeit in ihrem Lichte — — es ist *eure* Zeit, ihr Mittagsbrüder!
>
> (KSA 9:519)

[The sun of knowledge stands once again at midday: and the serpent of eternity lies coiled in its light — — it is *your* time, you brothers of midday!][18]

And the following sketch, fragment 11 [197], for a series of four books shows the extent of Nietzsche's conception of his project at this early stage:

Zum "Entwurf einer neuen Art zu leben."

Erstes Buch im Stile des ersten Satzes der neunten Symphonie. *Chaos sive natura:* "von der Entmenschlichung der Natur." Prometheus wird an den Kaucasus angeschmiedet. Geschrieben mit der Grausamkeit des Κράτος, "der Macht."

[For "Sketch for a new way of living."

[**First book** in the style of the first movement of the Ninth Symphony. *Chaos sive natura* [Chaos indistinguishable from Nature]: "On the dehumanization of nature." Prometheus is chained on to the Caucasus. Written with the cruelty of *kratos*, "the power."]

Presumably, the symphony referred to here is Beethoven's Ninth, in D minor (opus 125), composed in 1823.[19] Famous for its dramatic opening chords,[20] the symphony, in its final movement, contained a setting of Schiller's "An die Freude" ("Ode to Joy"), to which Nietzsche had alluded in *Die Geburt der Tragödie* (*GT* §1; KSA 1:29).

Playing on Spinoza's formulation of pantheism, *deus sive natura* (God indistinguishable from Nature), Nietzsche places chaos, not the deity, at the heart of nature. In another note from the *Nachlass*, he wrote: "Meine Aufgabe: die Entmenschung der Natur und dann die Vernatürlichung des Menschen, nachdem er den reinen Begriff 'Natur' gewonnen hat" (11[211]; KSA 9:525; "My task: the dehumanization of nature and then the naturalization of humanity, after it has gained the pure concept of 'nature'"). The reference to Prometheus, the man whom, according to Greek legend, Zeus chained to a lonely rock, so an eagle could feed by day on his liver, which was then restored again at night, might be explained, not just in light of the discussion of Prometheus in sections 9 to 11 of *Die Geburt der Tragödie,* but also in light of the fact that it was Goethe's poem "Prometheus" that sparked the so-called *Pantheismus-Streit* between Lessing and Jacobi, which centered on Spinoza's doctrines.[21] *Kratos,* "power," would offer Nietzsche a concept of global explanatory value when later theorized as the "will to power." He also envisaged a second book:

Zweites Buch. Flüchtig-skeptisch-mephistophelisch. "*Von der Einverleibung der Erfahrungen.*" Erkenntniss = Irrthum, der organisch wird und organisirt.

[**Second book**. Fleeting — sceptical — Mephistophelian. "On *the incorporation of experiences.*" Knowledge = error, which becomes organic and is organized.]

The skeptical and Goethean-"Mephistophelian" aspects of Zarathustra can be found in his apparent "nihilism";[22] while the section "Von den Verächtern des Leibes" ("On the Despisers of the Body"), actually in part 1, was to emphasize the bodiliness of identity and individuality. Nietzsche's (Goethean) view of knowledge as a form of "error" that is necessary for life is an idea that he would explore in further detail in *Jenseits von Gut und Böse* (*Beyond Good and Evil*, 1886):[23] "Die Falschheit eines Urtheils ist uns noch kein Einwand gegen ein Urtheil; darin klingt unsre neue Sprache vielleicht am fremdesten. Die Frage ist, wie weit es lebenfördernd, lebenerhaltend, Arterhaltend, vielleicht gar Art-züchtend ist" (*JGB* §36; KSA 5:18; "The falseness of a judgment is for us still not an objection to a judgment; in this respect our new language perhaps sounds strangest. The question is to what extent it is life-promoting, life-preserving, species-preserving, perhaps even species-cultivating"). What of the planned third book?

Drittes Buch. Das Innigste und über den Himmeln Schwebendste, was je geschrieben wird: "vom *letzten Glück des Einsamen*" — das ist der, welcher aus dem "Zugehörigen" zum "Selbsteignen" des höchsten Grades geworden ist: das vollkommene *ego:* nur erst *dies* ego hat *Liebe,* auf den früheren Stufen, wo die höchste Einsamkeit und Selbstherrlichkeit nicht erreicht ist, giebt es etwas anderes als Liebe.

[**Third book**. What is the most heartfelt and highest above the heavens that has ever been written: "On the *last happiness of the solitary one*" — that is the one who, from "one who belongs," has become "his own self" in the highest degree: the completed *ego:* only *this* ego has *love;* at the earlier stages, where the highest solitude and autocracy has not been reached, there is something other than love.]

The phrase "the last happiness of the solitary one" anticipates the figure of the Loneliest Man in "Vom Gesicht und Räthsel" ("On the Vision and the Riddle"), where the term will be used as a pseudonym for Zarathustra himself (*Z* III 2 §1; KSA 4:197). And "die Liebe" ("love"), we read in the preceding chapter, "ist die Gefahr des Einsamsten, die Liebe zu Allem, *wenn es nur lebt!*" (*Z* III 1; KSA 4:196; "is the danger of the loneliest one, love of everything *as long as it is alive!*"). And it is so precisely evocative of the egoistically gratifying love Goethe's Suleika celebrates as the motivating force of life and spirit:

Ach! wie schmeichelt's meinem Triebe,
Wenn man meinen Dichter preist:
Denn das Leben ist die Liebe,
Und des Lebens Leben Geist. (HA 2:75)

[Ah! How it flatters my own drive,
When people praise my poet.
For life is love,
And the life of life, spirit.][24]

Equally, other passages in part 3 pronounce such selfishness blessed — "die heile, gesunde Selbstsucht, die aus mächtiger Seele quillt:— / — aus mächtiger Seele, zu welcher der hohe Leib gehört" ("the sacred, healthy selfishness, which flows from the powerful soul, / from the powerful soul, to which belongs the high body") — and proclaim the ego healthy and selfishness blessed ("das Ich heil und heilig spricht und die Selbstsucht selig"; *Z* III 10 §2; KSA 4:238–40). This blessing is entirely consonant with both the context and the tone of, for example, Goethe's "confession" of 28 March 1830 to Kanzler von Müller of his own ego-drive: "Ich habe Natur und Kunst eigentlich immer nur egoistisch studirt, nämlich um mich zu unterrichten. Ich schrieb auch nur darüber, um mich weiter zu bilden. Was die Leute daraus machen, ist mir einerlei" (WA *Gespräche* 7:282–83; "Essentially I have always studied nature and art for purely egotistic reasons, namely in order to instruct myself. And I wrote about them, too, in order to continue to develop and grow. What people make of it all is no concern of mine").

Finally, a fourth book was planned:

Viertes Buch. Dithyrambisch-umfassend. "Annulus aeternitatis." Begierde, alles noch einmal und ewige Male zu erleben.

[**Fourth book**. Dithyrambic — all-embracing. "Ring of eternity." Desire to experience everything once more and an infinite number of times.]

In *Ecce Homo*, Nietzsche would write that "die Kunst des *grossen* Rhythmus, der *grosse Stil* der Periodik zum Ausdruck eines ungeheuren Auf und Nieder von sublimer, von übermenschlicher, Leidenschaft ist erst von mir entdeckt" (*EH* Warum ich so gute Bücher schreibe §4; KSA 6, 304–5; "the art of the *great* rhythm, the *great style* of periods to express a tremendous up-and-down of sublime, of superhuman passion, was first discovered by me"); and although he added that "mit einem Dithyrambus wie dem letzten des *dritten* Zarathustra, 'die sieben Siegel' überschrieben, flog ich tausend Meilen über das hinaus, was bisher Poesie hiess" ("with a dithyramb such as the last one of the third part of *Zarathustra*, entitled 'The Seven Seals,' I soared a thousand miles beyond what was hitherto called poesy"), part 4 would turn out to be particularly dithyrambic, partly through the inclusion of such songs as "Wer wärmt mich, wer liebt mich noch?" ("Who warms me, who loves me still?") and "Bei abgehellter Luft" ("In the dimmed air"), sung by the Magician (*Z* IV 5 §1 and 14 §3; KSA 4:312–17 and 371–74) and "Die Wüste wächst: weh dem, der Wüsten birgt!" ("The desert grows: woe to him who harbors deserts!") sung by the Shadow, later revised and included in the *Dionysos-Dithyramben* (*Dithyrambs of Dionysus*, written 1883–1888; assembled 1888–1889; published 1891), not to mention the dithyrambic elaboration of Zarathustra's roundelay, "Das Nachtwandler-Lied" ("Song of the Nocturnal Wanderer"). Moreover, in this fragment we find the idea of the abolition of linear eternity, through the embrace of the eternal recurrence — the desire for everything in one's life to recur again and again. Following this paragraph on the fourth book we find the comment: "Die unablässige *Verwandlung* — du musst in einem kurzen Zeitraume durch viele Individuen hindurch. Das Mittel ist *der unablässige Kampf*" ("The unremitting *transformation* — you must in a short period of time go through many individuals. The means is *the unremitting struggle*"). This statement, or perhaps the entire note, is dated — Sils-Maria, 26 August 1881. So between the beginning and end of August 1881, Nietzsche had worked out both the structure of a four-volume work, centered on a figure called Zarathustra, *and* the basic conception of the idea of the eternal recurrence, in terms redolent of Goethe's life-long insistence on the need for cyclical self-transformation, and couched in similarly biological images.[25]

Nietzsche's notebooks, published as volumes 10 and 11 of the KSA, are full of revealing sketches for the various parts of *Zarathustra*. For the time being, however, it seems no further progress was made. In a letter to Paul Rée at the end of August 1881, Nietzsche wrote about this intention to follow the completion of *Morgenröthe* with another work: "Und dieses selbe Jahr, das jenes Werk an's Licht brachte, soll nun auch das andre Werk an's Licht bringen, an dem ich im Bilde des Zusammenhanges und der goldnen Kette meine arme stückweise Philosophie vergessen darf!" (KSB 6:124; "And this same year which brought that work to light, must now bring the other work to the light in respect of which, in the image of the connection and the golden chain, I may forget my poor patchwork philosophy"!). But there is no evidence that he means here *Zarathustra;* and, in a letter to Köselitz of 25 January 1882, Nietzsche envisaged adding a further three parts to the five parts of *Morgenröthe* (KSB 6:159). Eventually, these formed the first four parts of *Die fröhliche Wissenschaft,* the last part of which, "Sanctus Januarius," was completed in Genoa in January 1882. But, during those months in the summer of 1881, Nietzsche continued to sketch scenarios and sentences that would later feed into what is arguably his most important work. For example, we find the psychological effect of the thought of the eternal recurrence, as it would be presented in *Die fröhliche Wissenschaft* (*FW* §341; KSA 3:570) and in *Also sprach Zarathustra* (*Z* III 2 §2; KSA 4:200–201), in this fragment, number 11 [206]: "Es ist Alles wiedergekommen: der Sirius und die Spinne und deine Gedanken in dieser Stunde und dieser dein Gedanke, daß Alles wiederkommt" (KSA 9:524; "Everything has recurred again; the Sirius star and the spider and your thoughts in this hour and even your thought that everything recurs"). And the emphasis, clearly stemming from Weimar Classicism,[26] placed by Nietzsche in his philosophy on the significance of the aesthetic is as unmistakable in this fragment, number 12 [29] —

> Wir kommen über die Ästhetik nicht hinaus — ehemals glaubte ich, ein Gott mache sich das Vergnügen, die Welt anzusehen: aber wir haben das Wesen einer Welt, welche die *Menschen* allmählich *geschaffen* haben: *ihre* Ästhetik.
>
> (KSA 9:581)
>
> [We cannot get beyond the aesthetic — previously I believed a God was indulging himself by looking at the world: but we have the existence of a world that *humans* have gradually *created: their* aesthetic.]

— as it is in this one, 12 [75]:

> Ich *wehre mich dagegen,* Vernunft *und Liebe,* Gerechtigkeit und Liebe von einander zu trennen, oder gar sich entgegenzustellen und der Liebe den höheren Rang zu geben! Liebe ist comes, bei Vernunft und Gerechtigkeit, sie ist die Freude an der Sache, Lust an ihrem Besitz, Begierde sie ganz zu besitzen und in ihrer ganzen Schönheit — die *aesthetische Seite* der Gerechtigkeit und Vernunft, ein Nebentrieb.
>
> (KSA 9:589)
>
> [I *put up a fight against* separating out reason *and love,* justice and love, or even setting them in opposition to each other and giving love the higher status! Love is "a companion," with reason and justice, it is joy in the thing, wanting to possess it, the desire to possess it entirely and in all its beauty — the *aesthetic aspect* of justice and reason, an accompanying drive.]

As Colli and Montinari have pointed out, the same notebooks from the Autumn of 1881 (namely, N V 7 and M III 4) that contain the preliminary versions of sections 68, 106, 125, 291, and 332 of *Die fröhliche Wissenschaft* also contain references to Zarathustra (KSA 14:280). The simultaneous genesis of parts of these two works points to the close connections between them.

In two of these fragments, 12 [79] and 15 [17], Nietzsche explicitly places himself in a tradition, stating in one, "Ich habe eine *Herkunft*" (KSA 9:590; "I have an *origin*") and explaining in the other: "In dem, was Zarathustra, Moses, Muhamed Jesus Plato Brutus Spinoza Mirabeau bewegte, lebe ich auch schon, und in manchen Dingen kommt in mir erst reif an's Tageslicht, was embryonisch ein paar Jahrtausende brauchte" (KSA 9:642; "In what moved Zoroaster, Moses, Mohammed, Jesus, Plato, Brutus, Spinoza, Mirabeau, there I am already living, and in some things what required a few millennia as an embryo is only now seeing the daylight in mature form, in me"). This rhetoric of aristocractic origins begins, whimsically if spookily, in *Menschliches, Allzumenschliches* (*Human, All Too Human*), where Nietzsche speaks of his "descent into Hades," and his conversations with four pairs of predecessors: Epicurus and Montaigne, Goethe and Spinoza, Plato and Rousseau, Pascal and Schopenhauer.[27] Later, in the more hyperbolic tones of *Ecce Homo,* Nietzsche places the metaphysical implications of his *Zarathustra* alongside or, rather, above the works of Goethe, Shakespeare, Dante, or the priests who wrote the Rig-Veda: "Dass ein Goethe, ein Shakespeare nicht einen Augenblick in dieser ungeheuren Leidenschaft und Höhe zu athmen wissen würde, dass Dante, gegen Zarathustra gehalten, bloss ein Gläubiger ist und nicht Einer, der die Wahrheit erst *schafft,* ein *weltregierender* Geist, ein Schicksal —, dass die Dichter des Veda Priester sind und nicht einmal würdig, die Schuhsohlen eines Zarathustra zu lösen, das ist Alles das Wenigste und giebt keinen Begriff von der Distanz, von der *azurnen* Einsamkeit, in der dies Werk lebt" (*EH Z* §6; KSA 6:343; "That a Goethe, a Shakespeare, would be unable to breathe even for a moment in this tremendous passion and height, that Dante is, compared with Zarathustra, merely a believer and not one who first *creates* truth, a *world-governing* spirit, a destiny — that the poets of the Veda are priests and not even worthy of tying the shoelaces of a Zarathustra — that is the least important thing and gives no idea of the distance, of the *azure* solitude in which this work lives"). Fragment 15[17] concludes, however, with a reference to a "new" aristocracy, which evokes the individuated nobility that Goethe and Schiller identified as the characteristic of achieved aesthetic form,[28] and to Nietzsche's own historicity of the kind that would later be included in *Also sprach Zarathustra* — "Darum, oh meine Brüder, bedarf es eines *neuen Adels*" (*Z* III 12 §11; KSA 4:254; "Therefore, O my brothers, a *new nobility* is needed") — and in *Ecce Homo* — "Erst von mir an giebt es auf Erden *grosse Politik*" (*EH* Warum ich ein Schicksal bin §1; KSA 6:366; "With me the earth knows *great politics* for the first time") — when he writes: "Wir sind die ersten Aristokraten in der Geschichte des Geistes — der historische Sinn beginnt erst jetzt" ("We are the first aristocrats in the history of the spirit — historical sense begins only now").

In another fragment, 12 [128] — "Du widersprichst heute dem, was du gestern gelehrt hast — Aber dafür ist gestern nicht heute, sagte Zarathustra" (KSA 9:598; "You are today contradicting what you taught yesterday — But that is why yesterday is not today, said Zarathustra") — we find an exchange that will have and echo in the second part of the completed *Zarathustra* (compare *Z* II 17; KSA 4:163), again suggesting a detailed working-out of some of the text two years before the actual composition of the work. By contrast, some other fragments never found their way into the final version.[29] In the case of fragments 12 [112] and 12 [225], the phrase "*Zarathustra's Müssiggang*" ("*Zarathustra's leisure*") anticipates a theme taken up in *Jenseits von Gut und Böse* (*JGB* §189; KSA 5:110–11) and in *Götzen-Dämmerung* (*Twilight of the Idols, GD* Sprüche §1; KSA 6:59). Indeed, 12 [112] provides early evidence of meditation on the theme of communication and reception as problematized, very much along the lines of Ottilie's reflections in Goethe's *Die Wahlverwandtschaften* (*Elective Affinities*) — "Sich mitzuteilen ist Natur; Mitgeteiltes aufzunehmen, wie es gegeben wird, ist Bildung" ("To communicate is natural, to receive what is communicated is an acquired art") — in *Zarathustra:* "Wenn Z[arathustra] die Menge bewegen will, da muß er der Schauspieler seiner selber sein" (KSA 9:596; "If Zarathustra wants to move the crowd, then he must become the actor of himself").[30] And 12 [225] contains a phrase, "So sprach Z[arathustra]," to be developed into the title and structural motif of the later work (KSA 9:616), while another formulation phrase in this fragment, "*ich klage nicht an, ich will selbst die Ankläger nicht anklagen*" ("*I do not accuse, I do not even want to accuse the accusers*"), would be taken up in the first section of Book 4 of *Die fröhliche Wissenschaft*, entitled "Zum neuen Jahre" ("For the New Year"): "Ich will nicht anklagen, ich will nicht einmal die Ankläger anklagen. *Wegsehen* sei meine einzige Verneinung! Und, Alles in Allem und Grossen: ich will irgendwann einmal nur noch ein Ja-sagender sein" (*FW* §276; KSA 3:521; "I do not want to accuse: I do not even want to accuse the accusers. May *looking away* be my only negation. And all in all and on the whole: I want some day to be only a Yes-sayer"). In turn, this passage anticipates the chapter "Vom Vorübergehen" ("On Passing By") in *Zarathustra*, with its conclusion, "wo man nicht mehr lieben kann, da soll man — *vorübergehen!*" (*Z* III 7; KSA 4:225; "where one can no longer love, there one should *pass by*"); indeed, the theme of Yes-saying permeates the entire work, emerging most noticeably in "Von den drei Verwandlungen" ("On the Three Transformations"; *Z* I §1; KSA 4:31) and "Die sieben Siegel" ("The Seven Seals"), subtitled "Oder: das Ja-und-Amen-Lied" ("Or: The Song of Yes and Amen"; *Z* III 16; KSA 4:287).

Above all, this section contains Nietzsche's commitment to an aesthetic, a Weimar Classical aesthetic, understanding of *amor fati*, one which would lie at the heart of the aesthetic gospel of *Zarathustra*: "Ich will immer mehr lernen, das Nothwendige an den Dingen als das Schöne sehen: — so werde ich Einer von Denen sein, welche die Dinge schön machen" (*FW* §276; KSA 3:521; "I want to learn increasingly to see what is necessary about things as what is beautiful: — in this way I shall become one of those who make things beautiful").[31] Between the end of 1881 and the summer of 1882, Nietzsche began, modified, and completed his work on *Die fröhliche Wissenschaft*, which was published in August 1882, and it is to this work we now turn.[32]

Die fröhliche Wissenschaft

Eine Kunst für Künstler, nur für Künstler!

An art for artists, only for artists!
(FW Vorrede §4; KSA 3:351)

Diese Griechen waren oberflächlich — aus Tiefe!

Those Greeks were superficial — out of profundity!
(FW Vorrede §4; KSA 3:352)

Nietzsche spent the summer of 1882 in Tautenburg, a village in the Thuringian forest, not far away from his birth-place, Röcken, and not far away either, as he realized, from Dornburg, the small town north of Weimar where Goethe had stayed from time to time in the later years of his life.[33] Nietzsche described the village as follows: "eine halbe Stunde abseits von der Dornburg, auf der der alte Goethe seine Einsamkeit genoß, liegt inmitten schöner Wälder Tautenburg" (KSB 6:210; "a half hour away from Dornburg, where the elderly Goethe enjoyed his solitude, lies Tautenburg, in the midst of lovely forests"). Here his sister, Elisabeth, he told his correspondent, had arranged for him "ein idyllisches Nestchen" ("an idyllic little nest"). The arrival of this correspondent herself in Tautenburg, however, was to make this quiet, secluded village rather less than idyllic, thanks to her endless quarrels with Nietzsche's sister. She was Lou von Salomé, to whom Nietzsche had been introduced earlier that year in Rome by his good friend (as he then was), Paul Rée. Meeting her for the first time in the splendid surroundings of St. Peter's Basilica in Rome, Nietzsche is reported to have greeted her as follows: "Von welchen Sternen sind wir hier einander zugefallen?" ("From what stars have we fallen to meet here?").[34] During his time with Lou in Tautenburg, Nietzsche made a resolution that would be echoed by Zarathustra: "Ich will nicht mehr einsam sein und wieder lernen, Mensch zu werden" (3 July; KSB 6:217; "I no longer want to be lonely and want to learn again to be human").[35]

Die fröhliche Wissenschaft, completed earlier in the year in Genoa,[36] anticipates the themes and motifs of its successor, *Also sprach Zarathustra,* in three important ways. First, it contains many reflections on art, which develop Nietzsche's thinking along the Weimar Classical aesthetic lines it had taken in *Die Geburt der Tragödie.* For example, in his *Vorrede* to the second edition, Nietzsche summarized his thinking on the Greeks:

> Oh diese Griechen! Sie verstanden sich darauf, zu *leben:* dazu thut Noth, tapfer bei der Oberfläche, der Falte, der Haut stehen zu bleiben, den Schein anzubeten, an Formen, an Töne, an Worte, an den ganzen Olymp des Scheins zu glauben! Diese Griechen waren oberflächlich — *aus Tiefe!* (*FW* Vorrede §4; KSA 3:352)
>
> [Oh, those Greeks! They knew how to live. What is required for that is to stop courageously at the surface, the fold, the skin, to adore semblance, to believe in forms, tones, words, in the whole Olympus of semblance. Those Greeks were superficial — *out of profundity.*]

Similarly, in the section entitled "Das Bewusstsein vom Scheine" ("The Consciousness of Semblance") Nietzsche took up again, in the context of a discussion of the relation between dreaming and reality, the question of *schöner Schein:* "Was ist mir jetzt 'Schein'! Wahrlich nicht der Gegensatz irgendeines Wesens, — [. . .] Schein ist für mich das Wirkende und Lebende selber" (*FW* §54; KSA 3:417; "What is 'semblance' for me now? Certainly not the opposite of some essence . . . Semblance is for me the very thing that is effective and is alive"). Then again, in the section "Unsere letzte Dankbarkeit gegen die Kunst" ("Our Ultimate Gratitude to Art"), he emphasized the importance of regarding the world as an aesthetic phenomenon: "Als ästhetisches Phänomen ist uns das Dasein immer noch *erträglich,* und durch die Kunst ist uns Auge und Hand und vor Allem das gute Gewissen dazu gegeben, aus uns selber ein solches Phänomen machen zu *können*" (*FW* §107; KSA 3:464; "As an aesthetic phenomenon existence is still *bearable* for us, and art furnishes us with eyes and hands and, above all, the good conscience to be *able* to turn ourselves into such a phenomenon"). Finally, in "Was man den Künstlern ablernen soll" ("What One Should Learn from Artists"), he read out of the possibility of aesthetic vision an existential implication:

> Sich von den Dingen entfernen, bis man Vieles von ihnen nicht mehr sieht und Vieles hinzusehen muss, *um sie noch zu sehen* — oder die Dinge um die Ecke und und wie in einem Ausschnitte sehen — oder sie so stellen, dass sie sich theilweise verstellen und nur perspectivische Durchblicke gestatten — oder sie durch gefärbtes Glas oder im Lichte der Abendröthe anschauen — oder ihnen eine Oberfläche und Haut geben, welche keine volle Transparenz hat: das Alles sollen wir den

Künstlern ablernen und im Uebrigen weiser sein, als sie. Denn bei ihnen hört gewöhnlich diese ihre feine Kraft auf, wo die Kunst aufhört und das Leben beginnt; *wir* aber wollen die Dichter unseres Lebens sein, und im Kleinsten und Alltäglichsten zuerst. (*FW* §299; KSA 3:538)

[Moving away from things until there is a good deal that one no longer sees and there is much that our eye has to add in order *still to see them;* or seeing things around a corner and as cut out and framed; or to place them so that they partially conceal each other and only permit us perspectival glimpses; or looking at them through tinted glass or in the light of the sunset; or giving them a surface and skin that is not fully transparent — all this we should learn from artists while in other matters being wiser than they are. For with them this subtle power usually comes to an end where art ends and life begins; but *we* want to be the poets of our life, and first of all in the smallest, most everyday matters.]

Second, *Die fröhliche Wissenschaft,* drawing on Nietzsche's experience of August 1881 and its subsequent treatment in his notebooks, anticipates the announcement in *Also sprach Zarathustra* of the thought of the eternal recurrence.

For in the section entitled "Das grösste Schwergewicht" ("The Greatest Weight") the motif of heaviness, taken up in *Zarathustra* in the shape of the *Geist der Schwere* (the spirit of gravity), expresses the existential drama of someone whom, as it were, not Mephistopheles himself, but one of his demons, visits:

Wie, wenn dir eines Tages oder Nachts, ein Dämon in deine einsamste Einsamkeit nachschliche und dir sagte: "Dieses Leben, wie du es jetzt lebst und gelebt hast, wirst du noch einmal und noch unzählige Male leben müssen; und es wird nichts Neues daran sein, sondern jeder Schmerz und jede Lust und jeder Gedanke und Seufzer und alles unsäglich Kleine und Grosse deines Lebens muss dir wiederkommen, und Alles in der selben Reihe und Folge — und ebenso diese Spinne und dieses Mondlicht zwischen den Bäumen, und ebenso dieser Augenblick und ich selber. Die ewige Sanduhr des Daseins wird immer wieder umgedreht — und du mit ihr, Stäubchen von Staube!" — Würdest du dich nicht niederwerfen und mit den Zähnen knirschen und den Dämon verfluchen, der so redete? Oder hast du einmal einen ungeheuren Augenblick erlebt, wo du ihm antworten würdest: "du bist ein Gott und nie hörte ich Göttlicheres!" Wenn jener Gedanke über dich Gewalt bekäme, er würde dich, wie du bist, verwandeln und vielleicht zermalmen; die Frage bei Allem und Jedem: "willst du diess noch einmal und noch unzählige Male?" würde als das grösste Schwergewicht auf deinem Handeln liegen! Oder wie müsstest du dir selber und dem Leben gut werden, um nach Nichts *mehr zu verlangen,* als nach dieser letzten ewigen Bestätigung und Besiegelung? — (*FW* §341; KSA 3:570)

[What if, some day or night, a demon were to steal after you into your loneliest loneliness and say to you: "This life as you now live it and have lived it, you will have to live once more and innumerable times more; and there will be nothing new in it, but every pain and every joy and every thought and sigh and everything unutterably small or great in your life will have to return to you, all in the same succession and sequence — even this spider and this moonlight between the trees, and even this moment and I myself. The eternal hourglass of existence is turned upside down again and again, and you with it, speck of dust!" Would you not cast yourself down and gnash your teeth and curse the demon who spoke thus? Or have you once experienced a tremendous moment when you would have answered him: "You are a god and never have I heard anything more divine." If this thought gained possession of you, it would change you as you are or perhaps crush you. The question in each and every thing, "Do you desire this once more and innumerable times more?" would lie upon your actions as the greatest weight. Or how well disposed would you have to be to yourself and to life *to crave nothing more fervently* than this ultimate eternal confirmation and seal?]

In this hypothetical situation, the transformative effect of the eternal recurrence is stressed.[37] The "moment" — both the *Augenblick* where the demon appears and the *Augenblick* where the interlocutor responds positively — appears later in *Zarathustra*, when he stands in conversation with the Spirit of Heaviness in front of the gate called "Augenblick." Furthermore, key details of the scenario here are, as we shall see, repeated later in part 3 of *Zarathustra*. In 1907, Georg Simmel (1858–1918) argued that the thought of the eternal recurrence functioned in a manner analogous to Kant's categorical imperative.[38] Similarly, one might argue that, because it is embedded in the context of an aesthetic culture, the eternal recurrence constitutes the formulation of, so to speak, not a moral but rather an aesthetic imperative of the kind formulated by Goethe in his poem "Vermächtnis" ("Legacy," 1828): "Dann ist Vergangenheit beständig, / Das Künftige voraus lebendig, / Der Augenblick ist Ewigkeit" ("Then the past is stable, / The future alive in anticipation, / The moment is eternity").[39]

In *Die Geburt der Tragödie*, Nietzsche had examined the problem of how to reintroduce tragedy into German culture and, by implication, how to reintroduce the aesthetic into life. After *Die fröhliche Wissenschaft*, and in *Also sprach Zarathustra* in particular, the emphasis comes to be placed, closely following two of Schiller's essays of 1795, "Von den nothwendigen Grenzen des Schönen" ("On the Necessary Limits of Beauty") and "Ueber die Gefahr ästhetischer Sitten" ("On the Danger of Aesthetic *Mores*"), on how to transmute life into the aesthetic mode. In one of the fragments from the *Nachlass* from this period, Nietzsche made clear the link between art, life, and the aesthetic:

> Wir wollen ein Kunstwerk immer wieder erleben! So soll man sein Leben gestalten, daß man vor seinen einzelnen Theilen denselben Wunsch hat! Dies der Hauptgedanke! Erst am Ende wird dann die *Lehre* von der Wiederholung alles Dagewesenen vorgetragen, nachdem die Tendenz zuerst eingepflanzt ist, etwas zu *schaffen,* welches unter dem Sonnenschein dieser Lehre hundertfach kräftiger *gedeihen* kann! (11[165]; KSA 9:505)

> [We want to experience a work of art again and again! In this way one should so shape one's life that one always has the same wish about its individual parts! This is the main thought! Only at the end is the *doctrine* of the repetition of all things that have been then expounded, after the tendency has first been planted to *create* something which, under the sunshine of this doctrine can *flourish* a hundred times more strongly!]

Or as Nietzsche also put it: "Die Kunst und nichts als die Kunst. Sie ist die große Ermöglicherin des Lebens, die große Verführerin zum Leben, das große Stimulans zum Leben . . ." (*WM* §853/11[415]; KSA 13:194; "Art and nothing but art! It is the great means of making life possible, the great seduction to life, the great stimulant of life"); compare: "Die Kunst [. . .] das große Stimulans des Lebens, ein Rausch am Leben, ein Wille zum Leben" (*WM* §851/15[10]; KSA 13:409; "Art . . . is the great stimulant of life, an intoxication of life, a will to life.") And elsewhere in his *Nachlass,* he wrote: "Die Wahrheit ist häßlich: *wir haben die Kunst,* damit wir nicht an der Wahrheit zu Grunde gehn" (*WM* §822/16[40]; KSA 13:500; "Truth is ugly: *we have art* so we do not perish of the truth").

Third, the internal structure of *Die fröhliche Wissenschaft* makes connections with themes and motifs that are more fully explored in *Zarathustra.* The section immediately following "Das grösste Schwergewicht," with its proleptic announcement of the doctrine of the Eternal Recurrence, is, significantly, entitled "*Incipit tragoedia*" and contains, with one minor variation only, the entire opening section of *Also sprach Zarathustra* (*FW* §342; KSA 3:571; compare *Z* Vorrede §1; KSA 4:11–12).[40] Finally, the penultimate section of the fifth and final book, entitled "Die grosse Gesundheit" ("The Great Health"), sets up, in precisely Schillerian terms, "das Ideal eines Geistes, der naiv, das heisst ungewollt und aus überströmender Fülle und Mächtigkeit mit Allem spielt, was bisher heilig, gut, unberührbar, göttlich hiess" ("the ideal of a spirit who plays naively — that is, spontaneously and from overflowing power and abundance — with all that was hitherto called holy, good, untouchable, divine"); and concludes, bringing together the

Faustian motif of the decisive clockhand and the imminence of Zarathustra's tragedy: "das Schicksal der Seele sich wendet, der Zeiger rückt, die Tragödie *beginnt . . .*" (*FW* §382; KSA 3:637; "the destiny of the soul changes, the hand moves forward, the tragedy *begins*").[41]

In an appendix added to the second edition of *Die fröhliche Wissenschaft* in 1887 the *Lieder des Prinzen Vogelfrei* (*Songs of Prince Vogelfrei*), the poem "Sils-Maria" highlights the central aesthetic themes of what was to be Nietzsche's next work. This poem draws on drafts dating back to 1882,[42] including the following:

> Ganz Meer, ganz Mittag, ganz Zeit ohne Ziel
> Ein Kind, ein Spielzeug
> Und plötzlich werden Eins zu Zwei
> Und Zarathustra gieng an mir vorbei.
> (4[145]; KSA 10:157)

> [All sea, all midday, all time without aim
> A child, a plaything
> And suddenly one turns into two
> And Zarathustra walked into my view.]

But the new title of this playful poem when its final version was published in 1887, alludes to the Swiss town near to which Nietzsche had his intuition of the idea of the eternal recurrence, and in which parts 2 and 3 of *Also sprach Zarathustra* were written:

Sils-Maria

> Hier sass ich, wartend, wartend, — doch auf Nichts,
> Jenseits von Gut und Böse, bald des Lichts
> Geniessend, bald des Schattens, ganz nur Spiel,
> Ganz See, ganz Mittag, ganz Zeit ohne Ziel.

> Da, plötzlich, Freundin! wurde Eins zu Zwei —
> — Und Zarathustra gieng an mir vorbei . . .
> (KSA 3:649)

> [Here I sat, waiting — not for anything —
> Beyond Good and Evil, fancying
> Now light, now shadows, all a game,
> All lake, all noon, all time without aim.

> Then, suddenly, woman-friend, one turned into two —
> And Zarathustra walked into my view.]

Various critics, probably unaware of the earlier and later versions, have interpreted this poem as a transcription of a psychological state or process. For example, C. G. Jung read the poem as an expression of an authentic archetypal experience.[43] More recently, René Girard saw in this poem a mysterious encounter with "le Double," describing it as "une veritable épiphanie du désir mimique" ("a true epiphany of mimetic desire").[44] Yet both Jung and Girard, as well as many others, fail to note that the poem deploys the key vocabulary of classical Weimar aesthetics: "Schatten," "Spiel," "ohne Ziel." Thus, in this text in the appendix to *Die fröhliche Wissenschaft*, *Zarathustra* is announced as an aesthetic experience. According to ancient Platonic-Thomist conceptions, Eternity is "the now that stands still."[45] The *nunc stans* (Everlasting Now) is reconceived by Nietzsche,[46] as it had been by Weimar classicism,[47] as an aesthetic phenomenon. The Goethean "permanence in change" ("Dauer im Wechsel"), which experience of the aesthetic illusion vouchsafes, yields both Dionysian import — "den Gehalt in deinem Busen" ("the content in your heart") — and Apollonian form — "die Form in deinem Geist" ("the form in your mind") — in the characteristically binary synthesis of art and beauty (HA 1:247–48). As Nietzsche had argued in *Die Geburt der Tragödie* and as Zarathustra would teach, the world is, after all, justified — but only as an aesthetic phenomenon.

We find Nietzsche, in a letter to Erwin Rohde on 22 February 1884, using Schiller's key-image of the dance, making — just as he would, four years later, in *Ecce Homo* — a claim of world-historical proportions for the significance of his *Zarathustra*. In particular, he claimed, there was an affinity in stylistic terms between his works and Goethe's:

> Ich bilde mir ein, mit diesem Z[arathustra] die deutsche Sprache zu ihrer Vollendung gebracht zu haben. Es war, nach *Luther* und *Goethe,* noch ein dritter Schritt zu thun —; sieh zu, alter Herzens-Kamerad, ob Kraft, Geschmeidigkeit und Wohllaut je schon in unsrer Sprache *so* beieinander gewesen sind. Lies Goethen nach einer Seite meines Buchs — und Du wirst fühlen, daß jenes "undulatorische," das Goethen als Zeichner anhaftete, auch dem Sprachbildner nicht fremd blieb. Ich habe die strengere, männlichere Linie vor ihm voraus, ohne doch, mit Luther, unter die Rüpel zu gerathen. Mein Stil ist ein *Tanz;* ein Spiel der Symmetrien aller Art und ein Überspringen und Verspotten dieser Symmetrien. Das geht bis in die Wahl der Vokale. — (KSB 6:479)

> [I think that with this Zarathustra I have brought the German language to its culmination. After *Luther* and *Goethe* there was a third step to be taken — consider, my dear comrade, whether power, suppleness and melodiousness have been *so* close together in our language. Read Goethe after a page of my book — and you will feel that that "undulat-

ing quality," which attached to Goethe the artist, did not remain foreign to the sculptor of language either. I have the advantage over him with regard to the stronger, more masculine line, but without, like Luther, ending up with the rabble. My style is a *dance;* a play of symmetries of all kinds and a jumping-across and mocking of these symmetries. This goes right into the choice of vowels.][48]

This passage clearly sets the tone for the kind of sophisticated appreciation of his work that Nietzsche would evoke in the rhetorically equally sophisticated auto-encomium of *Ecce Homo.*

Above all, throughout the years of composition (1883–85), and in the remaining years of Nietzsche's life, there remains a fundamental unity of function in the figure of Zarathustra, as Nietzsche stated in his note of August 1881 where, along with the thought of the eternal recurrence, he elaborated a "Philosophie der Gleichgültigkeit" ("philosophy of indifference"):

Was früher am stärksten reizte, wirkt jetzt ganz anders, es wird nur noch als *Spiel* angesehn und gelten gelassen (die Leidenschaften und Arbeiten) als ein Leben im Unwahren principiell verworfen, als Form und Reiz aber ästhetisch genossen und gepflegt, wir stellen uns wie die Kinder zu dem, was früher den *Ernst des Daseins* ausmachte. Unser Streben des Ernstes ist aber alles als werdend zu verstehen, uns als Individuum zu verleugnen; möglichst aus *vielen* Augen in die Welt sehen, *leben in* Trieben und Beschäftigungen, **um** damit sich Augen zu machen, *zeitweilig* sich dem Leben überlassen, um hernach zeitweilig über ihm mit dem Auge zu ruhen: die Triebe *unterhalten* als Fundament alles Erkennens, aber wissen, wo sie Gegner des Erkennens werden: in summa **abwarten**, wie weit das *Wissen* und die *Wahrheit* sich **einverleiben** können — und in wiefern eine Umwandlung des Menschen eintritt, wenn er endlich nur noch lebt, *um zu erkennen.* (KSA 9:494–95)

[What used to arouse the most strongly now has a completely different effect, it is now only seen and accepted as *play* (the passions and labours) as a life in untruth rejected in principle, but as form and stimulus aesthetically enjoyed and cultivated, we take the attitude of children to what used to constitute the *earnestness of existence*. All our striving in earnestness is, however, to be understood as becoming, in order to deny ourselves as individuals; as far as possible to see into the world with *many* eyes, to *live in* drives and activities, **in order** thus to create eyes for ourselves, *for a time* to abandon ourselves to life, in order afterward to contemplate it for a time: *to subordinate* the drives as the foundation of all knowing, but to know where they become opponents of knowing: in sum **to wait and see**, how far *knowledge* and *truth* can

be incorporated — and how far a transformation of the human individual takes place, when he or she finally only lives *in order to know*.]

The dialectic between *Ernst* and *Spiel,* derived from Goethe and Schiller and
alluded to persistently in *Zarathustra,*[49] is related here as in Weimar Classicism to the problem of "Schein," both in the sense of the phenomenal world
and of the "Schein des Scheins" ("ein Leben im Unwahren") *and* in the
sense of "Schein des Seins" or (aesthetic) play ("als Form und Reiz aber
ästhetisch genossen und gepflegt"), as Nietzsche had used them in *Die
Geburt der Tragödie.* In that work, Nietzsche had also analyzed the problem
of knowledge in relation to life, and the way in which, so he had argued, a
certain (Apollonian) kind of knowledge undermined life. The solution, he
had suggested, lies in understanding that the world is only justified "aesthetically," the same idea expressed here in the notion of (aesthetic) play and
in the pleasure of (aesthetic) intuition (*Anschauen*), an attitude which, from
an ethical point of view, must — as Goethe emphasized — appear as
"indifference":[50]

> Dies ist Consequenz von der Leidenschaft der Erkenntniß: es *giebt für
> ihre Existenz kein Mittel,* als die Quellen und Mächte der Erkenntniß,
> die Irrthümer und Leidensch[aften] auch zu erhalten, aus deren
> *Kampfe* nimmt sie ihre erhaltende Kraft. — Wie wird dies Leben in
> Bezug auf seine Summe von Wohlbefinden sich ausnehmen? *Ein Spiel
> der Kinder,* auf welches das Auge des Weisen blickt, Gewalt haben über
> *diesen* **und** *jenen* Zustand — und den Tod, wenn so etwas nicht
> möglich ist. — Nun kommt aber die schwerste Erkenntniß und macht
> alle Arten Lebens furchtbar bedenkenreich: ein absoluter Überschuß
> von Lust **muß** nachzuweisen sein, sonst ist die Vernichtung unser selbst
> in Hinsicht auf die Menschheit als Mittel der Vernichtung der
> Menschheit zu wählen. Schon dies: wir haben die Vergangenheit,
> unsere und die aller Menschheit, auf die Wage zu setzen und *auch* zu
> überwiegen — nein! dieses Stück Menschheitsgeschichte *wird* und
> muß sich ewig wiederholen, *das* dürfen wir aus der Rechnung lassen,
> darauf haben wir keinen Einfluß: ob es gleich unser Mitgefühl
> beschwert und gegen das Leben überhaupt einnimmt. Um davon nicht
> umgeworfen zu werden, darf unser Mitleid nicht groß sein. Die
> Gleichgültigkeit muß tief in uns gewirkt haben und der Genuß im
> Anschauen auch. Auch das Elend der zukünftigen Menschheit soll uns
> *nichts* angehn. Aber ob *wir* noch *leben wollen,* ist die Frage: und wie!
> (KSA 9:495)

[This is the consequence of the passion of knowledge: *there is for its existence no means* other than the sources and powers of knowledge to
sustain also errors and passions, from whose *struggle* it takes its sustain-
ing power. — How will this life look in relation to its sum of well-
being? *Like children's play,* on which the eye of the wise man looks, to

have power over *this* **and** *that* condition — and over death, when something like this is not possible. — Now there comes, however, the most difficult knowledge, and it makes all kinds of life terribly worthy of reflection: an absolute surplus of desire **must** be demonstrable, otherwise we must choose the destruction of ourselves with regard to humanity as the means to the destruction of humanity itself. This much is clear: we have to place the past, our own and that of all humanity, on the scales and *also* tip the balance — no! this piece of human history *will* and must repeat itself eternally, *that* we can leave out of account, over that we have no influence: even though it burdens our sympathy and turns it against life as such. In order not to be bowled over by this our sympathy should not be great. Indifference must have taken effect deep within us, and the pleasure in intuition (*Anschauen*) too. Also the misery of future humankind should *not* concern us. But whether *we* still *want to live,* that is the question: and what a question!]

The problem of why, given the idea of the eternal recurrence, we might still want to live, is explored — and answered — in *Also sprach Zarathustra,* which constitutes, in Goethean terms, an "Evangelium des Schönen" ("gospel of beauty"). Over and over again, at significant points in the development of his mature thought Nietzsche has recourse to the cardinal doctrines of Weimar Classicism. Clearly they exert a gentle, if sometimes unwitting, pressure on his conceptualization, even his formulations.[51] In the finished product of *Also sprach Zarathustra,* this literally formative influence is demonstrably at work, and discernibly so for all who have ears to hear it.

Notes

[1] Eventually, Nietzsche would express his dislike of academia with corrosive irony when, following his mental collapse, he would tell Jacob Burckhardt: "Zuletzt wäre ich sehr viel lieber Basler Professor als Gott" (6 January 1889; KSB 8:577; "In the end I would much rather be a Professor in Basel than God").

[2] For discussion of how to approach this text, see Gary Shapiro, "The Writing on the Wall: *The Antichrist* and the Semiotics of History," in Robert C. Solomon and Kathleen M. Higgins, eds., *Reading Nietzsche* (New York and Oxford: Oxford UP, 1988), 192–217, and "How One Becomes What One Is Not," in *Nietzschean Narratives* (Bloomington and Indianapolis: Indiana UP, 1989), 142–75; and Thomas Steinbuch, *A Commentary on Nietzsche's Ecce Homo* (Lanham, New York, London: UP of America, 1994).

[3] Compare with Nietzsche's remark in his letter to Heinrich Köselitz of 3 September 1883 (see note 17 below).

[4] For a picture of the "Zarathustra stone," see David Farrell Krell and Donald L. Bates, *The Good European: Nietzsche's Work Sites in Word and Image* (Chicago and London: U of Chicago P, 1997), 133.

[5] See his letter to Elisabeth Nietzsche of 7 July 1881 (KSB 6:98–99).

[6] Compare with Werther's letter of 10 May 1771 in *Die Leiden des jungen Werther* (*The Sorrows of Young Werther*, 1774/1787; HA 6:9); Johann Wolfgang von Goethe, *The Sorrows of Young Werther/Elective Affinities/Novella*, ed. David E. Wellbery, trans. Victor Lange and Judith Ryan, Goethe Edition, vol. 11 (New York: Suhrkamp, 1988), 6.

[7] In a postcard sent the previous day to Paul Rée, however, Nietzsche had written: "Mir ist mitunter als ob ich als Längst-Gestorbener mir die Dinge und Menschen anschaute — sie bewegen, erschrecken und entzücken mich, ich bin ihnen aber ganz ferne" (KSB 6:101–2; "It sometimes seems to me I am looking at things and people like someone who is long dead — they move, terrify, and delight me, but I am quite distant from them"). (Again, compare with Goethe's Werther, this time the letter of 18 August 1771 [HA 6:51–53; Goethe, *The Sorrows of Young Werther*, 36–37].) At the end of his letter, Nietzsche signed himself "der auf ewig Abhandengekommene" ("the one who has been lost for ever"), but added "und doch gerade Ihnen so Nahe: — In Treue F. N." ("and yet so close to you: — Truly, F. N.").

[8] His mother and his sister did send him a sausage, which arrived, however, broken and dried out (KSB 6:106); a second attempt proved more successful, although Nietzsche had to ask his mother not to send any more pears (KSB 6:110–11), and later no more sausages, either (KSB 6:114).

[9] Later, in 1887, Nietzsche noted Goethe's admiration for Spinoza, citing Goethe's letter to Knebel of 11 November 1784 (9[176]; KSA 12:439).

[10] As Nietzsche rightly says, he was ignorant of Spinoza, but not entirely: in *Menschliches, Allzumenschliches* (*Human, All too Human*), Nietzsche cites the *Tractatus Politicus* (MA I §93; KSA 2:91); refers to him, along with Kepler, as an instance of the "genius of knowledge" (MA I §157; KSA 2:147–48); describes him as "the purest sage" (MA I §475; KSA 2:310); and mentions him in a final passage discussed below. For a discussion of Spinoza in the context of the doctrine of the eternal recurrence, see note 7 from a sequence of notes entitled "Der europäische Nihilismus" ("European Nihilism"), dated 10 June 1887 (*WM* §55/5[71]; KSA 12:213–14).

[11] See the *Nachlass* from 1881 (11[193]; KSA 9:517–18), where Spinoza is cited from Kuno Fischer, *Geschichte der neuern Philosophie*, vol. 1, part 2, *Descartes' Schule: Geulinx, Malebranche. Baruch Spinoza* (2nd ed., Mannheim: F. Bassermann, 1865), which Nietzsche had asked Overbeck to send to him in Sils Maria.

[12] Compare FW §342 (KSA 3:571) and Z Vorrede §1 (KSA 6:11–12).

[13] 5[54]; KSA 7:106 (compare KSA 14:535); compare Max Müller, *Essays*, vol. 1, *Beiträge zur vergleichenden Religionswissenschaft*, vol. 2, *Beiträge zur vergleichenden Mythologie und Ethologie* (Leipzig: Wilhelm Engelmann, 1869), 1:145.

[14] Janz, *Friedrich Nietzsche: Biographie*, 2:230.

[15] "Zarathustra and his sacred texts were a major topic of excited discussion in philological circles at the end of the 1850s and first half of the 1860s" (Paul Kriwaczek, *In Search of Zarathustra: The First Prophet and the Ideas that Changed the World* (London: Weidenfeld and Nicolson, 2002), 45). For further discussion, see Michael

Stausberg, *Faszination Zarathushtra: Zoroaster und die europäische Religionsgeschichte der frühen Neuzeit,* 2 vols. (Berlin: Walter de Gruyter, 1998).

[16] See Emerson's essay on "Character": "We are born believers in great men. How easily we read in old books, when men were few, of the smallest action of the patriarchs. We require that a man should be so large and columnar in the landscape, that it should deserve to be recorded, that he arose, and girded up his loins, and departed to such a place. The most credible pictures are those of majestic men who prevailed at their entrance, and convinced the senses; as happened to the eastern magian who was sent to test the merits of Zertusht or Zoroaster. When the Yunani sage arrived at Balkh, the Persians tell us, Gushtasp appointed a day on which the Mobeds of every country should assemble, and a golden chair was placed for the Yunani sage. Then the beloved of Yezdam, the prophet Zertusht, advanced into the midst of the assembly. The Yunani sage, on seeing that chief, said, 'This form and this gait cannot lie, and nothing but truth can proceed from them.'" Emerson also refers to the figure of Zarathustra in his "Address Delivered Before the Senior Class in Divinity College, Cambridge" (15 July 1838) and his essays on "History." Compare also Nietzsche's comment on Emerson in KSA 9:588; and in another *Nachlass* note, Nietzsche refers to Emerson's portrayal of the "wise man" (KSA 10:512; compare KSA 15:693–94).

[17] For further discussion, see Manfred Mayrhofer, "Zu einer Deutung des Zarathustra-Namens in Nietzsches Korrespondenz," in Ruth Stiehl and Hans Erich Stier, eds., *Beiträge zur alten Geschichte und deren Nachleben: Festschrift für Franz Altheim zum 6.10.1968,* 2 vols. (Berlin: Walter de Gruyter, 1969), 2:369–74. Later, in response to a further query from Köselitz about the origin of the name, he wrote: "'Zarathustra' ist die ächte unverderbte Form des Namens Zoroaster, also ein *persisches* Wort. Von den Persern wird auf p. 81 Mitte [*Z* I 15; KSA 4:75] geredet" (20 May 1883; KSB 6:378; "'Zarathustra' is the pure unspoilt form of the name Zoroaster, thus a *Persian* word. The Persians are referred to in the middle of p. 81").

[18] Later, one of the most striking images of *Also sprach Zarathustra* would feature a serpent encircling the neck of an eagle. Janz suggests a poem by Shelley as a source for this image (Curt Paul Janz, *Friedrich Nietzsche: Biographie,* 3 vols. [Munich and Vienna: Hanser, 1978], 2:228–29; see also David Thatcher, "Eagle and Serpent in *Zarathustra,*" *Nietzsche-Studien* 6 [1977]: 240–60).

[19] For further discussion of the symphonic character or structure of *Also sprach Zarathustra,* see Janz, *Friedrich Nietzsche: Biographie,* 2:211–21.

[20] "The opening is one of sustained mystery and intensity. From a region in which all seems nebulous and ill-defined (a bare fifth on A in the second violins and cellos supported by horns) emerge the first faint foreshadowings of a theme which is presently hurled at us, with the force of Jove's thunderbolts, by the whole orchestra in union" (A. K. Holland, "Ludwig van Beethoven (1770–1827)," in Ralph Hill, ed., *The Symphony* [Melbourne, London, and Baltimore: Penguin, 1949], 92–125; here, 114–15).

[21] See Frederick Beiser, *The Fate of Reason: German Philosophy from Kant to Fichte* (Cambridge, MA and London: Harvard UP, 1987), 44–91.

[22] His "active" nihilism — of "der Geist, der stets verneint" ("the spirit that always says no"; *Faust I,* line 338) — that is, as opposed to "passive," to use Nietzsche's distinction as made in *Der Wille zur Macht:* "*Der Nihilism ein* **normaler** *Zustand.* [. . .]

Er ist **zweideutig**: (A) Nihilism als Zeichen der *gesteigerten Macht des Geistes:* als **activer Nihilism.** Er kann ein Zeichen von *Stärke* sein: [. . .] Sein **Maximum** von relativer Kraft erreicht er als gewaltthätige Kraft der **Zerstörung** [. . .] (B) Nihilism als *Niedergang und Rückgang der Macht des Geistes:* der **passive Nihilism:** als ein Zeichen von Schwäche [. . .] der müde Nihilism, der nicht mehr *angreift:* [. . .] die Kraft des Geistes kann ermüdet, *erschöpft* sein, so daß [. . .] die Synthesis der Werthe und Ziele (auf der jede starke Cultur beruht) sich löst, so daß die einzelnen Werthe sich Krieg machen: Zersetzung" (*WM* §22 and §23/9[35]; KSA 12:350–51; "Nihilism as a *normal* condition . . . It is *ambiguous:* (A) Nihilism as a sign of increased power of the spirit: as *active* nihilism. It can be a sign of strength . . . It reaches its maximum of relative strength as a violent force of destruction . . . (B) Nihilism as decline and decrease of the power of the spirit: as *passive* nihilism . . . the tired nihilism that no longer attacks . . . the power of the spirit can become weary, *exhausted,* so that . . . the synthesis of values and goals (on which every strong culture rests) dissolves, so that the individual values war against each other: subversion").

[23] See *Maximen und Reflexionen,* no. 33: "Der Irrtum verhält sich gegen das Wahre wie der Schlaf gegen das Wachen. Ich habe bemerkt, daß man aus dem Irren sich wie erquickt wieder zum dem Wahren hinwende" (HA 12:410; Johann Wolfgang von Goethe, *Maxims and Reflexions,* trans. Elizabeth Stopp, ed. Peter Hutchinson [London: Penguin, 1998], 39; "Error is related to truth as sleeping is to waking. I have observed that when one has been in error, one turns to truth as though revitalized"). In much the same spirit as Nietzsche's view of error as part of the process of knowledge acquisition, Goethe made the following remark to Kanzler von Müller on 8 March 1824: "Was sind travers? Falsche Stellungen zur Außenwelt. Wer hat sie nicht? Jede Lebensstufe hat die ihr eignen" (WA *Gespräche* 5:48; "What are frailties? Erroneous attitudes to the external world. Who doesn't have them? Every stage of life has its own").

[24] Johann Wolfgang von Goethe, *Poems of the West and East: West-Eastern Divan — West-Östlicher Divan: Bi-Lingual Edition of the Complete Poems,* trans. John Whaley (Bern, Berlin, Frankfurt am Main: Peter Lang, 1998), 291; translation adapted.

[25] See, for example, Goethe's conversation with Eckermann of 11 March 1828 on "wiederholte Pubertät" ("repeated puberty").

[26] For Schiller's highly differentiated view of the aesthetic as the highest level of human experience, see Elizabeth M. Wilkinson and L. A. Willoughby, "'The Whole Man' in Schiller's Theory of Culture and Society" [1969], in *Models of Wholeness: Some Attitudes to Language, Art and Life in the Age of Goethe,* ed. Jeremy Adler, Martin Swales, and Ann Weaver (Oxford, Bern, Berlin: Peter Lang, 2002), 233–68; here, 255–62.

[27] "Auch ich bin in der Unterwelt gewesen, wie Odysseus, und werde es noch öfter sein; und nicht nur Hammel habe ich geopfert, um mit einigen Todten reden zu können, sondern des eignen Blutes nicht geschont. Vier Paare waren es, welche sich mir, dem Opfernden nicht versagten: Epikur und Montaigne, Goethe und Spinoza, Plato und Rousseau, Pascal und Schopenhauer. Mit diesen muss ich mich auseinandersetzen, wenn ich lange allein gewandert bin, von ihnen will ich mir Recht und Unrecht geben lassen, ihnen will ich zuhören, wenn sie sich dabei selber untereinander Recht und Unrecht geben. Was ich auch nur sage, beschliesse, für

mich und andere ausdenke: auf jene Acht hefte ich die Augen und sehe die ihrigen auf mich geheftet" (*MA* II Vermischte Meinungen und Sprüche §408; KSA 2:533–34; "I too have been in the underworld, like Odysseus, and will often be there again; and I have sacrificed not only rams to be able to talk with the dead, but have not spared my own blood as well. There have been four pairs who did not refuse themselves to me, the sacrificer: Epicurus and Montaigne, Goethe and Spinoza, Plato and Rousseau, Pascal and Schopenhauer. With these I have to come to terms when I have wandered long alone, from them will I accept judgment, to them will I listen when in doing so they judge one another. Whatever I say, resolve, cogitate for myself and others: on these eight I fix my eyes and see theirs fixed upon me"). In *Morgenröthe*, Nietzsche set up a distinction between, on one hand, five of this group and, on the other, one of them (Schopenhauer) and Kant: "Vergleicht man Kant und Schopenhauer mit Plato, Spinoza, Pascal, Rousseau, Goethe in Absehung auf ihre Seele und nicht auf ihren Geist: so sind die erstgenannten Denker im Nachtheil: ihre Gedanken machen nicht eine leidenschaftliche Seelen-Geschichte aus, es giebt da keinen Roman, keine Krisen, Katastrophen und Todesstunden zu errathen, ihr Denken ist nicht zugleich eine unwillkürliche Biographie einer Seele, sondern, im Falle Kant's, eines *Kopfes*, im Falle Schopenhauer's, die Beschreibung und Spiegelung eines *Charakters* ('des unveränderlichen') und die Freude am 'Spiegel' selber, das heisst an einem vorzüglichen Intellecte" (*M* §481; KSA 3:285–86; "If you compare Kant and Schopenhauer with Plato, Spinoza, Pascal, Rousseau, Goethe with regard to their soul and not to their mind, then the former are at a disadvantage: their thoughts do not constitute a passionate history of a soul, there is nothing here that would make a novel, no crises, catastrophes, or death-scenes; their thinking is not at the same time an involuntary biography of a soul but, in the case of Kant, the biography of a *head*, in the case of Schopenhauer the description and mirroring of a *character* ('that which is unalterable') and pleasure in the 'mirror' itself, that is, in an excellent intellect").

[28] See the discussion by Wilkinson and Willoughby in the Glossary in their edition of Friedrich Schiller, *On the Aesthetic Education of Man in a Series of Letters* (2nd ed., Oxford: Clarendon P, 1982), 316–17.

[29] 12 [131], 12[136], 12[157], 15[50], and 15[52]; KSA 9:599, 603, 651, and 652. The *Nachlass* volumes of the KSA (vols. 10 and 11) are full of textual variants and sketches relating to *Zarathustra* (see the Appendix).

[30] *Maximen und Reflexionen*, no. 5 (HA 12:543; *Maxims and Reflexions*, 3 [adapted]).

[31] For Goethe's view of the aesthetic as the revelation of *necessary* laws, see *Maximen und Reflexionen*, no. 183: "Das Schöne ist eine Manifestation geheimer Naturgesetze, die uns ohne dessen Erscheinung ewig wären verborgen geblieben" (HA 12:467; *Maxims and Reflexions*, 21; "The beautiful is a surface manifestation of secret laws of nature, which would have remained for ever hidden from us but for this appearance" [adapted]).

[32] For publication details, see Raymond J. Benders, Stephan Oettermann et al, *Friedrich Nietzsche: Chronik in Bildern und Texten* (Munich and Vienna: Hanser/dtv, 2000), 527–28.

[33] See the so-called "Dornburger Gedichte," "Dem aufgehenden Vollmonde" [Dornburg, 25 August 1828] and "Früh wenn Thal Gebirg und Garten" [Dornburg, September 1828] (HA 1:391).

[34] Lou Andreas-Salomé, *Lebensrückblick,* ed. Ernst Pfeiffer (1951; repr. Frankfurt am Main: Insel-Verlag, 1974), 79–80; cited in Benders and Oettermann, *Chronik,* 511.

[35] Compare with Zarathustra's resolution in his Prologue: "Siehe! Dieser Becher will wieder leer werden, und Zarathustra will wieder Mensch werden" (Z I Vorrede §1; KSA 4:12; "Look! This cup wants to become empty again, and Zarathustra wants to become human again").

[36] According to Nietzsche in his letter to Hippolyte Taine of 4 July 1887 (KSB 8:107).

[37] Compare with the following passage from Nietzsche's *Nachlass* for the period Spring to Autumn 1881: "'Aber wenn alles nothwendig ist, was kann ich über meine Handlungen verfügen?' Der Gedanke und Glaube ist ein Schwergewicht, welches neben allen anderen Gewichten auf dich drückt und mehr als sie. Du sagst, daß Nahrung Ort Luft Gesellschaft dich wandeln und bestimmen? Nun, deine Meinungen thun es noch mehr, denn diese bestimmen dich zu dieser Nahrung Ort Luft Gesellschaft. — Wenn du dir den Gedanken der Gedanken einverleibst, so wird er dich verwandeln. Die Frage bei allem, was du thun willst: 'ist es so, daß ich es unzählige Male thun will?' ist das *größte* Schwergewicht" (11[143]; KSA 9:496; "'But when everything is necessary, what can I do about my actions?' Thought and belief is a heavy weight, which next to all other weights bears down on you and more than them. You say that nutrition, location, atmosphere, society transform and de-termine you? Well, your opinions do so even more, for they determine you in respect of this nutrition, location, atmosphere, society. — If you incorporate the thought of thoughts, then it will transform you. The question about everything that you want to do: 'Is this something that I want to do innumerable times?' is the *greatest* weight"; compare with a later *Nachlass* passage from Spring 1884, 25[7]; KSA 11:10–11). Nietzsche's *Nachlass* also offers the following variant: "[. . .] Welchen Zustand diese Welt auch nur erreichen *kann,* sie muß ihn erreicht haben und nicht einmal, sondern unzählige Male. So diesen Augenblick: er war schon einmal da und viele Male und wird ebenso wiederkehren, alle Kräfte genau so vertheilt, wie jetzt: und ebenso steht es mit dem Augenblick, der diesen gebar und mit dem, welcher das Kind des jetzigen ist. Mensch! Dein ganzes Leben wird wie eine Sanduhr immer wieder umgedreht werden und immer wieder auslaufen — eine große Minute Zeit dazwischen, bis alle Bedingungen, aus denen du geworden bist, im Kreislaufe der Welt, wieder zusammenkommen. Und dann findest du jeden Schmerz und jede Lust und jeden Freund und Feind und jede Hoffnung und jeden Irrthum und jeden Grashalm und jeden Sonnenblick wieder, den ganzen Zusammenhang aller Dinge. Dieser Ring, in dem du ein Korn bist, glänzt immer wieder. Und in jedem Ring des Menschen-Daseins überhaupt giebt [es] immer eine Stunde, wo erst Einem, dann Vielen, dann Allen der mächtigste Gedanke auftaucht, der von der ewigen Wiederkunft aller Dinge — es ist jedesmal für die Menschheit die Stunde des *Mittags*" (11[148]; KSA 9:498; "Whatever state this world *can* reach, it must have reached it, and not once, but innumerable times. Thus this moment: it was there once already and many times and will also recur, all powers distributed as they now

are: and thus it is with the moment that bore this one and with the one that is the child of the current one. Human! Your whole life is, like a sand-glass, turned upside down again and again and allowed to run out again and again — a great minute of time in the meantime, until all the conditions from which you have become, in the circulation of the world, come together again. And then you find again every pain and every pleasure and every friend and enemy and every hope and every error and every leaf of grass and every ray of sunshine, the entire connection of all things. This ring, in which you are a grain, gleams again and again. And in every ring of all human existence there is always an hour in which to one, then to many, then to all the most powerful thought surfaces, that of the eternal recurrence of all things — it is always for humanity the hour of *midday*"). "Midnight," by contrast, is Goethe's symbol of this heart-stopping moment (see his poem "Um Mitternacht" [HA 1:372–73]). See the moment when midnight becomes midday in *Also sprach Zarathustra* (*Z* IV 19 §10; KSA 4:402; discussed in chapter 3 below, especially endnotes 42 and 43).

[38] See Georg Simmel, *Schopenhauer und Nietzsche* (Leipzig: Duncker & Humblot, 1907); *Schopenhauer and Nietzsche*, trans. Helmut Loiskandl, Deena Weinstein, and Michael Weinstein (Urbana and Chicago: U of Illinois P, 1991).

[39] HA 1:370; in English, Johann Wolfgang von Goethe, *Selected Poems*, ed. Christopher Middleton, Goethe Edition, vol. 1 (Boston: Suhrkamp/Insel, 1983), 268, adapted from Middleton's translation.

[40] In his *Vorrede* to the second edition of *Die fröhliche Wissenschaft* of 1886, Nietzsche observed: "'Incipit *tragoedia*' — heisst es am Schlusse dieses bedenklich-unbedenklichen Buchs: man sei auf seiner Hut! Irgend etwas ausbündig Schlimmes und Boshaftes kündigt sich an: incipit *parodia*, es ist kein Zweifel . . ." (*FW* Vorrede §1; KSA 3:346; "'*Incipit tragoedia*' (let the tragedy begin) we read at the end of this unthinking book which makes you think. Beware! Something downright wicked and malicious is announced here: *incipit parodia* (let the parody begin), no doubt"). *Also sprach Zarathustra* is, in obvious respects, a parody (in its style of the Bible, in its *dramatis personae* of Schopenhauer, Wagner, and so on).

[41] The image of the clockhand informs another of Nietzsche's aphorisms, "Vom Stundenzeiger des Lebens" ("On the Hour-hand of Life"): "Das Leben besteht aus seltenen einzelnen Momenten von höchster Bedeutsamkeit und unzählig vielen Intervallen, in denen uns besten Falls die Schattenbilder jener Momente umschweben. Die Liebe, der Frühling, jede schöne Melodie, das Gebirge, der Mond, das Meer — Alles redet nur einmal ganz zum Herzen: wenn es überhaupt je ganz zu Worte kommt. Denn viele Menschen haben jene Momente gar nicht und sind selber Intervalle und Pausen in der Symphonie des wirklichen Lebens" (*MA* I §586; KSA 2:337; "Life consists of rare individual moments of the highest significance and countlessly many intervals in which at best the silhouettes of those moments hover about us. Love, spring, every beautiful melody, the mountains, the moon, the sea — each speaks truly to our heart only once: if they ever do in fact truly find speech. For many people never experience these moments at all but are themselves intervals and pauses in the symphony of real life").

[42] For a discussion of the dating, see Philip Grundlehner, *The Poetry of Friedrich Nietzsche* (New York and Oxford: Oxford UP, 1986), 134–36; and see, too, the

footnote in the translation by Walter Kaufmann (Friedrich Nietzsche, *The Gay Science* [New York: Vintage, 1974], 371).

[43] C. G. Jung, *Nietzsche's Zarathustra: Notes of the Seminar given in 1934–1939,* ed. James Jarrett, 2 vols. (London: Routledge, 1989), 1:10. For further discussion of the importance of Nietzsche for Jung, see Paul Bishop, *The Dionysian Self: C. G. Jung's Reception of Nietzsche* (Berlin and New York: Walter de Gruyter, 1995).

[44] René Girard, *Critiques dans un souterrain* (Paris: Grasset, 1976), 23 and 93. See also Grundlehner's commentary in *The Poetry of Friedrich Nietzsche,* 134–36.

[45] The idea can be found in St. Augustine, who says in his *Confessions,* Book 11, §13, that "eternity" is "supreme over time because it is a never-ending present," and that God is "at once before all past time and after all future time": "Your years are one day, yet your day does not come daily but is always today, because your today does not give place to any tomorrow nor does it take the place of any yesterday. Your today is eternity" (St. Augustine, *Confessions,* trans. R. S. Pine-Coffin [Harmondsworth: Penguin, 1961], 263). The Scholastic concept of the *nunc stans* is frequently found in St. Thomas Aquinas and derives from the *nunc permanens* of Boethius: "Nostrum nunc quasi currens tempus facit et sempiternitatem, divinum vero nunc permanens neque movens sese atque consistens aeternitatem facit" (Boethius, *De sancta trinitate,* ed. Stewart and Rand [London: 1918], 4:72–74, quoted in the entry on "Nunc stans," in Joachim Ritter and Karlfried Gründer, eds., *Historisches Wörterbuch der Philosophie,* 9 vols. [Basel: Schwabe, 1971–1995], 6:989–91; "Our Now brings about continuous time and perpetuity, whereas the divine Now, persistent and motionless and constant, brings about eternity"). For further discussion, see Jozef Wissink, *The Eternity of the World in the Thought of Thomas Aquinas and his Contemporaries* (Leiden and New York: E. J. Brill, 1990), especially 28–29.

[46] In his lecture "Wer ist Nietzsches Zarathustra?" ("Who is Nietzsche's Zarathustra?" 1953), Martin Heidegger notes that, in "Von der grossen Sehnsucht" ("On the Great Longing"), Zarathustra's opening words — "Oh meine Seele, ich lehrte dich 'Heute' sagen wie 'Einst' und 'Ehemals' und über alles Hier und Da und Dort deinen Reigen hinweg tanzen" (*Z* III 14; KSA 4:278; "O my soul, I taught you to say 'Today' as 'Once' and 'Formerly' and to dance away your dance over every Here and There and Over There") — recall the idea of the eternal Now, conceived as the eternal recurrence (*Vorträge und Aufsätze* (Pfullingen: Neske, 1954), 101–26; here, 106; translated by Bernd Magnus in David B. Allison, ed., *The New Nietzsche: Contemporary Styles of Interpretation* [Cambridge, MA and London: MIT Press, 1985], 64–79; here, 69). For further discussion, see Günter Wohlfart, "Wer ist Nietzsches Zarathustra?" *Nietzsche-Studien* 26 (1997): 319–30; and Laurence Paul Hemming, "Who is Heidegger's Zarathustra?" *Literature and Theology* 12 (1998): 268–93.

[47] For further discussion of the motif of the *nunc stans* in Goethe's work, see Pierre Hadot, "'The Present Alone is our Joy': The Meaning of the Present Instant in Goethe and in Ancient Philosophy," *Diogenes* 133 (1986): 60–82; and Andreas Anglet, *Der "ewige" Augenblick: Studien zur Struktur und Funktion eines Denkbildes bei Goethe* (Cologne, Weimar, and Vienna: Böhlau, 1991).

[48] In "Von der Seligkeit wider Willen" ("On Involuntary Bliss"), Zarathustra's words "Hinweg mit dir, du selige Stunde! Mit dir kam mir eine Seligkeit wider Willen" (*Z* III 3; KSA 4:206; "Away with you, blessed hour! With you bliss came to me against

my will") allude to Goethe's remark about his poetic talent in *Dichtung und Wahrheit* (part 4, bk. 16): "Ich war dazu gelangt, das mir inwohnende dichterische Talent ganz als Natur zu betrachten, um so mehr, als ich darauf gewiesen war, die äußere Natur als den Gegenstand desselben anzusehen. Die Ausübung dieser Dichtergabe konnte zwar durch Veranlassung erregt und bestimmt werden; aber am freudigsten und reichlichsten trat sie unwillkürlich, ja wider Willen hervor" (HA 10:80; "I had gotten to the point of viewing my indwelling poetic talent as nature, especially since I had been directed to look upon external nature as its subject matter. Of course, a specific occasion could move me to conceive this poetic gift for a particular purpose, but it was at its most joyous and opulent when it burst forth involuntarily, nay, *against* my will": Johann Wolfgang von Goethe, *From My Life: Poetry and Truth: Part Four/Campaign in France 1792. Siege of Mainz*, ed. Thomas P. Saine and Jeffrey L. Sammons, trans. Robert R. Heitner/Thomas P. Saine, Goethe's Collected Works, vol. 5 [New York: Suhrkamp, 1987], 525; compare KSA 14:312). In "Vom Geist der Schwere" ("On the Spirit of Gravity"), Zarathustra acknowledges the following about his style: "Mein Mundwerk — ist des Volks: zu grob und herzlich rede ich für die Seidenhasen. Und noch fremder klingt mein Wort allen Tinten-Fischen und Feder-Füchsen" (*Z* III 11 §1; KSA 4:241; "My tongue — is of the people: I speak too crudely and sincerely for those of fine sensibilities. And my speech sounds even stranger to all pettifogging pen-pushers"). In a letter to Lou von Salomé of August 1882 Nietzsche set out a number of related precepts entitled "Zur Lehre vom Stil" (1[109]; KSA 10:38–41, compare KSB 6:243–45). For discussion of Schiller's strategic use of the metaphor of dance, see the introduction and commentary by Wilkinson and Willoughby in their edition of Schiller, *On the Aesthetic Education of Man*, cxxxi–cxxxii, 235, and 300.

[49] See the commentary by Wilkinson and Willoughby in their edition of Schiller, *On the Aesthetic Education of Man*, 251; and see note 74 in chapter 3.

[50] One of the most important themes of the Goethe-Schiller correspondence of 1797, the idea of the necessity of "indifference," is given classic formulation by Goethe in the mouth of the Poet in the "Vorspiel auf dem Theater" ("Prelude in the Theater") of *Faust* Part One. Is it not the poet's office, he asks, to turn "indifferent" material into significant art (see line 143): "Wer flicht die unbedeutend grünen Blätter / Zum Ehrenkranz Verdiensten jeder Art?" (lines 154–55; "Who braids the insignificant green leaves / Into a garland of honor to merit of every kind?"). The same question is posed by Schiller in his *On the Aesthetic Education of Man* (in the footnote to Letter 21), where the "indifference" of the aesthetic state to any *specific* results is summed up as its "nullity" (*Null*) (see the introduction and commentary by Wilkinson and Willoughby in their edition of Schiller, *On the Aesthetic Education of Man*, clviii, clxxii, and 263).

[51] For a fuller account of the history of the composition of *Also sprach Zarathustra*, which is so revealing of the development of Nietzsche's thinking in this work, and further points of Weimar Classical influence in its development, see the appendix in this volume.

3: The Aesthetic Gospel of Nietzsche's *Zarathustra*

Man bedient sich als Symbol der Ewigkeit der Schlange, die sich in einem Reif abschließt, ich betrachte dieß hingegen als Gleichniß einer glücklichen Zeitlichkeit.

[People are fond of using, as a symbol of eternity, the snake, which turns into itself in a circle; I, however, like to consider it a representation of happiness in time.]

— Goethe, letter to F. W. H. von Trebra,
5 January 1814; WA 4.24:92

Die stillsten Worte sind es, welche den Sturm bringen. Gedanken, die mit Taubenfüssen kommen, lenken die Welt.

[It is the quietest words that bring the storm, thoughts that come on doves' feet guide the world.]

— Nietzsche, *Z* II §22; KSA 4:189

NIETZSCHE FREQUENTLY INSISTED ON THE centrality of *Zarathustra* amongst his philosophical works.[1] In *Ecce Homo*, for example, he wrote:

Innerhalb meiner Schriften steht für sich mein *Zarathustra*. Ich habe mit ihm der Menschheit das grösste Geschenk gemacht, das ihr bisher gemacht worden ist. Dies Buch, mit einer Stimme über Jahrtausende hinweg, ist nicht nur das höchste Buch, das es giebt, das eigentliche Höhenluft-Buch — die ganze Thatsache Mensch liegt in ungeheurer Ferne *unter* ihm —, es ist auch das *tiefste,* das aus dem innersten Reichthum der Wahrheit heraus geborene, ein unerschöpflicher Brunnen, in den kein Eimer hinabsteigt, ohne mit Gold und Güte gefüllte heraufzukommen. (*EH* Vorwort §4; KSA 6:259)

[Among my writings my *Zarathustra* stands on its own. With it I have given humankind the greatest gift that has been made to it so far. This book, with a voice that traverses centuries, is not only the highest book there is, the book that is truly characterized by the air of the heights — the whole fact of humankind lies *beneath* it at a tremendous distance — it is also the *deepest,* born out of the innermost wealth of truth, an inexhaustible well to which no pail descends without coming up again filled with gold and goodness.]

His later works were, to a great extent, conceived as explanations of *Zarathustra*. For example, Nietzsche told Jacob Burckhardt in a letter of 22 September 1886 that *Jenseits von Gut und Böse* (*Beyond Good and Evil*) "dieselben Dinge sagt, wie mein Zarathustra, aber anders, sehr anders" (KSB 7:254; "says the same things as my *Zarathustra,* but differently, very differently"). And, in the case of *Zur Genealogie der Moral* (*On the Genealogy of Morals*), he placed an aphorism from *Zarathustra* before the third essay, and invited the reader to interpret that essay as a commentary on that aphorism (*GM* Vorrede §8; KSA 5:255–56).

Zarathustra himself makes it clear that he brings a single message, doctrine, or teaching. This point has been clearly emphasized by Laurence Lampert who, however, sees Zarathustra's teaching as a founding fable inaugurating a new esoteric philosophy, not as continuing a firmly established aesthetic tradition. After the episode in the market-place with the motley fool, Zarathustra says to himself: "Ich will die Menschen den Sinn ihres Seins lehren: welcher ist der Übermensch, der Blitz aus der dunklen Wolke Mensch" (Vorrede §7; KSA 4:23; "I will teach humans the meaning of their existence — which is the superman, the lightning out of the dark cloud of humankind"). At the start of part 2, in "Das Kind mit dem Spiegel" ("The Child with the Mirror"), Zarathustra realizes that, as he puts it, "meine *Lehre* ist in Gefahr" (*Z* II 1; KSA 4:105; "my *teaching* is in danger"). In "Vom Geist der Schwere" ("On the Spirit of Heaviness"), Zarathustra summarizes his teaching in this form: "Das ist aber meine Lehre: wer einst fliegen lernen will, der muss erst stehn und gehn und laufen und klettern und tanzen lernen" (*Z* III 11 §2; KSA 4:244; "This is my teaching: whoever wants to learn to fly one day must first learn to stand and walk and run and climb and dance"); while the play here on "lernen" and "lehren" — "Man muss sich selber lieben lernen — also lehre ich" (KSA 4:242; "One must learn to love oneself — thus I teach") — is taken up and complexified in "Von alten und neuen Tafeln" ("On Old and New Tablets"): "Wollen befreit: denn Wollen ist Schaffen: so lehre ich. Und *nur* zum Schaffen sollt ihr lernen! / Und auch das Lernen sollt ihr erst von mir *lernen,* das Gut-Lernen!" (*Z* III 12 §16; KSA 4:258; "To want liberates: for to want is to create: thus I teach. And you should learn *only* in order to create. / And you should first *learn* from me how to learn, how to learn well!"). Then again, in "Die Begrüssung" ("The Welcome"), he tells the Higher Men: "Ich brauche reine glatte Spiegel für meine Lehren" (*Z* IV 11; KSA 4:350; "I need clean smooth mirrors for my teachings"). And in the penultimate chapter of part 4, the Ugliest Man proclaims: "Es lohnt sich auf der Erde zu leben: Ein Tag, Ein Fest mit Zarathustra lehrte mich die Erde lieben" (*Z* IV 19 §l; KSA 4:396; "It is worth while living on the earth: one day, one festival with Zarathustra, taught me to love the earth").[2] More important, *Zarathustra* concerns itself with the doctrine of art as it had been sketched out by Nietzsche in *Die Geburt der Tragödie* (*The Birth of Tragedy*).

Having examined, in chapter 1, the presence and function of the discourse of Weimar aesthetics in *Die Geburt der Tragödie* and, in chapter 2, the pressure it exerted on the genesis of *Also sprach Zarathustra*, let us see how the concepts of the Beautiful (and the Sublime) are used, in their fuller elaboration, in *Also sprach Zarathustra*. From this perspective, the chapters "Von der unbefleckten Erkenntniss" ("On Immaculate Perception") and "Von den Erhabenen" ("On the Sublime Ones") offer a helpful starting point. In his First Critique (1781; second edition, 1787), Kant examined the conditions for "pure" knowledge — "Kritik der *reinen* Vernunft." And in his Third Critique (1790), Kant defined Beauty as "der Gegenstand des Wohlgefallens ohne alles Interesse" ("the object of delight without any interest").[3] Both Kantian aesthetics and Kantian epistemology (together with the Christian faith it was able to underpin) are rejected by Zarathustra in the chapter entitled "On Immaculate Perception" (*Z* II 15; KSA 4:156–59).[4] The Man in the Moon, portrayed as a lustful monk, symbolizes that "pure knowledge" that comes only through the eye. Yet whilst their spirit may have convinced the men of pure knowing that the earthly is to be despised, their guts — their affective and instinctual aspects — still remain strong, so that they secretly and hypocritically desire what they hold in (visual) contempt. Immaculate perception sees Beauty, too, only through the eye. But such Beauty, says Zarathustra, is not real, and brings Beauty into disrepute: "Und was mit feigen Augen sich tasten lässt, soll 'schön' getauft werden! Oh, ihr Beschmutzer edler Namen!" (KSA 4:157; "And what allows itself to be touched by cowardly eyes should be baptized 'beautiful!' Oh, you soiler of noble names!"). In place of "immaculate perception," associated with the moon, Zarathustra teaches a knowledge of bodily sensuousness, symbolized by the sun. Images of thirst and hot breath, drinking and breasts, kissing and sucking, and "Unschuld und Schöpfer-Begier" ("innocence and creative desire") are associated with this knowledge.[5] Equally, with regard to this knowledge, Beauty is linked, not to weakness, but to the will: "Wo ist Schönheit? Wo ich mit allem Willen *wollen muss*" (KSA 4:157; "Where is beauty? Where I *must will* with all my will"). In other words, the intellectually controlled, purposively directed *will* must subordinate itself to voluntary, aesthetic *willing*. Aesthetically transformed, the will retains only its purposiveness, not its purpose.

Elsewhere, Zarathustra enlarges upon his concept of Beauty proper. At the end of his speech "On the Blissful Islands," Zarathustra brings Beauty together with the themes of creativity and the Superman:

Ach, ihr Menschen, im Steine schläft mir ein Bild, das Bild meiner Bilder! Ach, dass es im härtesten, hässlichsten Steine schlafen muss!

Nun wüthet mein Hammer grausam gegen sein Gefängniss. Vom Steine stäuben Stücke: was schiert mich das?

Vollenden will ich's: denn ein Schatten kam zu mir — aller Dinge Stillstes und Leichtestes kam einst zu mir!

Des Übermenschen Schönheit kam zu mir als Schatten. Ach, meine Brüder! Was gehen mich noch — die Götter an!

(Z II 2; KSA 4:111–12)[6]

[O humans, in the stone there sleeps an image, the image of my images! Alas, that it must sleep in the hardest, ugliest stone!

Now my hammer rages cruelly against its prison. Pieces of rock rain from the stone: what is that to me?

I want to perfect it; for a shadow came to me — the stillest and lightest of all things once came to me!

The beauty of the superman came to me as a shadow. O my brothers, what are to me now — the gods?]

In "Von den Tugendhaften" ("On the Virtuous"), Zarathustra reminds his followers: "Aber der Schönheit Stimme redet leise: sie schleicht sich nur in die aufgewecktesten Seelen" (Z II 5; KSA 4:120; "But the voice of beauty speaks softly: it creeps only into the most awakened souls"). And in "Vom Geist der Schwere," Zarathustra emphasizes: "Aber auch diese Kunst muss man lernen: Schale haben und schönen Schein und kluge Blindheit!" (Z III 11 §2; KSA 4:243; "But one must also learn this art: to have a shell and beautiful semblance and shrewd blindness").[7] Furthermore, these reflections on Beauty clarify Zarathustra's statements on the relationship between the Beautiful and the Sublime in the earlier chapter "Von den Erhabenen" (On the Sublime Ones"; Z II 13; KSA 4:150–52).

At the beginning of this chapter, Zarathustra describes the "Sublime Man" he has seen, whom he equates with "the penitent of the spirit" (Büßer des Geistes).[8] The Sublime Man is the hunter who has returned disappointed from the forest of knowledge, for he does not know two things: "Noch lernte er das Lachen nicht und die Schönheit" (KSA 4:150; "As yet he has not learnt laughter or beauty"). To those who follow the ancient line that de gustibus non est disputandum, Zarathustra replies, in another gesture of rejection towards that conventional aesthetic doctrine: "Aber alles Leben ist Streit um Geschmack und Schmecken!" (KSA 4:150; "But all of life is a dispute about taste and tasting!"). The Sublime Man, like the Pale Criminal in part 1, is still in hock to his contempt, and still prone to disgust.[9] For the Sublime Man, says Zarathustra, must forget his sublimity, jump over his own shadow (a symbol of self-overcoming, as well as a rejection of German proverbial wisdom)[10] and become a roaring white bull with the eye of an angel (a symbol of Apollonian calm and Dionysian energy). For only Beauty, as

Zarathustra says in his discourse on the Priests, should preach penitence (*Z* II 4; KSA 4:118). The Sublime Man must forget his will to be a hero, "ein Gehobener soll er mir sein und nicht nur ein Erhabener" (*Z* II 13; KSA 4:151; "he should be elevated, and not merely sublime"). Grace, Zarathustra adds, is a product of desire for the aesthetic, not surfeit: "Wahrlich, nicht in der Sattheit soll sein Verlangen schweigen und untertauchen, sondern in der Schönheit! Die Anmuth gehört zur Grossmuth des Grossgesinnten" (*Z* II 13; KSA 4:152; "Truly, it is not in satiety that his longing should be silenced and submerged, but in beauty! Gracefulness is part of the generosity of the magnanimous individual").[11] According to Zarathustra, the process in which power is rendered graceful and becomes visible is Beauty: "Wenn die Macht gnädig wird und herabkommt in's Sichtbare: Schönheit heisse ich solches Herabkommen" (KSA 4:152; "When power becomes gracious and descends into the visible: such a descent I call beauty"). Yet, as Zarathustra admits, it is hard for a hero to attain Beauty, for it is precisely the purposeful will that must be renounced: "Aber gerade dem Helden ist das *Schöne* aller Dinge Schwerstes. Unerringbar ist das Schöne allem heftigen Willen" (KSA 4:152; "But precisely for the hero the *beautiful* is the most difficult thing. The beautiful is unattainable for all violent wills"). In *Ueber die ästhetische Erziehung des Menschen* (*On the Aesthetic Education of Humankind*, 1795), Schiller had claimed that in aesthetic culture noble desire replaces the sublime will: "[Der Mensch] muss lernen *edler* begehren, damit er nicht nötig habe, *erhaben zu wollen.* Dieses wird geleistet durch ästhetische Kultur, welche alles das, worüber weder Naturgesetze die menschliche Willkür binden noch Vernunftgesetze, Gesetzen der Schönheit unterwirft und in der Form, die sie dem aüssern Leben gibt, schon das innere eröffnet" (Letter 23, §8; "Man must learn to desire *more nobly,* so that he may not need to *will sublimely.* This is brought about by means of aesthetic education, which subjects to laws of beauty all those spheres of human behavior in which neither natural laws, nor yet rational laws, are binding upon human caprice, and which, in the form it gives to outer life, opens up the inner").[12] Whilst Zarathustra had urged the Young Man in "Vom Baum am Berge" ("On the Tree on the Mountainside"), "wirf den Helden in deiner Seele nicht weg!" (*Z* I 8; KSA 4:54; "do not throw away the hero in your soul!"), at the end of this chapter he looks forward to the arrival of the Super-Hero (that is, the "One-Above-the-Hero"):

> Ja, du Erhabener, einst sollst du noch schön sein und deiner eignen Schönheit den Spiegel vorhalten.
>
> Dann wird deine Seele vor göttlichen Begierden schaudern; und Anbetung wird noch in deiner Eitelkeit sein!
>
> Diess nämlich ist das Geheimniss der Seele: erst, wenn sie der Held verlassen hat, naht ihr, im Träume, — der Über-Held.
>
> (*Z* II 13; KSA 4:152)

[Indeed, you sublime one, you shall yet become beautiful one day and hold up a mirror to your own beauty.

Then your soul will shudder with godlike desires; and there will be adoration even in your vanity!

For this is the secret of the soul: only when the hero has abandoned her, is she approached, in a dream, by — the super-hero.]

For Zarathustra, the Sublime is useful because it is a prerequisite of the aesthetic. In "Vom Krieg und Kriegsvolke" ("On War and Warriors"), he advises: "Ihr seid hässlich? Nun wohlan, meine Brüder! So nehmt das Erhabne um euch, den Mantel des Hässlichen!" (*Z* I 10; KSA 4:59; "You are ugly? Well then, my brothers, wrap yourselves in the sublime, the cloak of the ugly!"). And in part 4, during the "Eselsfest," Zarathustra asks the Ugliest Man: "Du dünkst mich verwandelt, dein Auge glüht, der Mantel des Erhabenen liegt um deine Hässlichkeit: *was* thatest du?" (*Z* IV 18 §1; KSA 4:392; "You seem changed to me, your eyes are glowing, the cloak of the sublime lies over your ugliness: *what* have you done?"). What has the Ugliest Man done? He has learned to laugh — "Eins aber weiss ich, — von dir selber lernte ich's einst, oh Zarathustra: wer am gründlichsten tödten will, der *lacht*" (KSA 4:392; "But one thing I do know; it was from you that I once learned it, O Zarathustra: whoever wants to kill most thoroughly, *laughs*"); something that the Sublime Man must also learn to do.[13] Furthermore, the attributes of *Heiterkeit* (or "serene cheerfulness") and distance constitute, as for many a German Classicist, from Wieland to Goethe and beyond, an important link between laughter and the category of the aesthetic.

Also sprach Zarathustra has a simple, if somewhat diffuse, plot. Zarathustra leaves his mountain in part 1 and goes to the town known as the Colorful Cow; by part 2, he has returned to his mountain but he descends again and visits the Blissful Islands; in part 3, he sails from the Blissful Islands and travels cross-country via the Great City and the Colorful Cow back to his mountain; and in part 4, he wanders through the mountains and forests, encountering the Higher Men whom he invites back to his cave. Interwoven into this plot, however, are numerous reminiscences and echoes of Goethe's *Faust*.[14] The Faustian elements of *Zarathustra* can be found at the very beginning of the text. Zarathustra's first address to the crowd in the market-place opens with the declamation — "*Ich lehre euch den Übermenschen*" (*Z* Vorrede §2; KSA 4:14; "*I teach you the superman*"). The very term "Übermensch" is, of course, borrowed from Goethe, where it occurs in the *Erdgeist* scene of *Faust I*.[15] There it is used ironically by the Earth Spirit, for whom Faust is no better than a *Wurm* ("worm"). The meaning of the term is, however, revalued in *Also sprach Zarathustra*. *Faust I* opens with Faust's existential despair and epistemological frustration. He expresses his contempt for learning: "Da steh ich nun, ich armer Thor! / Und bin so klug als wie zuvor" (lines 358–59; "And here, poor fool, I stand once more, / No wiser than I was before"). Likewise, Zarathustra tells the people in the market-place: "Was ist das Grösste, das ihr erleben könnt? Das ist die Stunde der grossen Verachtung. Die Stunde, in der euch auch euer Glück zum Ekel wird und ebenso eure Vernunft und eure Tugend" (*Z* Vorrede §3; KSA 4:15; "What is the greatest thing that you can experience? It is the hour of great contempt. The hour, in which even your happiness arouses your disgust, as do your reason and your virtue").[16] In the following lines, Zarathustra rejects as supreme values happiness, reason, virtue, justice, and pity. Later, in "Von der Wissenschaft" ("On Science"), the Conscientious Man of the Spirit presents a mainly negative account of science (but one which is subsequently rejected by Zarathustra; *Z* IV 15; KSA 4:375–78). In "Vom Lande der Bildung" ("On the Land of Education"), Zarathustra pours scorn on academics, calling them "halboffene Thore [. . .], an denen Todtengräber warten" ("half-open doors at which grave-diggers wait"), and he attributes to their reality the phrase with which, as "der Geist, der stets verneint" ("the spirit that always negates"), Mephistopheles characterizes his attitude to the universe: "Alles ist werth, dass es zu Grunde geht" ("Everything deserves to perish"; compare "alles, was entsteht, / Ist werth daß es zu Grunde geht" (*Z* II 14; KSA 4:154; "for all things that exist / Deserve to perish, and would not be missed"; also compare *Faust I*, 1339–40). Yet the term *der Erkennende* ("the one who knows") is used several times by Zarathustra largely in a positive sense. For example, when the friends of Zarathustra's followers mock: "'Seht nur Zarathustra! Wandelt er nicht unter uns wie unter Thieren?'" ("'Look at Zarathustra! Does he not go among us as if among animals?'"), Zarathustra corrects their words as follows: "Aber so ist es besser geredet: 'Der Erkennende wandelt unter Menschen *als* unter Thieren'" (*Z* II 3; KSA 4:113; "But it is better to say this: 'The enlightened man goes among humans *as* among animals'").[17] Unlike the pure in knowledge (and impure in heart) of "Von der unbefleckten Erkenntniss," the one who truly knows is regarded in the same way as "der Erwachte, der Wissende" ("the awakened, the knowing one") of "Von den Verächtern des Leibes" ("On the Despisers of the Body"; *Z* I 4; KSA 4:39). And even in the Prologue, the Old Man in the Forest says: "Verwandelt ist Zarathustra, zum Kind ward Zarathustra, ein Erwachter ist Zarathustra" (*Z* Vorrede §2; KSA 4:12; "Zarathustra has changed, Zarathustra has become a child, Zarathustra is an awakened one"). In a key passage from the chapter "Von der schenkenden Tugend" ("On the Gift-Giving Virtue"), Zarathustra announces: "Wissend reinigt sich der Leib; mit Wissen versuchend erhöht er sich; dem Erkennenden heiligen sich alle Triebe; dem Erhöhten wird die Seele fröhlich" (*Z* I 22 §2; KSA 4:100; "Through knowing the body purifies itself; experimenting with knowledge it elevates itself; to the one who knows, all drives become sacred; to the elevated, the soul becomes joyful"). Thus *der Erkennende* possesses a wisdom that the lonely Faust in his study at the beginning of the drama does not. As in Goethe's *Faust,* "erkennen" (or intellectual understanding) must be joined to "begreifen" (sensory understanding) in order to yield a higher (aesthetic) order of knowledge. This knowledge — of the aesthetic — must be acquired by Faust in the course of the play, and this same process, although more elusively, is undergone by Zarathustra.[18]

Faust features three central female figures: Gretchen, the earthly woman; Helena, the classical personification of Beauty; and the Eternal Feminine, embodied finally as the *Mater Gloriosa,* the symbol of Faust's aesthetic destiny. Correspondingly, three female personifications inhabit Nietzsche's text: Life, in "Das Tanzlied" ("The Dancing Song"; *Z* II 10; KSA 4:139–41) and "Das andere Tanzlied" ("The Other Dancing Song"), where she dances to the beat of Zarathustra's whip (*Z* III 15; KSA 4:282–86); Wisdom, who is wild in "Das Kind mit dem Spiegel" (*Z* II 1; KSA 4:107) and described affectionately as "diese tolle alte Närrin" ("this mad old foolish woman") in "Das andere Tanzlied" (*Z* III 15 §2; KSA 4:284); and Eternity, of whom he wrote, "Nie noch fand ich das Weib, von dem ich Kinder mochte, es sei denn dieses Weib, das ich liebe: denn ich liebe dich, oh Ewigkeit!" (*Z* III 16 §l; KSA 4:287; "Never yet have I found the woman from whom I wanted children, apart from this woman, whom I love: for I love you, O Eternity!"). In Goethe's dramatic poem, Faust makes his visit to the Mothers, "Gestaltung, Umgestaltung, / Des ewigen Sinnes ewige Unterhaltung" ("Formation, Transformation, / The eternal mind's eternal Recreation"; 6287–88); in *Die Geburt der Tragödie,* the personified figure of tragedy listens to the song of the Mothers of Being, "Wahn, Wille, Wehe" ("Delusion, Will, Woe"; *GT* §20; KSA 1:132); whilst Zarathustra, in his dream of the "Berg-Burg des Todes" ("the Mountain-Castle of Death"), is accompanied by three dismal female figures: "Helle der Mitternacht war immer um mich, Einsamkeit kauerte neben ihr; und, zudritt, röchelnde Todesstille, die schlimmste meiner Freundinnen" (*Z* II 19; KSA 4:173; "Brightness of Midnight was always around me, Solitude crouched next to her; and, as the third, the rasping Silence of Death, the worst of my three female friends"). Faust's words rejecting otherworldly projections and accepting the limits of knowledge, realizing that "Dem Tüchtigen ist diese Welt nicht stumm" (11446, compare 11443), recall Zarathustra's injunction: "*bleibt der Erde treu* und glaubt Denen nicht, welche euch von überirdischen Hoffnungen reden!" (*Z* Vorrede §3; KSA 4:15; "*remain true to the earth,* and do not believe those who speak of supercelestial hopes!"). And in act 1 of Part Two, Faust praises the earth for the encouragement it gives him "zum höchsten Dasein immerfort zu streben" (4685; "to strive on still towards supreme existence"). Finally, in the *Bergschluchten* ("Mountain Gorges") scene in act 5 of Part Two, we read: "Löwen, sie schleichen stumm- / Freundlich um uns herum" (11850–51; "Lions, they prowl around, / Gentle, without a sound"), corresponding to the traditional Christian iconography of the amiable lion as symbolizing sin transfigured. In the final chapter of *Zarathustra,* the laughing lion appears (*Z* IV 20; KSA 4:406).[19] Indeed, the final scene of *Zarathustra* is, like the aesthetic moment, timeless: "Diess Alles dauerte eine lange Zeit, oder eine kurze Zeit: denn, recht gesprochen, giebt es für dergleichen Dinge auf Erden *keine* Zeit —" (*Z* IV 20; KSA 4:407; "All this lasted a long time, or a short time: for, properly speaking, for such things there is on earth *no time*"). More important still, at the heart of Nietzsche's text, the import of the Faustian wager is reenacted.

The aesthetic transformation of the moment in *Faust* takes the form of the doctrine of the eternal recurrence in *Zarathustra*. In *Die Geburt der Tragödie,* Nietzsche spoke of the Dionysian drive of the artist who "[verschlingt] diese ganze Welt der Erscheinungen" ("devours this entire world of phenomena") to let us sense "eine höchste künstlerische Urfreude" (*GT* §22; KSA 1:141; "the highest artistic primordial joy"), reformulating Schiller's doctrine of "das eigentliche Kunstgeheimnis des Meisters" ("the real secret of the master in any art"), namely "*dass er den Stoff durch die Form vertilgt*" (Letter 22, §5; "*that he can make his form consume his material*"). Consonant with this view Zarathustra teaches: "Und wer ein Schöpfer sein muss im Guten und Bösen: wahrlich, der muss ein Vernichter erst sein und Werthe zerbrechen" (*Z* II 12; KSA 4:149; "And whoever must be a creator in good and evil: truly, must first be a destroyer and break apart values").[20] And, seen in Nietzsche's mirror, in a famous passage from the *Nachlass,* the world is envisaged as "meine *dionysische* Welt des Ewig-sich-selber-Schaffens, des Ewig-sich-selber-Zerstörens" (*WM* §1067/38[12]; KSA 11:611; "my *Dionysian* world of the eternally self-creating, the eternally self-destroying").

Thus the theme of *Verwandlung* or *Veredelung* — of Goethean "Stirb und werde!" ("Die and become!")[21] — runs throughout *Also sprach Zarathustra,* and deserves to be given greater prominence than it has received from critics and commentators. Indeed, the entire work could be described as a series of successive transformations, culminating in that transformation wrought by the acceptance of the eternal recurrence in the "Nachtwandler-Lied" ("Song of the Nocturnal Wanderer"). In the Prologue, Zarathustra is described by the Old Man in the Forest as transformed (*Z* Vorrede §2; KSA 4:12) and, in "Das Kind mit dem Spiegel," Zarathustra asks his animals: "Bin ich nicht verwandelt!" ("Am I not transformed?"; *Z* II 1; KSA 4:106). When Zarathustra first addresses the sun on the mountain, his heart is transformed (*Z* Vorrede §1; KSA 4:11); and at the end, in front of his cave, when he hears the roar of the lion, we read that "sein Herz verwandelte sich" (*Z* IV 20; KSA 4:406; "his heart was transformed"). In Zarathustra's central parable, the shepherd bites off the head of the snake and is transformed, becoming "ein Verwandelter, ein Umleuchteter, welcher *lachte*!" ("a transformed being, a radiant being, who *laughed!*"; *Z* III 2 §2; KSA 4:202). Moreover, a progressive sense of change in Zarathustra himself can be felt throughout the plot as it unfolds across the text. In "Von grossen Ereignissen" ("On Great Events"), Zarathustra's ghostly shadow cries: "'Es ist Zeit! Es ist die höchste Zeit!'" (*Z* II 18; KSA 4:171; "'It is time! It is high time!'"). In "Die stillste Stunde" ("The Stillest Hour"), the silent voice asks Zarathustra: "'*Du weisst es, Zarathustra?*—" (*Z* II 22; KSA 4:187; "'*Do you know it, Zarathustra?*'"), referring to the secret which, in "Das andere Tanzlied," Life is astonished to discover Zarathustra knows: "'Du *weisst* Das, oh Zarathustra? Das weiss Niemand. — —'" (*Z* III 15 §2; KSA 4:285 "'You *know* that, O Zarathustra? Nobody knows that'"). This secret is the doctrine of the eternal recurrence with its transformative effects, to which Zarathustra must give voice: "'Sprich dein Wort und zerbrich!'—" (*Z* II 22; KSA 4:188; "'Speak your word, and break into pieces!'").

Zarathustra's dream-like encounter in "Die stillste Stunde" begins with unmistakably Faustian motifs also used in *Die fröhliche Wissenschaft* (*The Gay Science; FW* §382; KSA 3:637): "Der Traum begann. / Der Zeiger rückte, die Uhr meines Lebens holte Athem" (*Z* II 22; KGW 4:187; "The dream began. / The hand moved forward, the clock of my life drew its breath"). Another set of images from the section "Vom grössten Schwergewicht" ("On the Greatest Weight"; *FW* §341; KSA 3:570) recurs in the nightmarish sequence in the second part of "Vom Gesicht und Räthsel" ("On the Vision and the Riddle"). In this episode Zarathustra, accompanied by the half-mole, half-dwarf figure of the *Geist der Schwere,* arrives at the great gate "Moment." At this gate, the two eternities of Past and Future intersect:

> "Siehe diesen Torweg! Zwerg! sprach ich weiter: der hat zwei Gesichter. Zwei Wege kommen hier zusammen: die gieng noch Niemand zu Ende.
>
> Diese lange Gasse zurück: die währt eine Ewigkeit. Und jene lange Gasse hinaus — das ist eine andre Ewigkeit.
>
> Sie widersprechen sich, diese Wege; sie stossen sich gerade vor den Kopf: — und hier, an diesem Thorwege, ist es, wo sie zusammen kommen. Der Name des Thorwegs steht oben geschrieben: "Augenblick."
>
> (*Z* III 2 §2; KSA 4:199–200)

> ["Behold this gateway! Dwarf!" I continued. "It has two faces. Two paths come together here: no one has ever reached their end.
>
> This long lane behind: it goes on for eternity. And this long lane in front — that is another eternity.

THE AESTHETIC GOSPEL OF NIETZSCHE'S ZARATHUSTRA ♦ 107

They oppose each other, these paths; they confront each other face to face; and it is here, at this gateway, that they come together. The name of the gateway is written above: "Moment."]

Just as in the section from *Die fröhliche Wissenschaft* the demon whispers in one's ear, in one's loneliest loneliness, that every moment of one's life — "und ebenso diese Spinne und dieses Mondlicht zwischen den Bäumen, und ebenso dieser Augenblick und ich selber" ("and even this spider and this moonlight between the trees, and even this moment and I myself") — will recur, so Zarathustra, the Loneliest Man, tells the Spirit of Heaviness:

> "Und diese langsame Spinne, die im Mondscheine kriecht, und dieser Mondschein selber, und ich und du im Thorwege, zusammen flüsternd, von ewigen Dingen flüsternd — müssen wir nicht Alle schon dagewesen sein?
>
> — und wiederkommen und in jener anderen Gasse laufen, hinaus, vor uns, in dieser langen schaurigen Gasse — müssen wir nicht ewig wiederkommen? —"
>
> (*Z* III 2 §2; KSA 4:200)

> ["And this slow spider crawling in the moonlight, and this moonlight itself, and I and you in the gateway, whispering together, whispering together of eternal things — must we not all have been here before?
>
> — and return and walk in that other lane, out there, before us, in this long, dreadful lane — must we not recur eternally?"]

At this point, Zarathustra says he was afraid of his own "Gedanken and Hintergedanken" ("thoughts and secret intentions"), for he is facing what he earlier described as the danger of the Loneliest One: "Die *Liebe* ist die Gefahr des Einsamsten, die Liebe zu Allem, *wenn es nur lebt!*" (*Z* III 1; KSA 4:196; "Love is the danger of the loneliest one: love of everything *as long as it is alive!*"). For the "moment" has not yet been aesthetically transformed.

The danger is that loving all things entails wanting all things in eternity — either as eternal Being or as recurring (Becoming) eternally.[22] This love of life, "wo Leben sich des Lebens freut" ("where life enjoys life"), was envisaged by Goethe in his poem entitled "Vermächtnis" ("Legacy," 1829) in the following terms: "Dann ist Vergangenheit beständig, / Das Künftige voraus lebendig, / Der Augenblick ist Ewigkeit" ("Then the past is stable, / The future alive in anticipation: / The moment is eternity").[23] In other words, the significance of the Eternal Recurrence does not lie in what form it takes — or might take. Rather, it lies in the response that it evokes in the individual who thinks this thought. To sustain the moment by loving its Beauty is the prerogative of the aesthetic: "Verweile doch! du bist so schön!" (*Faust I*, 1700; "Beautiful moment, do not pass away!"; compare *Faust II*,

11582). Seen in this light, the core of Zarathustra's message is clearly revealed as the injunction to bestow eternity on the moment through its aesthetic transformation.

This interpretation is supported in the key chapter of part 2 entitled
"Von der Erlösung" ("On Redemption") which, read carefully, may be said
to contain the aesthetic gospel of Zarathustra.[24] Earlier, in "Das Grablied"
("The Grave Song"), Zarathustra had emphasized the primacy of the Will:
"Ja, ein Unverwundbares, Unbegrabbares ist an mir, ein Felsensprengendes:
das heisst *mein Wille*. Schweigsam schreitet es und unverändert durch die
Jahre" (Z II 11/KSA 4:145; "Yes, something invulnerable, unburiable is
within me, something that explodes rocks: it is called *my will*. Silent and un-
changing it strides through the years").[25] And in "Auf den glückseligen
Inseln" ("On the Blissful Islands"), Zarathustra had related the Will to freedom: "Wollen befreit: das ist die wahre Lehre von Wille und Freiheit — so
lehrt sie euch Zarathustra" (Z II 2; KSA 4:111; "To will liberates: that is the
true doctrine of will and freedom — thus does Zarathustra teach you").[26] In
"Von der Erlösung," however, Zarathustra explains that the Will itself is a
prisoner:

> Wille — so heisst der Befreier und Freudebringer: also lehrte ich
> euch, meine Freunde! Und nun lernt diess hinzu: der Wille selber ist
> noch ein Gefangener.
> Wollen befreit: aber wie heisst Das, was auch den Befreier noch in
> Ketten schlägt?
>
> (*Z* II 20; KSA 4:179)

> [Will — that is what the liberator and bringer of joy is called: thus
> did I teach you, my friends! But now learn this as well: the will itself is
> still a prisoner.
> To will liberates: but what is it that puts even the liberator in fet-
> ters?]

On Zarathustra's account, what enslaves the Will is the past, the fact that
time flows in one direction only: "Dass die Zeit nicht zurückläuft, das ist
sein Ingrimm; 'Das, was war' — so heisst der Stein, den er nicht wälzen
kann" (*Z* II 20; KSA 4:180; "That time does not run backwards, that is the
cause of its [the Will's] anger: 'That which was' — that is what the stone it
cannot roll is called").[27] As a result, the reaction of the Will to the onward
flow of time is revenge: "Diess, ja diess allein ist *Rache* selber: des Willens
Widerwille gegen die Zeit und ihr 'Es war'" (KSA 4:180; "This, indeed this
alone, is *revenge* itself: the will's ill will towards time and its 'it was'").[28] Once
the moment has passed and is past, it can no longer be said to be willed. It
can, however, give rise to regret. In the culture of *ressentiment* that
Nietzsche, echoing Goethe's Mephistopheles (*Faust I,* 1339–40), diagnoses

as our own, this is all too often the case: "Und nun wälzte sich Wolke auf Wolke über den Geist: bis endlich der Wahnsinn predigte: 'Alles vergeht, darum ist Alles werth zu vergehn!'" (KSA 4:180; "And now cloud upon cloud rolled upon the spirit: until finally madness preached: 'Everything passes, therefore everything deserves to pass away'"). According to Zarathustra, this *ressentiment* is also the basis of morality: "'Sittlich sind die Dinge geordnet nach Recht und Strafe. Oh wo ist die Erlösung vom Fluss der Dinge und der Strafe 'Dasein'? Also predigte der Wahnsinn" (KSA 4: 181; "Things are ordered morally according to law and punishment. Oh, where is the redemption from the flux of things and from the punishment 'Being'?"). As a result, Zarathustra judges the Spirit of Revenge to be the central achievement of humanity so far: "*Der Geist der Rache:* meine Freunde, das war bisher der Menschen bestes Nachdenken; und wo Leid war, da sollte immer Strafe sein" (KSA 4:180; "*The spirit of revenge:* my friends, that was so far humankind's best subject of reflection; and where there was suffering, there should always be punishment").

In "Von den Taranteln" ("On the Tarantulas"), Zarathustra had described humanity's redemption from revenge as the bridge to his highest hope: "Denn *dass der Mensch erlöst werde von der Rache:* das ist mir die Brücke zur höchsten Hoffnung und ein Regenbogen nach langen Unwettern" (*Z* II 7; KSA 4:128; "For *that humankind be delivered from revenge:* that is for me the bridge to the highest hope and a rainbow after protracted storms").[29] For Goethe, hope was quite explicitly linked with aesthetic experience and, following on the evocation of the aesthetic in the term *scheinfrei* in the penultimate line of the penultimate stanza, he brought the poem "Urworte. Orphisch" ("Primal Words. Orphic"; 1820) to a close with the allegorical figure of Hope.[30] For Zarathustra, however, there remain the questions: how can humanity be redeemed from revenge? and how can the Will be freed from the past? For Zarathustra, the answer lies in the creativity of the Will; and, more precisely, in its ability to will, not so much the past, but that the past recur:

> Weg führte ich euch von diesen Fabelliedern, als ich euch lehrte: "der Wille ist ein Schaffender."
>
> Alles "Es war" ist ein Bruchstück, ein Räthsel, ein grauser Zufall — bis der schaffende Wille dazu sagt: "aber so wollte ich es!"
>
> — Bis der schaffende Wille dazu sagt: "Aber so will ich es! So werde ich's wollen!"
>
> [. . .]
>
> Die Vergangnen zu erlösen und alles "Es war" umzuschaffen in ein "So wollte ich es!" — das hiesse mir erst Erlösung!
>
> (*Z* II 20; KSA 4:181 and 179)

[I led you away from these fantasy-songs when I taught you: "the will is a creator."

All "it was" is a fragment, a riddle, a dreadful accident — until the creative will says to it, "But thus I willed it."

Until the creative will says to it, "But thus I will it! Thus I shall will it!"

[. . .]

To redeem those of the past and to recreate every "it was" into a "thus I willed it!" — that alone is what I would call redemption!]

The function of the thought of the Eternal Recurrence is now clear. This thought, the most terrible thought,[31] is also the thought that enables human beings to say — as Zarathustra tells the Spirit of Heaviness, and as the Ugliest Man tells Zarathustra: "'War *das* das Leben? Wohlan! Noch Ein Mal!'" (*Z* III 2 §1 and *Z* IV 19 §1/KSA 4: 199, 396; "'Was *that* life? Well then! One more time!'"). Thus Nietzsche replaces the medieval topos of *momento mori* with the injunction from *Wilhelm Meisters Lehrjahre*, "Gedenke zu leben" ("Remember to live").[32] In other words, the significance of the doctrine of the Eternal Recurrence lies not in its value as a cosmological hypothesis but in its effect as a psychological attitude conducive to the aesthetic experience.

In much the same way as the aesthetic does, the Eternal Recurrence bestows a necessity upon chance — and mere, capricious, desire![33] Goethe and Schiller argued that, seen aesthetically, relations "*appear* free" — in other words, as fortuitous or a matter of chance — while being, in fact, intentioned and willed.[34] And, in so appearing, these relations reveal a pattern of things — a "necessity" — unadulterated by human purpose.[35] For Zarathustra, the world is a gambling table at which the gods play (*Z* III 4, *Z* III 16 §3, *Z* IV 13 §14; KSA 4:210, 288, 363–64). Through the aesthetic, which for humanity confers eternity upon the moment just as, taken literally, the Eternal Recurrence would, Rough Approximation (a pun on the expression *von ohngefähr* [= "approximate," "accidental"; "unintended"]) may return to the world, not as a curse, but as a blessing; and all things, says Zarathustra, are liberated from their slavery to purpose. For, like the aesthetic moment, the Eternal Recurrence involves, in Kantian terms, a *Zweckmäßigkeit ohne Zweck*, a "purposiveness without purpose."[36]

Furthermore, the Eternal Recurrence is a necessary implication of aesthetic experience. Because life is beautiful, we want it again, or, as Zarathustra sings in his roundelay: "Alle Lust will Ewigkeit" ("All pleasure wants eternity"). Likewise, in *Faust II*, Lynceus the Watchman sings of "die ewige Zier" ("the eternal beauty"): "Es sei, wie es wolle, / Es war doch so schön!" (11297, 11302–3; "Let it be as it may, / It had beauty for me!"). Before the sun rises in part 3, Zarathustra pronounces his own blessing upon the world seen from this serene (*heiter*) point of view:

Wahrlich, ein Segnen ist es und kein Lästern, wenn ich lehre: "über allen Dingen steht der Himmel Zufall, der Himmel Unschuld, der Himmel Ohngefähr, der Himmel Übermuth."

"Von Ohngefähr" — das ist der älteste Adel der Welt, den gab ich allen Dingen zurück, ich erlöste sie von der Knechtschaft unter dem Zwecke.

Diese Freiheit und Himmels-Heiterkeit stellte ich gleich azurner Glocke über alle Dinge, als ich lehrte, dass über ihnen und durch sie kein "ewiger Wille" — will.

(Z III 4; KSA 4:209)

[Truly, it is a blessing and not a blasphemy when I teach: "Above all things stands the heaven of Chance, the heaven of Innocence, the heaven of Inexact Approximation, the heaven of High-spiritedness."

"Rough Approximation" — that is the most ancient nobility of the world, which I have given back to all things, I redeemed them from their slavery to Purpose.

This freedom and this heavenly cheerfulness I set like an azure bell over all things, when I taught that over them and through them no "eternal will" — wills.]

This blessing reformulates the thought expressed in the second stanza of Goethe's "Urworte. Orphisch," where "Chance" is not *just* chance (*Zufall*), but TYXHE ("inexactitude," "imprecision"), too: "Es ist ein Tand und wird so durchgetandelt" ("Life is a play-thing, and we play it through"). What, in other words, Nietzsche is trying here to articulate is the *casualness* of real art.[37] Within the economy of the dramatic plot, moreover, that Zarathustra himself belongs to the "causes" of the Eternal Recurrence is something he learns to "overcome."[38] As the convalescent, recovering from Faustian disgust and despair, he realizes that his presence in the world is a necessity for its aesthetic transformation:

Aber der Knoten von Ursachen kehrt wieder, in den ich verschlungen bin, — der wird mich wieder schaffen! Ich selber gehöre zu den Ursachen der ewigen Wiederkunft.

Ich komme wieder, mit dieser Sonne, mit dieser Erde, mit diesem Adler, mit dieser Schlange — *nicht* zu einem neuen Leben oder besseren Leben oder ähnlichen Leben:

— ich komme ewig wieder zu diesem gleichen und selbigen Leben, im Grössten und auch im Kleinsten, dass ich wieder aller Dinge ewige Wiederkunft lehre, —

— dass ich wieder das Wort spreche vom grossen Erden- und Menschen-Mittage, dass ich wieder den Menschen den Übermenschen künde.

(Z III 13 §2; KSA 4:276)

(But the knot of causes, in which I am entangled, recurs — it will create me again! I myself belong to the causes of the eternal recurrence.

I shall come again, with this sun, with this earth, with this eagle, with this snake — *not* to a new life or a better life or a similar life:

— I come back eternally to this same, selfsame life, in the greatest things and the smallest, to teach again the eternal recurrence of all things, —

— to speak again the word of the great noon of the earth and of humankind, to teach humankind again the Superman.

Like the central persona in Goethe's poem "Der Bräutigam" ("The Bridegroom," 1828), Zarathustra says: "Wie es auch sei, das Leben, es ist gut" ("Life's good, whatever it may entail").[39] And Faust's very words to the transitory moment — "Verweile doch, du bist so schön!" — are echoed in Zarathustra's great speech in "Das Nachtwandler-Lied." Here, for example, images from "Das grösste Schwergewicht" ("diese Spinne und dieses Mondlicht zwischen den Bäumen" ["this spider and this moonlight between the trees"]) and "Vom Gesicht und Räthsel" ("diese langsame Spinne, die im Mondscheine kriecht, und dieser Mondschein selber [. . .] Da, plötzlich, hörte ich einen Hund nahe *heulen*" ["this slow spider, crawling in the moonlight, and this moonlight itself . . . then, suddenly, I heard a dog nearby *howl*"]) are brought together: "Ach! Ach! Der Hund heult, der Mond scheint [. . .] Nun starb ich schon. Es ist dahin. Spinne, was spinnst du um mich?" (*Z* IV 19 §4; KSA 4:398; "Alas! Alas! The dog howls, the moon shines . . . Now I have died. It is over. Spider, why do you spin around me?"). In particular, the following section of Zarathustra's song, a dithyrambic address to the Higher Men, recapitulates many of the themes and motifs of the book and especially the Faustian ambivalent yearning for the moment to attain the quality of eternity:

Ihr höheren Menschen, was dünket euch? Bin ich ein Wahrsager? Ein Träumender? Trunkener? Ein Traumdeuter? Eine Mitternachts-Glocke?

Ein Tropfen Thau's? Ein Dunst und Duft der Ewigkeit? Hört ihr's nicht? Riecht ihr's nicht? Eben ward meine Welt vollkommen, Mitternacht ist auch Mittag, —

Schmerz ist auch eine Lust, Fluch ist auch ein Segen, Nacht ist auch eine Sonne, — geht davon oder ihr lernt: ein Weiser ist auch ein Narr.

Sagtet ihr jemals Ja zu einer Lust? Oh, meine Freunde, so sagtet ihr Ja auch zu *allem* Wehe. Alle Dinge sind verkettet, verfädelt, verliebt, —

— wolltet ihr jemals Ein Mal Zwei Mal, spracht ihr jemals "du gefällst mir, Glück! Husch! Augenblick!" so wolltet ihr *Alles* zurück!

— Alles von neuem, Alles ewig, Alles verkettet, verfädelt, verliebt, oh so *liebtet* ihr die Welt, —
— ihr Ewigen, liebt sie ewig und allezeit: und auch zum Weh sprecht ihr: vergeh, aber komm zurück! *Denn alle Lust will — Ewigkeit!*
(*Z* IV 19 §10; KSA 4:402)

[You Higher Men, what do you think? Am I a prophet? A dreamer? A drunkard? An interpreter of dreams? A midnight bell?

A drop of dew? A haze and fragrance of eternity? Do you not hear it? Do you not smell it? My world has just become perfect, midnight is also midday, —

Pain is also pleasure, a curse is also a blessing, night is also a sun, — go away, or you will learn: a wise man is also a fool.

Have you ever said Yes to a single joy? O my friends, then you said Yes as well to *all* woe. All things are chained, entwined, in love:

— if you ever wanted one time two times, if you ever said "You please me, happiness! instant! moment!" then you wanted *everything* back!

— everything new, everything eternal, everything chained, entwied, in love, O so you *loved* the world, —

— you eternal ones, love it eternally and evermore: and then to woe say too: go, but return! *For all pleasure wants — eternity.*][40]

Through the aesthetic, the moment has, then, become eternity. As one of Nietzsche's fragments from the *Nachlass* urges us: "Drücken wir das Abbild der Ewigkeit auf *unser* Leben!" (11[159]; KSA 9:503; "Let us imprint the image of eternity on *our* life!"). The image of the Great Noonday, when the reception of the doctrine of the Eternal Recurrence takes place, runs throughout the text as one of its main motifs.[41] Yet in the end it does not matter whether it is midday or midnight for, in the timeless unity of the aesthetic moment, they are the one and the same.[42] The problem of the "great noontide" of part 1 is answered by the "deep midnight" of Zarathustra's "Rundgesang," whose name is *Noch ein Mal* (One More Time) and whose meaning is "in alle Ewigkeit" (for all eternity; *Z* III 15 §3 and *Z* IV 19 §12; KSA 4:285–86 and 404).[43] This passage also highlights another of the major themes of Nietzsche's work: love.

At the end of "Die Metamorphose der Pflanzen" ("The Metamorphosis of Plants," 1798), Goethe wrote of love as a means to, and a product of, aesthetic experience: "Die heilige Liebe / Strebt zu der höchsten Frucht gleicher Gesinnungen auf, / Gleicher Ansicht der Dinge, damit in harmonischem Anschaun / Sich verbinde das Paar, finde die höhere Welt" ("Because holy love / Strives for the consummate fruit, marriage of minds, in the end, / One perception of things, that together, concerted in seeing, / Both to the higher world, truly conjoined, find their way").[44] Love, in a word, is both cause and effect of finding the world lovely. The theme of such creative love runs throughout *Also sprach Zarathustra*. In one of his first discourses, Zarathustra declared: "Es ist immer etwas Wahnsinn in der Liebe. Es ist aber immer auch etwas Vernunft im Wahnsinn" (*Z* I 7; KSA 4:49; "There is always some madness in love. But there is also always some reason in madness"). Later, in "Vom Wege des Schaffenden" ("On the Way of the Creative One"), Zarathustra told his disciples: "Schaffen will der Liebende, weil er verachtet! Was weiss Der von Liebe, der nicht gerade verachten musste, was er liebte!" (*Z* I 17; KSA 4:82; "The lover wants to create, because he despises! What does someone know of love who did not have to despise precisely what he loved!"); im "Vom Biss der Natter" ("On the Bite of the Adder"), Zarathustra asked: "Sagt, wo findet sich die Gerechtigkeit, welche Liebe mit sehenden Augen ist?" (*Z* I 19/KSA 4:88; "Tell me, where is the justice that is love with seeing eyes?"); in "Von den Mitleidigen" ("On the Pitying"), Zarathustra insisted: "Also redet alle grosse Liebe: die überwindet auch noch Vergebung und Mitleiden. [. . .] alle grosse Liebe ist noch über all ihrem Mitleiden: denn sie will das Geliebte noch — schaffen!" (*Z* II 3; KSA 4:115–16; "Thus speaks all great love: it overcomes even forgiveness and pity . . . all great love is even above all its pity: for it still wants to create the beloved!"); in "Vom Vorübergehen" ("On Passing By"), Zarathustra tells the Frothing Fool: "Aus der Liebe allein soll mir mein Verachten und mein warnender Vogel auffliegen: aber nicht aus dem Sumpfe! —" (*Z* III 7; KSA 4:224; "From love alone shall my contempt and my warning bird fly up: but not from the swamp!"); and in "Ausser Dienst" ("Retired from Service"), the Retired Pope tells Zarathustra that "der Liebende liebt jenseits von Lohn und Vergeltung" (*Z* IV 6; KSA 4:324; "the lover loves beyond reward and retribution"), an idea found elsewhere in Nietzsche's writings: "Was aus Liebe gethan wird, geschieht immer jenseits von Gut und Böse" (*JGB* §153; KSA 5:99; "Whatever is done out of love always happens beyond good and evil").[45] Finally, Zarathustra tells the Higher Men: "Wo eure ganze Liebe ist, bei eurem Kinde, da ist auch eure ganze Tugend!" (*Z* IV 13 §11; KSA 4:362; "Where your whole love is, with your child, there is also your whole virtue!"); and that: "Alle grosse Liebe *will* nicht Liebe: — die will mehr" (*Z* IV 13 §16; KSA 4:365; "All great love does not *want* love: — it wants more").

Furthermore, two of Zarathustra's speeches, playing on the phrase *dichten und trachten* (creating and striving), support the interpretation that the aesthetic transformation of the moment into what is lovely constitutes the heart of Zarathustra's message. In "Von der Erlösung" the future that Zarathustra beholds is perceived in terms of aesthetic vision (*Schau*):

Ich wandle unter Menschen als den Bruchstücken der Zukunft: jener Zukunft, die ich schaue.

Und das ist all mein Dichten und Trachten, dass ich in Eins dichte und zusammentrage, was Bruchstück ist und Räthsel und grauser Zufall.

Und wie ertrüge ich es, Mensch zu sein, wenn der Mensch nicht auch Dichter und Räthselrather und der Erlöser des Zufalls wäre!

Die Vergangnen zu erlösen und alles "Es war" umzuschaffen in ein "So wollte ich es!" — das hiesse mir erst Erlösung!

(*Z* II 20; KSA 4:179)

[I walk among humans as among the fragments of the future: that future, which I can see.

And this is all my creating and striving, that I create and bring together into one what is fragment and riddle and dreadful accident.

And how could I bear to be human if the human being were not also a poet and guesser of riddles and redeemer of chance?

To redeem those of the past and to recreate every "it was" into a "thus I willed it!" — that alone is what I would call redemption!]

When, in "Von alten und neuen Tafeln," Zarathustra looks back on and echoes this speech, he reflects as follows:

Ich lehrte sie all *mein* Dichten und Trachten: in Eins zu dichten und zusammen zu tragen, was Bruchstück ist am Menschen und Räthsel und grauser Zufall, —

— als Dichter, Räthselrather und Erlöser des Zufalls lehrte ich sie an der Zukunft schaffen, und Alles, das *war* —, schaffend zu erlösen.

Das Vergangne am Menschen zu erlösen und alles "Es war" umzuschaffen, bis der Wille spricht: "Aber so wollte ich es! So werde ich's wollen —"

— Diess hiess ich ihnen Erlösung, Diess allein lehrte ich sie Erlösung heissen. — —

(*Z* III 12 §3; KSA 4:248–49)

[I taught them all *my* creating and striving, to create and bring together into one what in the human being is fragment and riddle and dreadful accident, —

— as poet, guesser of riddles, and redeemer of chance, I taught them to create the future, and, by creating, redeem everything that *was*.

To redeem what is past in the human being and to recreate every "it was" until the will says, "Thus I willed it! Thus I shall will it —"

— This I called redemption, this alone I taught them to call redemption.]

At the beginning of part 4, this future is also described by Zarathustra in terms of "unser grosser Hazar, das ist unser grosses fernes Menschen-Reich, das Zarathustra-Reich von tausend Jahren" (*Z* IV 1; KSA 4:298; "our great *hazar*, our great distant human kingdom, the Zarathustra kingdom of a thousand years"). This Zarathustra *Reich* of 1000 years corresponds to the Third *Reich* of Schiller's *Aesthetic Letters*. For, in his final letter, Schiller envisioned the aesthetic impulse as being at work, building "ein drittes, fröhliches Reich des Spiels und des Scheins" ("a third, joyous kingdom of play and of semblance"; Letter 27, §8):

> Kein Vorzug, keine Alleinherrschaft wird geduldet, soweit der Geschmack regiert und das Reich des schönen Scheins sich verbreitet. Dieses Reich erstreckt sich aufwärts, bis wo die Vernunft mit unbedingter Notwendigkeit herrscht und alle Materie aufhört; es erstreckt sich niederwärts, bis wo der Naturtrieb mit blinder Nötigung waltet und die Form noch nicht anfängt. (Letter 27, §11)

> [No privilege, no autocracy of any kind, is tolerated where taste rules, and the realm of aesthetic semblance extends its sway. This realm stretches upwards to the point where reason governs with unconditioned necessity, and all that is mere matter ceases to be. It stretches downwards to the point where natural impulse reigns with blind compulsion, and form has not yet begun to appear.]

The two passages from *Zarathustra* quoted above emphasize the importance of the theme of creativity — by means of Beauty — within this work. In "Auf den glückseligen Inseln," Zarathustra declares: "Schaffen — das ist die grosse Erlösung vom Leiden, und des Lebens Leichtwerden. Aber dass der Schaffende sei, dazu selber thut Leid noth und viel Verwandelung" (*Z* II 2; KSA 4:110; "Creation — that is the great redemption from suffering, and makes life become light. But that the creator may be, that itself requires suffering and much transformation"). In his *Nachlass* notes, Nietzsche saw in Zarathustra "die große Synthesis des Schaffenden, Liebenden, Vernichtenden" ("the great synthesis of the creative, the loving, the destroying"; 31[3]; KSA 11:360).[46] Creativity is the dynamic of aesthetic transformation, replacing the "heaviness" of life as a burden with the incredible "lightness" of (aesthetic) being. Indeed, the central tenet of the "Evangelium des Schönen" is defined by Goethe in *Dichtung und Wahrheit* (part 3, bk. 13) in precisely these terms:

> Die wahre Poesie kündet sich dadurch an, daß sie, als ein weltliches Evangelium, durch innere Heiterkeit, durch äußeres Behagen, uns von den irdischen Lasten zu befreien weiß, die auf uns drücken. (HA 9:580)

[True poetry makes itself known by the fact that it, as a secular gospel, can free us from our oppressive earthly burdens by its inner serenity and external comfort.][47]

Likewise, the "activity" at the heart of *Zarathustra* is the creation of the aesthetic. Whereas, in *Die Geburt der Tragödie*, Nietzsche had looked forward to a new aesthetic discourse, the music of the future, *Zarathustra* provides this new kind of art through its sophisticated stylistic resourcefulness, reminiscent of the *schöner Vortrag* recommended and practiced by Schiller and Goethe.[48] In his "Versuch einer Selbstkritik" ("Attempt at a Self-Criticism"), Nietzsche wrote: "Sie hätte *singen* sollen, diese 'neue Seele' — und nicht reden!" (*GT* Versuch §3; KSA 1:15; "It should have *sung*, this 'new soul' — and not spoken!"). The song of the new soul is — *Also sprach Zarathustra* itself.

Now, *Zarathustra* constitutes this song in at least seven important respects. First, Nietzsche himself pointed to the dithyrambic nature of the work. Second, the issues of musical harmony and dissonance that Nietzsche raised in *Die Geburt der Tragödie* can also be applied to *Zarathustra*. Third, throughout the work, Zarathustra responds to an imperative to express himself. Fourth, and concomitantly, the importance of listening correctly is emphasized. Fifth, Zarathustra, as a poet, explains his complex attitude to poetry. Sixth, Zarathustra, as a rhetorician, draws on ancient stylistic resources of communication. And seventh, Zarathustra is explicit about his use of metaphor or *Gleichnis*. Let us examine these seven aspects in more detail.

In *Ecce Homo*, Nietzsche drew attention to the connection between the message of *Zarathustra* and its style. There he placed the solution of the psychological problem addressed in the work under the sign of Dionysus:

Das psychologische Problem im Typus des Zarathustra ist, [. . .] wie der, welcher die härteste, die furchtbarste Einsicht in die Realität hat, welcher den "abgründlichsten Gedanken" gedacht hat, trotzdem darin keinen Einwand gegen das Dasein, selbst nicht gegen dessen ewige Wiederkunft findet, — vielmehr einen Grund noch hinzu, das ewige Ja zu allen Dingen *selbst zu sein* [. . .]. *Aber das ist der Begriff des Dionysos noch einmal.*

(*EH Z* §6; KSA 6:345)

[The psychological problem in the type of Zarathustra is . . . how someone who has the hardest, most terrible insight into reality, who has thought the "most abysmal idea," nevertheless does not consider it an objection to existence, not even to its eternal recurrence — but rather one reason more *for being himself* the eternal Yes to all things . . . *But this is the concept of Dionysus once again.*]

Thus the most appropriate form of all for Zarathustra is the Dionysian dithyramb, whose significance Nietzsche had analyzed in detail in *Die Geburt der Tragödie:* "Welche Sprache wird ein solcher Geist reden, wenn er mit sich allein redet? Die Sprache des *Dithyrambus*" (*EH Z §7*; KSA 6:345; "What language will such a spirit speak when he speaks to himself? The language of the *dithyramb*"). Indeed, Nietzsche went so far as to describe himself as "der Erfinder des Dithyrambus" ("the inventor of the dithyramb"), citing the sections "Vor Sonnenaufgang" and "Das Nachtlied" ("The Night Song") as examples of his new dithyrambic artistry and thereby underlining the "musical" nature of his work; for, as he put it, "ein solches smaragdenes Glück, eine solche göttliche Zärtlichkeit hatte noch keine Zunge vor mir" (*EH Z §7*; KSA 6:345; "such an emerald happiness, such a divine tenderness did not have a tongue before me"). In *Die Geburt der Tragödie*, Nietzsche talks of Dionysian art as "dieses schwer zu fassende Urphänomen" (*GT §24*; KSA 1:152; "this primordial phenomenon that is difficult to grasp"), employing the term *Urphänomen* in the sense that Goethe, using *Abglanz* as in *Faust II* — "Am farbigen Abglanz haben wir das Leben" (4727; "In this colorful reflection we have our life"), applied it to Beauty: "Das Schöne ist ein Urphänomen, das zwar nie selber zur Erscheinung kommt, dessen Abglanz aber in tausend verschiedenen Äußerungen des schaffenden Geistes sichtbar wird und so mannigfaltig und so verschiedenartig ist als die Natur selber" ("Beauty is a primal phenomenon, which in itself never makes an appearance, but the reflection of which is visible in a thousand different utterances of the creative mind and is as manifold and various as Nature itself").[49]

In *Die Geburt der Tragödie*, Nietzsche had written that music in general and dissonance in particular could help us to understand in what sense the proposition that the world is justified as an aesthetic phenomenon might be understood: "Die Lust, die der tragische Mythus erzeugt, hat eine gleiche Heimat, wie die lustvolle Empfindung der Dissonanz in der Musik" (*GT §24*; KSA 1:152; "The pleasure that the tragic myth arouses has the same origin as the pleasurable sensation of dissonance in music").[50] One might say that *Zarathustra* contains many passages of dissonance — jarring and jagged prose, verbal slashes and stabs, veering images and alarming grotesqueries. Indeed, Zarathustra himself confesses to a certain crudity of style: "Mein Mundwerk — ist des Volks: zu grob und herzlich rede ich für die Seidenhasen. Und noch fremder klingt mein Wort allen Tinten-Fischen und Feder-Füchsen" (*Z III 11 §1*; KSA 4:241; "My tongue — is of the people: I speak too crudely and sincerely for those of fine sensibilities. And my speech sounds even stranger to all pettifogging pen-pushers"). Yet, by the same token, the text also contains moments of deep tranquility and beauty.[51] In an aphorism from *Die fröhliche Wissenschaft,* which offers a variant on Virgil's *sunt lacrimae rerum* (there are tears in things), Nietzsche defined "die

Musik der besten Zukunft" ("the music of the best future") in the following terms: "Der erste Musiker würde mir der sein, welcher nur die Traurigkeit des tiefsten Glückes kennte, und sonst keine Traurigkeit: einen solchen gab es bisher nicht" (*FW* §183; KSA 3:502; "The foremost musician for me would be the one who knew only the sadness of the most profound happiness, and no other sadness at all; but such a musician has never yet existed").[52] In the sense defined here, there can be little doubt that Zarathustra is a musician.

Throughout the work, we see Zarathustra's response to and struggle with the imperative to express himself. In "Das Kind mit dem Spiegel," Zarathustra says to his eagle and his snake: "Mund bin ich worden ganz und gar, und Brausen eines Bachs aus hohen Felsen: hinab will ich meine Rede stürzen in die Thäler. [. . .] Neue Wege gehe ich, eine neue Rede kommt mir" (*Z* II 1; KSA 4:106; "I have become entirely mouth, and the roar of a stream falling from high cliffs: I want to plunge my speech down into the valleys . . . I am traveling new paths, a new way of speaking is coming to me"). And in "Von der Selbst-Ueberwindung" ("On Self-Overcoming"), he emphasizes once again the necessity of expression: "Reden wir nur davon, ihr Weisesten, ob es gleich schlimm ist. Schweigen ist schlimmer; alle verschwiegenen Wahrheiten werden giftig" (*Z* II 12; KSA 4:149; "Let us speak of this, you wisest ones, even if it be bad. Silence is worse; all truths that are kept silent become poisonous"). At the same time, the importance of silence — likewise a central value for Goethe — is also recognized.[53] Again in conversation with his animals, Zarathustra admits: "Zu lange gehörte ich der Einsamkeit: so verlernte ich das Schweigen" (*Z* II 1; KSA 4:106; "For too long I belonged to solitude: thus I forgot how to be silent"), a phrase that is repeated with slight variation in "Die Heimkehr" ("The Home-Coming"; *Z* III 9; KSA 4:231). He tells his disciples in "Von der Erlösung": "'Es ist schwer, mit Menschen zu leben, weil Schweigen so schwer ist. Sonderlich für einen Geschwätzigen'" (*Z* II 20; KSA 4:182; "'It is difficult to live with people because silence is so difficult. Especially for someone talkative.'"). And in "Auf dem Oelberge" ("On the Mount of Olives"), Zarathustra attributes a special quality to his silence: "Meine liebste Bosheit und Kunst ist es, dass mein Schweigen lernte, sich nicht durch Schweigen zu verrathen. [. . .] Dass mir Niemand in meinen Grund und letzten Willen hinab sehe, — dazu erfand ich mir das lange lichte Schweigen" (*Z* III 7; KSA 4:220; "It is my favorite malice and art, that my silence has learned not to betray itself through silence . . . So that no one may see down into my ground and ultimate will, I have invented my long, bright silence").[54]

Yet Zarathustra's main mission is to speak. In part 2, his "stillste Stunde" ("stillest hour") tells him: "'Sprich dein Wort und zerbrich!'—" (*Z* II 22; KSA 4:188; "'Speak your word, and break!'"), and he remembers this moment when he returns home in part 2 (*Z* III 9; KSA 4:232). Upon his return, Solitude speaks to Zarathustra, reminding him of his special relationship to language: "Hier kommen alle Dinge liebkosend zu deiner Rede und schmeicheln dir: denn sie wollen auf deinem Rücken reiten. Auf jedem Gleichniss reitest du hier zu jeder Wahrheit" (*Z* III 9; KSA 4:231; "Here all things come caressingly to your discourse and flatter you: for they want to ride on your back. On every image you ride here to every truth").[55] In his solitude, Zarathustra realizes that, through him, both Being and Becoming are articulated: "Hier springen mir alles Seins Worte und Wort-Schreine auf: alles Sein will hier Wort werden, alles Werden will hier von mir reden lernen" (KSA 4:232; "Here the words and word stores of all Being spring open before me: here all Being wants to become word, here all Becoming wishes to learn from me how to speak"). Talking to the animals in his cave during his convalescence, Zarathustra praises the power of language to link what is otherwise separate:

> Wie lieblich ist es, dass Worte und Töne da sind: sind nicht Worte und Töne Regenbogen und Schein-Brücken zwischen Ewig-Geschiedenem?
>
> Zu jeder Seele gehört eine andre Welt; für jede Seele ist jede andre Seele eine Hinterwelt.
>
> Zwischen dem Ähnlichsten gerade lügt der Schein am schönsten; denn die kleinste Kluft ist am schwersten zu überbrücken.
>
> Für mich — wie gäbe es ein Ausser-mir? Es giebt kein Aussen! Aber das vergessen wir bei allen Tönen; wie lieblich ist es, dass wir vergessen!
>
> Sind nicht den Dingen Namen und Töne geschenkt, dass der Mensch sich an den Dingen erquicke? Es ist eine schöne Narrethei, das Sprechen: damit tanzt der Mensch über alle Dinge.
>
> Wie lieblich ist alles Reden und alle Lüge der Töne! Mit Tönen tanzt unsre Liebe auf bunten Regenbögen. —
>
> (*Z* III 13 §2; KSA 4:272)

> [How lovely it is, that there are words and sounds: are not words and sounds rainbows and bridges of semblance between things eternally apart?
>
> To every soul belongs another world; for each soul, every other soul is an afterworld.
>
> Between what is most similar, precisely their semblance tells lies most beautifully; for the smallest gap is the hardest to bridge.
>
> For me — how could there be an outside-me? There is no outside! But we forget this because of sounds; how lovely it is that we forget!
>
> Are not names and sounds given to things so that humankind might refresh itself with things? Speech is a beautiful folly: with it humankind dances over all things.
>
> How lovely is all speech, and all the lies of sounds! With sounds our love dances on many-hued rainbows.]

Because of its aesthetic and, in particular, its "musical" qualities, Zarathustra's language is a special language, his discourse a specific one; it is, in the words of "Das Kind mit dem Spiegel," no less than *eine neue Rede,* in that Beauty is always achieved specifically and, therefore, anew.

In order to understand this discourse, one must listen carefully. The central hermeneutic challenge of *Zarathustra* is symbolized by his warning in "Vom Lesen und Schreiben": "Sprüche sollen Gipfel sein: und Die, zu denen gesprochen wird, Grosse und Hochwüchsige" (*Z* I 7; KSA 4:48; "Aphorisms should be peaks: and those who are addressed, tall and lofty"). Later, Nietzsche elaborated on this claim in his preface to *Zur Genealogie der Moral:* "Die aphoristische Form [macht] Schwierigkeit: sie liegt darin, dass man diese Form heute *nicht schwer genug* nimmt. Ein Aphorismus, rechtschaffen geprägt und ausgegossen, ist damit, dass er abgelesen ist, noch nicht 'entziffert'; vielmehr hat nun erst dessen *Auslegung* zu beginnen, zu der es einer Kunst der Auslegung bedarf" (*GM* Vorrede §8; KSA 5:255; "The aphoristic form is difficult: this arises from the fact that today this form is *not taken seriously enough.* An aphorism, properly stamped and molded, has not been 'deciphered' when it has simply been read; rather, one has then to begin its *exegesis,* for which is required an art of exegesis").[56] Yet this art of interpretation is missing in all those who listen to Zarathustra. For example, his discourses in the market-place are greeted with incomprehension, and he realizes this: "Sie verstehen mich nicht: ich bin nicht der Mund für diese Ohren" (*Z* Vorrede §5; KSA 4:20; "They do not understand me: I am not the mouth for these ears").[57] Following the fall of the Tightrope-Walker, Zarathustra disposes of his corpse and goes in search of disciples: "Gefährten brauche ich und lebendige, — nicht todte Gefährten und Leichname, die ich mit mir trage, wohin ich will" (*Z* Vorrede §9; KSA 4:25; "Companions I need, living ones — not dead companions and corpses that I carry with me wherever I want"). Yet Zarathustra's disciples do not fully understand him, either. To them, he chooses to speak in a specific manner; the Inverse Cripple asks Zarathustra: "'Aber warum redet Zarathustra anders zu seinen Schülern — als zu sich selber?' —" (*Z* II 20; KSA 4:182; "'But why does Zarathustra speak differently to his pupils — than to himself?'"). Finally, Zarathustra realizes that even the Higher Men are not yet on his level: "'Aber noch fehlen mir meine rechten Menschen!'" (*Z* IV 20; KSA 4:406; "'But still I lack the right men'"). Nevertheless, the silence of Zarathustra's quietest hour reassures him of the effectiveness of his discourse:

> Und ich antwortete: "Noch versetzte mein Wort keine Berge, und was ich redete, erreichte die Menschen nicht. Ich gieng wohl zu den Menschen, aber noch langte ich nicht bei ihnen an."

Da sprach es wieder ohne Stimme zu mir: "Was weisst du *davon*! Der Thau fällt auf das Gras, wenn die Nacht am verschwiegensten ist." — [. . .]

Und ich antwortete: "Mir fehlt des Löwen Stimme zu allem Befehlen."

Da sprach es wieder wie ein Flüstern zu mir: "Die stillsten Worte sind es, welche den Sturm bringen. Gedanken, die mit Taubenfüssen kommen, lenken die Welt."

(Z II 22; KSA 4:188–89)

[And I answered: "As yet my words have moved no mountains, and what I said has not reached people. Indeed, I have gone to people, but as yet I have not arrived."

Then it spoke to me again without voice: "What do you know about *that*? The dew falls upon the grass when the night is at its most silent." [. . .]

And I answered: "I lack the lion's voice for commanding."

Then it spoke to me again as a whisper: "It is the quietest words that bring the storm, thoughts that come on doves' feet guide the world."]

Zarathustra's attitude to poetry, in both its strict and broadest senses, is, however, a complex one, as evinced in his speeches.

In "Auf den glückseligen Inseln," alluding to the final lines of Goethe's *Faust* and offering his own gloss on the Latin tag *poetae mentiuntur,* Zarathustra warns: "Alles Unvergängliche — das ist nur ein Gleichniss! Und die Dichter lügen zuviel" (Z II 2; KSA 4:110; "All that is intransitory — that is but a symbol! And the poets lie too much"). He repeats the first half of this conclusion at the beginning of the section entitled "Von den Dichtern" ("On the Poets"): "'[. . .] alles das 'Unvergängliche' — das ist auch nur ein Gleichniss'" (Z II 17; KSA 4:163; "'all that is 'intransitory' is also a mere symbol"). Then one of his disciples asks him why he had said that the poets lie too much. Zarathustra's response is crisp: "'Warum? [. . .] Du fragst warum? Ich gehöre nicht zu Denen, welche man nach ihrem Warum fragen darf'" (Z II 17; KSA 4:163; "'Why? . . . You ask why? I am not one of those whom one may ask about their why'").[58] But shortly afterwards he returns to the disciple's question — "'Doch was sagte dir einst Zarathustra? Dass die Dichter zuviel lügen? — Aber auch Zarathustra ist ein Dichter'" ("'But what was it Zarathustra once said to you? That the poets lie too much? — But Zarathustra too is a poet'") — and answers it with another: "'Glaubst du nun, dass er hier die Wahrheit redete? Warum glaubst du das?'" (KSA 4:163; "'Do you now believe that here he spoke the truth? Why do you believe that?'"). To the disciple's confession of faith in him, Zarathustra just shakes his head and laughs. Yet, even as he offers a searing critique of those poets who abandon the earth for airy ideals, Zarathustra nevertheless admits that he, too, is a poet. In "Von den Dichtern," the conclusion of *Faust II,* as well as Shakespeare's *Hamlet,* are used parodistically to assault Romantic notions of transcendence:

> Aber gesetzt, dass Jemand allen Ernstes sagte, die Dichter lügen zuviel: so hat er Recht, — *wir* lügen zuviel. [. . .]
> Und selbst nach den Dingen sind wir noch begehrlich, die sich die alten Weibchen Abends erzählen. Das heissen wir selber an uns das Ewig-Weibliche. [. . .]
> Ach, es giebt so viel Dinge zwischen Himmel und Erden, von denen sich nur die Dichter Etwas haben träumen lassen!
> Und zumal *über* dem Himmel: denn alle Götter sind Dichter-Gleichniss, Dichter-Erschleichniss!
> Wahrlich, immer zieht es uns hinan — nämlich zum Reich der Wolken: auf diese setzen wir unsre bunten Bälge und heissen sie dann Götter und Übermenschen:— [. . .]
> Ach, wie bin ich all des Unzulänglichen müde, das durchaus Ereigniss sein soll! Ach, wie bin ich der Dicher müde!
> (*Z* II 17; KSA 4:164–65)[59]

> [But suppose somebody said in all seriousness, the poets lie too much: he would be right — *we* do lie too much. . . .
> And we are still desirous even of those things the old women tell each other in the evening. That is what we ourselves call the Eternal Feminine. . . .
> Alas, there are so many things between heaven and earth of which only the poets have dreamed!
> And especially *above* the heavens: for all gods are poets' symbols, poets' prevarications!
> Truly, it draws us ever upward — that is, to cloud-land: on these we set our motley puppets and then call them gods and supermen:—
> . . .
> Alas, how weary I am of all the unattainable that is supposed to be event! Alas, how weary I am of the poets!]

Although Zarathustra uses a parody of Goethe to do so, he is attacking precisely the same notion of the aesthetic — namely, the Romantic — as did Goethe. For the contrast between the aesthetic view of the Romantics and that of the Weimar Classicists was summarized by Goethe as follows: "Meine unablenkbare Richtung [:] dem Wirklichen eine poetische Gestalt zu geben. Dagegen die Andern das Poetische zu verwirklichen suchten" ("My unalterable course: to give poetic form to reality. By contrast the others try to give reality to the poetic").[60] At the end of "Von den Dichtern," Zarathustra says the poets give rise to the penitent of the spirit —

"Verwandelt sah ich schon die Dichter und gegen sich selber den Blick gerichtet. / Büsser des Geistes sah ich kommen: die wuchsen aus ihnen" (KSA 4:166; "I have already seen the poets transformed, and their glances directed back on themselves. / Penitents of the spirit I saw approaching: they grew out of the poets") — that is, they give rise to the Sublime Men who must learn to laugh and to become beautiful.

Zarathustra is still a self-confessed poet in part 3, when he criticizes his own poetic techniques, ashamed "dass ich nämlich in Gleichnissen rede und gleich Dichtern hinke und stammle: und wahrlich, ich schäme mich, dass ich noch Dichter sein muss!" (*Z* III 12 §2; KSA 4:247; "that I have to speak in symbolic images and to limp and stammer like the poets: and truly, I am ashamed that I must still be a poet"). As a poet, however, Zarathustra is also a rhetorician.[61] Nietzsche understood the central importance of rhetorical communication, once remarking: "Es giebt keine unrhetorische 'Natürlichkeit' der Sprache, an die man appelliren könnte: die Sprache selbst ist das Resultat von lauter rhetorischen Künsten" ("There is no unrhetorical 'naturalness' of language to which one could appeal: language itself is the result of nothing but rhetorical devices").[62] Moreover, Nietzsche's work as a philologist had equipped him with a detailed knowledge of ancient rhetorical techniques, and rhetoric forms one of the principle stylistic techniques of *Zarathustra*. An analysis of Zarathustra's first speech provides examples of the many rhetorical devices used throughout the work (*Z* Vorrede §3; KSA 4:14–16). These devices include: *litotes,* for example, "Noch hat [die Tugend] mich nicht rasen gemacht"; *synonymia,* for example, "[die Seele] wollte [den Leib] mager, gräßlich, verhungert"; *enumeratio,* for example, "Verächter des Lebens sind es, Absterbende und selber Vergiftete," in both syndetic, for example, "Es ist Armut und Schmutz und ein erbärmliches Behagen," and asynedetic forms, here observing the law of increasing members: "Spracht ihr schon so? Schriet ihr schon so?"; alliteration, for example, "ein Zwiespalt und Zwitter von Pflanze und von Gespenst"; anaphora, for example, "Die Stunde, wo ihr sagt [. . .] / Die Stunde, wo ihr sagt [. . .]"; epiphora, for example, "[. . .] und ein erbärmliches Behagen! / [. . .] und ein erbärmliches Behagen!"; *anadiplosis* (or *reduplicatio*), for example, "Seht, ich lehre euch den Übermenschen! / Der Übermensch ist der Sinn der Erde"; *annomatio,* especially "figura etymologica," for example, "Ich lehre euch den Übermenschen. Der Mensch ist etwas, das überwunden werden soll. Was habt ihr getan, ihn zu überwinden?"; *polyptoton,* for example, "Was ist das Grösste, das ihr erleben könnt? Das ist die Stunde der grossen Verachtung"; and *repetitio,* for example, "Wo ist doch der Blitz, der euch mit seiner Zunge lecke? Wo ist der Wahnsinn, mit dem ihr geimpft werden müsstet? / Seht, ich lehre euch den Übermenschen: der ist dieser Blitz, der ist dieser Wahnsinn!"

Zarathustra's chief rhetorical and stylistic tool, however, is, as he recognizes, *Gleichnis* (metaphor, symbol, allegory, image).[63] At the end of part 1, Zarathustra — who came to bring humankind "ein Geschenk" ("a gift"; *Z* Vorrede §2; KSA 4:13) — accepts from the disciples the symbolic gift of a golden stick whose golden handle is decorated with the motif of a snake coiled around the sun. The gift becomes the occasion for Zarathustra to discourse on the relationship between "Gleichnis" and virtue (*Z* I 22 §1; KSA 4:97–99).[64] Zarathustra asks how gold came to be the highest value. Because, he says, gold is an "Abbild" ("copy," "representation," "image") of the highest virtue, and he lists the qualities of gold as follows: "Darum, dass es ungemein ist und unnützlich und leuchtend und mild im Glanze; es schenkt sich immer" ("Because it is uncommon and useless and gleaming and gentle in its splendor; it always gives of itself"). It is thus the aesthetic qualities of gold that make it valuable. And because gold, viewed aesthetically, "gives" or "bestows itself," Zarathustra concludes that "eine schenkende Tugend ist die höchste Tugend" (KSA 4:97; "a gift-giving virtue is the highest virtue"). Indeed, he suggests that all virtues or moral categories are, seen from the aesthetic perspective, symbolic: "Gleichnisse sind alle Namen von Gut und Böse: sie sprechen nicht aus, sie winken nur" (KSA 4:98; "Symbols are all names of good and evil: they do not articulate, they only point"). If we fail to understand this, we remain, like Faust, a fool ("ein Thor"); but our capacity to view aesthetically and, thereafter, *think* metaphorically represents the origin of a virtue, or our aesthetic redemption: "Achtet mir, meine Brüder, auf jede Stunde, wo euer Geist in Gleichnissen reden will: da ist der Ursprung eurer Tugend" (KSA 4:99; "Pay heed, my brothers, to every hour where your spirit wants to speak in symbols: there lies the origin of your virtue"). In other words, once aesthetic perception is gained, all other modes of thought and perception are derivative and (merely) metaphorical.

The text contains many examples of Zarathustra's talent for striking rhetorical images, *Gleichnisse,* and parables, derived from key symbols. In "Von der Keuschheit" ("On Chastity"), Zarathustra gives his disciples the following *Gleichnis:* "Nicht Wenige, die ihren Teufel austreiben wollten, fuhren dabei selber in die Säue" (*Z* I 13; KSA 4:70; "Not a few who sought to drive out their devil have themselves entered into the swine"). Later speeches comment on and play with this image. For example, "'Dem Reinen ist Alles rein' — so spricht das Volk. Ich aber sage euch: den Schweinen wird Alles Schwein!" (*Z* III 12 §14; KSA 4:256; "'To the pure all things are pure' — thus speak the people. But I say unto you: To the swine all things become swinish!"); or "Gab es Schmutzigeres bisher auf Erden als Wüsten-Heilige? Um *die* herum war nicht nur der Teufel los, — sondern auch das Schwein" (*Z* IV 13 §13; KSA 4:363; "Has there ever been anything filthier on earth than desert saints? Around *them* not only the devil was loose, but also the swine"). In "Von den Freuden- und Leidenschaften" ("On the Joys and Passions") Zarathustra tells one of his disciples: "Einst hattest du wilde Hunde in deinem Keller: aber am Ende verwandelten sie sich zu Vögeln und lieblichen Sängerinnen" (*Z* I 5; KSA 4:43; "Once you had wild dogs in your cellar: but in the end they changed into birds and lovely songstresses"), expanding on this image three chapters later: "Deine wilden Hunde wollen in die Freiheit; sie bellen vor Lust in ihrem Keller, wenn dein Geist alle Gefängnisse zu lösen trachtet. / Noch bist du mir ein Gefangener, der sich Freiheit ersinnt" (*Z* I 8; KSA 4:53; "Your wild dogs want freedom; they bark with joy in their cellar when your spirit plans to open all prisons. / To me you are still a prisoner who is plotting his freedom"). In "Der Blutegel" (The Leech"), Zarathustra offers the Conscientious Man of the Spirit the *Gleichnis* of the wanderer who, dreaming of distant things, accidentally steps on a dog asleep in the sun (*Z* IV 4; KSA 4:309). The most extended parable that Zarathustra tells is the *Gleichnis* of the Shepherd and the Snake, which concludes with four questions for his listeners (*Z* III 2 §2; KSA 4:202). Elsewhere, Zarathustra transmits his teaching in the form of such brief but vivid images as: "Einsamer, du gehst den Weg des Schaffenden: einen Gott willst du dir schaffen aus deinen sieben Teufeln!" (*Z* I 17; KSA 4:82; "Solitary one, you are going the way of the creative one: you want to create yourself a god from your seven devils!").

The aesthetic is, as Schiller had argued in his *Aesthetic Letters*, the prerequisite of free intellectual activity, but it involves our physical and instinctual capacities, too. Or, as Zarathustra opens his speech on the poets: "'Seit ich den Leib besser kenne [. . .] ist mir der Geist nur noch gleichsam Geist'" (*Z* II 17; KSA 4:163; "'Since I have come to know the body better . . . the spirit is to me only metaphorically spirit'"). Through the aesthetic, the merely intellectual capacities are themselves transfigured; as Zarathustra expresses it, we create the higher body in which mind inheres. In "Von den Hinterweltlern" (*Z* I 3; KSA 4:37; "On the Afterwordly"), Zarathustra hopes that the sick will become convalescents and overcomers and "einen höheren Leib sich schaffen" ("create a higher body for themselves"). And toward the end of part 1, he tells one of his disciples who wants to get married and have a child: "Einen höheren Leib sollst du schaffen" (*Z* I 20; KSA 4:90; "You should create a higher body").

For it is the aesthetic mode which, as a symbol and working (at least in part) through allegory, permits the creation of such a "higher body": "Erhöht ist da euer Leib und auferstanden" (*Z* I 22 §1/KSA 4 99; "There your body is elevated and resurrected").[65] As in Goethe's poem "Selige Sehnsucht" ("Blessed Longing," 1814) the aesthetic is the mode of thought and feeling that permits "höhere Begattung" ("higher copulation").[66] In the aesthetic mode, the intellectual and the sensuous faculties of the body are coordinated, permitting not just *erkennen* (intellectual awareness) but *begreifen* (experiential knowledge). In the tradition of Herder (in his *Plastik* [1778]) and Goethe (in the seventh of his *Römische Elegien* [1795]), this coordination is symbolically presented as a connection between the eye and the hand.[67] In "Das Nachtlied," Zarathustra sings: "Mein Auge quillt nicht mehr über vor der Scham der Bittenden; meine Hand wurde zu hart für das Zittern gefüllter Hände" (*Z* II 9; KSA 4:137; "My eye no longer wells over at the shame of those who beg; my hand has grown too hard for the trembling of filled hands"); and in "Von den Erhabenen," Zarathustra says of the Sublime Man who has not yet attained beauty: "Dunkel noch ist sein Antlitz; der Hand Schatten spielt auf ihm. Verschattet ist noch der Sinn seines Auges" (*Z* II 13; KSA 4:151; "His face is still dark; the shadow of the hand plays upon him. His eyesight is still in the shadows"). Significantly, in *Die fröhliche Wissenschaft* Nietzsche linked the hand and the eye to the notion of the aesthetic justification of the world in the aphorism entitled "Unsere letzte Dankbarkeit gegen die Kunst" ("Our Ultimate Gratitude to Art"): "Als ästhetisches Phänomen ist uns das Dasein immer noch *erträglich*, und durch die Kunst ist uns Auge und Hand und vor Allem das gute Gewissen dazu gegeben, aus uns selber ein solches Phänomen machen zu *können*" (*FW* §107; KSA 3:464; "As an aesthetic phenomenon existence is still *bearable* for us, and art furnishes us with eyes and hands and, above all, the good conscience to be *able* to turn ourselves into such a phenomenon").[68] Or, as Nietzsche put it in *Götzen-Dämmerung* (*Twilight of the Idols*): "In der Kunst geniesst sich der Mensch als Vollkommenheit" (*GD* Streifzüge §9; KSA 6:117; "In art human beings rejoice in their own perfection"). Indeed, Weimar Classicism declared as its chief objective the harmonious and productive coordination of human drives — by means of the aesthetic.[69]

The higher body belongs to a group of symbols in *Also sprach Zarathustra* that, drawing on Weimar classicism, represent the aesthetic. For example, there is the nexus of words built around the terms *veredeln* and *adeln* ("to ennoble"), which alludes to the Weimar classical theme of transformation.[70] Zarathustra uses both terms, saying: "Neues will der Edle schaffen und eine neue Tugend" (*Z* I 8; KSA 4:53; "The noble one wants to create something new and a new virtue"), as well as: "Darum, oh meine Brüder, bedarf es eines *neuen Adels*" ("Therefore, o my brothers, a *new aristocracy* is needed") and, as here, playing with them: "Vieler Edlen nämlich bedarf es und vielerlei Edlen, *dass es Adel gebe*" (*Z* III 12 §11; KSA 4:254; "For many who are noble are needed, and noble ones of many kinds, *that there may be aristocracy*"). He even uses the expression, *edle Seelen* (*Z* III 12 "noble souls"; *Z* III 12 §5; KSA 4:250), echoing the lines of Goethe's "Vermächtnis": "Denn edlen Seelen vorzufühlen / Ist wünschenswertester Beruf" ("For noble souls, feel out the way — / No task is more desirable").[71] Then again, there is the image of the dance, in which the activity of the body and the mind are, through the aesthetic, coordinated. In his

Aesthetic Letters, Schiller wrote: "Durch gymnastische Übungen bilden sich zwar athletische Körper aus, aber nur durch das freie und gleichförmige Spiel der Glieder die Schönheit" (Letter 6, §14; "Athletic bodies, it is true, can be developed by gymnastic exercises; beauty only through the free and harmonious play of the limbs"); "So wie sich ihm von aussen her [. . .] allmählich die Form nähert, so fängt sie endlich an, von ihm selbst Besitz zu nehmen und anfangs bloss den äussern, zuletzt auch den innern Menschen zu verwandeln. Der gesetzlose Sprung der Freude wird zum Tanz" (Letter 27, §6; "And as form gradually comes upon the individual from without . . . so finally it begins to take possession of the individual himself or herself, transforming at first only the outer, but ultimately the inner, human too. Uncoordinated leaps of joy turn into dance"). The same idea is expressed in his poem "Der Tanz" ("The Dance," 1795): "Es ist des Wohllauts mächtige Gottheit, / Die zum geselligen Tanz ordnet den tobenden Sprung" (NA 2.1:299; "It is the powerful deity of the melody, / Who orders the wild leap into the convivial dance"). In Nietzschean terms, the dance combines both Dionysian energy and Apollonian form. In *Die fröhliche Wissenschaft,* Nietzsche wrote: "— und ich wüsste nicht, was der Geist eines Philosophen mehr zu sein wünschte, als ein guter Tänzer. Der Tanz nämlich ist sein Ideal, auch seine Kunst, zuletzt auch seine einzige Frömmigkeit, sein 'Gottesdienst' . . ." (*FW* §381; KSA 3:635; "— and I really do not know what the spirit of philosopher might wish more to be than a good dancer. For the dance is his ideal, also his art, and finally also his piety, his 'divine service' . . ."). In *Ecce Homo,* Nietzsche said: "Zarathustra ist ein Tänzer" (*EH Z* §6/KSA 6:345; "Zarathustra is a dancer"). Some of the most startling images in *Zarathustra* use this topos of Weimar Classicism: "Man muss noch Chaos in sich haben, um einen tanzenden Stern gebären zu können" (*Z* Vorrede §5; KSA 4:19; "One must still have chaos in oneself to be able to give birth to a dancing star");[72] and: "Ich würde nur an einen Gott glauben, der zu tanzen verstünde" (*Z* I 7/KSA 4:49; "I would only believe in a god who knew how to dance"). Responding to Zarathustra's *Angst,* the Prophet tells Zarathustra to dance: "'du wirst tanzen müssen, dass du mir nicht umfällst!'" (*Z* IV 2; KSA 4:302; "'you will have to dance, lest you fall over!'"). And in "Das Grablied," Zarathustra links the dance with the stylistic technique of symbolism: "Nur im Tanze weiss ich der höchsten Dinge Gleichniss zu reden" (*Z* II 11; KSA 4:144; "Only in dance do I know how to speak the symbol of the highest things").

In *Zarathustra,* however, the chief symbol of the aesthetic is the child at play, first found in Nietzsche's discussion of Heraclitus (see chapter 1). Heraclitus's image of Time as a child at play is combined with Schiller's insight in the *Aesthetic Letters* that "der Mensch spielt nur, wo er in voller Bedeutung des Worts Mensch ist, und *er ist nur da ganz Mensch, wo er spielt*" (Letter 15, §9; "The human being only plays when he or she is in the fullest sense of the word a human being, and *a human being is only fully one when he or she plays*").[73] In one of his reflections in the *Nachlass* on the Eternal Recurrence, Nietzsche wrote: "Was früher am stärksten reizte, wirkt jetzt ganz anders, es wird nur noch als *Spiel* angesehn und gelten gelassen [. . .], wir stellen uns wie die Kinder zu dem, was früher *den Ernst das Daseins* ausmachte [. . .] Wie wird dies Leben in Bezug auf seine Summe von Wohlbefinden sich ausnehmen? *Ein Spiel der Kinder* [. . .]" (11[141]; KSA 9:494–95; "What used to arouse the most strongly now has a completely different effect, it is now only seen and accepted as *play* . . . we take the attitude of children to what used to constitute the *earnestness of existence* . . . How will this life look in relation to its sum of well-being? *Like children's play* . . .").[74] Like the individual who has accepted the Eternal Recurrence, the Child exists in a world where every moment is shot through with eternity. Indeed, the timeless world of children in an eternal present is emphasized by Nietzsche elsewhere in his *Nachlass,* in a review of *Der Werth des Lebens* (*The Value of Life*, 1865) by the philosopher and economist Eugen Dühring (1833–1921): "Das Kind ist viel mehr als ein bloßes Objekt der Erziehung. Die Pädagogen denken immer nur daran, was sie aus dem Kind zu *machen haben:* das Kind lebt in der Gegenwart, das ist der Contrast" (KSA 8:149; "The child is much more than a mere object of education. The pedagogues only ever think of what they *need to make out of the child:* the child lives in the present, that is the contrast"). At the beginning of part 1 of *Zarathustra,* in the chapter "Von den drei Verwandlungen" ("On the Three Transformations"), the spirit, which is laden down with the heaviness of life, is transformed into the camel. In its turn, the camel is transformed into the lion, which fights morality in the shape of the dragon "Du-sollst" ("Thou shalt") and creates sufficient freedom for aesthetic *Schaffen* ("creativity") to take place. Yet the lion must then be transformed into the Child, who is able to play creatively, affirmatively, and, above all, aesthetically:[75]

> Unschuld ist das Kind und Vergessen, ein Neubeginnen, ein Spiel, ein aus sich rollendes Rad, eine erste Bewegung, ein heiliges Ja-sagen.
>
> Ja, zum Spiele des Schaffens, meine Brüder, bedarf es eines heiligen Ja-sagens: *seinen* Willen will nun der Geist, *seine* Welt gewinnt sich der Weltverlorene.
>
> (*Z* I 1; KSA 4:31)

> [The child is innocence and forgetfulness, a new beginning, a game, a self-propelling wheel, a first movement, a sacred Yes.
>
> Yes, for the game of creation, my brothers, a sacred Yes is needed: *its* will is what the spirit now wills, *its* world is won by the one who had lost the world.]

The world gained by the Child at play is the world whose being is justified as an aesthetic phenomenon.

In his *Nachlass,* Nietzsche spoke of the world viewed through the aesthetic as a work of art giving birth to itself: "Die Welt als ein sich selbst gebärendes Kunstwerk" (*WM* §796/2[114]; KSA 12:119; "The world as a work of art that gives birth to itself"). Thus, in his last fragments, Nietzsche returned to a notion, founded in the aesthetics of Weimar Classicism, which he had elaborated in *Die Geburt der Tragödie* and to which he had given expression, as the "Evangelium des Schönen" *par excellence* in *Also sprach Zarathustra* — the idea of the aesthetic justification of the world.

Notes

[1] For previous commentaries on Zarathustra, see August Messer, *Erläuterungen zu Nietzsches Zarathustra* (Stuttgart: Strecker & Schröder, 1922); Hans Weichelt, *Zarathustra-Kommentar* (2nd ed., Leipzig: Felix Meiner, 1922); Arthur Pfeiffer, "Die Rollen des Zarathustra (Die Frage nach dem Ur-Zarathustra und seinen Problemen)," *Deutsches Vierteljahrsschrift für Literaturwissenschaft und Geistesgeschichte* 18 (1940): 61–111; Friedrich von der Leyen, "Friedrich Nietzsche: Die Sprache des 'Zarathustra,'" *Literaturwissenschaftliches Jahrbuch* 3 (1962): 209–38; Peter Wolfe, "Image and Meaning in 'Also sprach Zarathustra,'" *Modern Language Notes* 79 (1964): 546–52; C. A. Miller, "Nietzsche's 'Daughters of the Desert': A Reconsideration," *Nietzsche-Studien* 2 (1973): 157–95; K.-H. Volkmann-Schluch, "Die Stufen der Selbstüberwindung des Lebens (Erläuterungen zum 3. Teil von Nietzsches Zarathustra)," *Nietzsche-Studien* 2 (1973): 137–56; Anke Bennholdt-Thomsen, *Nietzsches "Also sprach Zarathustra" als literarisches Phänomen: Eine Revision* (Frankfurt am Main: Athenäum Verlag, 1974); Margot Paronis, *"Also sprach Zarathustra": Die Ironie Nietzsches als Gestaltungsprinzip* (Bonn: Bouvier, 1976); David S. Thatcher, "Eagle and Serpent in *Zarathustra,*" *Nietzsche-Studien* 6 (1977): 240–60; H. Miles Groth, "Nietzsche's Ontogenetic Theory of Time: The Riddle of the Laughing Shepherd," *American Imago* 37 (1980): 351–70; H. Miles Groth, "Nietzsche's Zarathustra: His Breakdown," *American Imago* 39 (1982): 1–20; Winfried Happ, *Nietzsches "Zarathustra" als moderne Tragödie* (Frankfurt am Main, Bern, New York: Lang, 1984); Adrian Del Caro, "The Immolation of Zarathustra: A Look at 'The Fire Beacon,'" *Colloquia Germanica* 17 (1984): 251–56; Kathleen Higgins, "The Night Song's Answer," and Robin Alice Roth, "Answer to 'The Night Song's Answer,'" *International Studies in Philosophy* 17 (1985): 33–50, 51–54; Hans-Georg Gadamer, "Das Drama Zarathustras," *Nietzsche-Studien* 15 (1986): 1–15; Laurence Lampert, *Nietzsche's Teaching: An Interpretation of "Thus Spoke Zarathustra"* (New Haven and London: Yale UP, 1986); Ernst Joós, *Poetic Truth and Transvaluation in Nietzsche's "Zarathustra": A Hermeneutic Study* (Bern, Frankfurt am Main: Lang, 1987); Kathleen Higgins, "Reading *Zarathustra,*" in Robert C. Solomon and Kathleen M. Higgins, eds., *Reading Nietzsche* (New York and Oxford: Oxford UP), 132–51; Kathleen Marie Higgins, *Nietzsche's "Zarathustra"* (Philadelphia: Temple UP, 1987); Michael Platt, "What does Zarathustra Whisper in Life's Ear?" *Nietzsche-Studien* 17 (1988): 179–94; Waller R. Newell, "Zarathustra's Dancing Dialectic," *Interpretation* 17 (1990): 415–32; Annemarie Pieper, *"Ein Seil geknüpft zwischen*

Mensch und Übermensch": *Philosophische Erläuterungen zu Nietzsches erstem "Zarathustra"* (Stuttgart: Klett-Cotta, 1990); Greg Whitlock, *Returning to Sils-Maria: A Commentary to Nietzsche's "Also sprach Zarathustra"* (New York, Frankfurt am Main: Lang, 1990); Roland Duhamel, *Nietzsches Zarathustra. Mystiker des Nihilismus: Eine Interpretation von Friedrich Nietzsches "Also sprach Zarathustra. Ein Buch für Alle und Keinen"* (Würzburg: Königshausen & Neumann, 1991); Joachim Köhler, *Zarathustras Geheimnis: Friedrich Nietzsche und seine verschlüsselte Botschaft: Eine Biographie* (Reinbek bei Hamburg: Rowohlt, 1992), 414–604; Francesca Cauchi, "Figures of *Funambule:* Nietzsche's Parable of the Ropedancer," *Nietzsche-Studien* 23 (1994): 42–64; Stanley Rosen, *The Mask of Enlightenment: Nietzsche's Zarathustra* (Cambridge: Cambridge UP, 1995); and Robert Gooding-Williams, *Zarathustra's Dionysian Modernism* (Stanford, CA: Stanford UP, 2001).

[2] In a draft found in the *Nachlass* from Autumn 1881, we find the warning: "Freunde, sagte Z[arathustra] [,] das ist eine neue Lehre und herbe Medizin, sie wird euch nicht schmecken" (15[50]; KSA 9:651; "Friends, said Zarathustra, this is a new doctrine and a bitter medicine, you will not like its taste").

[3] In Kant's First Critique, "pure" knowledge means knowledge without reference to experience. See also Kant, *Kritik der Urteilskraft;* in English, *Critique of Judgement,* trans. James Creed Meredith (Oxford: Clarendon, 1952), §5.

[4] For further discussion of this chapter, see Werner Frizen, "'Von der unbefleckten Erkenntniss': Zu einem Kapitel des *Zarathustra,*" *Deutsche Vierteljahrsschrift für Literaturwissenschaft und Geistesgeschichte* 58 (1984): 428–53. For an overview of Herder's doctrine of touch, which had a formative influence on Goethe and may well have been a shared, if mediated, source for Nietzsche's formulations, see Elizabeth M. Wilkinson and L. A. Willoughby, "The Blind Man and the Poet: An Early Stage in Goethe's Quest for Form" [1962], in *Models of Wholeness: Some Attitudes to Language, Art and Life in the Age of Goethe,* ed. Jeremy Adler, Martin Swales, and Ann Weaver (Oxford, Bern, Berlin: Lang, 2002), 99–125.

[5] Likewise, in "Von alten und neuen Tafeln" ("On Old and New Tablets") the earth is compared to a woman's breasts in terms of its usefulness and comfort: "Es giebt auf Erden viel gute Erfindungen, die einen nützlich, die andern angenehm: derentwegen ist die Erde zu lieben. / Und mancherlei so gut Erfundenes giebt es da, dass es ist wie des Weibes Busen: nützlich zugleich und angenehm" (*Z* III 12 §17; KSA 4:259; "There are many good inventions on earth, some of which are useful, some pleasing. / And there is such a variety of well-invented things that the earth is like a woman's breasts: useful and at the same time pleasing").

[6] Compare with the imagery of sculpture in Zarathustra's injunction in "Von alten und neuen Tafeln":

> "Die Schaffenden nämlich sind hart. Und Seligkeit muss es euch dünken, eure Hand auf Jahrtausende zu drücken wie auf Wachs, —
> — Seligkeit, auf dem Willen von Jahrtausenden zu schreiben wie auf Erz, — härter als Erz, edler als Erz. Ganz hart ist allein das Edelste.
> Diese neue Tafel, oh meine Brüder, stelle ich über euch: *werdet hart!*—"
> (*Z* III 12 §29; KSA 4:268)

[For creators are hard. And it must seem blessedness to you to impress your hand on millennia as on wax,
Blessedness to write on the will of millennia as on bronze — harder than bronze, nobler than bronze. Only the noblest is entirely hard.
This new tablet, O my brothers, I place over you: *become hard!*"]

In *Ecce Homo*, Nietzsche commented on this passage as follows: "An einer andren Stelle bestimmt [Zarathustra] so streng als möglich, was für ihn allein 'der Mensch' sein kann — *kein* Gegenstand der Liebe oder gar des Mitleidens — auch über den *grossen Ekel* am Menschen ist Zarathustra Herr geworden: der Mensch ist ihm eine Unform, ein Stoff, ein hässlicher Stein, der des Bildners bedarf" (*EH Z* §8; KSA 6:348; "In another passage Zarathustra defines as strictly as possible what alone 'humankind' can be for him — *not* an object of love or, worse, of the pity — Zarathustra has mastered the *great disgust* at humankind, too: humankind is for him a lack of form, a material, an ugly stone that needs the sculptor"). In *Jenseits von Gut und Böse*, Nietzsche used similar imagery in his argument against "Mitleid mit dem 'Geschöpf im Menschen'" ("pity for the 'creature in the human being'"): "Im Menschen ist *Geschöpf* und *Schöpfer* vereint: im Menschen ist Stoff, Bruchstück, Überfluss, Lehm, Koth, Unsinn, Chaos; aber im Menschen ist auch Schöpfer, Bildner, Hammer-Härte, Zuschauer-Göttlichkeit und siebenter Tag" (*JGB* §225; KSA 5:161; "In the human being *creature* and *creator* are united: in the human being there is material, fragment, excess, clay, dirt, nonsense, chaos; but in the human being there is also creator, form-giver, hammer-hardnesss, spectator-divinity, and seventh day"). Nietzsche gave his *Götzen-Dämmerung* (*Twilight of the Idols*) the subtitle "Wie man mit dem Hammer philosophirt" (KSA 6:55; "How one philosophizes with a hammer").

[7] On the importance of *schöner Schein*, see the following note in the *Nachlass* for winter 1884–85: "Zarathustra: man muß seinen Gott aus der Ferne sehen: nur so nimmt er sich gut aus. Darum hält sich der Teufel von Gott fern, denn er ist ein Freund des schönen Scheins" (31[46]; KSA 11:381; "Zarathustra: one must see one's God from a distance: only thus does he look good. For this reason the devil keeps away from God, for he is a friend of beautiful semblance").

[8] In "Von den Dichtern" ("On the Poets"), Zarathustra says that poets give rise to the Penitent of the Spirit (*Z* II 17; KSA 4:166); in Part Four, Zarathustra encounters the Sorcerer, who pretends to be the Penitent of the Spirit (*Z* IV 5 §2; KSA 4:318); and before he sings "Das Lied der Schwermuth" ("The Song of Melancholy"), the Sorcerer addresses the Higher Men as "'die freien Geister' [. . .] oder 'die Wahrhaftigen' oder 'die Büsser des Geistes' oder 'die Entfesselten' oder 'die grossen Sehnsüchtigen'" (*Z* IV 14 §2; KSA 4:370; "'the free spirits' . . . or 'the faithful' or 'the penitents of the spirit' of 'the unbound' or 'the great desirers'").

[9] For further discussion of the Pale Criminal, see Weichelt, *Zarathustra-Kommentar*, 17–20; Timothy Gould, "What Makes the Pale Criminal Pale: Nietzsche and the Image of the Deed," *Soundings: An Interdisciplinary Journal* 58 (1985): 510–36; Lampert, *Nietzsche's Teaching*, 43–44; Pieper, "*Ein Seil geknüpft*," 170–82; Köhler, *Zarathustras Geheimnis*, 441–43; Ronald Lehrer, *Nietzsche's Presence in Freud's Life and Thought: On the Origins of a Psychology of Dynamic Unconscious Mental Functioning* (Albany, NY: State U of New York P, 1995), 146–51; Rosen, *Mask of Enlight-*

enment, 87–99; and Paul Bishop, "Estrangement from the Deed and the Memory Thereof: Freud and Jung on the Pale Criminal in Nietzsche's *Zarathustra*," *Orbis Litterarum* 54 (1999): 424–38.

[10] In German, the expression "man kann nicht über seinen eigenen Schatten springen" means roughly the same as "a leopard cannot change its spots."

[11] See Schiller's essay "Ueber Anmuth und Würde" ("On Grace and Beauty," 1793). In the fifth letter of "Der Sammler und die Seinigen" ("The Collector and His Circle," 1799), Goethe wrote: "Das höchste Ziel der Kunst ist Schönheit und ihre letzte Wirkung Gefühl der Anmut" (HA 12:77; "The highest goal of art is beauty, and its ultimate effect is the feeling of grace"); Johann Wolfgang von Goethe, *Essays on Art and Literature,* ed. John Gearey, trans. Ellen von Nardroff and Ernest H. von Nardroff, Goethe Edition, vol. 3 (New York: Suhrkamp, 1986), 140 (translation modified).

[12] Cited from Friedrich Schiller, *On the Aesthetic Education of Man in a Series of Letters,* ed. and trans. Elizabeth M. Wilkinson and L. A. Willoughby (2nd ed., Oxford: Clarendon P, 1982). Citations from Schiller's *Aesthetic Letters* use the translation by Wilkinson and Willoughby, adapted where appropriate.

[13] Zarathustra constantly emphasizes the importance of laughter. As the Ugliest Man here reminds Zarathustra, in "Vom Lesen und Schreiben" ("On Reading and Writing") he says: "Nicht durch Zorn, sondern durch Lachen tödtet man" (*Z* I 7; KSA 4:49; "Not by anger does one kill, but by laughter"). In "Vom freien Tode" ("On Voluntary Death"), Zarathustra speculates that Jesus might have learnt to laugh (*Z* I 21; KSA 4:95); in "Der Wahrsager" ("The Prophet"), the disciple tells Zarathustra that "wahrlich, das Lachen selber spanntest du wie ein buntes Gezelt über uns" (*Z* II 20; KSA 4:175; "truly, you have spread laughter over us like a colorful tent"), a phrase which is echoed in "Von alten und neuen Tafeln" (*Z* III 12 §3; KSA 4:248); in "Die sieben Siegel" ("The Seven Seals"), Zarathustra claims: "— im Lachen nämlich ist alles Böse bei einander, aber heilig- und losgesprochen durch seine eigne Seligkeit" (*Z* III 16 §6; KSA 4:290; "for in laughter is all that is evil together, but proclaimed holy and absolved by its own bliss"); and the extracts from *Zarathustra* that Nietzsche quoted in his "Versuch einer Selbstkritik" ("Attempt at a Self-Criticism") in *Die Geburt der Tragödie* conclude as follows: "Diese Krone des Lachenden, diese Rosenkranz-Krone: euch, meinen Brüdern, werfe ich diese Krone zu! Das Lachen sprach ich heilig; ihr höheren Menschen, *lernt* mir — lachen!" (*Z* IV 13 §20; KSA 4:368; "This crown of whoever laughs, this rose-wreath crown: to you, my brothers, I throw this crown! Laughter I have pronounced holy; you higher men, *learn* from me — to laugh!"). To laughter belongs, as Zarathustra emphasizes, courage: "Ich will Kobolde um mich haben, denn ich bin muthig. Muth, der die Gespenster verscheucht, schafft sich selber Kobolde, — der Muth will lachen" (*Z* I 7; KSA 4:48; "I want to have goblins around me, for I am courageous. Courage that puts the ghosts to flight creates goblins for itself: — courage wants to laugh"; compare "Wenn Geister spuken, geh er seinen Gang, / Im Weiterschreiten find er Qual und Glück, / Er! unbefriedigt jeden Augenblick" (*Faust II*, 11450–53; "When spirits haunt him, let him walk his way, / Let both his pain and joy be in his forward stride — / Each moment leave him still unsatisfied"). In the formula used later by the Ugliest Man, courage is associated by Zarathustra in "Vom Gesicht und Räthsel"

with the acceptance of the Eternal Recurrence: "Muth nämlich ist der beste Todt-schläger, — Muth, welcher *angreift:* denn in jedem Angriffe ist klingendes Spiel. [. . .] Der schlägt noch den Tod todt, denn er spricht: 'War *das* das Leben? Wohlan! Noch Ein Mal!' / In solchem Spruche aber ist viel klingendes Spiel" (*Z* III 2 §1; KSA 4:199; "Courage is the best destroyer — courage, which *attacks:* for in every attack there is resounding play . . . It destroys even death, for it says: 'Was *that* life? Well then! One more time!' / In such sayings, however, there is much resounding play").

[14] References to *Faust* are by line number; and the following translations have been consulted: Johann Wolfgang von Goethe, *Faust: Part One,* trans. David Luke (Oxford and New York: Oxford UP, 1987); and *Faust: Part Two,* trans. David Luke (Oxford and New York: Oxford UP, 1994); and Johann Wolfgang von Goethe, *Faust: A Tragedy,* Norton Critical Edition, ed. Cyrus Hamlin, trans. Walter Arndt (2nd ed., New York and London: W. W. Norton, 2001).

[15] "Welch erbärmlich Grauen/ Faßt Übermenschen dich!" (489–90; "What pitiable fear / Seizes you, the superman!") the Earth Spirit mocks Faust (*Nacht*). Zarathustra's words "Ich liebe Den, welcher die Zukünftigen rechtfertigt und die Vergangenen erlöst: denn er will an den Gegenwärtigen zu Grunde gehen" (*Z* Vorrede §4; KSA 4:18; "I love him who justifies those of the future and redeems those of the past: for he wants to perish by those of the present") also allude to Faust's wager and his promise to Mephistopheles: "Dann will ich gern zu Grunde gehn!" (1702; "Then will I gladly perish!"). On the ambiguity of the phrase "zugrunde gehen" — meaning "to go to (the) ground (of Being)" as well as "to perish" — see Julian Roberts, *German Philosophy: An Introduction* (Cambridge: Polity, 1988), 231.

[16] Contempt is one of the great themes in *Zarathustra*. The first words that the Pale Criminal speaks are: "'Mein Ich ist Etwas, das überwunden werden soll: mein Ich ist mir die grosse Verachtung des Menschen'" (*Z* I 6; KSA 4:45; "My ego is something that must be overcome: my ego is to me the great contempt of humankind"); the Young Man tells Zarathustra in "Vom Baum am Berge": "'Meine Verachtung und meine Sehnsucht wachsen mit einander; je höher ich steige, um so mehr verachte ich Den, der steigt'" (*Z* I 8; KSA 4:52; "My contempt and my longing grow together; the higher I climb, the more I despise the person who climbs"); in "Von der verkleinernden Tugend" ("On the Virtue that Makes Small"), Zarathustra tells the people: "'Liebt immerhin euren Nächsten gleich euch, — aber seid mir erst Solche, die *sich selber lieben* — / — mit der grossen Liebe lieben, mit der grossen Verachtung lieben!" Also spricht Zarathustra, der Gottlose. — (*Z* III 5 §3; KSA 4:216; "'Always love your neighbor as yourselves, — but be first such as *love themselves* — / — loving with a great love, loving with a great contempt!" Thus speaks Zarathustra, the Godless); in "Von den drei Bösen" ("On the Three Evils") Zarathustra, speaking of "Herrschsucht" ("the lust to rule"), describes it as something "vor deren Blick der Mensch kriecht und duckt und fröhnt und niedriger wird als Schlange und Schwein: — bis endlich die grosse Verachtung aus ihm aufschreit —" (*Z* III 10 §2; KSA 4:238; "before the glance of which humankind crawls and bows and scrapes and becomes lower than the snake and the swine: — until at last the great contempt cries out from him"); in "Von der grossen Sehnsucht" ("On the Great Longing"), Zarathustra tells his soul: "Oh meine Seele, ich lehrte dich das Verachten, das nicht

wie ein Wurmfrass kommt, das grosse, das liebende Verachten, welches am meisten liebt, wo es am meisten verachtet" (*Z* III 14; KSA 4:278; "O my soul, I taught you the contempt that does not come as the gnawing of a worm, the great, the loving contempt that loves most where it despises most"); and in "Der hässlichste Mensch" ("The Ugliest Man"), Zarathustra says in his heart: "Ich liebe die grossen Verachtenden" (*Z* IV 7; KSA 4:332; "I love the great despisers"). In his preface to *Der Antichrist* (*The Antichrist*), Nietzsche wrote: "Man muss der Menschheit überlegen sein durch Kraft, durch *Höhe* der Seele, — durch *Verachtung . . .*" (KSA 6:168; "One must be above humankind in strength, in *loftiness* of soul — in contempt" . . .).

[17] Compare with Zarathustra's other speeches: "Nicht, wenn die Wahrheit schmutzig ist, sondern wenn sie seicht ist, steigt der Erkennende ungern in ihr Wasser" (*Z* I 13; KSA 4:70; "Not when truth is dirty, but when it is shallow, does the enlightened one dislike stepping into its waters"); "Und mit Bergen soll der Erkennende *bauen* lernen!" (*Z* II 8; KSA 4:134; "And the one who knows shall learn to *build* with mountains!"); and in "Von der Selbst-Ueberwindung" ("On Self-Overcoming"), Life tells the one who knows: "'Und auch du, Erkennender, bist nur ein Pfad und Fusstapfen meines Willens: wahrlich, mein Wille zur Macht wandelt auf den Füssen deines Willens zur Wahrheit!'" (*Z* II 12; KSA 4:148; "And you, too, the one who knows, are only a path and footstep of my will: truly, my will to power walks on the feet of your will to truth!'").

[18] See R. H. Stephenson, "The Diachronic Solidity of Goethe's *Faust*," in Paul Bishop, ed., *A Companion to Goethe's "Faust": Parts I and II* (Rochester, NY and Woodbridge, UK: Camden House, 2001), 243–79; here, 258–59.

[19] In "Von alten und neuen Tafeln," Zarathustra awaits the sign: "denn erst müssen mir die Zeichen kommen, dass es *meine* Stunde sei, — nämlich der lachende Löwe mit dem Taubenschwarme" (*Z* III 12 §l; KSA 4:246; "for first the signs must come to me that *my* hour is come: namely, the laughing lion with the flock of doves"); in "Die Begrüssung," Zarathustra declares: "*lachende Löwen* müssen kommen!" (*Z* IV 11; KSA 4:351; "*laughing lions* must come!"); finally, in the chapter entitled "Das Zeichen" ("The Sign"), the lion arrives: "'*Das Zeichen kommt,*' sprach Zarathustra und sein Herz verwandelte sich. Und in Wahrheit, als es helle vor ihm wurde, da lag ihm ein gelbes mächtiges Gethier zu Füssen und schmiegte das Haupt an seine Knie und wollte nicht von ihm lassen vor Liebe und that einem Hunde gleich, welcher seinen alten Herrn wiederfindet. Die Tauben aber waren mit ihrer Liebe nicht minder eifrig als der Löwe; und jedes Mal, wenn eine Taube über die Nase des Löwen huschte, schüttelte der Löwe das Haupt und wunderte sich und lachte dazu" (*Z* IV 20; KSA 4:406; "'*The sign is coming,*' said Zarathustra, and his heart was transformed. And in truth, when it became clear before him, there lay a mighty yellow animal at his feet and it pressed its head against his knees and out of love did not want to let go of him, behaving like a dog that finds its old master again. The doves, however, were no less eager in their love than the lion; and every time a dove glided over the lion's nose, the lion shook its head and was amazed and laughed"). In "Von den drei Verwandlungen" ("On the Three Transformations"), the camel is transformed into the lion, whose spirit says "Ich will" ("I will"), which, in the desert, fights the great dragon called "Du-sollst" ("Thou-shalt"; *Z* I 1; KSA 4:30). In the

final letter of *Ueber die ästhetische Erziehung des Menschen,* Schiller wrote that Nature had given the animals a surplus of possibility: "Wenn den Löwen kein Hunger nagt und kein Raubtier zum Kampf herausfordert, so erschafft sich die müssige Stärke selbst einen Gegenstand; mit mutvollem Gebrüll erfüllt er die hallende Wüste, und in zwecklosem Aufwand geniesst sich die üppige Kraft" (Letter 27, §3; "When the lion is not gnawed by hunger, nor provoked to battle by any beast of prey, his idle strength creates an object for itself: he fills the echoing desert with a roaring that speaks defiance, and his exuberant energy enjoys its *self* in purposeless display"). Yet in the penultimate section of that letter, Schiller added: "Die Kraft muss sich binden lassen durch die Huldgöttinnen, und der trotzige Löwe dem Zaum eines Amors gehorchen" (Letter 27, §11; "Strength must allow itself to be bound by the Graces, and the lion have its defiance curbed by the bridle of a Cupid"). For discussion of an alternative possible source of this image, see William Musgrave Calder III, "The Lion Laughed," *Nietzsche-Studien* 14 (1985): 357–59.

[20] Compare with Nietzsche's rhetorically hyperbolic discussion of this passage in the section of *Ecce Homo* entitled "Warum ich ein Schicksal bin" ("Why I am a Destiny"), §2, where he cites this passage as a summary of his world-historical significance: "Erst von mir an giebt es auf Erden *grosse Politik.* — Will man eine Formel für ein solches Schicksal, *das Mensch wird?* — Sie steht in meinem Zarathustra" (KSA 6:366; "With me the earth knows great politics for the first time. — Do you want a formula for such a destiny that *becomes human?* — It can be found in my *Zarathustra*").

[21] HA 2:18–19; Johann Wolfgang von Goethe, *Selected Poems,* ed. Christopher Middleton, Goethe Edition, vol. 1 (Boston: Suhrkamp/Insel, 1983), 207.

[22] As Nietzsche wrote in his *Nachlass* notes collected as *Der Wille zur Macht:* "Dem Werden den Charakter des Seins *aufzuprägen* — da ist der höchste *Wille zur Macht.* [. . .] Daß *Alles wiederkehrt,* ist die extremste *Annäherung einer Welt des Werdens an die des Seins: Gipfel der Betrachtung*" (*WM* §617/7[54]; KSA 12:312; "To *impose* upon Becoming the character of Being — that is the supreme *will to power . . .* That *everything recurs* is the closest *approximation of a world of Becoming to a world of Being: high point of meditation*"). In "Winckelmann und sein Jahrhundert" ("Winckelmann and His Century," 1805), Goethe described the unity of Being and Becoming as the goal of the universe in a symbolic portrait of the artist: "Wenn die gesunde Natur des Menschen als ein Ganzes wirkt, wenn er sich in der Welt als in einem großen, schönen, würdigen und werten Ganzen fühlt, wenn das harmonische Behagen ihm ein reines freies Entzücken gewährt, dann würde das Weltall, wenn es sich selbst empfinden könnte, als an sein Ziel gelangt aufjauchzen und den Gipfel des eigenen Werdens und Wesens bewundern. Denn wozu dient alle der Aufwand von Sonnen und Planeten und Monden, von Sternen und Milchstraßen, von Kometen und Nebelflecken, von gewordenen und werdenden Welten, wenn sich nicht zuletzt ein glücklicher Mensch unbewußt seines Daseins erfreut?" (HA 12:98; Goethe, *Essays on Art and Literature,* 101; "When man's nature functions soundly as a whole, when he feels that the world of which he is part is a huge, beautiful, admirable and worthy whole, when this harmony gives him pure and uninhibited delight, then the universe, if it were capable of emotion, would rejoice at having reached its goal and admire the crowning glory of its own evolution. For, what purpose would those countless suns

and planets and moons serve, those stars and milky ways, if a happy human being did not ultimately emerge unconsciously to enjoy existence?"). In a conversation of 1805 or 1806, probably with Sophie von Schardt, Goethe is recorded as saying (as he also states in his scientific writings): "Nichts ist, nichts ist geworden, alles ist stets im Werden, in dem ewigen Strom der Veränderung ist kein Stillstand" (WA 5.2:22; "Nothing is, nothing has become, everything is becoming, in the eternal stream of transformation there is no arrest").

[23] HA 1:370; in English, *Selected Poems,* 268, (adapted from Middleton's translation).

[24] The close relationship between these two chapters is clearly demonstrated by Martin Heidegger in his lecture "Wer ist Nietzsches Zarathustra?" (in *Vorträge und Aufsätze* [Pfullingen: Neske, 1954], 101–26; translated by Bernd Magus as "Who is Nietzsche's Zarathustra?" in David B. Allison, ed., *The New Nietzsche: Contemporary Styles of Interpretation* [Cambridge, MA and London: MIT Press, 1985], 64–79); see also "Nietzsches Wort 'Gott ist tot'" (in *Holzwege* [Frankfurt am Main: Klostermann, 1950], 248–95).

[25] In "Von der schenkenden Tugend," Zarathustra connected the Will with the Sublime and with virtue: "Wenn ihr erhaben seid über Lob und Tadel und euer Wille allen Dingen befehlen will, als eines Liebenden Wille: da ist der Ursprung eurer Tugend" (*Z* I 22 §1; KSA 4:99; "When you are sublime over praise and blame, and your will wants to command all things, like the will of a lover: that is the origin of your virtue"); and in the concluding section of "Von alten und neuen Tafeln," Zarathustra addresses the will thus: "O Wille, Wende aller Noth, du *meine* Nothwendigkeit! Spare mich auf zu Einem grossen Siege! — —" (*Z* III 12 §30; KSA 4:269; "O will, cessation of all need, who are *my* necessity! Save me for one great victory!"). What the (lover's) Will must will, however, is the aesthetic: "Wo ist Schönheit? Wo ich mit allem Willen *wollen muss*" (KSA 4:157; "Where is Beauty? Where I *must will* with all my will"). For further discussion of "Das Grablied," and an analysis of its pivotal function in the dramatic economy of *Also sprach Zarathustra,* see Paul Bishop, "'Yonder lies the grave-island, the silent island; yonder, too, are the graves of my youth': A Commentary on Zarathustra's Grave-Song," *Orbis Litterarum* 57 (2002): 317–42.

[26] This formula "Wollen befreit" is also found in "Von der Erlösung" (*Z* II 20; KSA 4:179) and in "Von alten und neuen Tafeln" (cited above, compare KSA 4:258).

[27] In "Vom Gesicht und Räthsel" ("On the Vision and the Riddle"), the image of the stone is applied by the Spirit of Heaviness to Zarathustra himself: "'Oh Zarathustra, raunte er höhnisch Silb' um Silbe, du Stein der Weisheit! Du warfst dich hoch, aber jeder geworfene Stein muss — fallen! [. . .] Verurtheilt zu dir selber und zur eignen Steinigung: oh Zarathustra, weit warfst du ja den Stein, — aber auf *dich* wird er zurückfallen!'" (*Z* III 2 §1; KSA 4:198; "'O Zarathustra,' he whispered mockingly, syllable by syllable, 'you stone of wisdom! You threw yourself up high, but every stone that is thrown must — fall! . . . Condemned to yourself and to your own stoning: O Zarathustra, far indeed have you thrown your stone — but it will fall back on *you*!'").

[28] In "Vom Nutzen und Nachtheil der Historie für das Leben" ("On the Uses and Disadvantages of History for Life"), Nietzsche had already analysed the curse of "es war": "Der Mensch hingegen stemmt sich gegen die grosse und immer grössere Last

des Vergangenen [. . .]. Deshalb ergreift es ihn, als ob er eines verlorenen Paradieses gedächte, die weidende Heerde oder, in vertrauterer Nähe, das Kind zu sehen, das noch nichts Vergangenes zu verläugnen hat und zwischen den Zäunen der Vergangenheit und der Zukunft in überseliger Blindheit spielt. Und doch muss ihm sein Spiel gestört werden: nur zu zeitig wird es aus der Vergessenheit heraufgerufen. Dann lernt es das Wort 'es war' zu verstehen, jenes Losungswort, mit dem Kampf, Leiden und Ueberdruss an den Menschen herankommen, ihn zu erinnern, was sein Dasein im Grunde ist — ein nie zu vollendendes Imperfectum" (*UB* II §1; KSA 1:249; "The human being, on the other hand, braces himself against the great and ever greater pressure of what is past . . . That is why it affects him like a vision of a lost paradise to see herds grazing or, in closer proximity to him, a child who, having as yet nothing of the past to shake off, plays in blissful blindness between the hedges of the past and the future. Yet its play must be disturbed; all too soon it will learn to understand the phrase 'it was,' that password that permits struggle, suffering, and satiety to approach the human being, so as to remind it of what its existence basically is — something imperfect that will never be completed"). On the significance of the symbol of the child, see below.

[29] The theme of "highest hope" runs through the whole of *Zarathustra*. In his third address to the crowd in the market-place, Zarathustra announces: "Es ist an der Zeit, dass der Mensch den Keim seiner höchsten Hoffnung pflanze" (*Z* Vorrede §5; KSA 4:19; "It is time for humankind to plant the seed of its highest hope"); in "Vom Baum am Berge," Zarathustra tells the Young Man: "Ach, ich kannte Edle, die verloren ihre höchste Hoffnung. [. . .] wirf den Helden in deiner Seele nicht weg! Halte heilig deine höchste Hoffnung!" (*Z* I 8; KSA 4:53–54; "Alas, I knew noble ones who lost their highest hope . . . do not throw away the hero in your soul! Keep holy your highest hope!"); in "Vom Krieg und Kriegsvolke," he cries: "Eure Liebe zum Leben sei Liebe zu eurer höchsten Hoffnung: und eure höchste Hoffnung sei der höchste Gedanke des Lebens!" (*Z* I 10; KSA 4:59; "Let your love of life be love of your highest hope: and let your highest hope be the highest thought of life!"); in the vision of the Great Noonday conjured up by Zarathustra at the end of Part One, humankind finds itself midpoint between animal and Superman, celebrating the way to evening as "seine höchste Hoffnung" ("its highest hope"; *Z* I 22 §3; KSA 4:102); in "Das Grablied," Zarathustra laments: "Ungeredet und unerlöst blieb mir die höchste Hoffnung!" (*Z* II 11; KSA 4:144; "Unspoken and unredeemed remain my highest hope"); in "Von der Seligkeit wider Willen" ("On Involuntary Bliss") Zarathustra addresses his rejoicing conscience: "Oh Nachmittag meines Lebens! Was gab ich nicht hin, dass ich Eins hätte: diese lebendige Pflanzung meiner Gedanken und diess Morgenlicht meiner höchsten Hoffnung!" (*Z* III 3; KSA 4:203; "O afternoon of my life! What did I not give to have one thing: this living plantation of my thoughts and this dawn of my highest hope"; repeated with a slight variation later in "Die Begrüssung," when Zarathustra says to the Higher Men: "'was gab ich nicht hin, / — was gäbe ich nicht hin, daß ich Eins hätte: *diese* Kinder, *diese* lebendige Pflanzung, *diese* Lebensbäume meines Willens und meiner höchsten Hoffnung!'" [*Z* IV 11; KSA 4:351; "'what did I not give, / what would I not give to have one thing: *these* children, *this* living plantation, *these* life-trees of my will and my highest hope!'"]); in "Von den drei Bösen," Zarathustra described sensual delight as the great simulacrum for higher happiness and highest hope: "Wollust: das grosse Gleichniss-Glück

für höheres Glück und höchste Hoffnung" (*Z* III 10 §2; KSA 4:237; "Sex: the happiness that is the great symbol of a higher happiness and the highest hope"); and, again in "Die Begrüssung," the King on the Right says of "die Menschen der grossen Sehnsucht, des grossen Ekels, des grossen Überdrusses" ("those who feel great longing, great disgust, great weariness of life'"): "'sie lernen von dir, oh Zarathustra, die grosse *Hoffnung*!'" (KSA 4:349; "'they learn from you, O Zarathustra, the great *hope*'").

[30] See the short essay "Inwiefern die Idee: Schönheit sei Vollkommenheit mit Freiheit, auf organische Naturen angewendet werden könne" ("The Extent to which the Idea 'Beauty is Perfection in Combination with Freedom' May Be Applied to Living Organisms," written 1794; HA 13:21–23; in English, Johann Wolfgang von Goethe, *Scientific Studies,* ed. and trans. Douglas Miller, Goethe Edition, vol. 12 [New York: Suhrkamp, 1988], 22–23). The final stanza of "Urworte. Orphisch" is entitled "ΕΛΠΙΣ, Hoffnung" ("ELPIS. Hope"; HA 1:360; *Selected Poems,* trans. Christopher Middleton, 231–33).

[31] "'Ach, abgründlicher Gedanke, der du *mein* Gedanke bist!" (*Z* III 3; KSA 4:205; "Alas, abysmal thought, you are *my* thought!"); "Herauf, abgründlicher Gedanke, aus meiner Tiefe!" (*Z* III 13 §1; KSA 4:270; "Up, abysmal thought, out of my depths!").

[32] Book Eight, chapter 5 (HA 7:540; Johann Wolfgang von Goethe, *Wilhelm Meister's Apprenticeship,* ed. and trans. Eric A. Blackall and Victor Lange, Goethe Edition, vol. 9 (New York: Suhrkamp, 1989), 331). In *Die fröhliche Wissenschaft,* Nietzsche expressed his wish to make the thought of life more worth thinking: "Es macht mich glücklich, zu sehen, dass die Menschen den Gedanken an den Tod durchaus nicht denken wollen! Ich möchte gern Etwas dazu thun, ihnen den Gedanken an das Leben noch hundertmal *denkenswerther* zu machen" (*FW* §278; KSA 3:523; "It makes me happy that human beings do not want to think at all the thought of death! I should very much like to do something that will make the thought of life a hundred times *more worthwhile thinking*"). In *Jenseits von Gut und Böse,* Nietzsche set up "das Ideal des übermüthigsten lebendigsten und weltbejahendsten Menschen, der sich nicht nur mit dem, was war und ist, abgefunden und vertragen gelernt hat, sondern es, *so wie es war und ist,* wieder haben will, in alle Ewigkeit hinaus, unersättlich da capo rufend, nicht nur zu sich, sondern zum ganzen Stücke und Schauspiele, und nicht nur zu einem Schauspiele, sondern im Grunde zu Dem, der gerade dies Schauspiel nöthig hat — und nöthig macht: weil er immer wieder sich nöthig hat — und nöthig macht — — Wie? Und dies wäre nicht — circulus vitiosus deus?" (*JGB* §56; KSA 5:75; "the ideal of the most high-spirited, liveliest, and most world-affirming human being, who has not only come to terms with and learned to get along with whatever was and is, but who wants to have *what was and is* repeated into all eternity, shouting insatiably *da capo* — not only to himself but to the whole play and spectacle, and not only to a spectacle but at bottom to him who needs precisely this spectacle — and who makes himself necessary because again and again he needs himself — — What? And would this not be — *circulus vitiosus deus* [god as vicious circle]?"). And in his *Nachlass,* Nietzsche emphasized the transformative effect of the thought of the Eternal Recurrence: "Meine Philosophie bringt den siegreichen Gedanken, an welchem zuletzt jede

andere Denkweise zugrunde geht. Es ist der große *züchtende* Gedanke: die Rassen, welche ihn nicht ertragen, sind verurtheilt; die, welche ihn als größte Wohlthat empfinden, sind zur Herrschaft ausersehn" (*WM* §1053/23[376]; KSA 11:250; "My philosophy brings the triumphant idea, of which every other mode of thought will ultimately perish. It is the great cultivating idea: the races that cannot bear it stand condemned; those who find it of the greatest benefit are chosen to rule").

[33] During his second visit to Rome, Goethe wrote in his correspondence included in the *Italienische Reise* (Part Three, 6 September 1787): "Diese hohen Kunstwerke [der Antike] sind zugleich als die höchsten Naturwerke von Menschen nach wahren und natürlichen Gesetzen hervorgebracht worden. Alles Willkürliche, Eingebildete fällt zusammen, da ist die Notwendigkeit, da ist Gott" (HA 11:395; Johann Wolfgang von Goethe, *Italian Journey,* ed. Thomas P. Saine and Jeffrey L. Sammons, trans. Robert R. Heitner, Goethe Edition, vol. 6 (New York: Suhrkamp, 1989), 316; "These sublime works of art [of antiquity] are also the sublimest works of nature, created by men following true and natural lives. Everything arbitrary, everything imaginary crumbles away, there we have necessity, there we have God"). Compare with Nietzsche's remark in *Jenseits von Gut und Böse:* "Die Künstler mögen hier schon eine feinere Witterung haben: sie, die nur zu gut wissen, dass gerade dann, wo sie Nichts mehr 'willkürlich' und Alles nothwendig machen, ihr Gefühl von Freiheit, Feinheit, Vollmacht, von schöpferischem Setzen, Verfügen, Gestalten auf seine Höhe kommt, — kurz, dass Nothwendigkeit und 'Freiheit des Willens' dann bei ihnen Eins sind" (*JGB* §213/KSA 5:148; "Artists may have a finer sensitivity here: for they know only too well that precisely when they no longer do anything 'arbitrarily' but do everything of necessity, their feeling of freedom, subtlety, authority, of creative placing, disposing, forming reaches its peak — in short, that necessity and 'freedom of the will' then become one in them").

[34] See Schiller's formulation in his *Kallias* letter (18 February 1773) of beauty as *Freiheit in der Erscheinung* ("freedom in appearance"), also referred to in his *Aesthetic Letters* (Letter 23, §7, n.1). For further discussion of the concept of freedom in appearance, see below; and see R. H. Stephenson, "Goethe's 'Sprüche in Reimen': A Reconsideration," *Publications of the English Goethe Society* 49 (1976): 102–30, especially 130.

[35] Another passage in Nietzsche's writings that explores the dialectic between lack of intention and necessity is the section "Hüten wir uns!" ("Let us beware!"; *FW* §109; KSA 3:467–69). There, Nietzsche distinguishes between the cosmos of "die astrale Ordnung, in der wir leben" ("the astral order in which we live") and the chaos of "der Gesammt-charakter der Welt" ("the total character of the world"). In "Urworte. Orphisch," "Scheinfreiheit" ("seeming freedom"; lines 31–32) transforms "Nötigung" (that is, "necessity") into the freedom of the final stanza (HA 1:360; *Selected Poems,* trans. Middleton, 232). For further discussion, see R. H. Stephenson, "On the Function of a Delphic Ambiguity in Goethe's 'Urworte. Orphisch' and Kafka's 'Ein Hungerkünstler,'" *Quinquereme* 10 (1987): 165–79.

[36] In his *Nachlass* for the period spring to summer 1883, Nietzsche noted: "Wichtigster Gesichtspunkt: *die **Unschuld** des Werdens zu gewinnen, dadurch daß man die **Zwecke** ausschließt*" (7[21]; KSA 10:245; "The most important point of view: *to gain the **innocence** of becoming by means of excluding **purposes**"*). In his *Kritik*

der Urteilskraft, Kant famously defined beauty as "Zweckmäßigkeit ohne Zweck" ("purposiveness without purpose"; Part One, Book 1, §10 and §17). For a discussion of Schiller's relation to Kantian aesthetics, see Dieter Henrich, "Der Begriff der Schönheit in Schillers Ästhetik," *Zeitschrift für philosophische Forschung* 11 (1957): 527–47; Eva Schaper, "Friedrich Schiller: Adventures of a Kantian," *British Journal of Aesthetics* 4 (1964): 348–62; John M. Ellis, *Schiller's "Kalliasbriefe" and the Study of his Aesthetic Theory* (The Hague and Paris: Mouton, 1969); and Eva Schaper, "Schiller's Kant: A Chapter in the History of Creative Misunderstanding," in *Studies in Kant's Aesthetics* (Edinburgh: Edinburgh UP, 1979), 99–117. Schiller himself acknowledged his debt and his divergence from Kant in one of his unpublished Xenien as follows: "Zwey Jahrzehende kostest du mir, zehn Jahre verlohr ich / Dich zu begreifen und zehn mich zu befreyen von dir" (NA 21:86; "Two decades you cost me, Ten years I lost / To understand you and then to free myself from you").

[37] Compare with the theory developed by Thorstein Veblen (1857–1929) of the high value of the *imperfect* (that is, handmade) object; for further discussion, see the chapter entitled "Pecuniary Canons of Taste" in his *The Theory of the Leisure Class* (1899; in Veblen, *The Portable Veblen,* ed. Max Lerner [New York: Viking P, 1948], 151–96), and *The Instinct of Workmanship* (1914).

[38] The central notion of *Selbstüberwindung* also has its source in Goethe. In the market-place, Zarathustra tells the crowd: "Der Mensch ist Etwas, das überwunden werden soll" (Vorrede §3; KSA 4:14; "Humankind is something that must be overcome"). Goethe's uncompleted epic poem, "Die Geheimnisse" ("The Mysteries"), contains the famous lines: "Von der Gewalt, die alle Wesen bindet, / Befreit der Mensch sich, der sich überwindet" (HA 2:276; "From the power that binds all beings / Those Liberate themselves who overcome themselves"). Similarly, Zarathustra's line in "Von den Taranteln," "Steigen will das Leben und steigend sich überwinden" (Z II 7; KSA 4:130; "Life wants to climb and, climbing, overcome itself") links *Selbstüberwindung* to another Goethean concept, *Steigerung.* Compare with the following passage: "Ich schliesse Kreise um mich und heilige Grenzen; immer Wenigere steigen mit mir auf immer höhere Berge, — ich baue ein Gebirge aus immer heiligeren Bergen. —" (Z III 12 §19; KSA 4:260; "I draw circles around myself, and sacred boundaries; fewer and fewer people climb with me up ever higher mountains: I am building a mountain range out of ever more sacred mountains").

[39] HA 1:386; *Selected Poems,* trans. Michael Hamburger, 267 [adapted]. In the section from *Menschliches, Allzumenschliches* (*Human, All Too Human*) entitled "Was von der Kunst übrigbleibt" ("What remains of Art"), Nietzsche used this line from Goethe as paradigmatic of the function of art: "Vor Allem hat [die Kunst] durch Jahrtausende hindurch gelehrt, mit Interesse und Lust auf das Leben in jeder Gestalt zu sehen und unsere Empfindung so weit zu bringen, dass wir endlich rufen: 'wie es auch sei, das Leben, es ist gut.' Diese Lehre der Kunst, Lust am Dasein zu haben und das Menschenleben wie ein Stück Natur, ohne zu heftige Mitbewegung, als Gegenstand gesetzmässiger Entwickelung anzusehen, — diese Lehre ist in uns hineingewachsen, sie kommt jetzt als allgewaltiges Bedürfniss des Erkennens wieder an's Licht" (MA I §222; KSA 2:185; "Above all, art has taught us for thousands of years to look upon life in all its forms with interest and pleasure, and to educate our sensibilities so far that at last we cry: 'however it may be, life is good!' This doctrine

of art, to take pleasure in life and to regard human life as a piece of nature, without being too involved in it, as an object of law-governed development — this doctrine has become part of us, it reemerges now into the light as an almighty requirement of knowledge").

[40] Nietzsche's thought is here is explained further in the following *Nachlass* note: "Gesetzt, wir sagen Ja zu einem einzigen Augenblick, so haben wir damit nicht nur zu uns selbst, sondern zu allem Dasein Ja gesagt. Denn es steht nichts für sich, weder in uns selbst, noch in den Dingen: und wenn nur ein einziges Mal unsre Seele wie eine Saite vor Glück gezittert und getönt hat, so waren alle Ewigkeiten nöthig, um dies Eine Geschehen zu bedingen — und alle Ewigkeit war in diesem einzigen Augenblick unseres Jasagens gutgeheißen, erlöst, gerechtfertigt und bejaht" (*WM* §1032/7[38]; KSA 12:307–8; "If we affirm one single moment, we thus affirm, not only ourselves, but all of existence. For nothing is self-sufficient, neither in us ourselves nor in things; and if our soul has just once trembled with happiness and sounded like a harp string, all eternity was needed to produce this one event — and, in this single moment of affirmation, all eternity was called good, redeemed, justified, and affirmed").

[41] " '*Todt sind alle Götter: nun wollen wir, dass der Übermensch lebe.*' — diess sei einst am grossen Mittage unser letzter Wille! —" (*Z* I 22 §3; KSA 4:102; " '*All gods are dead: now we want the Superman to live*' — at the great noontide let this be our last will!"); "Er kommt, er ist nahe, *der grosse Mittag*!" (*Z* III 5 §3; KSA 4:217; "It is coming, it is close, *the great noontide*!"); "Denn solche Feuersäulen müssen dem grossen Mittage vorangehn" (*Z* III 7; KSA 4:225; "For such pillars of fire must precede the great noontide"); "Aber denen Allen kommt nun der Tag, die Wandlung, das Richtschwert, *der grosse Mittag:* da soll Vieles offenbar werden! / Und wer das Ich heil und heilig spricht und die Selbstsucht selig, wahrlich, der spricht auch, was er weiss, ein Weissager: '*Siehe, er kommt, er ist nahe, der grosse Mittag!*'" (*Z* III 10 §3; KSA 4:240; "But for all these the day is now at hand, the transformation, the sword of judgment, *the great noontide:* much shall be revealed there! / And whoever proclaims the ego healthy and holy and selfishness blessed, truly he will also say what he, a prophet, knows: '*The great noontide is coming, it is close!*'"); and in the final chapter, Zarathustra announces: "'Dies ist *mein* Morgen, *mein* Tag hebt an: herauf nun, herauf, du grosser Mittag!'" (*Z* IV 20; KSA 4:408; "'This is *my* morning, *my* day is breaking: arise now, arise, you great noontide!'"). In *Zur Genealogie der Moral*, the second essay concludes with the hope for "der *erlösende* Mensch der grossen Liebe und Verachtung, der schöpferische Geist" ("the *redeeming* human of great love and contempt, the creative spirit") and looks forward to "dieser Glockenschlag des Mittags und der grossen Entscheidung, der den Willen wieder frei macht, der der Erde ihr Ziel und dem Menschen seine Hoffnung zurückgiebt" (*GM* II §24; KSA 5:336; "this bell-stroke of midday and of the great decision that liberates the will again, and that restores to the earth its goal and to humankind its hope").

[42] The perfection of the world, viewed aesthetically, is revealed at midday in the central chapter of part 4 entitled "Mittags" ("At Noon"; *Z* IV 10; KSA 4:342–45): "Wie? Ward die Welt nicht eben vollkommen?" (KSA 4:344; "What? Did the world not just become complete?"). Similarly, this chapter binds together phrases and mo-

tifs from the rest of the book. "Was geschah mir?" ("What happened to me?") is a question Zarathustra asks himself repeatedly; "'Siehe, jetzt eben ward die Welt vollkommen!' — also denkt ein jedes Weib, wenn es aus ganzer Liebe gehorcht" ("'Behold, the world has just become perfect' — thus thinks every woman when she obeys out of her entire love"), says Zarathustra in "Von alten und jungen Weiblein" ("On Old and Young Women"; ZI 18; KSA 4:85), and the maxim is repeated in §10 of "Das Nachtwandler-Lied" (the passage under discussion); "Oh des goldnen runden Balls!" ("O, the golden round ball!") recalls the golden ball that Zarathustra throws to his disciples (ZI 21; KSA 4:95–96); "Oh Himmel über mir!" ("O, heaven above me!") recalls "Vor Sonnen-Aufgang" (ZIII 4; KSA 4:207); "Oh meine Seele!" ("O, my soul!") recalls his conversation with his soul in "Von der grossen Sehnsucht" (ZIII 14; KSA 4:278–80); "Das Wenigste gerade, das Leiseste, Leichteste, einer Eidechse Rascheln, ein Hauch, ein Husch, ein Augen-Blick — *Wenig* macht die Art des *besten* Glücks" ("Precisely the least of things, the quietest, lightest, the rustling of a lizard, a breath, a darting move, the blink of an eye, a moment — *Little* things bring the best kind of happiness") recalls the passage under discussion; whilst "Oh des goldenen runden Reifs" ("O, of the round golden ring") recalls "der hochzeitliche Ring der Ringe, — der Ring der Wiederkunft" ("the conjugal ring-of-rings — the ring of return") with which, in "Die sieben Siegel," Zarathustra wishes to marry the only woman from whom he ever wanted to have children, Eternity, whom he loves (ZIII 16 §l; KSA 4:287). As an aesthetic moment, Zarathustra's vision is timeless: "Es möchte aber Einer daraus mit Recht abnehmen, dass Zarathustra damals nicht lange geschlafen habe" (Z IV 10; KSA 4:345; "From this one might, however, rightly conclude that at that time Zarathustra had not slept for long").

[43] Midnight is the scene of Faust's rejection of Anxiety (Part Two, 11384–510), and also the setting of the poems "Der Bräutigam" and "Um Mitternacht" (written 1818, published 1821; HA 1:372–73). See chapter 2, endnote 37.

[44] HA 1:201; in English, in *Selected Poems,* adapted from Hamburger's translation, 159.

[45] See also Nietzsche's discussion of love in his *Nachlass:* "Will man den erstaunlichsten Beweis dafür, wie weit die Transfigurationskunst des Rausches geht? Die 'Liebe' ist dieser Beweis, das, was Liebe heißt, in allen Sprachen und Stummheiten der Welt" (WM §808/14 [120]; KSA 13:299; "Do you want the most astonishing proof of how far the transfiguring art of frenzy extends? 'Love' is this proof, what love is called in all languages and silences of the world"); and the *Nachlass* fragment, "— *nur die Liebe soll richten* —" (25 [493]; KSA 11:143; "Only love should judge"). In another *Nachlass* note, Nietzsche observes: "Wirklich den Pessimismus *überwinden* —; ein Goethischer Blick voll Liebe und gutem Willen als Resultat" (WM §1032/9[177]; KSA 12:440; "Really to overcome *pessimism* —; a Goethean eye full of love and good will as the result").

[46] In his *Nachlass,* Nietzsche refers repeatedly to the theme of unifying the faculties: "Alles Schaffen ist Mittheilen. Der Erkennende der Schaffende der Liebende sind *Eins*" (4[23]; KSA 10:115; "All creation is communication. The one who knows, the one who creates, the one who loves, are *one*"); "der Schenkende der Schaffende der Lehrende — das sind Vorspiele des *Herrschenden*" (15[27]; KSA 10:486; "the one who gives, the who one creates, the one who teaches — these are preludes to *those*

who rule"); "Künstler (Schaffender), Heiliger (Liebender) und Philosoph (Erkennender) in *Einer Person* zu werden: — *mein praktisches Ziel!*" (16[11]; KSA 10:501; "To become the artist (the one who creates), the saint (the one who loves), and the philosopher (the one who knows) in *one person: my practical goal!*"; compare with his later notes: "Einheit des Schaffenden, Liebenden, Erkennenden in der Macht" [16[49]; KSA 10:514; "The unity of the one who creates, the one who loves, the one who knows in power"] and: "Die *Identität* im Wesen des *Eroberers, Gesetzgebers* und *Künstlers*" [25[94]; KSA 11:32; "The *identity* in essence of the conqueror, lawgiver and artist"]).

[47] Johann Wolfgang von Goethe, *From My Life: Poetry and Truth: Parts One to Three,* ed. Thomas P. Saine and Jeffrey L. Sammons, trans. Robert R. Heitner, Goethe Edition, vol. 4 (New York: Suhrkamp, 1987), 427. Compare with, in the *Tabulae Votivae* of Goethe and Schiller, "Der schöne Geist und der Schöngeist" ("The Aesthetic Spirit and the Aesthete"):

"Nur das Leichtere trägt auf leichten Schultern der Schöngeist,
Aber der schöne Geist trägt das Gewichtige leicht"

["Only what's easier is carried on light shoulders by the aesthete,
But the aesthetic spirit carries what's weighty with ease"]
(WA 1.5/i:305; see also *Aesthetic Letters,*
Letter 19, §12 and Letter 27, §8 and §11).

In "Urworte. Orphisch," Goethe attributes a similar lightness to Hope: "Aus Wolkendecke, Nebel, Regenschauer / Erhebt sie uns, mit ihr, durch sie beflügelt" (HA 1:360; "From heavy cloud, from fog, from squall of rain / She lifts us to herself, we're winged again": adapted from the translation by Middleton in Goethe, *Selected Poems,* 233); and in "Dauer im Wechsel" ("Permanence in Change"), Goethe urges: "Schneller als die Gegenstände / Selber dich vorüberfliehn" (HA 1:248; "Here, amid stampeding objects, / Be among the first to fly beyond yourself": adapted from the translation by John Frederick Nims in Goethe, *Selected Poems,* 169). This image of self-reflective lightness is carried through into *Zarathustra:* "Jetzt bin ich leicht, jetzt fliege ich, jetzt sehe ich mich unter mir, jetzt tanzt ein Gott durch mich" (Z I 7; KSA 4:50; "Now I am light, now I can fly, now I see myself beneath myself, now a god dances through me").

[48] See R. H. Stephenson, *Goethe's Wisdom Literature: A Study in Aesthetic Transmutation* (Bern, Frankfurt am Main, New York: Peter Lang, 1983), 157–208; *Goethe's Conception of Knowledge and Science* (Edinburgh: Edinburgh UP, 1995), 65–82; and "'Ein künstlicher Vortrag': Die symbolische Form von Goethes naturwissenschaftlichen Schriften," in Barbara Naumann and Birgit Recki, eds., *Cassirer und Goethe: Neue Aspekte einer philosophisch-literarischen Wahlverwandtschaft* (Berlin: Akademie Verlag, 2002), 27–42.

[49] See Goethe's conversation with Eckermann of 18 April 1827; *Conversations of Goethe with Johann Peter Eckermann,* ed. J. K. Moorhead, trans. John Oxenford (New York: Da Capo Press, 1998), 192 (translation adapted).

[50] Further on, Nietzsche repeats the view "dass nur als ein aesthetisches Phänomen das Dasein und die Welt gerechtfertigt erscheint" ("that existence and the world seem to be justified only as an aesthetic phenomenon"), explaining "dass selbst das

Hässliche und Disharmonische ein künstlerisches Spiel ist, welches der Wille, in der ewigen Fülle seiner Lust, mit sich selbst spielt" (*GT* §24; KSA 1:152; "that even the ugly and disharmonic is part of an artistic game, in which the will, in the eternal fullness of its pleasure, plays with itself"). Equally, ugliness was not excluded from Schiller's account of the aesthetic in his *On the Aesthetic Education of Man;* for ugliness is to be regarded as an absence of beauty, rather than being hypostatized into a separate category. In Kantian terms, beauty is a necessary postulate, whereas ugliness, by contrast, is merely a hypothetical postulate of Being. In his *Kritik der praktischen Vernunft* (*Critique of Practical Reason*), Kant describes a "Postulat der reinen praktischen Vernunft" ("postulate of pure, practical reason") as a "subjektive, aber doch wahre und unbedingte Vernunftnotwendigkeit" ("subjective, but still true and unconditioned necessity of reason"; "Vorrede," footnote 5).

[51] As a recent commentator who is hostile to Nietzsche has remarked: "Nietzsche's sometimes 'megalomanic' rhetorical mode has, as its concomitant, its comrade-in-arms, its distinctive 'minor literature' equivalent: namely, a site of operations deep within the most subtle, intricate, and overlooked levels of common language" (Geoff Waite, *Nietzsche's Corpse: Aesthetics. Politics. Prophecy, or, The Spectacular Technoculture of Everyday Life* [Durham and London: Duke UP, 1996], 130). Examples are such passages are "Das Nachtlied" (Z II 9; KSA 4:136–38), or the following lines from "Von den Dichtern":

> "Schon zuviel ist mir's, meine Meinungen selber zu behalten; und mancher Vogel fliegt davon.
> Und mitunter finde ich auch ein zugeflogenes Thier in meinem Taubenschlage, das mir fremd ist, und das zittert, wenn ich meine Hand darauf lege." (*Z* II 17; KSA 4:163)

> ["It is already too much for me to keep my own opinions to myself; and many a bird flies away.
> And now and then I also find a stray one flown into my dove-cot, one that is strange to me and that trembles when I lay my hand upon it."]

[52] Compare with Nietzsche's *Nachlass* fragment entitled "'*Musik*' — *und der große Stil*" ("'Music' — and the grand style"): "Die Größe eines Künstlers bemißt sich nicht nach den 'schönen Gefühlen' die er erregt [. . .]. Über das Chaos Herr werden das man ist; sein Chaos zwingen, Form zu werden; Nothwendigkeit werden in Form: logisch, einfach, unzweideutig, Mathematik werden; *Gesetz* werden —: das ist hier die große Ambition. Mit ihr stößt man zurück; nichts reizt mehr die Liebe zu solchen Gewaltmenschen — eine Einöde legt sich um sie, ein Schweigen, eine Furcht wie vor einem großen Frevel . . ." (*WM* §842/14[61]; KSA 13:246–47; "The greatness of an artist cannot be measured by the 'beautiful feelings' he arouses . . . To become master of the chaos one is; to compel one's chaos to become form: to become logical, simple, unambiguous, mathematics, *law* — that is the grand ambition here. — With it one repels; such men of force are no longer loved — a desert spreads around them, a silence, a fear as before some great sacrilege").

[53] For further discussion, see Victor Lange, "The Metaphor of Silence," in Elizabeth M. Wilkinson, ed., *Goethe Revisited* (London and New York: John Calder, 1983/84), 133–52.

⁵⁴ Compare with Nietzsche's remark in his letter to Carl von Gersdorff of circa 18 September 1871 about religion and philosophy: "Auch ist es eine edle Kunst, in solchen Dingen zur rechten Zeit zu *schweigen*" (KSB 3:227; "It is also a noble art to be *silent* about such things at the right time").

⁵⁵ Nietzsche quoted this passage in his famous discussion of the inspiration behind *Zarathustra* in *Ecce Homo* (*EH Z* §3; KSA 6:340).

⁵⁶ Compare with the discussion of the need to retrace the filiation of apparently paradoxical aphorisms in *Wilhelm Meisters Wanderjahre* (bk. 1, ch. 10): "Resultate waren es, die, wenn wir nicht ihre Veranlassung wissen, als paradox erscheinen, uns aber nötigen, vermittelst eines umgekehrten Findens und Erfindens rückwärtszugehen und uns die Filiation solcher Gedanken von weit her, von unten herauf wo möglich zu vergegenwärtigen" (HA 8:125; "These were conclusions which, if we did not know what occasioned them, would seem paradoxical, but which make us go backwards, by a process of reversed intuition or invention, to reconstruct as best we can the filiation of such ideas from the bottom up": Johann Wolfgang von Goethe, *Conversations of German Refugees/Wilhelm Meister's Journeyman Years or The Renunciants*, ed. Jane K. Brown, trans. Jan van Heurck/Krishna Winston, Goethe Edition, vol. 10 [New York: Suhrkamp, 1989], 181).

⁵⁷ In the Prologue, Zarathustra promises that "wer noch Ohren hat für Unerhörtes, dem will ich sein Herz schwer machen mit meinem Glücke" (*Z* Vorrede §9; KSA 4:27; "whoever still has ears for the unheard-of, his heart I shall make heavy with my happiness"); yet he realizes he is misunderstood: "Doch was rede ich, wo Niemand *meine* Ohren hat!" (*Z* III 5 §3; KSA 4:216; "But why do I speak when nobody has *my* ears?"); alluding to the Bible (Matthew 11.15, 13.9 and 43; Mark, 4.9 and 23; Luke, 8.8, 14.35), he cries: "Wer Ohren hat, der höre!" (*Z* III 2 §1 and *Z* III 12 §16; KSA 4:199 and 258; "Whoever has ears, let him hear!"); talking to the two Kings, Zarathustra refers to the ears of the ass they are driving before them and exclaims: "Ich bin entzückt, und, wahrlich, schon gelüstet's mich, einen Reim darauf zu machen: — / — mag es auch ein Reim werden, der nicht für Jedermanns Ohren taugt. Ich verlernte seit langem schon die Rücksicht auf lange Ohren" (*Z* IV 3 §1; KSA 4:306; "I am delighted, and truly, I already feel the desire to make a verse on this — / — even if it should be a verse not fit for everybody's ears. I have long become unaccustomed to any consideration for long ears"); hoping for good listeners in the Higher Men, he says: "oh Mensch, du höherer Mensch, gieb Acht! diese Rede ist für feine Ohren, für deine Ohren —" (*Z* IV 19 §4; KSA 4:398–99; "O man, Higher Man, take care! This speech is for delicate ears, for your ears —"); reacting to the disappointment of this hope, he realizes: "Das Ohr, das nach *mir* horcht, — das *gehorchende* Ohr fehlt in ihren Gliedern" (*Z* IV 20; KSA 4:405; "The ear that listens for *me*, the *obeying* ear, is lacking in their limbs"). In this respect, Zarathustra faces the same problem as Wagner, according to Nietzsche's analysis in "Richard Wagner in Bayreuth" ("Richard Wagner in Bayreuth," 1876): "Wenn aber die Sprache eines Volkes sich schon im Zustande des Verfalls und der Abnutzung befindet, so kommt der Wortdramatiker in die Versuchung, Sprache und Gedanken ungewöhnlich aufzufärben und umzubilden; er will die Sprache heben, damit sie wieder das gehobene Gefühl hervorklingen lasse, und geräth dabei in die Gefahr, gar nicht verstanden zu werden. Ebenso sucht er der Leidenschaft durch erhabene

Sinnsprüche und Einfälle Etwas von Höhe mitzutheilen und verfällt dadurch wieder in eine andere Gefahr: er erscheint unwahr und künstlich" (*UB* IV §9; KSA 1:488; "When the language of a people is already in a state of decay and deliquescence, however, the poet of the spoken drama falls prey to the temptation to give his thoughts and language unusual colors and to restructure them; he wants to elevate language so that it can again express exalted feelings and he thereby incurs the danger of not being understood at all. Likewise he seeks to lend the passions, through sublime aphorisms and conceits, some level of loftiness and thereby falls into another kind of danger: he appears false and artificial"). In *Jenseits von Gut und Böse,* Nietzsche complained that German books were not written for those with "das *dritte* Ohr" ("the *third* ear") (*JGB* §246; KSA 5:189; compare *JGB* §247; KSA 5:190–91).

[58] Compare with the following exchange in a fragment from the *Nachlass:* "Du widersprichst heute dem, was du gestern gelehrt hast — Aber dafür ist gestern nicht heute, sagte Zarathustra" (12[128]; KSA 9:598; "You are contradicting today what you taught yesterday — That's why yesterday is not today, said Zarathustra").

[59] The same lines from *Faust II* were parodied by Nietzsche in his poem "An Goethe" ("To Goethe"), the first of the "Lieder des Prinzen Vogelfrei" appended to *Die fröhliche Wissenschaft* (KSA 3:639). For a commentary on this poem, see Philip Grundlehner, *The Poetry of Friedrich Nietzsche* (New York and Oxford: Oxford UP, 1986), 150–57; and see also Ernst Rose, "Goethes 'Chorus Mysticus' als Anregung für Nietzsche und Rilke," *The Germanic Review* 17 (1942): 39–47.

[60] WA 1.29:277 (Apparat). In *Dichtung und Wahrheit* (part 4, bk. 18), Goethe attributed this remark to his friend Johann Heinrich Merck (HA 10:128; English translation from Johann Wolfgang von Goethe, *From My Life: Poetry and Truth. Part Four/Campaign in France 1792. Siege of Mainz,* ed. Thomas P. Saine and Jeffrey L. Sammons, trans. Robert R. Heitner/Thomas P. Saine, Goethe Edition, vol. 5 (New York: Suhrkamp, 1987), 560–61).

[61] For definitions of the rhetorical terms referred to here, see Heinrich Lausberg, *Handbuch der literarischen Rhetorik: Eine Grundlegung der Literaturwissenschaft,* 2 vols (2nd ed., Munich: Max Hueber, 1973). For further discussion, see Peter Gasser, *Rhetorische Philosophie: Leseversuche zum metaphorischen Diskurs in Nietzsches "Also sprach Zarathustra"* (Bern, Berlin, Frankfurt am Main: Lang, 1993).

[62] From Nietzsche's early lecture, known as "Darstellung der antiken Rhetorik" (Summer Semester 1874; KGW 2.4:425). Compare with Nietzsche's argument in his earlier essay "Ueber Wahrheit und Lüge im aussermoralischen Sinne" ("On Truth and Lying an an Extra-Moral Sense," 1872/1873; KSA 1:873–90). For further discussion, see Bernhard Greiner, *Friedrich Nietzsche: Versuch und Versuchung in seinen Aphorismen* (Munich: Wilhelm Fink, 1972), "Nietzsches Stellung zur Rhetorik" (213–19).

[63] Goethe, famously, called himself the "Gleichnismacher" and, besides such rhetorical forms as metaphor, his concept of "Gleichnis" (or "likeness") includes the seeming, symbolic similarity between aesthetic patterns in art and those at work in life. See Stephenson, *Goethe's Conception of Knowledge and Silence,* 47–63.

[64] See Gary Shapiro's analysis of this chapter in *Nietzschean Narratives* (Bloomington and Indianapolis: Indiana UP, 1989), 39–70.

[65] In a fragment from the *Nachlass* from the period November 1882 to February 1883 we find the Zarathustrian note: "Ihr sollt eure Sinne nicht tödten sondern heiligen — unschuldig machen" (4[94]; KSA 10:142; "You should not kill your senses but sanctify them — make them innocent").

[66] Goethe, "Selige Sehnsucht," HA 2:19; in English, *Selected Poems,* adapted from the translation by Hamburger, 207.

[67] "Das Auge ist nur Wegweiser, nur die Vernunft der Hand; die Hand allein gibt *Formen,* Begriffe dessen, was sie *bedeuten,* was in ihnen *wohnet* [. . .] Durch [den] Zaubertrug [des Malers] sollte Gesicht Gefühl werden, so wie bei ihm das Gefühl Gesicht ward" (Johann Gottfried Herder, *Plastik,* sections 4 and 1, §2, in *Werke,* 10 vols (Frankfurt am Main: Deutscher Klassiker Verlag, 1985–2000), 4:280 and 251; "The eye is only the guide, only the reason of the hand; the hand alone gives *forms* concepts of what they *mean,* what *dwells* in them . . . Through the magical deception of the painter vision should become feeling, just as, for him feeling became vision"); and compare with the coordination of eye and hand celebrated in Goethe's seventh poem in the *Römische Elegien* (*Roman Elegies*) cycle: "Dann versteh' ich den Marmor erst recht: ich denk' und vergleiche, / Sehe mit fühlendem Aug', fühle mit sehender Hand" (HA 1:160; "Only thus I appreciate marble; reflecting, comparing, / See with an eye that can feel, feel with a hand that can see" translation by Hamburger, in *Selected Poems,* 107).

[68] In *Der Antichrist,* Nietzsche evokes the topos of the hand and the eye when he laments what has happened to the achievements of classicism: "Was wir heute, mit unsäglicher Selbstbezwingung — denn wir haben Alle die schlechten Instinkte, die christlichen, irgendwie noch im Leibe —, uns zurückerobert haben, den freien Blick vor der Realität, die vorsichtige Hand, die Geduld und den Ernst im Kleinsten, die ganze *Rechtschaffenheit* der Erkenntniss — sie war bereits da! vor mehr als zwei Jahrtausenden bereits! *Und,* dazu gerechnet, der gute, der feine Takt und Geschmack! *Nicht* als Gehirn-Dressur! *Nicht* als 'deutsche' Bildung mit Rüpel-Manieren! Sondern als Leib, als Gebärde, als Instinkt, — als Realität mit Einem Wort . . . *Alles umsonst!* Über Nacht bloss noch eine Erinnerung!" (*AC* §59; KSA 6:248; "What we today have again conquered with immeasurable self-mastery — for each of us still has the bad instincts, the Christian ones, in his system — the free eye in the face of reality, the careful hand, patience and seriousness in the smallest matters, the whole *honesty* in knowledge — that had already been there once before! More than two thousand years ago! *And,* in addition, the good, the delicate sense of tact and taste. *Not* as brain drill! *Not* as 'German' education with loutish manners! But as body, as gesture, as instinct — in a word, as reality. *All in vain!* Overnight nothing but a memory!").

[69] For further discussion, see Elizabeth M. Wilkinson and L. A. Willoughby, "'The Whole Man'" in Schiller's Theory of Culture and Society," in *Models of Wholeness: Some Attitudes to Language, Art and Life in the Age of Goethe,* ed. Jeremy Adler, Martin Swales, and Ann Weaver (Oxford, Bern, Berlin: Peter Lang, 2002), 233–68.

[70] Beginning with his review of Bürger's *Gedichte, veredeln* was a central notion within Schillerian aesthetics (compare *On the Aesthetic Education of Man,* Letters 4, §2 and 13, §5; and see Wilkinson and Willoughby's glossary [316–17], where they suggest that this is one of the concepts Schiller derived from Goethe's natural sci-

ence). The term has alchemical implications, which would probably also have been known to Nietzsche. For further discussion, see Richard Perkins, "Nietzsche's *opus alchymicum*," *Seminar* 23 (1987): 216–26, where he points out: "Beginning in 1882, Nietzsche frequently and fairly insistently poses as an inner alchemist, privately in euphoric notebook entries, confidentially in frantic letters to Franz Overbeck, and publicly in *Also sprach Zarathustra,* a frankly chrysopoetic work culminating in a golden nature won through transmutation" (216); and Graham Parkes, *Composing the Soul: Reaches of Nietzsche's Psychology* (Chicago and London: U of Chicago P, 1994), where he argues that *Zarathustra* is "a text that contains dozens of images that figure importantly in alchemy — and especially in alchemy understood as a symbol system for psychological transformation — such as chaos; the stone, fire, sun, and moon; the dragon, eagle, lion, serpent, and ouroborus; the child; and of course lead and gold" (166). The transmutation wrought by Zarathustra is, however, not alchemical as such, but rather, as in Goethe and Schiller, aesthetic.

[71] HA 1:370; *Selected Poems,* trans. Middleton, 269.

[72] Compare with Nietzsche's remark in "Vom Nutzen und Nachtheil der Historie für das Leben": "Dies ist ein Gleichniss für jeden Einzelnen von uns: er muss das Chaos in sich organisiren, dadurch dass er sich auf seine ächten Bedürfnisse zurückbesinnt" (*UB* II §10; KSA 1:333; "This is a parable for each one of us: he or she must organize the chaos within him or her by thinking back to his or her real needs").

[73] In the last letter of his *On the Aesthetic Education of Man,* Schiller emphasized: "In [dem] Gebiete [des Geschmacks] muss auch der mächtigste Genius sich seiner Hoheit begeben und zu dem Kindersinn vertraulich herniedersteigen" (Letter 27, §11; "In the kingdom of taste even the mightiest genius must divest itself of its majesty, and stoop in all humility to the mind of the little child").

[74] The reciprocal opposition between *Ernst* and *Spiel* is frequently found in Goethe and Schiller (see the note by Wilkinson and Willoughby in their edition of *On the Aesthetic Education of Man,* 251). See further Goethe's "Der Sammler und die Seinigen," Letter 8, §6 (HA 12:96; *Essays on Art and Literature,* 159); the Prologue to Schiller's *Wallensteins Lager* (1798): "Ernst ist das Leben, heiter ist die Kunst" (NA 8:6; "Life is serious, but art is cheerful"); and, in *On the Aesthetic Education of Man,* Letters 9, §7; 15, §5-§7; and 22, §2. In a passage from "Vom Lesen und Schreiben" that Nietzsche also uses as a motto for part 3, Zarathustra says: "Wer von euch kann zugleich lachen und erhoben sein? / Wer auf den höchsten Bergen steigt, der lacht über alle Trauer-Spiele und Trauer-Ernste" (*Z* I 7; KSA 4:49; "Who among you can laugh and be elevated at the same time? / Whoever climbs the highest mountains laughs at all tragic plays and tragic seriousness").

[75] Although Zarathustra is described by the Old Man in the Forest as having become a child (*Z* Vorrede §2; KSA 4:12), he must still make progress in the aesthetic; in "Die stillste Stunde," Zarathustra hears the silence tell him: "'Du musst noch Kind werden und ohne Scham. / Der Stolz der Jugend ist noch auf dir, spät bist du jung geworden: aber wer zum Kinde werden will, muss auch noch seine Jugend überwinden'" (*Z* II 22; KSA 4:189; "'You must yet become a child and without shame. / The pride of youth is still upon you, you have become young late: but whoever wants to become a child must overcome even youth"). Elsewhere, Zarathustra places great emphasis on the inner child: "Im ächten Manne ist ein Kind

versteckt: das will spielen" (ZI 18; KSA 4:85; "In the real man a child is hidden: it wants to play"); and: "[. . .] im Manne ist mehr Kind als im Jünglinge" (ZI 21; KSA 4:95; "in the man there is more of the child than in the youth"). The link between children and play is humorously made at the end of "Von den Tugendhaften," when the tide has taken away his disciples' toys: "Wahrlich, ich nahm euch wohl hundert Worte und eurer Tugend liebste Spielwerke; und nun zürnt ihr mir, wie Kinder zürnen. / Sie spielten am Meere, — da kam die Welle und riss ihnen ihr Spielwerk in die Tiefe: nun weinen sie" ("Truly, I have taken away from you a hundred words and the dearest playthings of your virtue; and now you are angry with me, as children are angry. / They were playing by the sea, and a wave came and carried off their play-things to the depths: now they are crying"). But, instead, the sea will provide new (aesthetic) seashells to play with: "Aber die selbe Welle soll ihnen neue Spielwerke bringen und neue bunte Muscheln vor sie hin ausschütten! / So werden sie getröstet sein; und gleich ihnen sollte auch ihr, meine Freunde, eure Tröstungen haben — und neue bunte Muscheln! —" (ZII 5; KSA 4:123; "But the same wave shall bring them new playthings and shower new, colorful sea-shells before them! / Thus they will be consoled; and, like them, you too, my friends, shall have your consolations — and new, colorful sea-shells!"). At the end of the book, the sign of the laughing lion tells Zarathustra that his children are near (Z IV 20; KSA 4:408).

4: From Leucippus to Cassirer: Toward a Genealogy of "Sincere Semblance"

Freuet euch des wahren Scheins,
Euch des ernsten Spieles:
Kein Lebendiges ist ein Eins,
Immer ist's ein Vieles.

[Take delight in this true illusion,
In this serious play:
No living thing is One,
It is always Many.]
— Goethe, "Epirrhema"

THERE IS MUCH IN THE long history of reflection on beauty in art and nature to support the view that Weimar Classicism is advocating a perennial aesthetic. It is not just that it has recently been claimed "that the aesthetic is [. . .] the dynamic center of the whole speculative enterprise" of philosophy.[1] There are also innumerable indications across the whole cultural spectrum, from theology to drama, to suggest a succession of anticipations of Goethe's and Schiller's position. For instance, Leucippus, the atomist materialist philosopher of the fifth century B.C.E., is reported to have taught that "true happiness is the purpose of the soul," and that "happiness is procured by beautiful things."[2] Diogenes of Sinope, the Cynic philosopher of the fourth century B.C.E., is recorded as asking of someone: "Why do you live, if you are not concerned to make your life beautiful?"[3] Moreover, the lure of semblance is attested to in the biblical Apocrypha, where King Solomon writes that "[men] are persuaded by appearances because what they see is so beautiful."[4] And the meditation of the second-century Roman emperor and Stoic philosopher Marcus Aurelius on the pleasure afforded by "the things that follow after the things that are produced according to nature" sounds, in its down-to-earth illustration, very close indeed to what Goethe and Schiller had in mind when they spoke of the "manifest freedom" of an aesthetic object: "For instance, when bread is baked some parts are split at the surface, and the parts which thus open, and have a certain fashion *contrary to the purpose of the baker's art,* are beautiful in a manner." For, according to Aurelius, it is precisely the result of such apparently unintended consequences that "*seem* [. . .] to be in a manner disposed so as to give pleasure."[5] Similarly, when St. Thomas Aquinas, in a passage in the *Summa Theologica* that Stephen Dedalus seeks to defend in *A Portrait of the Artist as a Young Man* (1914–15) by James Joyce (1882–1941), argues that beauty is a matter of the particular "quiddity" of things "which please when seen," rather than of numerals,[6] we are surely justified in registering an overlap with Weimar Classicism's staunch insistence on the concretion of aesthetic experience. Strong evidence also suggests that an association of both *frei* (free) and *Schein* (illusion) with the notion of beauty was established in German usage long before Schiller used the term *Freiheit in der Erscheinung* (freedom in appearance) to cover his own distinctive, finely elaborated concept. According to the Grimms' *Deutsches Wörterbuch,* the collocation goes back to Middle High German, a view that Keith Spalding's *Historical Dictionary of German Figurative Usage* supports. Shakespeare's equation of "sweet semblance" with "beauty" in Sonnet 13, like Cervantes' sophisticated play with the nuances of Appearance and Reality in *Don Quixote,*[7] seems to corroborate the pedigree of Weimar aesthetics, in much the same way that a recent account of Rubens's New Aesthetic as a view of beauty as "growth into form" resonates precisely with Goethe's view of art as (second) nature.[8] Indeed, the very collocation of "free illusion" is, according to the Grimms, to be found in Lessing, Kant, and Moses Mendelssohn, who held "that only full awareness of the fact that it is illusion creates aesthetic pleasure" —[9] a precipitate, perhaps, of a theory of aesthetic experience as being grounded in a coordination of sense and thought that seems to owe a good deal to the pervasive influence of the Scottish School, particularly Thomas Reid (1710–96), on German thought in the eighteenth century.[10]

Despite the fact that, as Johan Huizinga reminds us, "there are few subjects about which tradition is so defective as the aesthetic sentiment of past ages,"[11] it is nonetheless possible to discern a line of descent to Goethe and Schiller, to Nietzsche, and beyond, which is clearly marked by a divergence from the aesthetic idealism of Plato and his followers, particularly from that taught by Plotinus. Socrates' reporting of Diotima's declarations that "the beauty in every form is one and the same," and that "the beauty of the mind is more honorable than the beauty of the outward form"[12] stands in stark opposition to the position taken by Weimar Classicism, like his argument to Phaedrus — presented to such ironic effect by Thomas Mann (1875–1955) in his *Der Tod in Venedig* (*Death in Venice,* 1912) — about beauty as "der Weg des Fühlenden zum Geiste, — nur der Weg, ein Mittel nur" ("the beauty-lover's way to the spirit, but only the way, only the means").[13]

By contrast with Plato's assertion in part 5 of *The Republic* that "the lovers of sounds and sights [are] incapable of seeing or loving absolute beauty,"[14] for Goethe and Schiller, just as the spell of poetry is cast by the enchantment of sound, sense, and their interaction, so, too, the magic of any and every aesthetic relation is essentially, if not wholly, a physical, sensuous, phenomenon. Indeed, even the word "relation" is far too abstract for the awkward, odd, "quiddity" of the aesthetic experience as they envisage it. For by virtue of its sheer (sensuous) particularity, it fits no neat compartmentalization of the intellect. It would, in fact, be no exaggeration to say that Weimar Classicism represents a stance of resistance to Platonism of all kinds. Socrates' famous lines in *Phaedrus* about the human fate of being imprisoned in the living tomb of the body "like an oyster in his shell" is the perfect foil to Goethe's, and Schiller's, conviction that the artist must tenderly explore the bodiliness of his (frankly limited and limiting) chosen medium, in order to give expression to what would otherwise entirely go without saying.[15] As Goethe's careful coming-to-terms with Plotinus' aesthetics, in a series of aphorisms that eventually found their way into *Wilhelm Meister,* shows, the position he shared with Schiller does not entail tracing the "beauty that is in bodies" (as if that were different from that "which is in the soul") to its source in the "eternal intelligence," "the beauty outside of sense"; "the beauty [. . .] not in the concrete object," which Plotinus extols, simply does not exist for Weimar Classicism, except as a metaphor.[16] Goethe could hardly be more forthright, or more in the tune with the spirit of his collaboration with Schiller, in wholly rejecting the fundamental tenet of Plato's theory of beauty:

> Im Ästhetischen tut man nicht wohl zu sagen: die Idee des Schönen; dadurch vereinzelt man das Schöne, das doch einzeln nicht gedacht werden kann. Vom Schönen kann man einen Begriff haben, und dieser Begriff kann überliefert werden.

> [In the context of aesthetics it is not appropriate to speak of "the idea of beauty"; in this way you isolate the concept of beauty, which surely cannot be thought of as a separate entity. You can have a concept of what is beautiful and this concept can be transmitted.][17]

For Weimar Classicism beauty is a sensuous matter, irreducible to the Ideal.

Nowhere is this divergence from the Platonic tradition clearer than in respect of the key idea of aesthetic illusion (*aufrichtiger Schein* [sincere semblance]) as Goethe and Schiller developed it. The frank illusion of a *trompe l'oeil* (such as the drawing of a cube on a flat surface) lacks the aesthetic ingredient of appearing to be unintended, and thus "alive" in the sense of self-generating, although confusion of "the perceptual quality of liveliness" with merely "making things look real" has traditionally dogged art-criticism.[18] There is no such confusion in Weimar Classicism. Long before his work with Schiller, Goethe had anticipated his friend's views in, for instance, his reflections on "Frauenrollen auf dem Römischen Theater durch Männer gespielt" ("Women's Parts Played by Men in the Roman Theatre"), written in 1788 during his Italian journey. Aware that the roles are being played by men, the audience is not deceived by this particular mode of cross-dressing; but neither is the illusion entirely destroyed as it would be by, say, clumsy actors. The concept of art, Goethe concludes, remains a living one, and skilful play (*Spiel*) produces a self-conscious, "frank and honest," illusion.[19]

It was Goethe's and Schiller's shared conviction that objectification of the inner life is the distinctive function of all art. "The poet," as Johann Gottfried Herder (1744–1803) had it in opposition to Lessing, "should express feelings."[20] In the eighteenth century "feeling" had a much wider meaning than it has today, encompassing what T. S. Eliot called "felt-thought," the whole continuum from tactile sensation to thought: in other words, thought not yet reduced to the either-or categories of discursive language and thus highly ambivalent. A work of art, like any other aesthetic phenomenon, articulates such feeling by providing, for our contemplation, an analogue of the felt-life within, something that can be achieved only if this analogue, this "semblance" (*Schein*), exhibits the same sensuous-abstract quality as the felt-thought it is designed to express. Where this illusion is achieved, the direct benefit for our minds is twofold. On the one hand we gain in self-awareness and self-control. On the other, aesthetic insight is knowledge and, like any form of freshly acquired knowledge, enables us to conceive the world with a new tool. Commonly shared but dimly apprehended feelings become, through aesthetic experience, no less shared but now articulated "convictions" or "attitudes" (*Gesinnungen*) on which we act and base our reasoning, but to which (because they are still in part tethered to sensation) we find it impossible to give adequate intellectual expression. Such sensuous-abstract schemata permit us to "see into the life of things." *Gehalt* — "content" in the sense of "import" — is that aspect of our felt-life that the work of art "contains" for us. Feeling, Susanne K. Langer (1895–1985) argues, has distinctive patterns; it exhibits what she, very much in the spirit of Goethe, calls a "morphology":[21] the structure of the inner life is an organic, developmental one in which thinking-feeling-bodily sensation is coalesced. And it is in constant interaction with the external world: we internalize ideas and expressions — what Goethe and Schiller called *Stoff* ("content" in the sense of material) — by aligning them with the felt, dynamic, patterns at work within us. Because of different life-experiences the felt-life of one individual will, to a lesser or greater extent, differ from that of another. But, because we share the same, or at least similar, natural, cultural, or social environment, the overlap will be considerable. The more fundamental and encompassing the felt-thought an aesthetic object articulates, the more "universal" its appeal will be, the greater its significance. Now, if what is within us is to be projected outwards on to it, the aesthetic phenomenon must exhibit the same organic structure as the morphology of our inner life; it must, as Schiller argued, evince "manifest freedom" (*Freiheit in der Erscheinung*): it must appear to be both self-regulating and self-regulated. In order to achieve this peculiarly aesthetic illusion, the relations established in the aesthetic object must inhere in the medium used, so that its aesthetic order does not appear to be imposed from the outside, but *seems* rather to be immanent in the object itself; to be, as Nietzsche has it, *von Ohngefähr* — casual and unintended.

What the intellect separates as incompatible Either-Or's, aesthetic form binds together and reconciles as congruent co-existents, held in the precarious synthesis of a polar interplay within a shared, sensuous, medium. Thus aesthetic experience is essentially playful and comic, even when concerned with the gravest import. And the detachment and inherent comedy of sincere seeming vouchsafes "serenity" (*Heiterkeit*) in the ancient sense of *euthumia* — "the lightness of being," as Milan Kundera calls it — which makes life, even at its darkest moments, seem worthwhile.[22] For beauty does not appear to be at all purposive, but merely — as if by grace — necessarily present; it seems to be, and actually is, dependent on the patterned interaction of contingent factors, sustained for the brief duration of the aesthetic experience. To put it simply, in psychological terms that have become the veriest commonplaces of modernity: the Self, in the sense of one's felt inner life, speaks only in this transient, though recurrent, aesthetic mode; the Ego, in the sense of the thinking subject wrestling with purposive, prosaic reality, can express itself only in the discursive mode of "serious" intent.

Freiheit in der Erscheinung, manifest freedom, consists for Schiller in the *apparently* self-regulating structure of an aesthetic object. And this, in turn, means that no rule should be discernible in the object that can be translated into general conceptual terms and extracted. For such a rule would imply the imposition, by a mind, of order from outside the work.[23] By establishing perceptible relations between specific physical features of the medium, the artist ensures that no such rule can be deduced, and no such intention inferred. The result is that, like a product of nature, the art-object seems free, autonomous:

> Das Gesetz, das in die Erscheinung tritt, in der größten Freiheit, nach seinen eigensten Bedingungen, bringt das objektiv Schöne hervor, welches freilich würdige Subjekte finden muß, von denen es aufgefaßt wird.

> [Law which is made manifest, in the greatest freedom, according to its very own conditions, gives rise to objective beauty, which must, admittedly, find worthy subjects to apprehend it.][24]

Artistic finesse consists precisely in the exploitation of the detail of the medium to form an apparently autonomous pattern, expressive of import. In the case of poetry, it is the pattern created between semantic elements and the outward forms of individual words that "appears" utterly fortuitous, free, in Schiller's sense. And since no evidence of intent is available, the virtual object created by these coordinations cannot be ascribed to a rhetorical persona, since a persona is, by definition, the "mind" implied by rule-bound use of language. It must be ascribed, rather, to the writer himself. For the aesthetic structure seems to be the unconscious, and unintentional, precipitate of the meeting of mind with medium;[25] and, for that reason, appears to bear his stamp, and seems sincere.[26] For Goethe and Schiller, as for André Breton (1896–1966), *les mots font l'amour* (words make love); poetry, like all art, has a body in which it has its being.[27]

But the manifest freedom of aesthetic form is also deployable in the sphere of human action. As Goethe articulates Schiller's concept of *schöner Umgang* (handsome behavior) in, for example, the last two stanzas of his "Urworte. Orphisch" ("Primal Words. Orphic," 1817–18), it is precisely the frank illusion of "seeming free" that gives meaning to human life:

ΑΝΑΓΚΗ, Nötigung

25 Da ist's denn wieder, wie die Sterne wollten:
26 Bedingung und Gesetz; und aller Wille
27 Ist nur ein Wollen, weil wir eben sollten,
28 Und vor dem Willen schweigt die Willkür stille;
29 Das Liebste wird vom Herzen weggescholten,
30 Dem harten Muß bequemt sich Will' und Grille.
31 So sind wir scheinfrei denn nach manchen Jahren
32 Nur enger dran, als wir am Anfang waren.

ΕΛΠΙΣ, Hoffnung

33 Doch solcher Grenze, solcher eh'rnen Mauer
34 Höchst widerwärt'ge Pforte wird entriegelt,
35 Sie stehe nur mit alter Felsendauer!
36 Ein Wesen regt sich leicht und ungezügelt:
37 Aus Wolkendecke, Nebel, Regenschauer
38 Erhebt sie uns, mit ihr, durch sie beflügelt;
39 Ihr kennt sie wohl, sie schwärmt durch alle Zonen;
40 Ein Flügelschlag — und hinter uns Äonen!

ΑΝΑΓΚΗ, Necessity

Then back it comes, what in the stars was written;
Law and circumstance; each will is tried,
All willing simply forced, by obligation:
In face of it, caprice's tongue is tied.
Man's heart forswears what most was loved by him,
To iron "Must" comply both will and whim.
It only seems we're free, years hem us in,
Constraining more than at our origin.

ΕΛΠΙΣ, Hope

Yet the repulsive gate can be unbolted
Within such bounds, their adamantine wall,
Though it may stand, that gate, like rock for ever;
A being moves, unchecked, ethereal:
From heavy cloud, from fog, from squall of rain
She lifts us to herself, we're winged again,
You know her well, to nowhere she's confined —
A wingbeat — aeons vanish far behind.[28]

The ambiguity of the word *scheinfrei* (line 31), meaning both "merely illusorily free" and "manifestly free," yields a rich reading. The poem traces the development of an individual from birth to maturity. In this, a pattern is discerned. In the opening stanza, "Dämon," the fixity of what is innate and "given" is evoked; in the second, "Das Zufällige," the freedom of adolescent dalliance; in the third, "Liebe," the intoxication of love, which carries within it the seeds of commitment. In the fourth stanza, quoted above, the topic is again fixity — this time that imposed by commitment. Here the individual is caught between external necessity (*Bedingung*) and what is traditionally referred to as moral "freedom," namely the recognition of a law within (*Gesetz*) to which our will is subject — often differentiated in eighteenth-century German usage from freedom proper by the term *Freiwilligkeit*.[29] Certainly, this will curb caprice (line 28) and enables us to renounce (line 29); but it is itself an inner compulsion (line 30). Hence the horribly bleak conclusion (lines 31–32) follows as naturally as the little words "so" and "denn" indicate. We have, it is true, an intuition of freedom conceded in the second element of the pregnant compound *scheinfrei*. But it is a mere "illusion," and in two ways: it does not exist in the world (note the imperfect subjunctive in line 27); and, as an *Urwort*, as a necessary presupposition of the equally fundamental notion of Necessity,[30] it only intensifies our sense of constraint and frustration, underlined by poetic play on the polyptoton, linking the notions of "will," "moral obligation," and "mere caprice." For, in addition to environmental pressure, we now have an absolute obligation of stern Duty (lines 26–27), one that we cannot possibly satisfy because of our contingency (line 32).

Yet, if this already complex and subtle thought were all there were to *scheinfrei*, the next and final stanza of the cycle would indeed be what numerous critics take it to be: a wholly incoherent and sentimental flourish — one of these endings that Goethe is so often accused of adding to mitigate his realistic vision of the harshness of the human condition. In fact, this last stanza makes sense as an integral part of the poem only if we give to the term the additional meaning of "aesthetically free."

The change to Hope remains sudden, but not unprepared for. In the midst of despair a thing of beauty sets us free, according to Schiller, by engaging both our abstractive powers and our senses in playful coordination:

> Sobald [. . .] zwei entgegengesetzte Grundtriebe in [dem Menschen] tätig sind, so verlieren beide ihre Nötigung, und die Entgegensetzung zweier Notwendigkeiten gibt der *Freiheit* den Ursprung.

> [As soon as two opposing fundamental drives are active within [the human being], both lose their compulsion, and the opposition of two necessities gives rise to *Freedom*.][31]

Just as a poet coordinates the sounds and rhythms of his language to create a network of palpable resemblances and contrasts that, in turn, establishes apparently free and spontaneous coordinate relations within the semantic content, so anyone who, having glimpsed his or her moral freedom, is desperate to give it expression may will to behave aesthetically (Letter 26, §§1 and 7). This he or she may do by using his or her imagination to coordinate into an interlacing texture those outward, physical, and observable aspects of his or her milieu and person that are already subordinated to on-going purposive action. She or he thereby establishes, like the poet, a perceptible aesthetic form, one that "clothes" and sustains activity, and onto which she or he (and others) can project, and release, the free and dynamic play of the inner life. Whatever she or he undertakes, she or he now undertakes in a free way. Moreover, the aesthetic contemplation basic to aesthetic behavior awakens us to the primacy and priority of formal relationships in the outside world: "Sobald es Licht wird in dem Menschen, ist auch ausser ihm keine Nacht mehr" (Letter 25, §2; "As soon as light dawns within the human being, there is no longer any night without"). Objects no longer seem hard, lifeless, and static; they seem in process and "living." What to the frustrated will seemed monolithic and rigid is revealed as a self-regulating whole, a network of mutually related and intricately interconnected channels of filiation. We are, as in Plato's *Phaedrus,* "given wings" by the contemplation of beauty; but not as the result of any merely intellectual contemplation of the Ideal.[32] What releases us, in Goethe's and Schiller's view, is rather the very earthy experience of an onrush of felt life, engendering that familiar human attitude of Hope (lines 36–38) — intimately connected, as Goethe made explicit, with aesthetic awareness:

> Schön nennen wir ein vollkommen organisiertes Wesen, wenn wir uns bei seinem Anblicke denken können, *daß ihm ein mannigfaltiger freier Gebrauch aller seiner Glieder möglich sei, sobald es wolle,* das höchste Gefühl der Schönheit ist daher mit dem Gefühl von Zutraun und Hoffnung verknüpft.

[We call a perfectly organized creature beautiful when we can entertain the thought while looking at it that it is capable of a manifold, free use of all its limbs as promptly as it likes. The highest feeling of beauty is therefore linked to the feeling of trust and hope.][33]

The enjoyment of aesthetic freedom anticipates the absolute freedom that the Will is set on, for the satisfaction so gained is inherent in the *process* of a life so led, and thus promises a "final" *product* of the same order. We move in, and interact with, the world — once it is aesthetically transformed — with ease and grace. And our mind, now released from the dreariness of a merely conditioned existence, ranges freely and serenely through space and time (lines 38–40; see Letter 25, §7).

Once again what we are dealing with here is Weimar Classicism's reformulation of an age-old aesthetic doctrine. "The necessary technique of seeming," as Yeats — himself deeply influenced by Goethe and Schiller — called it, is the essence of that long tradition of the aristocrat, whether by blood or talent, as an artist of the self.[34] The Self, both Schiller and Goethe knew as well as C. G. Jung (1875–1961), is beyond conceptualization. It is, they held, an aesthetic construct, freely expressed in the style of one's living. And, lest unavoidable associations with the aristocratic tradition of *paraître* should mislead, it is important to note that it is, in their view, in the nature of aesthetic valuation to attach the highest significance to what, from the perspective of the intellect, is "low": the particular, the local, and the close at hand,[35] or what Nietzsche in his writings called the "nearest things."[36] In a passage from *Dawn*, Nietzsche had asked himself:

> Wohin will diese ganze Philosophie mit allen ihren Umwegen? Thut sie mehr, als einen stäten und starken Trieb gleichsam in Vernunft zu übersetzen, einen Trieb nach milder Sonne, heller und bewegter Luft, südlichen Pflanzen, Meeres-Athem, flüchtiger Fleisch-, Eier- und Früchtenahrung, heissem Wasser zum Getränke, tagelangen stillen Wanderungen, wenigem Sprechen, seltenem und vorsichtigem Lesen, einsamen Wohnen, reinlichen, schlichten und fast soldatischen Gewohnheiten, kurz nach allen Dingen, die gerade mir am besten schmecken, gerade mir am zuträglichsten sind? Eine Philosophie, welche im Grunde der Instinct für eine persönliche Diät ist? Ein Instinct, welcher nach meiner Luft, meiner Höhe, meiner Witterung, meiner Art Gesundheit durch den Umweg meines Kopfes sucht? (*D* §553; KSA 3:323)

> [Where does this whole philosophy, with all its circuitous paths, want to go? Does it do more than translate an enduring and strong drive, so to speak, into reason, a drive for gentle sunlight, bright and buoyant air, southerly vegetation, the breath of the sea, fleeting meals of flesh, fruit and eggs, hot water to drink, daylong silent wanderings, little talk-

ing, infrequent and careful reading, solitary living, clean, simple and almost soldierly habits, in short, for all those things that *to me* taste best and are most beneficial? A philosophy that is deep down the instinct for a personal diet? An instinct that seeks my own air, my own heights, my own kind of health and weather, by the circuitous path of my head?]

As if in answer to his own question, in *Die fröhliche Wissenschaft* (*The Gay Science*) Nietzsche wrote that philosophy, as he conceived it, had the following aim: "*Wir* aber wollen die Dichter unseres Lebens sein, und im Kleisten und Alltäglichsten zuerst" (*FW* §299; KSA 3:538; "*We* want to be the poets of our life, and first of all in the smallest, most everyday matters"). For the object of aesthetic perception, the beautiful particular, can only be attained by transcending the generalizing type-concept, which is the closest that intellect, operating alone, comes to a real grasp on reality. The particular, which aesthetic perception endows with universal significance, becomes an individual entity of value.

This emphatically un-Platonic, indeed materialistic, temper of Weimar aesthetics is perhaps at its most blatant in Goethe's *Reineke Fuchs* (1794) which, like *Hermann und Dorothea* (1798), celebrates the aesthetic pleasures of "idyllic-Homeric" domesticity.[37] For what heightens the rhetoric, and behavior, of Goethe's Reineke by contrast with his predecessors is not so much the erotic undertones that are a long-standing motif of the traditional fable but rather his aesthetic impulse. His exuberant and crafted lying is undertaken with that "good conscience" that, according to Nietzsche's claim in *Die fröhliche Wissenschaft* defines the true artist (*FW* §107; KSA 3:464; compare *FW* §§361 and 366; KSA 3:608 and 616). By skilful amendment of his sources, in which only desultory mention is made of Reynard's arts, Goethe consistently creates the impression that everything that his Reineke does is not just more acutely intelligent than the beliefs and behavior of his fellow-animals but is, in some sense, artistic. He adds, for instance, the adjective *künstlich* — "artificial," but retaining, too, especially in late eighteenth-century usage, connotations, as in canto 6, line 324, of "skill-as-art" — to Gottsched's description of Reineke's well-fortified home, Malpertus (canto 1, line 24);[38] in canto 8 (lines 12–13) the aesthetic connotations of Reineke's self-confessed duping of the king are far stronger than in Gottsched's much plainer formulation (79); in Goethe's version, Reineke's zestful playing of the game for the sheer aesthetic pleasure of it contrasts tellingly with the crabbed, self-serving, utilitarian motivations of the other characters (exemplified in Goethe's addition in canto 10, line 320); Reineke's speech is believed by all who hear it, not simply because of its feigned *gravitas* (as in Gottsched, 17), but because of the beauty of his description of the fictitious treasure (canto 10, line 422); his audience is beguiled in Goethe's account, but not in Gottsched's (118), by the art of Reineke's tissue of lies (canto 10, lines 460–62); and the "knot tied with art" (*Ich habe den Knoten / Künstlich geknüpft*) that seals both the sack containing Lampe's head and Bellyn's fate is Goethe's supplementation of Gottsched (65), and applies to Reineke's way of doing everything (canto 6, lines 323–24). It is this aesthetic flair of Reineke's that, in Goethe's text, lends authority to the monkey's description, added by Goethe, of Reineke's kind as "noble" in the same sense as Nietzsche's "Von Ohngefähr" ("Lord Chance," "Rough Approximation"; canto 9, line 350).

Reineke's rhetoric deploys the traditional topoi of argumentation, such as the appeal to kinship (canto 3, lines 284–85) and the *argumentum ad pecuniam* (canto 4, lines 237–40), that Goethe found in his sources. But Goethe's Reineke is an artist, a spellbinding teller of tales that give pleasure to the imagination by means of the delights of aesthetic discourse. In Gottsched (39) the adroitness and skill of Reineke's oratory is duly noted; but his uncanny ability to lend to what he says "the appearance of truth" (canto 4, lines 78–81) and to project good-natured warmth (canto 4, lines 153–54) is not a feature of Gottsched's account (60). Just as, in their various escapades involving Reineke, the other animals are foolishly taken in by his ruses, so, as listeners, they lack the ironic distance that Goethe's (imprecise) hexameters invite his own readers to maintain, in order to be in a position to distinguish fantasy from fact, aesthetic illusion from prosaic truth-telling. And so they bear witness to the principle, enunciated by Goethe, very much in the sober spirit of La Rochefoucauld, in an aphorism: "Man wird nie betrogen, man betrügt sich selbst" ("One is never deceived, one deceives oneself").[39] Yet, in spite of his listeners' obtuse confusion of fact and aesthetic fantasy, Reineke's rhetoric has the great virtue of restoring to them that "belief in humanity" of which the stress of the war of each against each robs them.[40] If the story-within-the-story about the snake, driven by hunger to kill and eat its rescuer, articulates a pessimistic view of humanity's lot (canto 11, lines 221–66), Reineke's rhetoric fills his auditor with hope for an alternative, fairer way of being. This is the burden of Goethe's addition of Reineke's sincere hopefulness even on the scaffold (canto 4, lines 183 and 198). Above all, the positive, life-giving, indeed *enlightening,* influence of Reineke's words (and behavior) is brought out in Goethe's rendition by the much greater emphasis he places on comedy, which, in this text, functions, as social anthropologists like Mary Douglas have argued, as a real, or imagined, shared social phenomenon. Goethe often adds the motif of laughter (for example, canto 2, lines 192, and canto 3, lines 338–40), which, like that provoked by Reineke in canto 11 (line 377), is linked to exposure not of weakness and failure as such but of the social secret, namely hypocrisy. In Goethe's text, shame derives from *believing* a falsehood (for example, canto 6, lines 382–83); and shame is something that can be learned (canto 10, line 375), for it is essentially the awareness of the (often embarrassing) discrepancy between one's own behavior and the beliefs one holds. Shortly before his death in 1832, Goethe assured the young poet Melchior Meyr that "the Muses like to accompany prudent circumspection."[41] This is certainly shown to hold in respect of his Reineke — "the free man" (canto 3, lines 180; not in Gottsched) — who, in the freedom with which he conducts himself, symbolizes the liberation that flows from aesthetic awareness.

Aesthetic illusion vouchsafes the revelation of Being in the midst of Becoming: what, to the intellect, is the mere paradox of Permanence-in-Change ("Dauer im Wechsel") is revealed in aesthetic experience as a stable process; Being is, as Goethe's "Urworte. Orphisch" has it, "unlatched" (*entriegelt*), in what Stephen Dedalus calls "the luminous silent stasis of aesthetic pleasure."[42] Appealing in its beauty, such frank illusion is also satisfying in its linking of subjective with objective, making the individual feel by such "creative apperception" that life is worth living.[43] Unlike the high abstraction of Platonic beauty which, according to Mrs. Dalloway in *To the Lighthouse* (1927) by Virginia Woolf (1882–1941), "stilled life — froze it,"[44] beauty as conceived by Weimar Classicism is closer to "that great and saving illusion that shone with an unearthly glow in the darkness" that, not without ambiguity, offers consolation at the end of *Heart of Darkness* (1899) by Joseph Conrad (1857–1924).[45] For beauty is, on Goethe's and Schiller's understanding, dynamic, and on two counts: it creates a nisus to activity, and it facilitates such activity once undertaken, the content of which is determined by other, non-aesthetic — practical, moral, intellectual — factors.

Certainly, the concept of freedom as self-regulation finds its classical metaphysical formulation in Spinoza: "That thing is called free, which exists solely by the necessity of its own nature, and of which the action is determined by itself alone."[46] The insistence in Weimar Classicism, however, on the highly significant role of a material medium in the achievement of such freedom is the defining characteristic of the temper of its aesthetic, and broader cultural, theory. And wherever such decisive deviation from Platonic abstraction is detectable in thinking about art and beauty, we may well be justified in suspecting at least a trace of the genealogical chain of ideas to which Goethe and Schiller felt their own aesthetics belonged.

In the case of aesthetic discussion which has followed that of Goethe and Schiller, evidence of a non-Platonic stance may well indicate the filiation of their characteristic thought. Everything depends in this context on the morphology of ideas. That is to say, it would seem reasonable to assume that, where the form of conceptualization in Weimar Classicism and in a later writer is similar, as distinct from merely verbal likeness, it is possible to discern answers to the question, posed over thirty years ago in the limited scope of a short article restricted to just a handful of illustrative instances, to which to date no satisfactory answer has been given: namely, "whatever happened to Weimar Classicism?"[47] With the deconstructive turn has come, in the meantime, some recognition of the acute relevance of Weimar Classicism's key ideas, in particular the concepts of play and illusion, to contemporary thinking on aesthetico-cultural matters, although undifferentiated assumptions of overlap often threaten to obscure the (very important) differences that obtain between, say, Derrida's concept of *jeu* and Goethe's and Schiller's *Spiel,* or Baudrillard's *simulacrum* and Weimar Classicism's *Schein.*[48] Moreover, historical investigation of the descent of Weimar classicism has been inhibited by postmodernist tendencies, fostered by the all-pervasive critique of "grand narratives," to assume discontinuity. A severe version of this trend has been called *Gegenwartsfetischismus* (fetishism of the present-day) in contemporary German discourse — a variant of that temporal parochialism that, confusing modernity and relevance, dogmatically insists on the absolute status of (inevitably artificial) periodizations and the "obsoleteness" of all but the most recent past.[49]

With this question and with this heuristic criterion in mind, what follows is a sketch-outline, almost exclusively limited to English and German-speaking writings, which seeks — by means of a sampling that is by no means either fully representative or merely random, but determined by expectation and experience — to reintroduce into our contemporary debate instances of apparent continuation, mediated and unmediated, of Weimar aesthetics.[50] As distinct from the purely pragmatic value of the method of historical morphology, its *methodological* justification (derived, by analogy, from Kant's principle, enunciated in the preface to the *Critique of Practical Reason*) is the "necessity" for coherent thinking of presuming continuity while entertaining the "hypothetical" possibility of discontinuity.[51] Despite differences, and discontinuities, of development, it is possible, by means of such morphological comparison and contrast, to discern, even in such a limited sample, the hermeneutic potential of an enormously rich family relationship of aesthetic ideas stretching from the late eighteenth and early nineteenth to the twenty-first century. In order to adumbrate its ongoing influence with appropriate brevity, it is helpful to single out four conjunctions of the reception history of "sincere semblance" that are particularly revealing of its persistent relevance, not easy to calculate, to succeeding generations of cultural and aesthetic reflection, including Nietzsche. They are, first, its immediate reception in the late eighteenth and early nineteenth century; second, its sporadically explicit, and its mostly tacit, presence in the nineteenth-century philosophical tradition; third, its general reception among non-philosophers; and fourth, its function in some key twentieth-century thinking about aesthetics. Each conjuncture opens up a fresh perspective on the history of modern aesthetics.

The Immediate Reception in Germany
and Transmission to Britain

The mixed reception on publication of Schiller's letters *Ueber die ästhetische Erziehung des Menschen* (*On the Aesthetic Education of Humankind*, 1795) seems to have owed a good deal to the central role played in his theory by the unsettling idea of "sincere semblance."[52] While it was predictable that Rationalists of the stamp of Friedrich Nicolai (1733–1811) should baulk at such paradoxes, it is at first sight surprising that Jean Paul (1763–1825), in the preface to the second edition of *Quintus Fixlein* of 1796, should find the concept, in its relatedness to play, frivolous. His commitment to intellectual wit may help explain this rejection, just as it seems plain that Hölderlin's objections to the same concept (in letters to his brother of 2 November 1797 and 1 January 1799), despite his indebtedness to Schiller in so many other respects, are due to his Platonic view of the poet as a seer. The relative neglect into which the *Aesthetic Letters* fell (pretty well until the early 1920s, when C. G. Jung picked them up again with enthusiasm) may be attributed to the centrality of what appeared to many to be a highly dubious idea. It certainly sat uneasily with the public image foisted on to Schiller of *the* great moral-didactic writer, an image that Nietzsche deftly caricatured as the "Moral-Trompeter von Säckingen" ("The moral-trumpeter of Säckingen") in his *Götzen-Dämmerung* (*Twilight of the Idols; GD* Streifzüge §1; KSA 6:111). Schiller's sophisticated doctrine of the need for an aesthetic *Umweg* of indirection to mediate between moral, intellectual, practical, political, and other realms of life was clearly incompatible with such a simple, straightforward view of the poet's office. Nonetheless, as we have seen, despite — or perhaps, rather, because of — this widespread public repudiation of "sincere seeming," it exerted a powerful influence over Nietzsche's conception of art in particular and aesthetics in general. But on the few occasions when Schiller's doctrine of illusion was noted it merely served to attract either the support of the extreme political Right (commending such apolitical disengagement with reality) or the condemnation of the extreme Left (on the same grounds).

Understandably, no such heat was generated outside Germany by Schiller's aesthetic theories. The enthusiastic response of Wilhelm von Humboldt (1767–1835) had the ironic effect of reinforcing the tendency of British (and French) colporteurs of contemporary German culture to an undifferentiated conflation of quite disparate positions amongst the German thinkers of the time: Humboldt's views, heavily reliant as they were on Goethe's as well as Schiller's, became in many a mind indistinguishable from theirs. Humboldt's interest was focused on practical, educational points, not on the central issue of frank illusion (see his letter to Schiller of 7 November 1794).[53] Just as Madame de Staël's *De l'Allemagne* (1810), though it made

Schiller known throughout Europe, paid little attention to the heady "meta-physics," including his aesthetic theory, that she had come across on her German tour of two years earlier, so also Thomas Carlyle (1795–1881), above all, in his *Life of Schiller* of 1869, likewise had little or no appreciation of his aesthetic tenets, least of all his doctrine of illusion, for all that he saw the principled profundity of Schiller's thinking. Schiller's play-drive (*Spieltrieb*) was translated by Carlyle, clearly affronted by such reliance on trifling, as "sport-impulse," thus avoiding any, for him, disturbing connections with dissembling.[54] So Schiller, shorn of the key element of his entire thesis and thus its relation to the political sphere, appeared before the English public as if he were advocating not an aesthetic theory but the kind of substitute religion of individual self-improvement for which Humboldt's position, increasingly identified with Schiller's, was to be impugned.[55] Nevertheless, Schiller's idea of "freedom-in-appearance" found other channels of transmission to Britain, and to France. Although the question of the exact degree and nature of the assimilation of German thought by Samuel Taylor Coleridge (1772–1834), which clearly led to a naturalization of German ideas in William Morris (1834–96), Matthew Arnold (1822–88), F. R. Leavis (1895–1978) and the New Critics,[56] remains an open one, there is considerable evidence of his familiarity with Weimar Classicism, including internal evidence that he read the *Aesthetic Letters*,[57] especially with regard to that "autonomy" that Schiller saw as characteristic of achieved aesthetic experience.[58] But in the case of Coleridge we seem to have a transformation of Schiller's thought in the opposite direction to that distortion effected by Carlyle. For Coleridge seems to have had no problem with the physicality of Schiller's account of the creation of "living form" (Letter 26, §7). Rather, Coleridge's version of the Aesthetic State, set out in *On the Constitution of Church and State* (1839), tends, like his (enormously influential) doctrine of imagination, to accentuate unduly, by comparison with Schiller's view of the aesthetic mode of understanding, the concrete, not in the sense of manipulable medium, but rather in the common-sense meaning of everyday, practical perception. Thus the illusion component is downgraded in both instances, to be replaced by pragmatic policy-making in the former and, in the latter, a theory that does not really distinguish the aesthetic from any other modality of imagination.[59]

By contrast, John Stuart Mill (1806–73), in his reflective essays on Bentham and Coleridge (1838–40), where he sought to reconcile the English utilitarian tradition and the humanizing tendencies of "the German-Coleridgian school," comes closest of all the major English thinkers of the period in his grasp of the need for flexible articulation between the distinct though separate spheres of cultural and political life.[60] His familiarity with German letters was profound, as is clear from the following statement in his *Autobiography* (1873): "I was deriving much from Coleridge and from the writings of Goethe and other German authors which I read during those years [1828–33]."[61]

Mill particularly admired the solid grounding in ultimate principle in his German authors,[62] and he grasped the distinct contribution aesthetic play could make, in co-operation with intellectual and moral development, to develop feeling (although he overlooked Schiller's insistence on the reciprocal subordination of feeling and thought).[63] Nonetheless, it seems clear that Mill's often aggressively anti-Platonic stance against one-sided intellectualism, entirely understandable given the rigorously intellectualist education he received from his father from a very early age, enabled him to discern Schiller's conception of aesthetic experience as a special type of illusion, and to see its far-reaching potential for life.

The following generation — John Ruskin (1819–1900), William Morris, Sir Edward Burne-Jones (1833–98), as well as Walter Pater (1839–94) and, through him, Oscar Wilde (1854–1900) — was also open to Schiller's influence, albeit more selectively. Ruskin, who found Schiller's theories, rightly, uncongenial to his emphasis on the moral message of art, had no conscious realization of what the idea of "sincere seeming" might mean, so intent was he on the direct effect of beauty on right conduct. But there is, even here, evidence that he owed to Schiller — specifically, his idea of "manifest freedom" — more than he ever realized, especially with regard to his account of the artist's shaping power.[64] William Morris's commitment to the quasi-religious function of "joy-in-craft" seems to have left little room for intellectual reflection in general, let alone for tricky notions like "frank illusion." But it was seized upon by Pater and his followers, though they overlooked the fact that, although Schiller *distinguished* the aesthetic and moral, his whole concern was not to *separate* them, but rather, precisely by means of judicious use of "sincere seeming" in flexible articulation with ethics (and intellect, and politics, and so on), to sustain a dynamic interplay. Though Pater's championing in *The Renaissance* (1893) of the aesthetic transformation of daily life, like his (and Wilde's) advocacy of art for art's sake, may sound very like some of Schiller's (and Goethe's) down-to-earth formulations, as both Pater and Wilde liked to point out, both men lack what, for Schiller, is a vital condition of successful living. The whole point of aesthetic experience is that it is *not* an ultimate, Platonic, end in itself (although it must *seem* so); its justification lies in the fact that aesthetic freedom is the necessary condition of that rebirth of the personality as a whole that energizes us sufficiently to face as best we can the moral, and many other, challenges of this world. That is why the apparently dubious concept of "true illusion" is central to the whole cultural program of Weimar Classicism: it alone can set us free, to be open to formative, civilizing — indeed, civic — influence.[65]

The Nineteenth-Century Philosophical Tradition

Hegel, like Kant, was enthusiastic about the *Aesthetic Letters* on their appearance; they were, he told Schelling in a letter (16 April 1795) "ein Meisterstück" ("a masterpiece").[66] And in the very next year, in collaboration with Schelling and Hölderlin, he produced the so-called "Ältestes Systemprogramm des deutschen Idealismus" ("Oldest Systematic Program of German Idealism"), setting out the new Romantic attitude to art, science, and philosophy.[67] The influence of Schiller's ideas is obvious; but so, too, is their subordination to the Platonic Idea of beauty as the highest reason.[68] Hegel soon moved away from this assimilation (which remained a key feature of Schelling's "Identity-Philosophy") of modes of intellectual activity to the aesthetic. But Hegel's indebtedness to Schiller remained great, in particular for the manner of philosophical presentation: for the employment of "paradoxology and tautology, the deferment of a solution to the problem posed, the subordination of linear argument and logical progression, the 'turning with similar words again and again around the same point,' the uncovering of the limitations of a thought by exhibition of its one-sidedness, the reliance on the internal relations of the language within the totality of the whole"[69] — and, perhaps most notoriously, "Hegel adopted and greatly expanded the technique of multiple reference by serious punning that Schiller had developed."[70] In addition Hegel seems to have drawn on Schiller heavily, as does Marx, for his discussions of such issues as human wholeness and the question of "alienation."[71] And even his formulations — such as his definition of beauty as "das sinnliche Scheinen der Idee" ("the sensuous appearance of the idea") — can, at first sight at least, sound very close indeed to Weimar Classicism's conception.[72]

But, in fact, poetry is the highest art form of modernity for Hegel only because it enjoys the most detached relationship to its medium of language, which is a mere inessential convention. Poetry's dignity consists in its striving to become philosophy, and its increasing revelation of the linguistic medium as "gänzlich gleichgültiges und wertloses Zeichen" ("utterly indifferent and valueless sign").[73] For Hegel, religion transcends art, because religion thinks the Absolute, whereas art merely presents it in figurative form. "Sensuous appearance of the idea" is clearly a long way from Schiller and very near to Plato. Unlike Kierkegaard, for whom, like Goethe and Schiller, "the first immediacy is the aesthetic,"[74] for Hegel the first immediacy is the Idea (*Geist*). This idealistic aesthetic pervades his thought, and makes even the most Goethean- or Schillerian-sounding of his statements about art and culture subtly, but significantly, different from the stance taken by Weimar Classicism. For example, in his *Vorlesungen über die Philosophie der Geschichte* (*Lectures on the Philosophy of History*, 1821–31) it may be tempting (and correct) to detect the influence of Weimar Classicism in Hegel's praise of the beauty of Greek athleticism as a first expression of human freedom, when he writes: "so zeigt doch der Mensch in dieser Übung der Körperlichkeit seine Freiheit, daß er den Körper nämlich zum Organ des Geistes umgebildet habe" ("yet in this exercise of his physical powers man shows his freedom, viz. that he has transformed his body to an organ of the spirit").[75] Not only is this embodiment of spirit more reminiscent in its purposiveness of Carlyle's "sport" than of Schiller's *Spiel,* but the context also makes quite plain that the model Hegel has in mind is body as (disposable) container of the content of spirit rather than Weimar Classicism's conception of import inhering in concrete form: "In der griechischen Schönheit ist das Sinnliche nur Zeichen, Ausdruck, Hülle, worin der Geist sich manifestiert" ("In Greek beauty the sensuous is only a sign, an expression, an envelope, in which the spirit manifests itself").[76]

Clearly, conceptual content is incontrovertibly more "serious" than aesthetic form — for Weimar Classicism, a heresy that reduces interest in the work of art to an adventitious concern with the material (*Stoff*) out of which the artist has fashioned the art-symbol. For Hegel, however, any tender regard for the quiddity of form would constitute a betrayal of the onward rush of the Spirit towards the Absolute, would constitute indeed an *illusion* (but with a negative accent); even in the loveliest of paintings "dies Wahre [ist], wie es *erscheint,* nur in der Weise eines Sinnlichen, nicht in seiner ihm selbst gemäßen Form" ("this element of truth as thus exhibited is manifested only in a sensuous mode, not in its appropriate form").[77] The Spirit cannot tarry in the aesthetic realm, for that is only a step to the next levels, those of Religion and Philosophy. In no other case, perhaps, is the morphological method more potentially revealing of the contrasting characteristics of both elements of the comparison than in the case of Hegel and Weimar Classicism. And it testifies emphatically to the power of the formulations of Weimar Classicism to exert pressure on the rhetorical form of even the most alien ideas.

The orthodox Marxist view of Weimar Classicism's attachment to *Schein* as a regrettable, if understandable, escapism in the face of Germany's social and political misery in the late eighteenth and early nineteenth centuries is encapsulated in the condemnation of Schiller's flight from political reality by Friedrich Engels (1820–95) in terms of "die Vertauschung der platten mit der überschwenglichen Misère" ("the exchange of prosaic for highflown misery").[78] Yet this view does not chime with Karl Marx's well-documented admiration for, and indebtedness to, Goethe and Schiller. In particular, in its crudity it expunges the many telltale traces, in formulation as well as in conceptualization, of the powerful hold that Weimar Classicism's modes of thought seem to have had over Marx. The remarkable passage, for instance, in the introduction to the *Grundrisse* (1858) where Marx turns not only Hegel but the philosophical tradition on its head — by the simple expedient of reversing the usual hierarchy of abstraction: high, concretion: low — is a continuation of a tradition in which Goethe, Schiller, and Coleridge, participate:[79]

> Hegel geriet [. . .] auf die Illusion, das Reale als Resultat des sich in sich zusammenfassenden, in sich vertiefenden und aus sich selbst bewegenden Denkens zu fassen, während die Methode vom Abstrakten zum Konkreten aufzusteigen, nur die Art für das Denken ist, sich das Konkrete anzueignen [. . .][80]

> [Hegel fell into the illusion of conceiving the real as the product of thought concentrating itself, probing its own depths, and unfolding itself out of itself, whereas the method of rising from the abstract to the concrete is only the way in which thought appropriates the concrete . . .]

Marx seems to be juxtaposing here, in terms reminiscent of Weimar Classicism's oppositions of "true (frank, sincere) semblance" and "false (logical) semblance," a kind of concreteness (Hegelian) that is false with another kind that is true-to-reality (and therefore higher than mere abstraction):

> Das Konkrete ist konkret, weil es die Zusammenfassung vieler Bestimmungen ist, also Einheit des Mannigfaltigen. Im Denken erscheint es daher als Prozeß der Zusammenfassung, als Resultat, nicht als Ausgangspunkt, obgleich es der wirkliche Ausgangspunkt und daher auch der Ausgangspunkt der Anschauung und Vorstellung ist.

> [The concrete is concrete because it is the concentration of many determinations, hence unity of the manifold. It appears in the process of thinking, therefore, as a process of concentration, as a result, not as a point of departure, even though it is the point of departure in reality and hence also the point of departure for observation (*Anschauung*) and representation.][81]

Could it be, in other words, that Marx is working with a sophisticated doubling of his favored metaphor of the "veil" of illusion? One in the sense of (Hegelian) "false consciousness," the other in the sense of the true veil of aesthetic consciousness in Schiller's sense? Certainly Marx's insistence on the "autonomy" of the real individual, existing outside the abstractions of thought, would, like his use of that key term of Weimar Classicism, *Anschauung*, seem to suggest so: "Das reale Subjekt bleibt nach wie vor außerhalb des Kopfes in seiner Selbständigkeit bestehn" ("The real subject retains its autonomous existence outside the head just as before").[82] The fact that this reading is also supported by Marx's distinction, developed in the same text, between negative, illusory *Verdinglichung* (reification) and positive, real *Vergegenständlichung* (objectification in the popular psychoanalytic sense of "self-realization") surely speaks for the hermeneutic potential of its further investigation.[83]

General Reception among Non-Philosophers

Given the established channels of transmission between the two countries it is hardly surprising that the English Romantics should have been indebted to Weimar Classicism for some of their most "original" aesthetic doctrines. The concept of psychical distance, elaborated by Schiller in his review of Bürger's poetry (and in the twenty-second of his *Aesthetic Letters*) surfaces, for example, in chapter 15 of Coleridge's *Biographia Literaria;* and Coleridge is, no doubt, the conduit for the famous version, articulated by Wordsworth (1770–1850), of the principle of "emotion recollected in tranquillity" (though, for Schiller, the dominant element in the perception and creation of beautiful illusion is neither "recollection" nor "tranquillity," but "distance"). Similarly, Coleridge's theory of genius in terms of "the balance or reconciliation of opposite or discordant qualities" at the end of chapter 14 of *Biographia Literaria* may owe more to Schiller than, as is often assumed, to Schelling. Although not schooled in contemporary German thought, John Keats (1795–1821) was likewise deeply indebted to the (German-influenced) *Essay on the Principles of Human Action* (1805) by William Hazlitt (1778–1830) in formulating his doctrine of "negative capability," which is very reminiscent of but not quite identical with that state of absolute determinability (Schiller's *Nullpunkt;* see Letter 21, §4 and §5) into which sincere semblance lures the percipient.[84] And it is difficult to imagine a closer, more precise evocation of aesthetic perception, of *Anschauung,* as Goethe and Schiller understood it, than the primordial realism of the *Suspiria de Profundis* (1845) by Thomas De Quincey (1785–1859):

> Far more of our deepest thoughts and feelings pass to us through perplexed combinations of *concrete* objects, pass to us as *involutes* (if I may coin that word) in compound experiences incapable of being disentangled, than ever reach us *directly,* and in their own abstract shapes.[85]

All that is missing here is an explicit statement of what is implied by such "concrete" perception: since quality inheres in felt contrasts and likenesses between things, any attempt to articulate the qualitative aspect of experience will require a form that is equally dynamic and concrete, or at least *appears* to be so: the frank illusion of living form.

Less expected, though in fact entirely understandable in the light of the to-and-fro of cultural interchange between America and Europe in the course of the nineteenth century, as well as the personal interest in Goethe of Herman Melville (1819–91), is the astonishing similarity between the narrator's description of the beauty of the whale's tail-fin in *Moby Dick*

(1851) and the image of an undulating wave that Goethe employed on occasion to evoke instances of "sincere seeming" as he and Schiller envisaged it, "where infantileness of ease undulates through Titanism of power": "Real strength never impairs beauty or harmony, but it often bestows it; and in everything impossibly beautiful, strength has to do with the magic [. . .] the subtle elasticity [. . .] invariably marked by exceeding grace."[86] This is no more the anemic (Platonic) "line of beauty" that some eighteenth-century Enlightenment figures fondly thought contained the secret of beauty than is Goethe's description of a thing of beauty in terms of the human body, "when it moves as a beautiful undivided whole, in undulating life, before our eyes" (*sich* [. . .] *als ein schönes ungetrenntes Ganze in lebendigen Wellen vor unserm Auge bewegt*).[87] *Lebende Gestalt* has, like the tail-fin, the strength of life and the vanishing delicacy of exquisite form.

Works by two very different novelists are similarly shot through with formulations evocative of the key concepts of Weimar Classicism: Stendhal (the pseudonym of Henri Beyle, 1783–1842) and Marcel Proust (1871–1922). We recognize, for example, the account that Goethe and Schiller offer of a mode of experience that is not in any way divided or duplicitous in character. For it has the same quality of authenticity as the sensations provoked by chamber music in summer that Proust describes, perhaps under the influence of his intense study of *Dichtung und Wahrheit*, in the following passage: "Elle n'en réveille pas seulement l'image dans notre mémoire, elle en certifie le retour, la présence effective, ambiente, immédiatement accessible" ("It not only awakens their image in our memory, it guarantees their return, their actual, persistent, immediately accessible presence").[88] On Weimar Classicism's account this is just how the frank illusion of aesthetic apperception feels — originary and unreconstituted. In the case of Stendhal, what we have in his *De l'Amour* (*Love*, 1822) is the application of Goethe's (and Schiller's) principles of *Steigerung* ("refinement") and *Spezifikation* ("crystalization") to the case of love, "cette passion dont tous les développements sincères ont un caractère de beauté" ("this passion whose every genuine manifestation is characterized by beauty");[89] it is saturated with references to the two German writers.[90] Its burden is the need to sustain "cet ensemble d'illusions charmantes que nous avons appelé [. . .] cristallisations" ("that pattern of exquisite illusion which we have called crystallization") in order to keep sensuous, not Platonic, love alive.[91] And everything depends on distinguishing firmly between false affectation, which is fatal to the process, and the sincere artifice needed to project the impression of being natural.[92] It is all a matter of the most refined cultivation of both form and feeling: "L'amour est le miracle de la civilisation" ("Love is civilization's miracle").[93] Outside the writings of Oscar Wilde, it is difficult to imagine a more faithful presentation of all that *schöner Schein* means in the theory and practice of living.

It seems natural, too, and for similar reasons, that close parallels should be found between, say, Schiller's notion (in his letter to Goethe of 27 March 1801) of "objectifying a state of feeling" (*"einen Empfindungszustand in ein Objekt legen"*) and the theory of the "objective correlative" developed by T. S. Eliot (1888–1965) — for all Eliot's well-known reservations about Goethe.[94] Likewise, albeit for different reasons — above all, his apostrophe of Schiller as "schönheitslehrer und erzieher • als verfasser der Ästhetischen Erziehung • der seinem volk auch heute noch fremd ist und vermutlich noch lange bleibt" ("teacher of beauty and educator • as the author of the *Aesthetic Education* • who still remains a stranger to his people and will probably remain so for some time") — the borrowing of *schöner Schein* by Stefan George (1868–1933) to bolster his, and his Circle's, campaign for "pure" poetry is quite understandable.[95] Schiller, however, could never have approved of tendencies to assert aggressively the distinctiveness of art to the point where it ceases to have relevance for life, no more than he could have stomached the ruthless identification of the indifference of the material to the artist with that of the people to the statesman (*Führer*) made by Joseph Goebbels (1897–1945) in his novel *Michael* (1929), where the central character declares: "Der Staatsmann ist auch ein Künstler. Für ihn ist das Volk nichts anderes, als was für den Bildhauer der Stein ist. Führer und Masse, das ist ebensowenig ein Problem wie etwa Maler und Farbe" ("The statesman is also an artist. For him the people are no different from what the stone is for the sculptor. The leader and the masses, that is no more of a problem than are the artist and his choice of color").[96] Indeed, in respect of Weimar Classicism's undoubted role in modernist poetry's concern, from Baudelaire to Benn, with the conscious aspect of the creative process, it is important to bear in mind not only some significant differences but also the common source of the "perennial aesthetic."[97]

But if making such assumptions of continuity has all the "naturalness" fostered by well-known (and well-worn) perspectives — as, perhaps, most eminently in the case of Thomas Mann's carefully and deeply cultivated relation to his own German-cum-European heritage — this is emphatically not the case with most recent writing. A case in point is Franz Kafka (1883–1924). It is only when the pervasive prejudice of assuming the twentieth century to constitute a "disinherited mind" is overcome — that is, once we entertain the postulate of continuity — that the ongoing life of Weimar Classicism's concept of "sincere seeming" comes into focus, in Kafka and, by extension, throughout the last century. All that is needed is to direct attention to the large volume of scholarly work that has sought to dismantle the myth of discontinuity by documenting Kafka's intimate acquaintance with the German classics, and his perennial concern with Goethe in particular, in that most conservative of German cultural enclaves, Prague — a cultural climate that engendered the atmosphere that Kafka's thought breathed.[98] Consider the "rather astonishing last paragraph of *Ein Hungerkünstler* that has embarrassed many critics":[99]

> "Nun macht aber Ordnung!" sagte der Aufseher, und man begrub den Hungerkünstler samt dem Stroh. In den Käfig aber gab man einen jungen Panther. Es war eine selbst dem stumpfsten Sinn fühlbare Erholung, in dem so lange öden Käfig dieses wilde Tier sich herumwerfen zu sehn. Ihm fehlte nichts. Die Nahrung, die ihm schmeckte, brachten ihm ohne langes Nachdenken die Wächter; nicht einmal die *Freiheit schien* er zu vermissen; dieser edle, mit allem Nötigen bis knapp zum Zerreißen ausgestattete Körper *schien* auch die *Freiheit* mit sich herumzutragen; irgendwo im Gebiß *schien* sie zu stecken; und die Freude am Leben kam mit derart starker Glut aus seinem Rachen, daß es für die Zuschauer nicht leicht war, ihr standzuhalten. Aber sie überwanden sich, umdrängten den Käfig und wollten sich gar nicht fortrühren.

> ["Now let's tidy up," said the supervisor, and the hunger-artist was buried along with the straw. A young panther was, however, put into the cage. It was a palpable relief to even the most insensitive of people to see this wild animal throwing itself about in a cage that had been desolate for so long. It lacked for nothing. The keepers brought it the food it liked without a second thought; it didn't even *seem* to miss its *freedom;* this noble body, equipped almost to bursting with everything it needed also *seemed* to carry *freedom* around with itself; it *seemed* to be set somewhere in its teeth; and its passion for life came with such strong ardor from its maw that it was difficult for the onlookers to bear it. But they overcame their reluctance, surrounded the cage, and were unwilling to move on.][100]

As the italics indicate, what is of interest here is the fact that Kafka employs locutions that, in the mind of anyone familiar with Weimar Classicism, echo that key concept of Weimar aesthetics — *Freiheit in der Erscheinung* (manifest freedom). To assume that this is indeed what Kafka had in mind makes perfect sense. The panther, far from being, as Heinz Politzer has it, "out of place," turns out — once this resonance is heard — to be an instance of what Politzer rightly describes as "the irony [Kafka] was able to derive from seemingly insignificant details." For although it is true that the question of art "commands Kafka's attention in the story,"[101] we go very wrong if we overlook the narrator's subtle irony with regard to his hunger-"artist," so clearly evident, if only in the parodistic echoes of Goethe's *Faust* — "'Wer es nicht fühlt, dem kann man es nicht begreiflich machen" (135; compare *Faust* Part One, line 534; "Anyone who can not feel it, will not be able to grasp it") — and of Luther's reputed declaration at Worms — "Weil ich hungern muß, ich kann nicht anders" (136; "Because I must starve, I can do nought else"). For all the grandiosity of his ambition (130), the hunger-artist cannot show anyone, even his guards (128–29), what it is he has "achieved": he arouses pity as a martyr, not admiration as an artist (130). Such "artistry" as there is in his act is provided by the impresario's pretence that what the hunger-artist does with consummate ease is difficult (130–32) — a deception which, in the ironic words of the narrator, provides the hunger-artist with a number of years of "scheinbarer Glanz" ("deceptive glory"; 131). Now, this "Verdrehung der Wahrheit" ("perversion of truth"; 132) is a remarkably exact reversal of Schiller's theory of what constitutes beauty in art as in life (Letter 15). In L. A. Willoughby's succinct formulation, according to Schiller "a work of art was beautiful when [. . .] the laws which conditioned its existence obtruded so little on the observer that the object 'appeared' to be free from constraint, and to be the spontaneous product of nature."[102] How very different from the hunger-artist! He is out not to engage the disinterested play-drive but to have his purposeful record-breaking taken seriously (131); and he admits to being driven not by any love of sheer semblance, but by what Nietzsche saw as characteristic of all *décadents* — disgust and lack of "taste": he did it "weil ich nicht die Speise finden konnte, die mir schmeckt" ("because I couldn't find any food to my taste"; 136). But, by the same token, how like the panther: it not only appears oblivious of its captivity but, like Melville's whale, evinces an almost overpowering vitality (137) by virtue of just that manifest freedom that is the mark of the healthy "product of nature," an ambiguity that throws the futile, fanatical (133), efforts of the hunger-artist into ironic, indeed amusing, relief.

Some Key Twentieth-Century Contexts

Despite the reported remark of Alfred North Whitehead (1861–1947) in 1939, to the effect that he preferred Schiller's down-to-earth thought to Goethe's more exalted "Romantic" flights, there is much in his philosophy that seems identical with Goethe's (and Schiller's) fundamental tenets: "Goethe's thinking is too special, and [. . .] the world would be better off for the sound, sane, sensible, second-rate sentiments of Schiller. They never rise beyond a certain level but they are safe and serviceable."[103] Since Whitehead held, like Goethe and Schiller, that "an actual fact is a fact of aesthetic experience," and that "all aesthetic experience is feeling arising out of the realization of contrast under identity,"[104] he may have had no more in mind (if he is being correctly reported) than that, of the two Weimar Classicists — as Schiller himself generously acknowledged — Goethe had the greater scope and, therefore, the greater ("Romantic") tendency to lead too far afield. However that may be, the remark, once read in the context of Whitehead's own philosophy, nicely makes the point that the aesthetic theorizing of Weimar Classicism is profoundly realistic in firmly setting art, and aesthetic experience in general, in their often subordinate, "second-rate" place within the broad framework of human needs and aspirations. Like Goethe and Schiller, Whitehead, too, saw "the animal body" as "the great central ground underlying all symbolic reference":[105] since every occasion of experience is dipolar, integrating mental experience with physical experience, all experience, at whatever level, is in some sense a physical-mental synthesis, that is, it is aesthetic.[106] The following statement of his own position, like the chapter entitled "Appearance and Reality" in his *Adventures of Ideas* (1933), makes the overlap of Whitehead's philosophy with Weimar Classicism plainly incontrovertible:

> The metaphysical doctrine, here expounded, finds the foundations of the world in the aesthetic experience, rather than — as with Kant — in the cognitive and conceptive experience. All order is therefore aesthetic order, and the moral order is merely certain aspects of aesthetic order. The actual world is the outcome of the aesthetic order, and the aesthetic order is derived from the immanence of God.[107]

To what extent Goethe and Schiller would have welcomed a ("Romantic") metaphysics of the aesthetic, let alone one derived from a theology of immanence, is a question which, if tackled, would throw into relief the deeper foundations of Weimar Classicism, along with many other "second-rate" issues, no doubt. It would also probably reveal the extent to which Whitehead succeeded in achieving a synthesis of Platonism, to which he is committed, with the empirical process-philosophy which he seeks to articulate.

In many ways Whitehead's whole enterprise recalls that of Charles Peirce (1839–1914), not least in their shared immersion in Weimar aesthetics. Peirce's reading in philosophy had begun with Schiller's *Aesthetic Letters,* and the positive impression they made on him was life-long. Like Whitehead, and like Schiller, Peirce also sought to ground logic and ethics in aesthetics. A morphological comparison of Peirce and Schiller, as Elizabeth M. Wilkinson and L. A. Willoughby suggest, might well throw penetrating light — like the comparison of Whitehead and Goethe or Schiller — on Weimar Classicism's predilection for shifting hierarchies, facilitated in their reciprocal subordinations by judicious and timely "regression" to the pure determinability of candid aesthetic illusion.[108]

In general the philosophical discourse of the twentieth century, certainly in the case of the major thinkers of the time, has not concerned itself chiefly with aesthetics. Whitehead is a rarity in this respect, as is his pupil Susanne K. Langer. On the whole, twentieth-century philosophy has stood under the sign of what Hegel called, in a famous remark defining the task of the modern novel, the "prose of circumstance" — in "the conflict with the poetry of the heart" (*den Konflikt zwischen der Poesie des Herzens und der entgegenstehenden Prosa der Verhältnisse*).[109] Uncommon indeed is the sociologically-minded scholar who, like Herbert Spencer (1820–1903) in his *Principles of Psychology* (1870–72), publicly declares the need of an aesthetic theory to link conceptually the public and private spheres. Far more typical, indeed the very model of a modern thinker, is Max Weber (1864–1920) who, in his *Zwischenbetrachtung* (1915), declared unambiguously that, in a world of unceasing rationalization of life, art (and, by implication, aesthetics) is degraded to the ancillary role of providing a pseudo-salvation from the prosaic and soul-destroying constraints of everyday life, and especially from the pressures of theoretical and practical rationalism. Art has a redemptory function, but without the faith that had sustained earlier ages. The tendency to ivory-tower aestheticism at the turn of the nineteenth to the twentieth century is a mere symptom of the shift from the now unsustainable moral to the aesthetic evaluation of conduct, a touching if doomed resistance to the crushing machinery of society.

And yet, as a sampling of some of the representative thinkers of the era indicates, Weimar Classicism's doctrine of the "freedom-in-appearance" of frank illusion is still detectably at work in not unimportant junctures of their thought. Take, for example, the case of Martin Heidegger (1889–1976). There is much in "Der Ursprung des Kunstwerks" ("The Origins of the Work of Art"), written 1935–36 and published in 1950, to confirm the widespread view that his mode of Existentialism entails an open antipathy to aesthetics. His stated aim is ontological: "Die ganze Abhandlung 'Der Ursprung des Kunstwerks' bewegt sich wissentlich und doch unausgesprochen auf dem Wege der Frage nach dem Wesen des Seins" ("The whole essay 'The Origins of the Work of Art' moves, knowingly but tacitly, on the trail of the question of the nature of being").[110] Drawing on his major work, *Sein und Zeit* (*Being and Time*, 1927), and in particular on the concept he developed there of *Welt* (world) as the framework in which human being (*Dasein*) develops sophisticated self-interpretation (30; 44–45), Heidegger introduces a complementary concept in this essay of *Erde* (earth; 19 and 28; 34 and 42). What art does, Heidegger seems to be saying, is "set up" (*aufstellen;* 31; 45–46) a tension between "world" and the "earth" (in the sense of non-interpreted, naive, experience) which it also "sets forth" (*herstellen;* 31; 45) reflecting, as it were, Earth's eruption into our otherwise bland worldview. Art manifests what happens when this tension happens. The work of art, of which Poetry is the paradigm (59–64; 73–78), is, then, a historical *event* of truth (26 and 63–64; 41 and 77–78), in the materialist, even Marxist sense — and in much the same way as a political state and a philosopher's questionings (48 and 61; 61–62 and 75). Heidegger insists that, despite the testimony of the great artists (45; 58), art is a form of knowing, not making: it is a form of *revelation*. "Createdness"

(*Geschaffensein;* 53; 66–67), the "artificiality" in art and all human production, always reveals — or, better, "unconceals" — that uncanny conflict between (phenomenal) "world" and (ontic) "earth" that he calls *der Riss* ("the
rift," "rupture"; 40, 49, 50; 54–55, 63, 64). Art calls forth "preservation"
(*Bewahren*), and those who preserve it (the recipients) participate in the
event of its truth, and pass it on as a living thing in the context of (materialist) cultural history: *Bewahrung* consists in "letting the work be a work" (*das
Werk ein Werk sein lassen;* 53; 66–67).

In the present context the foregoing exposition, however inadequate to
the rich subtleties of Heidegger's thought it may be, brings out the fact that
his discourse on aesthetics, for all that it is presented not as an aesthetic theory, but as an ontology (70; 86) — and, as such, a *resistance* to traditional
metaphysics (of, say, the Whitehead variety, and certainly of Plato) — is
redolent of some of the key positions of Weimar Classicism (see, for instance, 23, 26–27, 54, 56, 58 and 64; 38, 41, 68, 69, 72 and 78 — and, in
particular, 2–3; 18–19). For, although Heidegger's purpose is ontological,
his method is, like Goethe's and Schiller's, phenomenological. Art is an
"event of truth" (22, 24, 26–27 and 58; 38, 39, 41 and 71): it sets out to
show us, as for example in Van Gogh's painting of 1886, *A Pair of Shoes,* the
truth of things;[111] philosophy seeks only to point, through the medium of
language at full stretch, to such existent objects. But the suspicion is widespread that Heidegger's identification of art with poetry, and poetry with
(even philosophical) language — and language with Being — seems to viti-
ate this distinction, leaving us with no differentiated account of art: "die
Sprache selbst ist Dichtung" (60; 74; "language itself is poetry").

Could it be, however, that, just as the term *bewahren* takes us into
Goethe's central idiom (see line 4 of the great poem "Vermächtnis" ["Testament"], for instance),[112] such terms as *Gestalt* and *Erscheinen,* on which
Heidegger puts heavy emphasis, reveal a continuity with the "frank illusion"
of Weimar Classicism, whose aim, after all, is to "preserve" the authenticity
of "earthy" experience? Statements such as "Kunst ist das Feststellen der sich
einrichtenden Wahrheit in die Gestalt" (57; 71; "Art is the secure setting of
self-positing truth into form") and, above all perhaps, "das Erscheinen ist —
als dieses Sein der Wahrheit im Werk und als Werk — die Schönheit" (67;
81; "appearance is — as this being of truth in the work and as work —
beauty") suggest, at least at the level of verbal resonance, the exciting possibility that this could be the case. Careful morphological comparison and
contrast might in addition disclose that Heidegger's (much-criticized) ma-
nipulation of the German language, to the point of untranslatability,[113] owes
less to, say, Hamann's (and Hölderlin's) identification of poetry with truth
and rather more to Schiller (and to Herder). In particular, it may well be indebted to Schiller's theory of *schöner Vortrag* (aesthetic discourse), on which
Goethe drew in his scientific and cultural prose in order both to communi-

cate a message and to match, in the linguistic texture itself, at least to some degree, the subtle delicacy of connectedness that characterizes the products of both art and nature.[114]

In the case of Theodor W. Adorno (1903–69) the links with Weimar Classicism, on the surface at least, are even more striking. If Weber's melancholy analysis of modernity gave rise to the Frankfurt School's critique of instrumental reason (*Zweckrationalität*) and of the "repressive tolerance" of mass culture, it also stimulated a theory of art and aesthetic value that shares the faith of Weimar Classicism in what Whitehead called "the efficacy of beauty."[115] For all his animus against (Platonic) ideals of harmony and plenitude, and for all his (and Horkheimer's) insistence on the need to resist the established status quo,[116] Adorno also expresses what some might say is an almost "theological" belief in art's capacity to reveal insight, in an epiphany or "*apparition*."[117] Unlike the subordination by the mass media of aesthetic effect to the mythical reification of reality, art — as in Schiller — has an emancipatory function. A work of art is the site of "promise" (*Versprechen*), of *sensuous,* child-like, happiness: for art transcends, in a utopian fashion, the (Weberian) constraints of existence (though such joyful realization is constantly ruptured).[118] And it does this by virtue of its autonomy (as a kind of "windowless monad"), which is a vital form of resistance to the social system. The "seriousness of works of art" consists precisely in their enigmatic quality of never being fully reducible to interpretation;[119] in the fact that, in terms Weimar Classicism employed to make the same point, their "import" (*Gehalt*) is not reducible to their "content" (*Inhalt*).

As Jürgen Habermas has pointed out, Adorno's (and Horkheimer's) recourse to the notion of "mimesis" is open to the criticism that it is a regression to an occult property, analogous to "a piece of unpenetrated nature" (*ein undurchschautes Stück Natur*), an "organic cuddling-up to the Other" (*organische Anschmiegung ans Andere*).[120] But, while the underlying notions of truth and reason may in general be, as Martin Jay has suggested, very nebulous in Critical Theory,[121] what is important in the present context is that Adorno was concerned, like Herbert Spencer before him, to make room in sociological thinking for aesthetic experience, and in terms that are strikingly familiar to readers of Goethe and Schiller.[122] The shift of focus, away from Marxist class-conflict, to that between humankind and nature,[123] can plausibly seem like a return to Goethe, especially since it is precisely the function of art to "reconcile" this contradiction and to keep us in remembrance of natural being (*Eingedenken der Natur*).[124]

Could it be that the apparently moralistic seriousness of the Frankfurt School's castigation of twentieth-century popular culture has hidden, at least from historical morphological investigation, Critical Theory's reliance on Weimar Classicism's (profoundly serious) concept of playful frank illusion? Adorno's rhetorical dependence on the German Classical tradition is incontrovertible: his texts are saturated in the key-terms of Weimar Classicism. What needs to be investigated are the indications of a *conceptual* indebtedness, suggested, for example, in his theory of the moment of sublimation (*Vergeistigung*) in works of art providing epiphany. Is this Schiller's *Veredelung* and Goethe's *Steigerung*?[125] And, if so, are there significant differences as well as continuities? Only close comparative study of the relevant corpus of texts, in the appropriate context of the perennial aesthetic, seems to hold out the prospect of an illuminating answer.

One of the differences between Adorno and Weimar Classicism seems to be that, for Adorno, escape from Weber's famous "iron cage" (*eisernes Gehäuse*) of social repression is unreliably fleeting and transient, while for Schiller and Goethe the application of "frank illusion" to social activity (*schöner Umgang*) promises sustained personal liberty. On this latter point, Habermas is far closer to Weimar Classicism than the Frankfurt School (and than he himself seems to recognize). After all, the whole burden of Habermas's concern is the question of how to defend what he calls "the lifeworld" of intrinsically meaningful forms of life that are endangered in his view by the "colonializing" encroachments of the purposive rationality of the socioeconomic "system." Like Habermas, Schiller aims "to mark out within the positive State an area in which personal and social contact is governed by criteria other than those of law, politics, or the received morality of public opinion."[126] But for Habermas the "expressive" function of the aesthetic is no more than a distinctive species of "communicative action."[127] This much is clearly revealed in his "Exkurs zu Schillers Briefen über die ästhetische Erziehung des Menschen" ("Excursus on Schiller's *Letters on the Aesthetic Education of Humankind*") in *"Hegels Begriff der Moderne"* ("Hegel's Concept of Modernity," 1984), where Habermas reduces Schiller's concept of art and aesthetics to his own Hegelian notions, and, above all, Schiller's complex notion of "beautiful communication" (*schöne Mitteilung*) to his own of communicative action.[128] As Schiller made clear (for example, in his letter to Körner of 10 November 1794), the aesthetic in his view does *not* appeal to universalizing Reason at all, but rather to that "generalisierte Individualität" ("generalized individuality") which the coordination of sensuous delight and mental apprehension that constitutes aesthetic experience alone can bring forth. Hence what Schiller means by "thinking presentationally" (*darstellend denken*) is far away indeed from the kind of abstract rationalizing Habermas obviously has in mind.[129]

Yet, despite Habermas's acceptance of the thesis of Walter Benjamin (1892–1940), to the effect that art has in the modern era lost its "aura" (of aesthetic semblance?) and its "classical" autonomous status,[130] he still seems attached to certain key concepts of Weimar Classicism (even if he does not always seem alive to their full implications). For example, he sees "sincerity" (*Wahrhaftigkeit*) as the defining criterion of aesthetic value. Admittedly, he sees such "authentic expression" as a *reason* to be adduced for the validity of aesthetic judgment, one which can be "measured"[131] — as opposed to Schiller's and Goethe's insistence that such sincerity could only ever be appreciated in terms of the aesthetic form, the *schöner Schein,* giving it articulation. In the light, however, of his overriding concern for lifeworld values, for transparent, mutual understanding between individual people in terms of *Verständigungsformen,* and, above all, of his concept of "drama-turgical action" as a form of self-presentation, derived from the mediation of the play concept via Ernest Goffman and T. R. Sorbin, his distance from Schiller seems much reduced.[132] A morphological comparison might, if only by highlighting differences, do much to bring out anew the serious political and social engagement driving Weimar Classicism's commitment to aesthetic play.

Perhaps the most promising context of all in which to seek to establish the ongoing relevance of "sincere semblance" to twentieth-century thought is the work of Ernst Cassirer (1874–1945). Cassirer's intensive coming-to-terms with Goethe was a life-long, direct, intimate preoccupation with every aspect of the *œuvre* and the life, which has been eloquently dubbed an "eavesdropping" on Goethe.[133] Throughout the elaboration of his own phi-losophy of symbolic form, Cassirer was "as it were in dialogue with Goethe," without ever confusing the distinct, albeit ultimately related, areas in Goethe's thought of *Anschauung* (aesthetic perception) and *Erkenntnis* (in-tellectual cognition). Essential elements of Cassirer's thought derive from Goethe's reflections on the role of symbolism in the presentation of his sci-ence and in his poetic output, which Cassirer re-presented in a peculiarly ef-fective way by blending his own commentary with Goethe's distinctive voice, employing Goethe's figures of speech and thought in a reciprocal interplay between his own theoretical positions and Goethe's, to the mutual clarifica-tion of both. He is also close to Goethe in his awareness of the limits of dis-cursive language; in his belief in a more fundamental, "natural" symbolism; in his interest in the expressive symbol's sensory body containing "a meaning which it presents"; and in his taking bodily feelings to be themselves "sym-bolically pregnant" — in Goethe's sense of "full of import" (*Gehalt*).[134]

The striking similarities between Cassirer's and Goethe's and, by implication, Schiller's thinking seem less remarkable, perhaps, when one recalls what a sensitive, as well as critical, reader of Goethe Cassirer was.[135] Cassirer's openness to Goethe's interest in the aesthetic aspects of nature enabled him to appreciate Goethe's science in a way that was not available to predominantly positivistic-minded nineteenth-century commentators (nor, for that matter, to twentieth-century rationalists), particularly in respect of both Goethe's *Anschauung,* which Cassirer rightly understood as a process, and his conception of the *Urphänomen* as a self-regulating activity.[136] But perhaps most significantly, Cassirer is rare among German commentators of his era in his emphatic appreciation for what Goethe called "tender empiricism" (*zarte Empirie*), a loving regard for the smallest detail of life that is at the very heart of Weimar Classicism's theory of sincere form.[137] Cassirer brings out this quality with great delicacy in a lecture he gave in Sweden in 1941, entitled "Goethes geistige Leistung" ("Goethe's Intellectual Achievement"):

> Der kleinste Gegenstand, die flüchtigste Stimmung kann künstlerisch behandelt und geformt werden — sofern es nur gelingt, nicht nur sie selbst auszusprechen, sondern an ihr und durch sie das Ganze der Persönlichkeit, die Tiefe der Individualität sichtbar zu machen. Nur was in dieser Weise aus dem inneren Leben des Künstlers quillt, hat Wahrheit — und hat damit echte Schönheit.

> [The smallest object, the most fugitive of moods, can be treated and given form aesthetically, so long as the artist succeeds, not only in expressing the mood itself but in making manifest in and through the mood the wholeness of his personality, the depth of his individuality. Only what flows in this way from the inner life of the artist has truth — and with it genuine beauty.][138]

This sensitivity, it seems, enables Cassirer to see that for Weimar Classicism actual creativity is self-discovery: "[a poet] only comes to understand himself in the concrete form he has created" (*begreift sich selbst erst in seinem Gebilde*).[139]

In tackling the question of how something sensuous becomes a carrier of meaning, Cassirer developed a theory of symbolism that is remarkably close, at all major points, to Goethe's (and, in some ways, to Whitehead's) conception. For Cassirer, as for Goethe — and Herder — the body-soul relationship is the prototype of symbolization: the body, as for Goethe and Whitehead, is "the seat of meaning." Taking his cue from Gestalt psychology (itself indebted to Goethe), Cassirer attempts to develop a general theory of the image in its most basic sense, the perceptual *Gestalt*, in barely translatable terms that are redolent of Goethe's and Schiller's formulations of the "living form" of the aesthetic symbol:

> Die spezifische Besonderung der "Praegnanz" begründet und ermöglicht erst die spezifische Verschiedenheit der "Gestalten"; alle Vergegenwärtigung ist immer Vergegenwärtigung in einem bestimmten "Sinne."

> [The specific particularization of "Praegnanz" is what first founds and makes possible the specific differences among "Gestalten"[;] all representation is always representation {literally "making present"} in a specific "sense."][140]

One great benefit of Cassirer's approach is that, in conscious opposition to contemporary trends emphasizing the authentic inner *Erlebnis* (experience) that, for example, Wilhelm Dilthey and Stefan George alleged were expressed in Goethe's works (and life), he is able to identify and elaborate Goethe's interest in, and openness to, philosophical ideas. On closer scrutiny, Goethe's utterances on philosophy and philosophers "convey the selfsame fundamental tendency which Goethe stuck to from the beginning to the end" (*"alle diese Äußerungen [bilden] ein und dieselbe Grundtendenz, die Goethe von Anfang bis zu Ende festgehalten hat"*).[141] For Cassirer, predominantly interested as he was in reconstructing Goethe's intellectual biography, "it was the poet's figures of thought that possessed actuality and vitality" (*"für Cassirer besitzen die Gedankenfiguren des Dichters Aktualität und Lebendigkeit"*). Although here closer to Kant, for whom "symbols are always 'indirect presentations of the concept,'"[142] than to Goethe, for whom symbols can have an inherently sensuous meaning, Cassirer is yet respectful of the boundaries marking poetry off from science.[143] Out of this subtle tension Cassirer conceives the notion of *symbolische Prägnanz* (symbolic pregnance):

> "Symbolische Prägnanz" als Wechselbstimmung und Bewegung ist für Cassirer einmal · durch Unhintergehbarkeit charakterisiert und ist insofern apriorisch. Sie ist jedem Symbolisierungsprozeß und damit in Cassirers Sinn jedem Bedeutungsprozeß inhärent.

> ["Symbolic pregnance" as reciprocal determination and movement is for Cassirer characterized by ultimate impenetrability and is to that extent *a priori*. It is inherent in every process of symbolization and, as a consequence, in Cassirer's sense, inherent in every production of meaning.][144]

In developing the theoretical and philosophical implications in Goethe's own position, Cassirer develops Goethe's thought further than Goethe had himself, at least explicitly, aligning his own "basic phenomena" (*"Basisphänomene"*), "phenomena of symbolic pregnance," with Goethe's concept of the *Urphänomen*.[145]

Cassirer's profound insight into the nature and significance of Weimar Classicism's doctrine of sincere seeming may be summed up in the following remark, taken from *Freiheit und Form:* "[Goethe] hat das Spiel des Werdens als 'wahrer Schein' durchschaut, als einen Schein, der das Wesen nicht verhüllt, sondern offenbart" ("Goethe penetrated the play of becoming as 'true' illusion, as a semblance that does not conceal, but reveal, Being").[146] The question of whether Cassirer has really succeeded in giving adequate intellectual articulation to his intuition of what Goethe and Schiller had in mind with their theory of living form is a question whose resolution must await the full comparative analysis, already begun, that the position of his work in the perspective of the "perennial aesthetic" so compellingly invites.[147]

Conclusion

If we have learned anything from the "poststructuralist" turn with which Nietzsche is often associated, it is surely to appreciate the chaotic nature of culture, in both its synchronic and diachronic dimensions. We have learned to see culture as a collection of ill-sorted fragments in collision and intersection with each other, in struggles for power and domination.[148] Indeed, this has now hardened into a would-be self-evident commonplace, a cliché even. But insight into (Dionysian) chaos as the inevitable concomitant of (Apollonian) order is at least as old as the Western tradition itself, as Nietzsche himself reminds us. And its newly minted versions should not blind us to the fact that some degree of order is necessary to the organization of our knowledge. In the case of the past, one such concept available to us is that of "tradition." In part this is inevitably an historian's construct, brought to bear on the data. But in part, too, it is more than "extrinsic" in this sense; it must, if it is to carry persuasion, subsume one or more "intrinsic" traditions, that is, filiations, demonstrable and sometimes acknowledged, between the utterances of one writer and those of another. Such intrinsic traditions may well be, indeed often are, *implicit,* in the sense that a writer will frequently address a traditional matter or question without explicitly naming many, or any, of the predecessors whose thought on the matter has made or kept it traditional, and with which the writer and/or his or her readership is undoubtedly familiar. It is obviously part of the task of a historian of ideas constructing an external tradition, however sketchy, to put significant contributors to a chain of ideas in line with each other. But, again, only a part: traditions are often piecemeal and discontinuous — chaotic, even — and that, too, needs to be taken into account.

The purpose of trying to make out ever-greater order in our common cultural history since the Age of Goethe is a theoretical one. Structure and genesis are, as modes of thought, mutually interdependent: the structure of our ideas is derived from and conditioned by the story we tell ourselves about their genesis, and vice versa. An example of the conceptual obfuscation that is occasioned by historical confusion is afforded by the early English (and, in some degree, German) reception of Schiller's ideas: the conflation of what was taken to be Humboldt's untrammeled individualism and subjectivism with Schiller's utterly different views on the relation of the State and the Individual has led to still-persistent prejudices, on demonstrably false grounds, against Weimar Classicism.[149] Even more problematic is the undifferentiated use of terms like "harmony" and "totality" in respect of Weimar Classicism, above all at a time of "resistance" to dominant ideologies and the repudiation of all "grand narratives." Here, too, more discrimination is needed, if we are not to be debarred from making cultural use of the Weimar Classical inheritance. For the totality at which Schiller aimed in his *Aesthetic*

Letters (Letter 6, §15), and which Nietzsche affirmed in the Delphic tones of Zarathustra, bears simply no relation to the totality so routinely attacked in much contemporary cultural theory. Wholeness for Weimar Classicism and for Nietzsche is neither Platonic perfection nor the universality promoted by the German Romantics and systematically codified by Hegel. Whatever term may be used, totality/harmony for Goethe, Schiller, and Nietzsche means the imperfect unique integrity of a *particular*. It is difficult to see how this, or any other, defining characteristic of a body of thought from the past could be grasped without an orderly historical framework in which to set it.[150]

So much more work remains to be done in this field, and yet more refined conceptual analysis will surely bring to light further differentiation.[151] While the evidence adduced here is very far from certainty, its pretensions to probability, at least in part, may, we hope, prove a provocation to further investigation of the genesis — and, by implication, the structure and function — of the notion of "sincere semblance," one of the key ideas of the whole length of the European tradition of reflection on aesthetics.

Notes

[1] Robert Wood, *Placing Aesthetics: Reflections on the Philosophical Tradition* (Illinois: Ohio UP, 2000), xv.

[2] Jean-Paul Dumont, Daniel Delattre, Jean-Louis Poirier, eds., *Les Présocratiques* (Paris: Gallimard, 1988), 745.

[3] Diogenes Laertius, *Lives and Opinions of Eminent Philosophers*, 6.65 (In German, Diogenes Laertius, *Leben und Meinungen berühmter Philosophen*, trans. Otto Apelt and Hans Günter Zekl [Hamburg: Felix Meiner, 1998], 1:327).

[4] *The Wisdom of Solomon*, 13:7: "[Men] believe their sight: because the things are beautiful that are seen" (King James Version); "[Men] fall victim to appearances, seeing so much beauty" (Jerusalem Bible).

[5] Marcus Aurelius, *Meditations*, trans. Maxwell Staniforth (Harmondsworth: Penguin, 1964), bk. 3, §2 (54), translation adapted.

[6] Thomas Aquinas, *Summa Theologica*, First Part, Q. 5, Art. 4; James Joyce, *A Portrait of the Artist as a Young Man* (1916; repr. London: Jonathan Cape, 1930), 234–38, 241–42.

[7] For an indication of the deep interest in Hispanic culture common to Goethe, Schiller, and the German Romantics, see Patricia Zecevic, *The Speaking Divine Woman: López de Úbeda's "La pícara Justina" and Goethe's "Wilhelm Meister"* (Oxford: Peter Lang, 2001), especially 15 and 117; compare Hilde Domin, ed., *Doppelinterpretationen* (Frankfurt am Main: Athenäum, 1966), on "der die ganze Moderne bestimmende Einfluß der Franzosen und Spanier" (3; "the determining influence of the French and the Spanish on the whole of modernism").

[8] See Paul Oppenheimer, *Rubens: A Portrait* (New York: Cooper Square Press, 2002), 7; and R. H. Stephenson, *Goethe's Conception of Knowledge and Science* (Edinburgh: Edinburgh UP, 1995), 70 and 75–76.

[9] Walter Hinck, "Man of the Theatre," in Elizabeth M. Wilkinson, ed., *Goethe Revisited: A Collection of Essays*, 153–69; here, 168 (London: John Calder, 1984).

[10] See R. H. Stephenson, "Weimar Classicism's Debt to the Scottish Enlightenment" in Nicholas Boyle and John Guthrie, eds., *Goethe and the English-Speaking World* (Rochester, NY, and Woodbridge, UK: Camden House, 2002), 61–70; here, 68.

[11] Johan Huizinga, *The Waning of the Middle Ages: A Study of the Forms of Life, Thought, and Art in France and the Netherlands in the Fourteenth and Fifteenth Centuries* [1919], trans. F. Hopman [1924] (London: Edward Arnold, 1937), 243.

[12] Plato, *The Symposium*, trans. Christopher Gill (Harmondsworth: Penguin, 1949), 211 b (49), 210 b (48) (translation adapted).

[13] Thomas Mann, *Die Erzählungen* (Frankfurt am Main: Fischer, 1986), 547; compare Plato, *Phaedrus and the Seventh and Eighth Letters*, trans. Walter Hamilton (Harmondsworth: Penguin, 1973), 250 b–251 a (56–57).

[14] Plato, *The Republic*, trans. Desmond Lee, 2nd ed. (Harmondsworth: Penguin, 1974), 476 b (269).

[15] Plato, *Phaedrus*, 250 c (57); see R. H. Stephenson, "'Ein künstlicher Vortrag': Die symbolische Form von Goethes naturwissenschaftlichen Schriften," in Barbara Naumann und Birgit Recki, eds., *Cassirer und Goethe: Neue Aspekte einer philosophisch-literarischen Wahlverwandtschaft* (Berlin: Akademie Verlag, 2002), 25–42; here, 41.

[16] Plotinus, *The Six Enneads*, trans. Stephen Mackenna, revised B. S. Page, 4th ed. (London: Faber and Faber, 1969), Fifth Ennead, Eighth Tractate: "On the Intellectual Beauty," §§1–4 (422–25); Goethe, *Maximen und Reflexionen*, ed. Max Hecker, nos. 633–43 (HA 12:491; HA 8:462–64).

[17] *Maximen und Reflexionen*, no. 376 (HA 12:468); *Johann Wolfgang von Goethe: Maxims and Reflexions*, trans. Elizabeth Stopp, ed. Peter Hutchinson (London: Penguin, 1998), 44 (translation adapted).

[18] Rudolf Arnheim, review of E. H. Gombrich, *Art and Illusion: A Study in the Psychology of Pictorial Representations* (London: Phaidon Press, 1960), *Art Bulletin* 44 (1962): 75–79; here, 76; compare Richard Wollheim, "Art and Illusion," *British Journal of Aesthetics* 3 (1963): 15–37; here, 30.

[19] WA 1.47:269–74; see Hinck, "Man of the Theatre," 167–69.

[20] See Elizabeth M. Wilkinson, "Schiller's Concept of *Schein* in the Light of Recent Aesthetics," *The German Quarterly* 28 (1955): 219–27; here, 225.

[21] Susanne K. Langer, *Philosophy in a New Key: A Study in the Symbolism of Reason, Rite, and Art* (1942; repr. New York: Mentor Books, 1961), 92 and 202.

[22] Milan Kundera, *The Unbearable Lightness of Being*, trans. Michael Henry Heim (1984; repr. London and Boston: Faber and Faber, 1985). The novel makes repeated reference to Goethe and Nietzsche.

[23] See his letter to Körner, 18 February 1773; compare, too, Elizabeth M. Wilkinson and L. A. Willoughby, "Glossary," to Friedrich Schiller, *On the Aesthetic Education of Man in a Series of Letters,* 2nd ed. (Oxford: Clarendon P, 1982), 327–29.

[24] *Maximen und Reflexionen,* no. 1346 (HA 12:470); English translation adapted from *Maxims and Reflexions,* 171.

[25] The phrase derives from Edward Bullough's "Mind and Medium in Art," in *Aesthetics: Lectures and Essays,* ed. Elizabeth M. Wilkinson, 131–58 (Stanford, CA: Stanford UP, 1957). Goethe called the aesthetic patterning of the "sound-look" of language "the veil of poetry" (*der Dichtung Schleier*), drawing on a long-standing tradition that goes back at least as far as the sixth century C.E.. For a discussion of Olympiodorus's use of the veil-metaphor in aesthetic contexts, see Katherine Everett Gilbert and Helmut Kuhn, *A History of Esthetics* (New York: Macmillan, 1939), 165; and R. H. Stephenson and Patricia D. Zecevic, "Goethe and the Divine Feminine in the Light of the Spanish Kabbalah," *Quaderni di Lingue e Letterature Straniere* 12 (2003): 299–333; here, 318–19.

[26] For an outline of the long history of the notion of "sincerity" in Western literature, see Paul Bishop, "Sincerity," in Chris Murray and Frank Northen Magill, eds., *The Encyclopaedia of Literary Critics and Criticism,* 2 vols.(London and Chicago: Fitzroy Dearborn, 1999), 2:1030–31.

[27] André Breton, "Les mots sans rides," in *Littérature,* 2nd series, 1 December 1922, 12–14; reprinted in *Œuvres complètes,* ed. Marguerite Bonnet, 3 vols. (Paris: Gallimard, 1988–99), 1:284–86; here, 286.

[28] HA 1:360; compare Johann Wolfgang von Goethe: *Selected Poems,* ed. Christopher Middleton, *Goethe's Collected Works,* vol. 1 (Boston: Suhrkamp/Insel, 1983), 231–33, adapted from Christopher Middleton's translation. For the consensus view of the difficulty of the poem, see Johannes A. E. Leue, "Goethes 'Urworte. Orphisch,'" *Acta Germanica* 2 (1967): 1–10; for further discussion, see John M. Krois, "Urworte: Cassirer als Goethe-Interpret," in Enno Rudolph and Bernd-Olaf Küppers, eds., *Kulturkritik nach Ernst Cassirer* (Hamburg: Felix Meiner, 1995), 297–324; Erika Swales, "Johann Wolfgang von Goethe, 'Urworte. Orphisch,'" in Peter Hutchinson, ed., *Landmarks in German Poetry* (Oxford: Lang, 2000), 57–71; and Dennis F. Mahoney, "Primeval Formation: Teaching *Wilhelm Meisters Lehrjahre* with the Help of Goethe's *Urworte. Orphisch,*" in Jeffrey L. High, ed., *Die Goethezeit: Werke—Wirkung—Wechselbeziehungen: Eine Festschrift für Wilfried Malsch* (Göttingen: Verlag von Schwerin, 2001), 202–14.

[29] See, for example, J. C. Adelung's laconic remark in his *Versuch eines vollständigen grammatisch kritischen Wörterbuchs der hochdeutschen Mundart in beständiger Vergleichung der übrigen Mundarten* (Leipzig, 1807): "Eine Handlung kann freywillig seyn, ohne eben alle Mahle frey zu seyn" ("An action can be free-willed without always being free"). For a clear discussion of the ambiguity of moral freedom, see David L. Norton, *Personal Destinies: A Philosophy of Ethical Individualism* (Princeton, NJ: Princeton UP, 1976): "We may say [. . .] interchangeably 'He wants to do,' or 'He is where he must be, doing what he must do'" (222).

[30] Compare Alfred North Whitehead, *Process and Reality: An Essay in Cosmology* [1929], corrected edition by David Ray Griffin and Donald W. Sherburne (New York: The Free P, 1978), 133.

[31] Friedrich Schiller, *Ueber die ästhetische Erziehung der Menschen in einer Reihe von Briefen* [1795]; *On the Aesthetic Education of Man in a Series of Letters*, ed. and trans. Elizabeth M. Wilkinson and L. A. Willoughby, 2nd ed. (Oxford: Clarendon P, 1982), Letter 19, §12 (henceforth cited in the text with reference to letter and section number). See, too, Letter 27, §§8 and 11, where the vocabulary, like that of the other later letters, is strongly reminiscent of Goethe's in the final stanza here.

[32] Plato, *Phaedrus*, 251 a–252 d (57–58).

[33] "Inwiefern die Idee: Schönheit sei Vollkommenheit mit Freiheit, auf organische Naturen angewendet werden könne" (1794; HA 13:23; "To what Extent the Idea 'Beauty is Perfection in Combination with Freedom' may be applied to Living Things").

[34] See Donna C. Stanton, *The Aristocrat as Art: A Study of the 'Honnête Homme' and the Dandy in Seventeenth- and Nineteenth-Century French Literature* (New York: Columbia UP, 1980).

[35] "Ernst Stiedenroth, Psychologie zur Erklärung der Seelenerscheinungen. Erster Teil. Berlin 1824" (HA 13:42; "Ernst Stiedenroth, *A Psychology in Clarification of Phenomena of the Soul* (part 1, Berlin: 1824)").

[36] "Es giebt eine erheuchelte Missachtung aller der Dinge, welche thatsächlich die Menschen am wichtigsten nehmen, *aller nächsten Dinge*. Man sagt zum Beispiel 'man isst nur, um zu leben,' — eine verfluchte *Lüge*, wie jene, welche von der Kinderzeugung als der eigentlichen Absicht aller Wollust redet. Umgekehrt ist die Hochschätzung der 'wichtigsten Dinge' fast niemals ganz ächt: die Priester und Metaphysiker haben uns zwar auf diesen Gebieten durchaus an einen heuchlerisch übertreibenden *Sprachgebrauch* gewöhnt, aber das Gefühl doch nicht umgestimmt, welches diese wichtigsten Dinge nicht so wichtig nimmt, wie jene verachteten nächsten Dinge" (*MA*, II, "Wanderer und sein Schatten," §5; KSA 2:541; "There exists a feigned contempt for all the things which we in fact take most seriously, *for all the things nearest to them*. One says, for example, 'one eats only in order to live' — which is a damned *lie*, as is that which speaks of the begetting of children as the real objective of all lust. Conversely, the high esteem in which the 'most serious things' are held is almost never quite genuine: the priests and metaphysicians, to be sure, have in these domains altogether accustomed us to a hypocritically exaggerated *linguistic usage*, but they have not converted the feeling that refuses to take these most serious things as seriously as those despised nearest things"); "Wir müssen wieder *gute Nachbarn der nächsten Dinge* werden und nicht so verächtlich wie bisher über sie hinweg nach Wolken und Nachtunholden hinblicken. In Wäldern und Höhlen, in sumpfigen Strichen und unter bedeckten Himmeln — da hat der Mensch als auf den Culturstufen ganzer Jahrtausende allzulange gelebt, und dürftig gelebt. Dort hat er die Gegenwart und die Nachbarschaft und das Leben und sich selbst *verachten gelernt* — und wir, wir Bewohner der *lichteren* Gefilde der Natur und des Geistes, bekommen jetzt noch, durch Erbschaft, Etwas von diesem Gift der Verachtung gegen das Nächste in unser Blut mit" (*MA,* II, "Wanderer und sein Schatten," §16;

KSA 2:551; "We must again become *good neighbours to the nearest things* and cease from gazing so contemptuously past them at clouds and monsters of the night. In forests and caves, in swampy regions and under cloudy skies — this is where human-kind has lived all too long, and lived poorly, as on the cultural steps of whole millen-nia. There he has *learned to hold in contempt* the present and nearness and life and himself — and we, who dwell in the *brighter* fields of nature and the spirit, we too have inherited in our blood something of this poison and contempt for what is near-est"); and compare the dialogue between the Wanderer and the Shadow at the end of this book, where the Shadow says: "Von Allem, was du vorgebracht hast, hat mir Nichts *mehr* gefallen, als eine Verheissung: ihr wollt wieder gute Nachbarn der näch-sten Dinge werden" (KSA 2:703; "Of all you have said nothing has pleased me *more* than a promise: you want again to become good neighbors to the things nearest to you"). Nietzsche returns to this theme in *Ecce Homo* when he argues that "diese kleinen Dinge" ("these little things"), such as diet, location, climate, recreation, "die ganze Casuistik der Selbstsucht" ("the entire casuistry of selfishness"), are, in fact, "über alle Begriffe hinaus wichtiger als Alles, was man bisher wichtig nahm" ("incon-ceivably more important than everything hitherto considered of importance"; *EH* Warum ich so klug bin §10; KSA 6:295).

[37] Goethe, *Campagne in Frankreich. 1792* (1820–1821, pub. 1822; HA 10:256).

[38] Alexander Bieling, ed., *Gottscheds Reineke Fuchs* (Halle: Max Niemeyer, 1886). Henceforth referred to in the text as "Gottsched," with page references. For a fuller reading, see R. H. Stephenson, "The Political Import of Goethe's *Reineke Fuchs,*" in Kenneth Varty, ed., *Reynard the Fox: Cultural Metamorphoses and Social Engagement in the Beast Epic from the Middle Ages to the Present,* 2nd ed., 191–207 (Oxford: Berghahn, 2003).

[39] Goethe, *Maximen und Reflexionen,* no. 681 (HA 12:522); *Maxims and Reflexions,* 92.

[40] Goethe, *Campagne in Frankreich* (HA 10:203).

[41] "[Die] holden Göttinnen [. . .] stehen [. . .] auch der umsichtigen Klugheit gerne zur Seite" ("Für junge Dichter — Wohlgemeinte Erwiderung" [1832; HA 12:359]).

[42] Joyce, *A Portrait of the Artist as a Young Man,* 242.

[43] See Anthony Storr, *The School of Genius* (London: André Deutsch, 1988), 71.

[44] Virginia Woolf, *To the Lighthouse* [1927] (Harmondsworth: Penguin, 1992), 193.

[45] Joseph Conrad, *Heart of Darkness* (Harmondsworth: Penguin, 1986), 119.

[46] Benedict de Spinoza, *On the Improvement of the Understanding/The Eth-ics/Correspondence,* trans. R. H. M. Elwes (New York: Dover, 1955), part 1 ("Con-cerning God"), Definition 7, page 46). For further discussion, see Sabine Roehr, "Freedom and Autonomy in Schiller," *Journal of the History of Ideas* 64 (2003): 119–34.

[47] Elizabeth M. Wilkinson and L. A. Willoughby, "Missing Links or Whatever Hap-pened to Weimar Classicism?" in Hinrich Siefken and Alan Robinson, eds., *Erfah-rung und Überlieferung: Festschrift for C. P. Magill* (Cardiff: Trivium Special Publica-tions, 1974), 57–74.

[48] See Robert R. Wilson, "Play, Transgression and Carnival: Bakhtin and Derrida on *Scriptor Ludens*," *Mosaic* 19 (1986): 73–89; Juliet Sychrava, *Schiller to Derrida: Idealism in Aesthetics* (New York: Cambridge UP, 1989); and compare R. H. Stephenson, "Theorizing to Some Purpose: 'Deconstruction' in the Light of Goethe and Schiller's Aesthetics — the Case of *Die Wahlverwandtschaften*," *The Modern Language Review* 84 (1989): 381–92.

[49] Compare Volker Gerhardt, *Individualität: Das Element der Welt* (Munich: Beck, 2000), 13–17 and 184–89; for Gerhardt's views on "particularity" and "beauty," which are at least consonant with Weimar Classicism, see, too, 217–18 and 223.

[50] For an illuminating example of the meticulous application of the method of morphological comparison, see Heidi Robinson, "Der gesellschaftsfeindliche 'innere' bzw. 'ganze Mensch': Mißdeutungen in der englischen Rezeption und Überlieferung von Schillers Kulturtheorie," *Arcadia* 15 (1980): 129–48; and her unpublished doctoral thesis, "The Growth of a Myth: An Examination of English Responses to Schiller's Theory of Culture," University of London, 1981, especially 2 and 5–19. Compare the similarly enlightening use of the method of comparative morphology in respect of a selected, but central, cluster of ideas, in Wladyslaw Tatarkiewicz, *A History of Six Ideas: An Essay in Aesthetics* (The Hague: Martinus Nijhoff, 1980).

[51] Immanuel Kant, "Vorrede," *Kritik der praktischen Vernunft* [1788] (Frankfurt am Main: Insel, 1976), 107.

[52] For surveys of the reception history, see René Wellek, *History of Modern Criticism: 1750–1950*, 8 vols (New Haven: Yale UP, 1955–1992), 1:254–55; Schiller, NA 27:232–40; Elizabeth M. Wilkinson and L. A. Willoughby, introduction to Schiller, *On the Aesthetic Education of Man*, cxxxiii–cxcvi.

[53] See Robinson, "Der gesellschaftsfeindliche 'innere' bzw. 'ganze Mensch,'" 129, 136–37, and 140; and Robinson, "The Growth of a Myth," 20–42.

[54] Thomas Carlyle, *Critical and Miscellaneous Essays*, 7 vols. (London: Chapman and Hall, 1872), 3:97.

[55] See Robinson, "The Growth of a Myth," ch. 3, 67–93.

[56] See David Simpson's introduction to his edition, *German Aestheic and Literary Criticism: Kant, Fichte, Schelling, Schopenhauer, Hegel* (Cambridge: Cambridge UP, 1984), 20.

[57] See Rosemary Ashton, *The German Idea: Four English Writers and the Reception of German Thought 1800–1860* (Cambridge: Cambridge UP, 1980), especially ch. 1; Elinor Shaffer, *"Kubla Khan" and the Fall of Jerusalem* (Cambridge: Cambridge UP, 1975); Robinson, "The Growth of a Myth," 67–93; and James Simpson, *Matthew Arnold and Goethe* (Liverpool: Liverpool UP, 1979).

[58] *The Notebooks of Samuel Taylor Coleridge*, ed. Kathleen Coburn, 4 vols. (London: Routledge and Kegan Paul, 1957), vol. 1 1794–1804, part 2, no. 1705.

[59] See Robinson, "Der gesellschaftsfeindliche 'innere' bzw. 'ganze Mensch,'" 145.

[60] See Robinson, 132–33, 142, and 147; and Robinson, "The Growth of a Myth," 95–124.

[61] John Stuart Mill, *Autobiography* (1873; repr. London: Oxford UP, 1971), 72.

[62] F. R. Leavis, ed., *Mill on Bentham and Coleridge* (London: Chatto and Windus, 1950), 129.

[63] Robinson, "Der gesellschaftsfeindliche 'innere' bzw. 'ganze Mensch,'" 147.

[64] Wilkinson and Willoughby, introduction to Schiller, *On the Aesthetic Education of Man,* clvi; and their note to Letter 26, §8 ("Commentary," 286).

[65] See Robinson, "The Growth of a Myth," 126–83; compare, too, L. A. Willoughby, "Oscar Wilde and Goethe," in Elizabeth M. Wilkinson and L. A. Willoughby, *Models of Wholeness: Some Attitudes to Language, Art and Life in the Age of Goethe* [British and Irish Studies in German Language and Literature, 30], ed. Jeremy Adler, Martin Swales, and Ann Weaver (Oxford: Peter Lang, 2002), 195–226 (especially 220–22).

[66] G. W. F. Hegel, *Briefe von und an Hegel* [Hegel, *Sämtliche Werke,* vols. 27–30], ed. Johannes Hoffmeister, 4 vols (Hamburg: Felix Meiner, 1952–1960), 1:25.

[67] G. W. F. Hegel, "Ältestes Systemprogramm des deutschen Idealismus," first edited and published by Franz Rosenzweig (1886–1929) in *Sitzungsberichte der Heidelberger Akademie der Wissenschaften: Philosophisch-historische Klasse* 5 (1917), 5–7; the text and detailed commentary on it are available in Christoph Jammes and Helmut Schneider, eds., *Mythologie der Vernunft: Hegels "ältestes Systemprogramm des deutschen Idealismus"* (Frankfurt am Main: Suhrkamp, 1984); it is translated in H. S. Harris, *Hegel's Development: Toward the Sunlight, 1770–1801* (Oxford: Clarendon P, 1972), 510–12.

[68] Compare Wellek, *History of Modern Criticism,* 2:367–69. For an account of the divergence between Schelling's aesthetics and those of Weimar Classicism, see R. H. Stephenson, *Goethe's Conception of Knowledge and Science,* 27–31.

[69] Wilkinson and Willoughby, "Missing Links," 66.

[70] M. H. Abrams, *Natural Supernaturalism: Tradition and Revolution in Romantic Literature* (New York: Oxford UP, 1971), 353.

[71] For a thorough investigation of the question whether it is really justifiable to claim Schiller as the originator or precursor of later doctrines of 'alienation' such as those of Hegel and Marx, see Vicky Rippere, *Schiller and "Alienation"* (Bern: Peter Lang, 1981), 145–73.

[72] See Georg Lasson, *Die Idee and das Ideal* (Leipzig: F. Meiner, 1931), 163.

[73] Lasson, *Die Idee und das Ideal,* 133.

[74] Søren Kierkegaard, *Fear and Trembling,* trans. Alastair Hannay (1843; repr. Harmondsworth: Penguin, 1985), 109 (Problema 3).

[75] Georg Wilhelm Friedrich Hegel, *Vorlesungen über die Philosophie der Geschichte* (1961; repr. Stuttgart: Reclam, 1997), 345.

[76] Hegel, *Vorlesungen,* 341.

[77] Hegel, *Vorlesungen,* 550.

[78] Friedrich Engels, *Deutscher Sozialismus in Versen und Prosa* [1847], in Karl Marx/Friedrich Engels, *Werke,* 6 vols. (Berlin/DDR: Dietz, 1972), 4:207–47; here, 232.

[79] See R. H. Stephenson, "The Cultural Theory of Weimar Classicism in the Light of Coleridge's Doctrine of Aesthetic Knowledge," in Paul Bishop and R. H. Stephenson, eds., *Goethe 2000: Intercultural Readings of his Work* (Leeds: Northern UP, 2000), 149–69 (especially 161–62), where the raising by all three poet-thinkers of the traditional "lower" faculty of sense and imagination to the top of the hierarchy of faculties is discussed.

[80] Karl Marx, *Grundrisse der Kritik der politischen Ökonomie* (Berlin: Akademie Verlag, 1953), 22 (our italics).

[81] Marx, *Grundrisse,* 21–22.

[82] Marx, *Grundrisse,* 22.

[83] Marx, *Grundrisse,* 208. Recent work on Schopenhauer suggests a similar reversal of our habitual assumptions for, once Schopenhauer's "nothingness" is seen from the perspective of Schiller's *Nullpunkt,* it seems less like the ground for a call to art for death's sake, an escape from the will into Nirvana, than a call to fullness of life (see Paul Bishop, "Social Critique and Aesthetics in Schopenhauer," *History of European Ideas* 29 [2003]: 411–35).

[84] See Wilkinson and Willoughby, introduction to Schiller, *On the Aesthetic Education of Man,* clxvi–clxvii, clxviii, clxx–clxxii.

[85] Thomas De Quincey, *Confessions of an English Opium-Eater,* ed. Malcolm Elwin (London: Macdonald, 1956), 466; compare Stephenson, *Goethe's Conception of Knowledge and Science,* 55 and 66.

[86] Herman Melville, *Moby Dick, or The White Whale* (Boston: Page, 1851), 354; compare Stephenson, *Goethe's Conception of Knowledge and Science,* 7.

[87] Goethe, "Einleitung in die Propyläen" (HA 12:43).

[88] Marcel Proust, *À la recherche du temps perdu,* vol. 1, *Du Coté de chez Swann* (1914; repr. Paris: Gallimard, 1954), 83.

[89] Stendhal, *De l'Amour* (Paris: Garnier-Flammarion, 1965), bk. 1, ch. 7, 31; in English, *Love,* trans. Gilbert and Suzanne Sale (Harmondsworth: Penguin, 1975), 43.

[90] See, for example, *De l'Amour,* bk. 1, ch. 29; bk. 2, ch. 59; Fragment §61 (101, 239–40 and 257; *Love,* 95, 209 and 229).

[91] *De l'Amour,* bk. 1, ch. 39 (ii), 143; *Love,* 128; compare bk. 1, ch. 2, 34–35; *Love,* 45.

[92] *De l'Amour,* bk. 1, ch. 32, 114–15 and 117; *Love,* 105–6 and 108.

[93] *De l'Amour,* bk. 1, ch. 26, 86; *Love,* 83.

[94] Eliot's apparent assimilation of Weimar aesthetics while repudiating most of what he thought Goethe ("the sage") stood for is exactly analogous to Carlyle's repugnance for the frivolous-sounding idea of playful illusion co-existing with his (surely Schiller-inspired) conviction that "sincerity" and reproductive "creativity" go hand in hand: "A man can believe, and make his own, in the most genuine way, what he has received from another [. . .] The merit of originality is not novelty; it is sincerity. The believing man is the original man; whatever he believes he believes for himself, and not for another" (Thomas Carlyle, *On Heroes, Hero-Worship and the Heroic in History,* The Works in Thirty Volumes [London: Chapman and Hall, 1841], 6:25–26).

[95] Stefan George, "Vorrede zur zweiten Ausgabe," in Stefan George and Karl Wolfskehl, eds., *Deutsche Dichtung*, vol. 3, *Das Jahrhundert Goethes*, 7 (Berlin: Georg Bondi, 1910).

[96] Joseph Goebbels, *Michael: Ein deutsches Schicksal in Tagebuchblättern* 6th ed. (Munich: Verlag Franz Eber Nachfolger, 1935), 21. Compare "Der Künstler ist Gott zu vergleichen. Beide geben dem Stoff Form" (22; "The artist can be compared to God. Both give form to material").

[97] Wilkinson and Willoughby, introduction to Schiller, *On the Aesthetic Education of Man*, cxli–cxlii, clx, clxiv, and clxxii–clxxiii. The genealogy of Yeats's "necessary technique of seeming" — forged, inter alia, from Wilde's theory of masks and the role of *Schein* in Goethe's *Wilhelm Meister* — was sketched by L. A. G. Strong, in his article "Reminiscences of W. B. Yeats," *The Listener*, 22 April 1954 (cited in Wilkinson and Willoughby, introduction to Schiller, *On the Aesthetic Education of Man*, clx).

[98] See, for instance, the chapter "Prag um die Jahrhundertwende" in Klaus Wagenbach, *Franz Kafka: Eine Biographie seiner Jugend 1883–1912* (Bern: Francke, 1958), 65–98; and Bert Nagel, *Kafka und die Weltliteratur: Zusammenhänge und Wechselwirkungen* (Munich: Winkler, 1983), 171–72. We are grateful to our departmental colleague Bernard Ashbrook for advice and information in connection with this point.

[99] The remark is Roy Pascal's, in his *Kafka's Narrators: A Study of his Stories and Sketches* (Cambridge: Cambridge UP, 1982), 113.

[100] Franz Kafka, *Das Urteil und andere Erzählungen* (Frankfurt am Main: Fischer, 1952), 136–37. Further references to this edition are in parenthesis in the text.

[101] Heinz Politzer, *Franz Kafka: Parable and Paradox* 2nd ed. (Ithaca: Cornell UP, 1966), 308, 59–60, and 302. Roy Pascal's analysis of the narrator as a "coarse showman" (113) needs to be qualified: rather, he is a cultivated man who uses the language of show business to ironic effect.

[102] L. A. Willoughby, *The Classical Age of German Literature, 1748–1805* (New York: Russell and Russell, 1966), 107.

[103] Lucien Price, *The Dialogues of Alfred North Whitehead* (Boston: Little, Brown and Company, 1954), 125.

[104] Whitehead, *Process and Reality*, 280; compare Stephenson, *Goethe's Conception of Knowledge and Science*, 26–27.

[105] Whitehead, *Process and Reality*, 170.

[106] Compare with Ralph Waldo Emerson's statement that "Beauty is the normal state" (*The Conduct of Life* [London: George Routledge and Sons, 1913], 283). This is exactly the position of Weimar Classicism (see Stephenson, *Goethe's Conception of Knowledge and Science*, 7). Besides the Great Victorians, one of the formative influences on Whitehead's high estimation of aesthetics may have been Samuel Alexander, a philosopher Whitehead held in the highest esteem, who, especially in his *Beauty and Other Forms of Value* (London: Macmillan, 1933) gave vivid and precise expression to many of the central doctrines of Weimar Classicism. Compare the following with Goethe's and Schiller's view of art as a sensuous-mental object: "The work of art

is a particular concrete thing, and everything that it means is embodied in this particular material" (51).

[107] Alfred North Whitehead, *Religion in the Making* (1926; repr. New York: Fordham UP, 1999), 104–5.

[108] Compare Wilkinson and Willoughby, introduction to Schiller, *On the Aesthetic Education of Man,* clxxxviii–clxxxix.

[109] Georg Wilhelm Friedrich Hegel, *Sämtliche Werke,* ed. Hermann Glockner, 26 vols. (Stuttgart: Fromann, 1927–1930), 14:396.

[110] Martin Heidegger, "Der Ursprung des Kunstwerks," in *Holzwege* (Frankfurt am Main: Vittorio Klostermann, 1950), 70; in English, "The Origin of the Work of Art," in Martin Heidegger, *Poetry, Language, Thought,* trans. Albert Hofstadter (New York: Harper and Row, 1971), 86 (translation modified). Further references to this edition and this translation (sometimes modified) appear in parenthesis in the text.

[111] For further discussion, see Meyer Schapiro, "The Still Life as Personal Object — A note on Heidegger and Van Gogh," in Marianne L. Simmel, ed., *The Reach of Mind: Essays in Memory of Kurt Goldstein* (New York: Springer, 1968), 203–9; this essay as well as Heidegger's analysis is discussed at length by Jacques Derrida in *La Vérité en peinture* (Paris: Flammarion, 1978), 291–436; in English, Jacques Derrida, *The Truth in Painting,* trans. Geoff Bennington and Ian McLeod (Chicago and London: U of Chicago P, 1987), 255–382.

[112] "Das Sein ist ewig; denn Gesetze / Bewahren die lebend'gen Schätze / Aus welchen sich das All geschmückt" (HA 1:369; "Being is deathless; For law / Preserves living wealth / With which the All adorns itself"; compare the translation by Christopher Middleton in *Selected Poems,* 267).

[113] See Kenneth Maly, "Translating Heidegger's Works into English: The History and the Possibility," *Heidegger Studies* 16 (2000): 115–38.

[114] See Stephenson, *Goethe's Conception of Knowledge and Science,* 65–67.

[115] Alfred North Whitehead, *Adventures of Ideas* (1933; repr. New York: The Free P, 1961), 285.

[116] Theodor W. Adorno, *Negative Dialektik* (Frankfurt am Main: Suhrkamp, 1966).

[117] Theodor W. Adorno, *Ästhetische Theorie* (Frankfurt am Main: Suhrkamp, 1970), 125.

[118] Adorno, *Ästhetische Theorie,* 205.

[119] Adorno, *Ästhetische Theorie,* 190.

[120] Jürgen Habermas, *Theorie des kommunikativen Handelns,* 2 vols., 2nd ed. (Frankfurt am Main: Suhrkamp, 1987), 1:512.

[121] Martin Jay, *The Dialectical Imagination: A History of the Frankfurt School and the Institute of Social Research, 1923–1950* (Boston: Little, Brown and Company, 1973), 63.

[122] See Jay, *The Dialectical Imagination,* 82.

[123] See Jay, *The Dialectical Imagination,* 256 and 179.

[124] See Jay, *The Dialectical Imagination,* 270. In *Dialektik der Aufklärung: Philosophische Fragmente* (1944; *Dialectic of Nature: Philosophical Fragments*)

Adorno and Horkheimer speak of "[das] Eingedenken der Natur im Subjekt" (*Dialektik der Aufklärung* (Frankfurt am Main: Fischer, 1988), 47; "remembrance of Nature in the subject"); in his *Theorie des kommunikativen Handelns,* Habermas focuses on this phrase (1:516), which echoes Sigmund Freud's comment in *Das Unbehagen in der Kultur* (1930; *Civilization and its Discontents*), which speaks of "ein Stück der unbesiegbaren Natur" ("a piece of invincible Nature") in terms of "unserer eigenen psychischen Beschaffenheit" ("our own psychic disposition"; Sigmund Freud, *Gesammelte Werke: Chronologisch geordnet,* 19 vols. (Frankfurt am Main: S. Fischer, 1962–1987), 14:445).

[125] Adorno, *Ästhetische Theorie,* 125–27.

[126] Wilkinson and Willoughby, introduction to Schiller, *On the Aesthetic Education of Man,* clvi.

[127] Habermas, *Theorie des kommunikativen Handelns,* 1:42 and 251.

[128] Jürgen Habermas, *Der philosophische Diskurs der Moderne* (Frankfurt am Main: Suhrkamp, 1984), 59–63.

[129] For further discussion, see Frances Birrell, "'Abenteuerlich mißverstanden'? Habermas's Reception and Interpretation of Schiller," *German Life and Letters* 49 (1996): 297–310; and "An Investigation of the Theoretical Insights of Jürgen Habermas in Relation to the Aesthetic Writings of Friedrich Schiller," doctoral thesis, University of Strathclyde, 1997 (especially 185, 189, 196 and 232, on the differences between Schiller's and Weber's "aesthetic state").

[130] Jürgen Habermas, "Bewußtmachende oder rettende Kritik — Die Aktualität Walter Benjamins," in *Kultur und Kritik* (1972; repr. Frankfurt am Main: Suhrkamp, 1973), 302–51; *Legitimationsprobleme im Spätkapitalismus* (Frankfurt am Main: Suhrkamp, 1973), 120.

[131] Habermas, *Theorie des kommunikativen Handelns,* 1:41–42. Habermas's phrase "authentischer Ausdruck einer exemplarischen Erfahrung" ("authentic expression of an exemplary experience") seems to take aesthetics back to the presentation of the typical associated with the didacticism of a Boileau or a Gottsched.

[132] See Habermas, *Theorie des kommunikativen Handelns,* 1:128, 135 and 140.

[133] Barbara Naumann, *Philosophie und Poetik des Symbols: Cassirer und Goethe* (Munich: Wilhelm Fink, 1998), 14.

[134] John Michael Krois, "Cassirer's 'Prototype and Model' of Symbolism: Its Sources and Significance," *Science in Context* 12 (1991): 531–47 (532, 534, 539, and 540); John Michael Krois, *Cassirer: Symbolic Forms and History* (New Haven: Yale UP, 1987), 5–9, 53–54, 57–62, 80–81, and 86–88.

[135] See Krois, *Cassirer,* 176–81.

[136] Ernst Cassirer, *Freiheit und Form: Studien zur deutschen Geistesgeschichte* (Berlin: Bruno Cassirer, 1916), 208–9 and 242–56.

[137] Goethe, *Maximen und Reflexionen,* no. 565; *Maxims and Reflections,* 75.

[138] Ernst Cassirer, *Goethe-Vorlesungen,* ed. John M. Krois (Hamburg: Felix Meiner, 2003), 257. Volume 2 of Cassirer, *Nachgelassene Manuskripte und Texte,* ed. John M. Krois and Oswald Schwemmer.

[139] Cassirer, *Freiheit und Form,* 278.

[140] Quoted by Krois in "Cassirer's 'Prototype and Model,'" 535, from "Praegnanz, symbolische Ideation," an undated manuscript in the Beinecke Rare Book and Manuscript Library, Yale University (Gen. Mss. 98, Box 23, folder 424), and translated by him.

[141] Cassirer, *Freiheit und Form*, 252.

[142] Immanuel Kant, *Kritik der Urteilskraft*, ed. Karl Vorländer, Die philosophische Bibliothek, vol. 39a (Hamburg: Felix Meiner, 1974), B 256; quoted by Naumann, *Philosophie und Poetik des Symbols*, 61.

[143] Naumann, *Philosophie und Poetik des Symbols*, 11, 12, 73, and 146.

[144] Naumann, *Philosophie und Poetik des Symbols*, 94.

[145] Naumann, *Philosophie und Poetik des Symbols*, 94–96 and 99; for a (partial) divergence from Naumann's reading, see R. H. Stephenson, "'Eine zarte Differenz': Cassirer on Goethe on the Symbol," in Cyrus Hamlin and John M. Krois, eds., *Symbolic Forms and Cultural Studies: Ernst Cassirer's Theory of Culture* (New Haven: Yale UP, 2004).

[146] Cassirer, *Freiheit und Form*, 256.

[147] The fruitfulness of Weimar Classicism's theory of the aesthetic was not lost on Ernst Cassirer's pupil, Susanne Langer (who, significantly, also counted that metaphysician of the aesthetic, A. N. Whitehead, as her other great intellectual mentor). She was thus well placed to develop a *Philosophy in a New Key* (1942), culminating in the monumental three-volume study, *Mind: An Essay on Human Feeling*, 3 vols. (Baltimore: Johns Hopkins UP, 1967–1970). Langer's dissatisfaction with her own theory of illusion, up to and including *Feeling and Form: A Theory of Art Developed from Philosophy in a New Key* (London: Scribner's, 1953), is made quite explicit in *Mind* 1:230 (compare Wilkinson and Willoughby, introduction to Schiller, *On the Aesthetic Education of Man*, clxv).

[148] See Philip Smith, *Cultural Theory: An Introduction* (Oxford: Blackwell, 2001), 121.

[149] See Robinson, "Der gesellschaftsfeindliche 'innere' bzw. 'ganze Mensch,'" 136–38; and see Richard Sheppard, "Two Liberals: A Comparison of the Humanism of Matthew Arnold and Wilhelm von Humboldt," *German Life and Letters* 24 (1971): 219–33.

[150] See Robinson, "Der gesellschaftsfeindliche 'innere' bzw. 'ganze Mensch,'" 143–45.

[151] For instance, a conception of "sincerity" seems required that is more complex than "the degree of congruence between feeling and avowal" with which the debate was stimulated over thirty years ago by Lionel Trilling (in his *Sincerity and Authenticity* [London: Oxford UP, 1972], 7).

Appendix:
The Composition of *Zarathustra*

IF THE FIRST OF THE TWO KEY CONCEPTS that dominate Nietzsche's account in *Ecce Homo* of the composition of *Zarathustra* is the idea of the eternal recurrence (see chapter 2), the second is "inspiration" (*EH Z* §3; KSA 6:339). In his pseudo-autobiography, Nietzsche offered the following description of the kind of inspiration he had in mind:

> — Hat Jemand, Ende des neunzehnten Jahrhunderts, einen deutlichen Begriff davon, was Dichter starker Zeitalter *Inspiration* nannten? Im andren Falle will ich's beschreiben. — Mit dem geringsten Rest von Aberglauben in sich würde man in der That die Vorstellung, bloss Incarnation, bloss Mundstück, bloss medium übermächtiger Gewalten zu sein, kaum abzuweisen wissen. Der Begriff Offenbarung, in dem Sinn, dass plötzlich, mit unsäglicher Sicherheit und Feinheit, Etwas *sichtbar*, hörbar wird, Etwas, das Einen im Tiefsten erschüttert und umwirft, beschreibt einfach den Thatbestand. Man hört, man sucht nicht; man nimmt, man fragt nicht, wer da giebt; wie ein Blitz leuchtet ein Gedanke auf, mit Nothwendigkeit, in der Form ohne Zögern, — ich habe nie eine Wahl gehabt.
>
> (*EH Z* §3; KSA 6:339)

> [Has anyone, at the end of the nineteenth century, a clear idea of what poets of strong ages called *inspiration*? If not I will describe it. — With even the slightest remnant of superstition one could hardly reject the idea that one is merely incarnation, merely mouthpiece, merely the medium of overpowering forces. The concept of revelation, in the sense that suddenly, with indescribable certainty and subtlety, something becomes *visible*, audible, something that shakes one to the core and bowls one over, merely describes the facts. One hears, one does not seek; one takes, one does not ask who is giving; like lightning a thought flashes up, with necessity, without hesitation in its form — I never had any choice.]

"Dies," wrote Nietzsche, "ist *meine* Erfahrung von Inspiration; ich zweifle nicht, dass man Jahrtausende zurückgehn muss, um Jemanden zu finden, der mir sagen darf 'es ist auch die meine'" (KSA 6:340; "This is *my* experience of inspiration; I do not doubt that one has to go back thousands of years to find anyone who could say to me, 'it is also mine'").[1] (Of course,

Nietzsche had only to turn back to Goethe, for whom such *aperçus* were the foundation of all creativity.)[2] At about the same time, in his letter to Georg Brandes of 10 April 1888, Nietzsche made a similar point about the suddenness and rapidity of composition when he claimed that each part of *Zarathustra* was written in about 10 days ("jeder Theil in ungefähr zehn Tagen"), and he noted: "Vollkommener Zustand eines 'Inspirirten,' Alles unterwegs, auf starken Märschen concipirt: absolute Gewißheit, als ob jeder Satz Einem zugerufen wäre. Gleichzeitig mit dem Gefühl größter körperlicher Elasticität und Fülle" (KSB 8:287; "Perfect state of an 'inspired one,' everything conceived out and about, on long walks: absolute certainty, as if every sentence has been shouted out to one. Simultaneous with the feeling of the greatest bodily elasticity and fullness").[3]

Yet, as we have seen in chapter 2, preparations for *Zarathustra* had begun as early as 1881, and there can be no doubt that Nietzsche had been meditating for at least two years on the possibility of a work of the substance and style of *Zarathustra*.[4] (In fact, it is possible that the material for some episodes lay much further back in Nietzsche's past.)[5] Furthermore, there are indications in Nietzsche's correspondence that he was aware that something was on its way. In the draft of a letter to one of his friends, the writer Malwida von Meysenbug (1816–1903), probably written on 13 July 1882 from Tautenburg, Nietzsche, completing the proof-reading of *Die fröhliche Wissenschaft,* wrote of a sense of "crisis": "Dieses Jahr, welches in mehreren Hauptstücken meines Lebens eine neue Crisis bedeutet (Epoche ist das richtige Wort, ein Mittelzustand zwischen 2 Crisen, eine hinter mir eine vor mir) ist mir durch den Glanz und die Anmuth dieser jungen, wahr[haft] heroischen Seele sehr verschönt worden" ("This year, which represents in many areas of my life a new crisis (*epoch* is the right word, a condition of being between two crises, one behind, one in front of me) has been brightened up by the glamour and grace of this young, truly heroic soul") — that young, heroic soul being, of course, Lou von Salomé (KSB 6:223–24). Then again, in a letter to Franz Overbeck, written from Leipzig on 9 September 1882, he realized that the fourth book of *Die fröhliche Wissenschaft* amounted to a caesura in his thought and in his life (which, in the case of Nietzsche, virtually amounted to the same thing):

> Wenn Du den Sanctus Januarius gelesen hast, so wirst Du gemerkt haben, daß ich einen *Wendekreis* überschritten habe. Alles liegt neu vor mir, und es wird nicht lange dauern, daß ich auch das *furchtbare* Angesicht meiner ferneren Lebens-Aufgabe zu sehen bekomme. Dieser lange reiche Sommer war für mich eine *Probe*-Zeit; ich nahm äußerst muthig und stolz von ihm Abschied, denn ich empfand für diese Zeitspanne wenigstens die sonst so häßliche Kluft zwischen Wollen und Vollbringen als *überbrückt.* Es gab *harte* Ansprüche an meine Menschlichkeit, und ich bin mir im Schwersten genug geworden.

Diesen ganzen Zwischenzustand zwischen sonst und einstmals nenne ich "in media vita"; und der Dämon der Musik, der mich nach langen Jahren wieder einmal heimsuchte, hat mich gezwungen, auch in Tönen davon zu reden.

(KSB 6:255)

[If you have read "Sanctus Januarius" you will have noticed that I have gone through a *turning-point.* Everything lies new before me, and it will not be long before I am also able to see the *terrible* face of my more distant life-task. This long, rich summer was, for me, a time for *rehearsal;* I took my leave from it with great courage and pride, for I sensed that, at least for this period of time, the otherwise ugly gap between willing and accomplishing was *bridged.* There were *hard* demands on my humanity, and in the most difficult circumstances I found I was sufficient unto myself. This entire intermediate condition between what was and what will be I call "in media vita"; and the daemon of music, that afflicted me again after many years, has forced me also to speak of this in resonant notes.]

And, in a letter to the composer and conductor Hans von Bülow (1830–94), written from Rapallo, a small town on the Italian Riviera where he was staying at the end of December 1882, Nietzsche invoked the idea of the "second nature" he had developed:[6]

Die veränderte Art zu denken und zu empfinden, welche ich seit 6 Jahren auch schriftlich zum Ausdruck brachte, hat mich im Dasein *erhalten* und mich beinahe gesund *gemacht.* Was geht es mich an, wenn meine Freunde behaupten, diese meine jetzige "Freigeisterei" sei ein excentrischer, mit den Zähnen festgehaltener *Entschluß* und meiner eigenen Neigung abgerungen und angezwungen? Gut, es mag eine "zweite Natur" sein: aber ich will schon noch beweisen, daß ich mit dieser zweiten Natur erst in den eigentlichen *Besitz* meiner ersten Natur getreten bin.

(KSB 6:290)[7]

[This changed way of thinking and feeling, which I have been expressing in written form for 6 years, has *preserved* me in my existence and almost *made* me healthy. What does it concern me, if my friends claim that my present "free-spiritedness" is an excentric *decision,* held in my teeth and wrung and forced from my own inclination? Well, it may be a "second nature": but I still want to prove that it is only with this second nature that I have actually taken *possession* of my first nature.]

And, further on in this letter, Nietzsche evoked an image that would be central to *Zarathustra,* the idea of pregnancy; yet the image also captures his sense of expectancy: "Genug, ich bin wieder Einsiedler und mehr als je; und denke mir — folglich — etwas Neues aus. Es scheint mir, daß allein der

Zustand der *Schwangerschaft* uns immer wieder an's Leben anbindet. —" (KSB 6:290; "Enough, I am a hermit again and more than ever before; and I think up — therefore — something new. It seems to me that only the condition of *pregnancy* binds us to life again and again").

This notion of "pregnancy" — ubiquitous in Goethe's writing, and perhaps paradigmatically expressed in his poem "Auf dem See" ("On the Lake," 1795) — had been preoccupying Nietzsche throughout the summer, too, as this note, 21 [11], from the *Nachlass* from Summer 1882 shows: "Im Zustande der Schwangerschaft verbergen wir uns und sind furchtsam: denn wir fühlen, daß es uns schwer fällt, uns jetzt zu vertheidigen, noch mehr daß es dem, was wir mehr lieben als uns selber schädlich sein würde, wenn wir uns vertheidigen müßten" (KSA 9:686–87; "In the condition of pregnancy we hide ourselves and are afraid: for we feel that it is difficult for us to defend ourselves now, and even more that it would be harmful for what we love more than ourselves, if we had to defend ourselves"). In *Zarathustra*, such "pregnancy" would turn out to be one of the work's key images: "Dass der Schaffende selber das Kind sei, das neu geboren werde, dazu muss er auch die Gebärerin sein wollen und der Schmerz der Gebärerin" [*Z* II 2; KSA 4:111; "To be the child who is newly born, the creative one must also want to be the birth-giver and want the pangs of the birth-giver"), Zarathustra teaches on the blissful islands; "zum Blitze bereit im dunklen Busen und zum erlösenden Lichtstrahle, schwanger von Blitzen, die Ja! sagen, Ja! lachen, zu wahrsagerischen Blitzstrahlen: — / — selig aber ist der also Schwangere!" (*Z* III 16 §1; KSA 4:287; "Ready for the lightning in its dark bosom, and for the redeeming flash of light, pregnant with lightning bolts that say Yes! and laugh Yes!, ready for soothsaying lightning bolts — / — blessed is he who is pregnant in this way!"), he pronounces at the end of part 3; for "man ist nur für das eigne Kind schwanger" (*Z* IV 13 §11; KSA 4:362; "one is only pregnant with one's own child"). As Graham Parkes has shown, the imagery of pregnancy is a telling one in Nietzsche's works, not least because it echoes numerous motifs in Platonic texts, such as Diotima's characterization in the *Symposium* of the activity of love (*eros*) as "giving birth in beauty both in mind and body."[8] Nietzsche himself seems to have been alert to the way *Zarathustra* "emerged" from his previous writings; for example, in a letter to Köselitz of 1883, Nietzsche would observe that he had written the commentary before the text ("den *Commentar* früher geschrieben als den Text"), and that his previous works, including "Schopenhauer als Erzieher" ("Schopenhauer as an Educator") and *Menschliches, Allzumenschliches,* had been leading up to *Zarathustra:* "Wenn Sie jetzt einen Augenblick an die 'fröhl[iche] Wiss[enschaft]' zurückdenken wollen, so werden Sie lachen, mit welcher Sicherheit, ja impudentia darin die *bevorstehende Geburt* 'annoncirt' wird" (21 April 1883; KSB 6:364; "If you think back for a moment to the 'gay science,' then you will laugh at the certainty, the impudence even with which the *imminent birth* is 'announced'").[9]

In biographical terms, these references to loneliness could have several explanations: his itinerant existence as a retired, and sick, academic; his break with Richard Wagner, whom he had last seen in Sorrento in 1876, and who was soon to die, just after the completion of part 1 of *Zarathustra,* in February 1883, affecting Nietzsche deeply;[10] the increasing distance from his mother and his sister; or the disastrous relationship with Lou von Salomé (1861–1937), which also ended his friendship with Paul Rée. According to Ida Overbeck (1848–1933), the wife of the Basel theologian, the relationship with Lou von Salomé had a direct influence on the composition of *Zarathustra:* "Der Schmerz und die Entsagung, keinen Sohn zu haben, nie einen zu haben, waren in ihm lebendig geworden. Er hat im Sommer 1882 ausgesprochen, daß er deshalb auf die Idee gekommen sei, eine Sohnesgestalt künstlerisch zu schaffen" ("He had started to feel the pain and the renunciation of having no son, of never having one. In the summer of 1882 he said that for this reason he had had the idea of creating the form of a son artistically").[11] Rightly, Ida Overbeck adds the important rider: "Man darf den Wert solcher Konfidenzen nicht übertreiben. Den Zarathustra umzuwerten, der ihm ein Vertreter des Wertmessers Gut und Böse war, in der ältesten Geschichte der Menschheit, war ja der eigentliche Gedanke" ("One should not exaggerate the value of such remarks. To revalue Zoroaster, who for him was the representative of the values of good and evil, in the most ancient history of humankind, was the real thought"). However, she insists that "trotz verschiedener, einander in die Hände arbeitender Anlässe zum Zarathustra, hat doch Lou den direkten Anteil daran, Nietzsche zum philosophisch-religiösen und moralisch-prophetischen Ausdruck eines Ersatzes für Religion und Moral gebracht zu haben" ("despite the various causes that worked together to produce Zarathustra, Lou nevertheless was directly involved in making Nietzsche express in a philosophical-religious and moral-prophetic way a substitute for religion and morality").[12] Yet, in her biography of Nietzsche, written in 1894, Lou herself has relatively little to say about *Zarathustra;*[13] and, as we have seen, preparations for *Zarathustra* go back at least a year before Nietzsche's first meeting with Lou in Rome at the end of April 1882.

Zarathustra I

These preparations, however unconscious, came to fruition in the small Italian town of Rapallo, in January 1883. Not far from Rapallo lies Portofino, and in the summer/autumn of 1882 Nietzsche gave the name of this town on the Genovese and Ligurian coast to the following short poem, the earliest version of "Sils-Maria," as its title:

Portofino

Hier sitz ich wartend — wartend? Doch auf nichts,
Jenseits von gut und böse, und des Lichts
Nicht mehr gelüstend als der Dunkelheit,
Dem Mittag Freund und Freund der Ewigkeit.

(3[3]; KSA 10:107–8)

[Here I sit, waiting — waiting? But for nothing,
Beyond good and evil, and for the light
No more longing than for the darkness,
To midday a friend, and a friend of eternity.]

Another sketch of the poem, emphatically expressive of Goethe's and Schiller's influence, this time from the notebooks for November 1882 to February 1883, is untitled, but even closer to the final text:

Hier saß ich wartend —
Jenseits von gut und böse, bald des Lichts
Genießend bald des Schattens: ganz nur Spiel
Ganz Meer, ganz Mittag, ganz Zeit ohne Ziel.

(4[121]; KSA 10:150)

[Here I sat waiting —
Beyond good and evil, now the light
Enjoying, now the shadow: all a game
All sea, all midday, all time without aim.]

But if, at the end of 1882, he was not ready to "walk into" this poem, the figure of Zarathustra "walked into view" for 10 days in January 1883. In *Ecce Homo,* Nietzsche would offer the following account:

Den darauf folgenden Winter lebte ich in jener anmuthig stillen Bucht von Rapallo unweit Genua, die sich zwischen Chiavari und dem Vorgebirge Porto fino einschneidet. Meine Gesundheit war nicht die beste; der Winter kalt und über die Maassen regnerisch; ein kleines Albergo, unmittelbar am Meer gelegen, so dass die hohe See nachts den Schlaf unmöglich machte, bot ungefähr in Allem das Gegentheil vom Wünschenswerthen. Trotzdem und beinahe zum Beweis meines Satzes, dass alles Entscheidende "trotzdem" entsteht, war es dieser Winter und diese Ungunst der Verhältnisse, unter denen mein Zarathustra entstand. — Den Vormittag stieg ich in südlicher Richtung auf der herrlichen Strasse nach Zoagli hin in die Höhe, an Pinien vorbei und weitaus das Meer überschauend; des Nachmittags, so oft es nur die Gesundheit erlaubte, umgieng ich die ganze Bucht von Santa Margherita bis hinter nach Porto fino. [. . .] — Auf diesen beiden

Wegen fiel mir der ganze erste Zarathustra ein, vor Allem Zarathustra
selber, als Typus: richtiger, er *überfiel mich* . . .

(*EH Z* §1; KSA 6:336–37)[14]

[The following winter I stayed in that charming quiet bay of Rapallo,
not far from Genoa, which is cut out between Chiavari and the foothills
of Portofino. My health was not particularly good; the winter was cold
and excessively rainy; my small *albergo,* situated right by the sea so that
the high tide made it impossible to sleep at night, was in just about
every way the opposite of what one might wish. In spite of this and almost as proof of my proposition that everything decisive comes into being "in spite of," it was that winter and under these unfavorable
circumstances that my *Zarathustra* came into being. In the morning I
would walk in a southerly direction on the splendid road to Zoagli, going up past pines to gain a magnificent view of the sea; in the afternoon, whenever my health permitted it, I walked around the whole bay
from Santa Margherita all the way to Portofino. . . . — It was on these
two walks that the whole of *Zarathustra I* occurred to me, and above
all Zarathustra himself as a type: rather, he *fell upon me.*]

In a letter written on Christmas Day 1882, Nietzsche had told Franz Overbeck: "Wenn ich nicht das Alchemisten-Kunststück erfinde, auch aus diesem — Kothe *Gold* zu machen, so bin ich verloren" (KSB 6:312; "If I
cannot pull off the alchemists' trick of turning this — *filth* into gold, then I
am lost").[15] A few days later, on New Year's Eve, he had told Overbeck: "Ich
bin nun einmal nicht Geist und nicht Körper, sondern etwas drittes. Ich
leide immer am Ganzen und im Ganzen" (KSB 6:313; "I am simply neither
spirit nor body, but some third thing. I am suffering from everything and in
everything"). And, plagued by illness and insomnia, on 20 January 1883 he
complained: "Gefroren habe ich diesen Winter wie noch nie, auch nie so
schlecht gegessen. Übrigens geht die Gesundheit *stark* rückwärts" (KSB
6:318; "I have been frozen this winter as never before, and have never eaten
so badly. By the way, my health is getting *seriously* worse"). No more letters
followed for eleven days. Then, in his letter to Köselitz of 1 February 1883,
Nietzsche suddenly, and jubilantly, announced the completion of *Also sprach
Zarathustra: Ein Buch für Alle und Keinen* (A Book for All and None):

Es handelt sich um ein ganz kleines Buch — hundert Druckseiten etwa.
Aber es ist mein *Bestes,* und ich habe einen schweren Stein mir damit
von der Seele gewälzt. Es giebt nichts Ernsteres von mir und auch
nichts Heiteres; ich wünsche von Herzen, daß *diese* Farbe — welche
nicht einmal eine Mischfarbe zu sein braucht — immer mehr zu meiner
"Natur"farbe werde. [. . .] Mit diesem Buche bin ich in einen neuen
"Ring" eingetreten — von jetzt ab werde ich wohl in Deutschland
unter die Verrückten gerechnet werden. Es ist eine wunderliche Art
von "Moral-Predigten." (KSB 6:321)

[It is quite a small book — about a hundred printed pages. But it is my *best*, and with it I have lifted a heavy weight from my mind. There is nothing more serious by me and also nothing more cheerful; I wish from the heart that *this* color — which does not even need to be mixed with other colors — will increasingly become my "natural"-color. . . . With this book I have entered a new "circle" — from now I will be counted in Germany among the mad. It is a strange kind of homily.]

Later, on 17 April 1882, he admitted to Köselitz: "Seine Entstehung war eine Art *Aderlaß*, ich verdanke ihm, daß ich nicht erstickt bin. Es war etwas Plötzliches, die Sache von 10 Tagen" (KSB 6:361; "Its composition was a kind of *blood-letting*, I owe to it that I did not suffocate. It was something sudden, a matter of 10 days"). On 1 February, he also wrote to Overbeck:

> Jetzt hatten wir Regenwetter: aber vorher gab es eine ganze Reihe vollkommen reiner Tage, die ich gut benützt habe. [. . .] Inzwischen, im Grunde in ganz wenig Tagen, habe ich mein *bestes Buch* geschrieben, und, was mehr sagen will, jenen entscheidenden Schritt gethan, zu dem ich im vorigen Jahre noch nicht den Muth hatte. Diesmal hatte ich alle meine zehn Kräfte nöthig — und sie waren auch zu meinen Diensten. Ich bin jetzt noch ein Paar Tage mit der "Nagelprobe" beschäftigt, eine Sache des feinen *Hörens*, für die man nicht einsam genug sein kann. (KSB 6:324)

> [Now we had rain: but before that there was a whole series of completely clear days, which I used well. [. . .] In the meantime, basically in just a few days I have written my *best book*, and, what is more, taken that decisive step for which in the previous year I did not yet have the courage. This time I needed all my ten faculties — and they were at my service. Now I am occupied for a few days with the "acid test," a matter of fine *hearing*, for which one cannot be solitary enough.]

And he was now sleeping much better, "jetzt gegen 14 Tage hintereinander — oh *welche* Wohlthat!" ("now for almost 14 days in a row — o *what* a blissful relief!").

Just over a week later, however, his gloom had returned: "Es ist wieder Nacht um mich; mir ist zu Muthe, als hätte es geblitzt — ich *war* eine kurze Spanne Zeit *ganz* in meinem Elemente und in meinem Lichte. Und nun ist es vorbei" (10 February 1883; KSB 6:325; "Once again it is night around me; it seems to me as if there was lightning — I *was* for a short span of time *entirely* in my element and in my light. And now it is past"). Nevertheless, on 13 February Nietzsche proceeded to contact his publisher in Chemnitz, Ernst Schmeitzner, to discuss publication of the work, describing it as "eine 'Dichtung,' oder ein fünftes 'Evangelium' oder irgend Etwas, für das es noch keinen Namen giebt" ("a 'work of literature,' or a 'fifth gospel,' or something for which there is as yet no name"),[16] and predicting for it a wide

audience as "bei weitem das Ernsteste und *auch* Heiterste meiner Er-
zeugnisse, und Jedermann zugänglich" (KSB 6:327; "by far the most serious
and *also* the most cheerful of my productions, and accessible to everyone").[17]
As his letters to Franz Overbeck of 6 and 22 March show, Nietzsche (now in
Genoa) soon grew increasingly impatient about the publication of his book
(KSB 6:339 and 348) — and increasingly despondent about the extent to
which the book succeeded in its aims;[18] and on 25 March he fired off an angry letter to Schmeitzner, followed by a calmer one on 1 April (KSB 6:351–
52). Although the publisher's reply has been lost, Nietzsche explained the
delay in his next letter to Köselitz:

> Zarathustra kommt *jetzt* an die Reihe. Was stand ihm im Wege? Eine
> halbe Million christlicher Gesangbücher, die Teubner bis Osten fertig
> machen mußte. Unter welche Rubrik gehört eigentlich dieser
> "Zarathustra"? Ich glaube beinahe, unter die "Symphonien." Gewiß ist,
> daß ich damit in eine andere Welt hinübergetreten bin — der
> "Freigeist" ist *erfüllt.* Oder? (KSB 6:353)

> [It's *now* the turn of Zarathustra. What was standing in its way? Half a
> million Christian hymnbooks, which Teubner had to have ready by
> Easter. To which category does this "Zarathustra" actually belong? I
> am tempted to believe to the "symphonies." What is certain is that with
> it I have stepped into another world — the "free spirit" is *fulfilled.*
> Don't you agree?]

And in a letter, written at about the same time, to Franz Overbeck,
Nietzsche repeated the ironic anecdote about the delay caused to
Zarathustra by half a million hymnbooks and, in response to an alleged remark by his old colleague at Basel, Jacob Burckhardt, that he, Nietzsche,
ought "Weltgeschichte ex professo zu dociren" ("to lecture on world history
ex professo"), added: "Aber warten wir erst noch Zarathustra ab: ich fürchte,
keine Behörde der Welt wird mich *darnach* noch zum Lehrer der Jugend
haben wollen" ("But let us first wait and see about Zarathustra: I fear that
afterward no authority in the world will let me become a teacher of youth
again"). In the conclusion to this letter, Nietzsche speculated that
Zarathustra had opened up a new stage in his development, and that, with
this work, he had finally taken his leave of philology:

> Es ist **möglich**, daß ich mit diesem Winter in eine neue Entwicklung
> eingetreten bin. Zarathustra ist etwas, das kein lebendiger Mensch
> außer mir machen kann. Vielleicht habe ich jetzt erst meine beste Kraft
> entdeckt. Selbst als "Philosoph" habe ich meine wesentlichsten
> Gedanken (oder "Tollheiten") noch nicht ausgesprochen — ach, ich
> bin so schweigsam, so versteckt! Aber gar als "Dichter"! Meine
> Philologie habe ich *vergessen;* ich hätte was Besseres in meinen 20-ger
> Jahren *lernen* können! Ach, was ich unwissend bin! — (KSB 6:355)

[It is **possible** that with this winter I have entered upon a new development. Zarathustra is something no human being alive apart from me can produce. Perhaps I have only now discovered my best power. Even as a "philosopher" I have still not yet spoken my most essential thoughts (or "follies") — oh, I am so discreet, so furtive! And even as a "poet"! My philology I have *forgotten;* I could have *learnt* something better during my twenties! Oh, the things I am ignorant of! —]

In response to a letter from his publisher, who had obviously expressed concern about the possible political implications of the work he was publishing, Nietzsche also wrote at this time: "Mag man mich zu den 'Anarchisten' rechnen, wenn man mir übel will: aber gewiß ist, daß ich europäische Anarchien und Erdbeben in ungeheurem Umfange *voraussehe.* Alle Bewegungen führen *dahin* — Ihre antijüdische eingerechnet" (2 April 1883; KSB 6:355–56; "One may well count me among the 'anarchists,' if one wishes me ill: but what's certain is that I *foresee* European anarchies and earthquakes on a terrible scale. All movements are leading *in that direction* — your anti-Semitic ones included"). (In the rest of the letter, Nietzsche discussed the appearance of the title page, advertising strategy, and — somewhat optimistically, as it turned out — his royalties.)

To judge from his correspondence, Nietzsche understood the completion of *Zarathustra* to represent a major change in his life. He referred repeatedly to a "decisive step" ("entscheidenden Schritt"; KSB 6:327 and 357); and if, when writing to Malwida von Meysenbug, he affirmed his identity in theological terms — "Wollen Sie einen neuen Namen für mich? Die Kirchensprache *hat* einen: ich bin — — — — — — — — der *Antichrist*" (3/4 April 1883; KSB 6:357; "Do you want a new name for me? Ecclesiastical language *has* one: I am — — — — — — — — the *Antichrist*") — he had also discovered a new identity, as he told Köselitz, as a *father* — the "father of Zarathustra": "Aber ich bin ein Soldat: und dieser Soldat ist zuguterletzt noch der *Vater* Zarathustra's geworden! Diese Vaterschaft war seine Hoffnung; ich denke, Sie empfinden jetzt den Sinn des Verses an den Sanctus Januarius 'der du mit dem Flammenspeere meiner Seele Eis zertheilt, daß sie brausend nun *zum Meere ihrer höchsten Hoffnung* eilt' — — Und auch den Sinn der Überschrift 'incipit tragoedia'" (6 April 1883; KSB 6:358; "But I am a soldier: and this soldier has in the end become Zarathustra's *father!* This fatherhood was his hope; I think you can now sense the meaning of the verses to Saint Januarius, 'You who with a flaming spear broke up the ice of my soul, so that it **rushes** *towards the ocean of its highest hope*' — — And also the meaning of the heading 'incipit tragoedia'").[19] Here Nietzsche recalls a text written in Genoa exactly a year before the composition of *Zarathustra,* the poem "Sanctus Januarius" that opens the fourth and penultimate book of *Die fröhliche Wissenschaft.*[20] This poem, written in obvious imitation of a famous text by Goethe,[21] alludes to the notion of the "highest hope" (*höchste Hoffnung*), a key motif of *Zarathustra*.[22] And this letter perhaps explains, at least in part, a passage that can be found in the chapter "Von den Taranteln" ("On the Tarantulas") from part 1 of *Zarathustra:* "Was der Vater schwieg, das kommt im Sohne zum Reden; und oft fand ich den Sohn als des Vaters entblösstes Geheimniss" (*Z* II 7; KSA 4:129; "What the father kept silent, speaks in the son; and I often found the son to be the father's unveiled secret"). At the same time, concerns about the reception of his work, even before it had been published, began to appear. "Mich ekelt davor, daß Z[arathustra] als Unterhaltungs-Buch in die Welt tritt" ("I find it disgusting that *Zarathustra* goes into the world as a work of entertainment"), Nietzsche reflected at the end of this letter; "wer ist ernst genug dafür!" (KSB 6:359; "who is serious enough for it!"). And over a week or so later he wrote: "Mit 'Zarathustra' gerathe ich nun gar noch unter die 'Litteraten' und 'Schriftsteller,' und das Band, das mich mit der Wissenschaft verknüpfte, wird als zerrissen *erscheinen*" (17 April 1883; KSB 6:360; "With 'Zarathustra' I will now end up even among the *litterateurs* and 'writers,' and the tie that bound me to scholarly discourse will *appear* to be torn").

Zarathustra II

Time and again in the letters from this period, Nietzsche reflects on the significance of what he had written in *Also sprach Zarathustra* (consisting of "Zarathustra's Vorrede" and the subsequent 22 chapters of what is now known as part 1). Writing on 17 April 1883 to Franz Overbeck, who had suggested he return to teaching, he wondered whether he had fulfilled his life's task: "*Lehrer* sein: ach ja, es wäre wohlthätig genug jetzt für mich [. . .]. Aber es giebt etwas *Wichtigeres,* gegen das gerechnet mir auch ein nützlicher und wirkungsvoller Lehrer-Beruf nur als Erleichterung des Lebens, als Erholung gelten dürfte. Und erst, wenn ich *meine Hauptaufgabe erfüllt* habe, werde ich auch das gute Gewissen für eine solche Existenz [. . .] finden. — Aber vielleicht *habe* ich sie erfüllt?" (KSB 6:362; "To be a *teacher:* oh yes, that would be beneficial enough for me now [. . .] But there is something *more important,* counted against which even a useful and effective teaching job could only be considered a relief in life, a relaxation. And only when I *have fulfilled my main task* will I find the good conscience for such an existence[. . .]. — But perhaps I *have* fulfilled it?"). And the reference in *Die fröhliche Wissenschaft* to "Sanctus Januarius" — the saint whose blood, preserved in a vial in the cathedral in Naples, becomes liquid again on his feast day — becomes clearer in light of his remarks to Köselitz (see above) and Overbeck, whom he told here about correcting the text:

Inzwischen kam Zarathustra, langsam, Bogen für Bogen, zum Vorschein. Ja, ich lernte ihn jetzt erst kennen! In jenen 10 Tagen seiner Entstehung hatte ich *dazu* keine Zeit. [. . .] Es scheint mir mitunter, als ob ich gelebt, gearbeitet und gelitten hätte, um dies kleine Buch von 7 Bogen machen zu können! ja als ob mein Leben damit eine nachträgliche Rechtfertigung erhalte. Und selbst auf diesen schmerzhaftesten aller Winter sehe ich seitdem mit andern Augen: wer weiß, ob nicht erst eine *so große* Qual nöthing war, mich zu jenem *Aderlaß* zu bestimmen, als welcher dies Buch [= *Zarathustra*] ist? Du versteht, es ist sehr viel Blut in diesem Buche. (KSB 6:362).[23]

[In the meantime Zarathustra came, sheet by sheet, into appearance. Yes, I was just getting to know him then! In the 10 days of his creation I had no time *for that*. . . . Sometimes it seems to me as if I had lived, worked, and suffered, to be able to make this small book of 7 pages! indeed, as if my life thereby received its retrospective justification. And even on this most painful of all winters I have ever since looked with different eyes: who knows whether *so much* torment was not actually necessary to destine me for the *blood-letting* that is this book? You know, there is a lot of blood in this book.]

To Malwida von Meysenbug, on the other hand, he spoke of his book in terms of its response to religion: "Ich habe alle Religionen herausgefordert und ein neues 'heiliges Buch' gemacht! Und, in allem Ernste gesagt, es ist so ernst als irgend eines, ob es gleich das Lachen mit in die Religion aufnimmt" (20 April 1883; KSB 6:363; "I have challenged all religions and made a new 'holy book'! And, in all seriousness, it is as serious as any other, even though it makes laughter part of religion"); an idea that the next day he restated, with renewed concern about the reception of his work, to Köselitz: "*Jetzt* erst, nach der Veröffentlichung des Zarathustra, wird *das Ärgste* kommen, denn ich habe, mit meinem 'heiligen Buche,' alle Religion herausgefordert" ("Only *now*, after the publication of Zarathustra, will *the worst* come, for with my 'holy book' I have challenged all religions"). He had never, he confided, been guided by other people's opinions about himself, although, he added: "aber mir *fehlt* die Menschenverachtung und die glückliche Mitgift des Bärenfells — und so bekenne ich, zu allen Zeiten des Lebens sehr an der Meinung über mich *gelitten* zu haben" (KSB 6:365; "but I *lack* the contempt for humanity and the happy inheritance of a thick skin — and so I confess that I have at all times of my life suffered greatly from opinions about me").[24]

Whilst waiting for the copies of *Zarathustra* to arrive, and for the presentation copies to be sent to his friends, Nietzsche had moved, at the suggestion of Malwida von Meysenbug, to Rome; but, disappointed with the "eternal city," he now looked forward to making new friends over the summer, and contented himself with trying out the white trousers his mother had sent him.[25] Nietzsche's letters from this period show him becoming increasingly impatient about the delay in the publication of *Zarathustra*. It was during this stay in Rome, according to *Ecce Homo*, that Nietzsche wrote "Das Nacht-Lied" ("The Night Song"), a chapter of what would be a second part of *Zarathustra*, from a *loggia,* high above the Piazza Barberini, with a fine view of the city and the sound of the *fontana* splashing below (*EH Z* §4; KSA 6:340–41).[26] Did Nietzsche's plans for a second part fuel his impatience with the delay in the appearance of the first? Or was it vice versa?

In this period, we also find the idea emerging that, with *Zarathustra,* Nietzsche intends that his protagonist should replace him, while he "disappears." To Overbeck he talked about "die oft schon brieflich angedeutete 'Weltflucht'" (20 May 1883; KSB 6:379; "the 'flight from the world' often already mentioned in my letters"); and to Marie Baumgartner he spoke of "ein Entschluß, der seit Jahren kommt und geht und wiederkommt und endlich — jetzt! — mich reif findet und stark genug: der Entschluß, auf ein paar Jahre zu 'verschwinden'" (28 May 1883; KSB 6:381; "a decision, which for years has been coming and going, and coming again and — now! — finds me ripe and strong enough: the decision to 'disappear' for a few years"). By the end of June 1883, Nietzsche found himself back in Sils-Maria — his third visit to the Engadine and his second stay in Sils-Maria — once again receiving food parcels from his mother and his sister,[27] and still waiting for *Zarathustra* to appear in printed form. If the publication of *Zarathustra* was to bring about the beginning of the disappearance of Nietzsche, it was also, he suggested, the end of his silence — "die Zeit des Schweigens ist *vorbei*" ("the time of remaining silent is *over*") — and the emergence of his true identity — "Es ist ein Anfang, mich zu erkennen zu geben — nicht mehr!" ("It is the start of revealing my identity — not more!"):

> Mein Zarathustra, der Dir in diesen Wochen übersandt sein wird, möge Dir verrathen, *wie* hoch mein Wille seinen Flug genommen hat. Laß Dich durch die legendenhafte Art dieses Büchleins nicht täuschen: hinter all den schlichten und seltsamen Worten steht mein *tiefster Ernst* und meine *ganze Philosophie.* [. . .] Ich weiß ganz *gut*, daß Niemand lebt, der so Etwas machen könnte, wie dieser Zarathustra ist — (KSB 6:386)

> [My Zarathustra, which will be sent to you in the coming weeks, may reveal to you *how* high my will has taken flight. Do not let the legendary style of this little book deceive you: behind all these smooth and strange words stand my *deepest earnestness* and my *entire philosophy*. . . . I know quite *well* that no living person could write something like this Zarathustra —]

Up until now, Nietzsche had referred to the text that we now know as part 1 of that work as *Also sprach Zarathustra*. In other words, it seems that part 1 was intended to be the whole work, beginning with Zarathustra's descent from the mountain and ending with his decision to depart in "Von der schenkenden Tugend" ("On the Gift-Giving Virtue") and the dramatic words: "'*Todt sind alle Götter: nun wollen wir, dass der Übermensch lebe.*' — diess sei einst am grossen Mittage unser letzter Wille! —" (*Z* I §22; KSA 4:102; "'*All gods are dead: now we want the Superman to live*' — at the great noontide let this be our last will!").

In this letter to his friend Carl von Gersdorff (1844–1904), however, we find the first indication in his correspondence that there might be more of *Zarathustra* to come: "Ach, was liegt noch Alles verborgen in mir und will Wort und Form werden! Es kann gar nicht still und hoch und einsam genug um mich sein, daß ich meine innersten Stimmen vernehmen kann!" (KSB 6:386; "Oh, how everything still lies hidden in me and wants to become word and form! It cannot be still and high and solitary enough around me so that I can hear my inmost voices!"). His impatience about the continuing delay at the publisher's — now a consignment of anti-Semitic pamphlets was causing the problem[28]— takes on a particular significance in the light of the fact that, by mid-July 1883, the manuscript of the second part of *Zarathustra* was complete. Far from being the complete work, the book waiting to be sent out from Leipzig was, in fact, just the first installment of what was turning out to be — or maybe had always been conceived as — a much larger project.

On 6 July, he wrote to his sister that she should tell Schmeitzner "daß er den 2ten Theil Zarathustra *unverzüglich* in Druck giebt, **sobald** das Manuscript in seine Hände kommt" ("that he should *immediately* print the second part of Zarathustra, **as soon as** he has the manuscript in his hands"), adding:

> Ich will damit zu Ende kommen und von dieser Expansion des Gefühls erlöst sein, die solche Produktionen mit sich führen: es ist mir öfter der Gedanke gekommen, daß ich an so Etwas plötzlich sterbe. [. . .] Aus Allem wirst Du errathen, daß besagter 2ter Theil wirklich existirt: Du kannst Dir von der *Vehemenz* solcher Entstehungen nicht leicht einen zu großen Begriff machen. Darin aber liegt ihre Gefahr. (KSB 6:392)

> [I want to make an end of it and be released from this expansion of feeling that such productions bring in their train: I have frequently had the thought that I could suddenly die from something like this . . . From all this you will guess that the aforementioned second part in fact exists: you cannot easily form too much of an idea of the *vehemence* of such compositions. Therein, however, lies their danger.]

On 10 July, he wrote to her again, this time with a palpable sense of relief, to confirm that the manuscript would soon be complete. Despite the misery and despite his illness, he saw in this work, he told her, a justification of the recent weeks and months:

> Damit, daß ich diesen 2ten Theil *gemacht habe,* ist das ganze Jahr schon gerechtfertigt, insbesondere die Reise nach dem Engadin: und sogar auch die Reise nach Rom bekommt nun eine neue Bedeutung: es war ein tiefes Ausruhen in diesem römischen Aufenthalt; und gerade auch in der Zerstreuung und dem Lärm meiner Wohnung lag etwas *Nützliches,* ebenso in dem Klumpfuß auf der Eisenbahn und dem vielen verdorbenen Magen und schlechten Nächten. *Alles* hinderte mich zu arbeiten und nachzudenken; und es ist kaum zu sagen, *wie schwer* es ist, mich von mir selber wegzuziehn. (KSB 6:394–95)

> [With the fact that I *have written* this second part the whole year is already justified, particularly the journey to the Engadine: and even the journey to Rome now takes on a new meaning: I was able to rest deeply during this stay in Rome; and precisely in the distraction and in the noise of my flat there was something *useful,* just as there was in the club foot at the railway station and in my frequently upset stomach and bad nights. *Everything* prevented me from working and reflecting; and I hardly know how to say *how difficult* it is for me to get away from myself.][29]

So, unlike the serene cheerfulness that, according to Nietzsche, had accompanied the composition of part 1, the biographical background to part 2 was one of considerable ill-health and physical discomfort (letter to Overbeck of 9 July 1883; KSB 6:393–94). As already suggested, Nietzsche's attitude, by contrast, toward the writing of part 2 was much more robust: "Mit Einem Male hatte ich die Conception zum *zweiten* Theile Zarathustra — und *nach* der Conception auch die Geburt: Alles mit der größten Vehemenz. (Dabei ist mir der Gedanke gekommen, daß ich wahrscheinlich an einer *solchen* Gefühls-Explosion und -Expansion einmal sterben werde: hol' mich der Teufel!)" (to Köselitz, 13 July 1883; KSB 6:397; "In one fell swoop I had the conception for the *second* part of Zarathustra — and *after* the conception the birth, too: everything with the greatest vehemence. (With it I had the thought that I will probably die of *such* an expansion and explosion of feeling: the devil take me!)"). Moreover, the bitterness about the delay in publication of the first part had also remained, and is clearly detectable in his letter to his sister: "Im letzten Winter habe **ich** Alles so eingerichtet, daß der erste Theil Zarathustra *Ostern* in den Händen meiner Leser sein konnte: und habe den höchsten Fleiß nöthig gehabt, um es *so* einzurichten. Ein verlornes halbes Jahr der *Wirkung meiner* Gedanken kommt *recht sehr* in Betracht, namentlich in Hinsicht auf die Dauer meines eignen Lebens" (10 July; KSB 6:395; "Last winter **I** so arranged everything that the first part of Zarathustra could be in the hands of my readers by *Easter:* and I needed the greatest effort *so* to arrange things. A lost half-year of the *effect of my* thoughts is *really* considerable, especially with regard to the length of my own life"). Given that part 2 was nearing completion, it seems likely that this sense of urgency to publish part 1 was, in part, driven by an awareness at a much earlier stage that yet further installments of *Zarathustra* would be written.

After all, Nietzsche now treated the words at the end of part 1 — "und erst, wenn ihr mich Alle verleugnet habt, will ich euch wiederkehren. / Wahrlich, mit andern Augen, meine Brüder, werde ich mir dann meine Verlorenen suchen; mit einer anderen Liebe werde ich euch dann lieben" (*Z* I 22; KSA 4:101–2; "and only when you have all denied me will I return to you. / Truly, with different eyes, my brothers, shall I then seek my lost ones; with a different love shall I then love you") — not so much as a conclusion as a link to part 2: "Die ist das *Motto* zum zweiten Theil: aus ihm ergeben sich, was dem Musiker zu sagen fast unschicklich ist, andre Harmonien und Modulationen, als im ersten Theile" ("This is the *motto* for the second part: out of it develop, and it is almost improper to say this to a musician, other harmonies and modulations than in the first part"). Furthermore, Nietzsche now envisaged a third part, too: "In der Hauptsache galt es, *sich auf die zweite Stufe zu schwingen,* — um von dort aus noch die *dritte* zu erreichen (deren Name ist: 'Mittag und Ewigkeit': das sagte ich Ihnen schon einmal? Aber ich bitte Sie inständig, davon gegen Jedermann zu schweigen! Für den dritten Theil will ich mir Zeit lassen, vielleicht *Jahre* —)" (to Köselitz, 13 July; KSB 6:397; "The main thing is *to reach the second level,* — in order to get from there to the *third* (whose name is 'Midday and Eternity': have I already told you this? But I implore you to be silent about this with everyone! For the third part I want to leave myself time, perhaps *years* —)"). The putative name for this third part goes right back, of course, to Nietzsche's earliest sketches for *Zarathustra* in Summer 1881, where he had drafted a plan for a work in no less than four parts. For all his talk of spontaneous inspiration, then, it seems that Nietzsche may well have been, to a greater extent than is often appreciated, working to a predetermined plan of composition. Nor would it be years before the third part of *Zarathustra* was written.

Zarathustra III

In the "real" time of Nietzsche's biography, the ensuing months were pre-occupied with the emotional fallout from the end of his affair with Lou von Salomé; with his continuing ill-health; and, later on, with his furious reaction to his sister's decision to marry an anti-Semite, Bernhard Förster (1843–89). To Ida Overbeck he wrote in mid-July 1883: "In der That, ohne die *Ziele* meiner Arbeit und die *Unerbittlichkeit* solcher Ziele lebte ich nicht mehr. In so ferne heißt mein Lebensretter: Zarathustra, mein Sohn Zarathustra! —"

(KSB 6:406; "Indeed, without the *goals* of my work and the *relentlessness* of such goals I would not still be alive. To this extent the savior of my life is called: Zarathustra, my son Zarathustra! —"). At the end of July, however, he told her that he was planning to complete "eine größere philos[ophische] Abhandl[ung]" ("a fairly large philosophical treatise") by the autumn, with no reference to further work on *Zarathustra* (KSB 6:411). If, as he told her in yet another letter, he had in no other year reached "*diese* Höhen der Empfindung" (the "heights of sensation" that he had reached when completing the second part of *Zarathustra*), it seems that, at times, he now feared he would never be able to reach them again (13–14 August 1883; KSB 6:423). Physical reality and the world of Zarathustra had seemed, however, to intersect for a moment when, on 28 July 1883, an earthquake struck the island of Ischia, in the Gulf of Naples. As Nietzsche told Köselitz, no sooner had he finished the manuscript of part 2 than areas of the island that had served as a model for the "blissful islands" were completely destroyed by a tremor, just as Wagner's death had also coincided with the completion of part 1 (to Köselitz, 16 August 1883; KSB 6:429).

In mid-August 1883, Nietzsche may have described "Zarathustra I and II" as "Licht- und heiterer-Himmel-Ausgeburten" ("the spawn of light and clear skies"; KSB 6:431), but part 2 was still being proofread (by Köselitz), and part 1 had still not yet appeared. This did not prevent him from envisaging, in a letter to his sister, the composition the next year of another, perhaps final, installment: "[D]aß ich nächstes Jahr hier oben meinen *Zarathustra-Schluß* mache — der Gedanke daran, wie er mir vorschwebt, macht mich fast schwindeln, die Aufgabe ist *ungeheuer schwer* und *einstweilen* weit über das Maaß meiner Kräfte gehend" (KSB 6:431; "that next year I might write my *conclusion to Zarathustra* up here — the thought of it, as crosses my mind, almost makes me dizzy; the task is *incredibly weighty* and *for the time being* greatly exceeds the extent of my powers").

Towards the end of August the first review of *Zarathustra* appeared; the accusation that he was the "Antichrist," not surprisingly, pleased Nietzsche greatly.[30] He celebrated the recognition of the fact that he was "einer der furchtbarsten Gegner des Christenthums" ("one of the most terrible opponents of Christianity") and that he had even gone one step further than Voltaire: "Seit Voltaire gab es kein solches *Attentat* gegen das Christenthum — und, die Wahrheit zu sagen, auch Voltaire hatte keine Ahnung davon, daß man es **so** angreifen könne" (KSB 6:436 and 438; "There has not been such an outrageous *attack* on Christianity since Voltaire — and, to tell the truth, even Voltaire had no idea that one could attack it in **this** way"). And this publication of part 1, at a cost of 3.30 Marks per copy, gave Nietzsche the opportunity, six months after its composition, to reflect on its significance.[31] To his sister he wrote on 29 August: "Jedes Wort meines Zarathustra ist ja siegreicher Hohn und mehr als Hohn über die

Ideale dieser Zeit; und fast hinter jedem Wort steht ein persönliches Erlebniß, eine Selbst-Überwindung ersten Ranges. Es ist ganz *nothwendig*, daß ich **mißverstanden** werde; mehr noch, ich muß es dahin bringen, *schlimm* verstanden und *verachtet* zu werden" (KSB 6:439; "Every word of my Zarathustra is triumphant scorn and more than scorn at the ideals of this age; and behind almost every word there stands a personal experience, a self-overcoming of the highest order. It is quite *necessary* that I be **misunderstood**; even more, I must succeed in being *badly* understood and *despised*").[32] At the same time, work on the publication of part 2 was proceeding apace; about it, Nietzsche wrote to Köselitz at the end of August 1883:

> Ich bin noch nicht zu einem *objektiven* Eindruck des Ganzen gelangt; doch wollte es mir scheinen, daß es einen nicht geringen *Sieg* über den "Geist der Schwere" darstelle, in Hinsicht darauf, *wie* schwer die Probleme, um die es sich handelt, darzustellen sind. Daß der erste Theil einen *Ring* von Gefühlen umfaßt, der für den Ring von Gefühlen, die den zweiten Theil ausmachen, eine *Voraussetzung* ist — auch das erscheint mir leicht erkennbar und "*gut* gemacht," um wie ein Tischlermeister zu reden. (KSB 6:442)

> [I have still not yet arrived at an *objective* impression of the whole, but it seems to me that it represents a not insignificant *victory* over the "spirit of heaviness," when I consider *how* difficult the problems it deals with are to represent. That the first part takes in a *circle* of feelings that is a *presupposition* for the circle of feelings that constitute the second part — that too seems easily recognizable to me and "*well*-made," as a carpenter might say.]

And he felt confident enough to look ahead again to the rest of the *Zarathustra* project, telling Köselitz in the same letter:

> Im Übrigen habe ich alles Schwere und Schwerste noch vor mir. Nach einem ziemlich genauen architektonischen Überschlag des Ganzen giebt es noch ebenso viel als bisher — ungefähr noch 200 Seiten. Gelingt es mir so, wie mir — trotz der fürchterlichsten Gegnerschaft, die ich im Herzen gegen das gesammte Zarathustra-Gebilde mit mir herumschleppe — die ersten zwei Theile gelungen *erscheinen*, so will ich ein Fest feiern und vor Vergnügen dabei sterben. Pardon! (KSB 6:442–43)

> [By the way, I still have all the difficult and most difficult things in front of me. According to a fairly precise architectonic estimate of the entirety, there is still as much to come as there has already been — approximately 200 pages. If I can succeed in this, as — despite the most terrible opposition which I carry around in my heart to the whole con-

struct of Zarathustra — the first two parts *seem* successful to me, then I will have a celebration and die from pleasure. Excuse me!]

The phrase here, "architectonic estimate," implies a plan of composition; and, for the first time, Nietzsche sounds a note of resistance to the whole project of *Zarathustra*. All in all, however, he expressed satisfaction — almost relief — with what he had achieved in 1883:

> *Wahrscheinlich* hätte ich, wenn ich dieses ganze Jahr meine Seele heiter und hell gehabt hätte, aus *artistischen* Motiven die Farben der beiden ersten Theile dunkler, finsterer und greller gewählt — in Hinsicht auf das, was den *Schluß* macht. Aber dies Jahr war mir das Labsal heitrerer und luftigerer Farben *zum Leben* **nothwendig;** und so habe ich im zweiten Theile beinahe wie ein Possenreißer meine Sprünge gemacht. — Im Einzelnen ist unglaublich Vieles persönlich Erlebte und Erlittne darin, das nur mir verständlich ist, — manche Seiten kamen mir fast *blutrünstig* vor. Es gehört für mich übrigens zu den noch räthselhaften Thatsachen, *daß* ich wirklich in diesem Jahre beide Theile gemacht habe. Ein Bild, das fast in allen meinen Schriften einmal vorkommt "über sich selber erhaben" — ist zur Wirklichkeit geworden — und — oh wenn Sie wüßten, *was* hierbei *sich selber* zu bedeuten hat! (KSB 6:443)

[If I had had a cheerful and bright soul throughout this year, I would probably have chosen colors for the two first parts that were darker, more sinister and more garish, from *artistic* motives — taking into consideration what brings it to a close. But this year the refreshment of more cheerful and airier colors was **necessary** *to keep me alive;* and so in the second part I have made my leaps almost like a buffoon. — In individual respects it contains an unbelievable amount of what I have personally experienced and suffered, which is comprehensible only to me — some pages seem to me almost *bloodthirsty*. By the way one of the still mysterious facts for me is *that* I really wrote both parts this year. An image that crops up in nearly all my writings, "elevated above himself" has become reality — and — oh, if you knew *what* this *"self"* means here!]

Examination of the *Nachlass* from this period confirms a vast amount of drafting and planning activity. If earlier notebooks contain material relating to part 1 (see the notebooks for Summer and Autumn 1882 in KSA 10) and to part 2 (see the notebooks for May-June, June-July, Summer 1883 in KSA 10), the notebooks for Summer and Autumn, Autumn, and the end of 1883 (see KSA 10) reveal much about Nietzsche's progress on part 3. For example, in one fragment we find this presentation of the idea of the eternal recurrence: "Wenn nur Ein Augenblick der Welt wiederkehrte, — sagte der *Blitz* — so müßten alle wiederkehren" (15[3]; KSA 10:479; "If just one moment of the world were to recur, says the *lightning,* then they would all have to recur"); in another, this response to the eternal recurrence: "Zarathustra's Consequenz ist daß der Mensch, um den Gedanken nicht zu fühlen, zum Thier *zurück* sich bilden muß. Oder zum Übermenschen" (15[4]; KSA 10:479–80; "Zarathustra's conclusion is that humankind, in order not to feel the thought, must educate itself *back* to the animal. Or to the superman"). Some drafts envisage a structure based on Zarathustra's "seven solitudes" (16[7], 16[9]; KSA 10:498 and 500–501), which might conclude: "*Alle Bedenken sind Zeichen des Willens zum Leiden, ein Vertiefen des Schmerzes: als der Schmerz am höchsten ist, wirft ihn Zarathustra ab: größter Schluß-Moment* (der Löwe): **ich will!!!**" (16[64]; KSA 10:522; "*All doubts are signs of the will to suffer, a deepening of pain; when the pain is at its highest, Zarathustra throws it off: great concluding moment* (the lion): **I will!!!**").

In a letter written to Köselitz at the beginning of September, Nietzsche suggested there might be a compensatory relationship between his depressions and the cheerfulness exhibited by Zarathustra — "Dergestalt hat Z[arathustra] sich auf meine Kosten *erheitert,* und ich habe mich auf seine Kosten *verdüstert*" (KSB 6:444; "In this way Zarathustra has *cheered* himself up at my expense, and I have grown *darker* at his expense"). Indeed, it sometimes seems as if the empirical Nietzsche, who wrote these sad, sometimes wearisome, letters, was the kind of Christian figure against whom the literary persona, Nietzsche-Zarathustra, wrote. Yet as he expanded on his plan for part 3 Nietzsche predicted, drawing explicitly on Weimar Classicism's notion of "serious play," that things were about to change:

> Übrigens muß ich Ihnen, nicht ohne Betrübniß, melden, daß jetzt, mit dem dritten Theile, der arme Z[arathustra] wirklich in's Düstere geräth — so sehr, daß Schopenhauer und Leopardi nur als Anfänger und Neulinge gegen *seinen* "Pessimismus" erscheinen werden. So will es der *Plan.* Um aber *diesen* Theil machen zu können, brauche ich selber erst tiefe, himmlische Heiterkeit: denn das Pathetische der höchsten Gattung wird mir nur als *Spiel* gelingen. (Zum Schluß wird **Alles** *hell.*)
>
> (KSB 6:445)

> [By the way I must tell you, not without sadness, that now, with the third part, Zarathustra really descends into gloom — so much so that Schopenhauer and Leopardi will seem no more than debutants and novices compared with *his* "pessimism." This is according to the *plan.* To be able to write *this* part, however, I myself need deep, celestial cheerfulness: for I can only make the pathos of the highest kind successful as *play.* (At the end **everything** becomes *bright.*)]

Faced with the horror of the idea of the eternal recurrence in "Vom Gesicht und Räthsel," Zarathustra experiences his bleakest moments in "Der Genesende" ("The Convalescent"; (*Z* III 13 §1; KSA 4:270–71), before he learns to "justify" the world as (aesthetic) play. The conclusion to part 3 turned out to be the "Ja-and-Amen-Song" of "The Seven Seals."

In September and October, Nietzsche traveled to Naumberg (where he endured further confrontation with his sister and his mother; 5 September–2 October), to Frankfurt am Main with Franz Overbeck (4–6 October), visiting the Overbeck home in Basel (7–9 October), then, via Genoa, to La Spezia (12–21 October), back to Genoa, and finally to Nice for the winter (2 December–20 April 1884). From Genoa on 9 November, Nietzsche, promising a copy of part 2 to Franz Overbeck, told him: "lies ihn als einen zweiten Theil von *vieren* d.h. verstehe, daß Mancherlei darin erst im *Sinne des Ganzen* seine Nothwendigkeit bekommen wird" ("as a second part of *four,* i.e., understand that the necessity of many things in it can only been seen in the *sense of the whole*"). On Nietzsche's account, then, the earlier parts of *Zarathustra* were written with the *whole,* that is, the four-part, text in mind. "Im Übrigen wirst Du wissen," he commented to Overbeck, "wie unsäglich fern ich mit diesem Z[arathustra] von allem eigentlich *Litterarischen* bin. Es handelt sich um eine ungeheure Synthesis, von der ich glaube, daß sie noch in keines Menschen Kopf und Seele gewesen ist. Bringe ich sie so an's Licht, wie ich sie auf Augenblicke vor mir gesehn habe, so will ich ein Fest feiern und sterben" (KSB 6:455; "By the way, you will know how indescribably far away I am with this 'Zarathustra' from all that is in fact *literary.* It is really an immense synthesis, which I believe has never yet been in any human's head and soul. If I can bring it to light, as I have envisaged it for moments, then I will have a celebration and die").

Nietzsche, not greatly enamored of Nice, tried to brave out the winter in the French town and, in particular, tried to recapture some of the cheerfulness he associated with Sils-Maria: "Von allen guten Dingen, die ich gefunden habe, will ich am wenigsten die 'Fröhlichkeit der Erkennens' wegwerfen oder verloren haben [. . .]. Nur muß ich jetzt, mit meinem Sohne Zarathustra zusammen, zu einer *viel höheren* Fröhlichkeit *hinauf,* als ich sie je bisher in Worten darstellen konnte" ("Of all the good things that I have found I want least of all to throw away or have lost the 'joyfulness of knowing' . . . It's just that I must now, together with my son Zarathustra, go *up* to a *much higher* joyfulness than I could previously represent in words"). For "das Glück," he continued, "welches ich in der 'fröhlichen Wissenschaft' darstellte, ist wesentlich das Glück eines Menschen, der sich endlich *reif* zu fühlen beginnt für eine ganz große Aufgabe, und dem die Zweifel über sein Recht *dazu* zu schwinden anfangen" (to Franz Overbeck, 6 December 1883; KSB 6:460; "The happiness that I represented in the 'Gay Science' is essentially the happiness of someone who at last is beginning to feel *mature enough* for a really large task, and whose doubts about his right *to do this* are beginning to disappear"). And Nietzsche must have succeeded, at least to some extent, in recapturing the mountain air of Switzerland in this port-town of France for shortly afterwards, on 18 January 1884, he announced to his publisher, Ernst Schmeitzner: "[M]ein Zarathustra ist *fertig:* — es bedarf der Abschrift — es bedarf des *Drucks*" (KSB 6:465; "My Zarathustra is *finished:* — it needs copying — it needs *publishing*"). Looking back in *Ecce Homo*, Nietzsche presents the composition of part 3 as another one of those "halcyon" periods of his life:

> Viele verborgene Flecke und Höhen aus der Landschaft Nizza's sind mir durch unvergessliche Augenblicke geweiht; jene entscheidende Partie, welche den Titel "von alten und neuen Tafeln" trägt, wurde im beschwerlichsten Aufsteigen von der Station zu dem wunderbaren maurischen Felsenneste Eza gedichtet, — die Muskel-Behendheit war bei mir immer am grössten, wenn die schöpferische Kraft am reichsten floss. Der *Leib* ist begeistert: lassen wir die "Seele" aus dem Spiele . . . Man hat mich oft tanzen sehn können; ich konnte damals, ohne einen Begriff von Ermüdung, sieben, acht Stunden auf Bergen unterwegs sein. Ich schlief gut, ich lachte viel —, ich war von einer vollkommnen Rüstigkeit und Geduld. (*EH Z* §4; KSA 6:341)[33]

> [Many obscure spots and heights in the landscape around Nice are hallowed for me by unforgettable moments; that decisive passage that bears the title "On Old and New Tablets" was composed during the most onerous ascent from the station to the wonderful Moorish bastion at Èzé — the suppleness of my muscles has always been greatest when my creative energies were flowing most abundantly. The *body* is inspired; let us keep the "soul" out of it . . . Often one could have seen me dance; in those days I could walk in the mountains for seven or eight hours without a trace of weariness. I slept well, I laughed a lot — my vigor and patience were perfect.]

As usual, and understandably enough, Nietzsche's mood on completion as reflected in his correspondence was one of triumph, if of a rather self-alienated kind: "Ich bin glücklich und, wie schon oft in meinem Leben, von mir selber über mich selber 'überrrascht' [. . .] Dieser dritte Akt meines Dramas (besser sollte ich vom Finale meiner Symphonie reden)" ("I am happy and, as so often in my life, have 'surprised' myself about myself. This third act of my drama [it would better if I spoke of the finale of my symphony]"), he told Schmeitzner, "enthält mancherlei 'Unglaubliches'" ("contained many 'unbelievable things'"; KSB 6:465–66). A similar tone of triumph is detectable in a letter of 25 January 1884 to Overbeck, and these, as well as other letters,[34] suggest that Nietzsche now regarded *Zarathustra* as complete in three parts:

Das Ganze ist somit genau im Verlaufe *eines* Jahrs entstanden: im strengeren Sinne sogar im Verlaufe von 3 x 2 Wochen. — Die letzten zwei Wochen waren die glücklichsten meines Lebens: ich bin **nie** mit solchen Segeln über ein solches Meer gefahren; und der ungeheure Übermuth dieser *ganzen* Seefahrer-Geschichte, welche so lange dauert als Du mich kennst, 1870, kam auf seinen Gipfel. [. . .] Die Vollendung meines Zarathustra hat meiner Gesundheit *sehr wohl* gethan. (KSB 6:466–67)

[The whole thus came into being in the course of *one* year: strictly speaking just in three two-week periods. — The last two weeks were the happiest of my life: I have **never** voyaged across such a sea under such sails; and the incredible high spirits of this *entire* seafarer's story, which has been going on for as long as you have known me, since 1870, reached its zenith. . . . The completion of my Zarathustra has done my health *very much good.*]

The sea-faring image used in this letter was one of Nietzsche's favorites; one thinks, for example, of the poem "Nach neuen Meeren" ("Toward New Seas"), which begins "Dorthin — *will* ich" (KSA 3:649; "To go there — is my *will*").[35] In this letter, Nietzsche expresses his sense of completion, not just with his *Zarathustra,* but with his entire philosophical project, beginning with his work on tragedy in the 1870s. On the evidence of this and other letters, at least Nietzsche himself saw his work in terms of an overarching continuity.[36] And the battle, he suggested, was still not yet over: "Alter lieber Freund, das Nächste, was ich projektire, *zur Erholung!* ist ein großer **Front-Angriff** auf *alle* Arten des *jetzigen* deutschen Obscurantismus" (KSB 6:467; "Dear old friend, the next thing I would like to do, *as relaxation!* is a great **frontal-attack** on *all* kinds of *current* German obscurantism"). At about this time, part 2 of *Zarathustra* appeared, costing 3 Marks per copy.[37]

Immediately, part 3 went into production. There were to be no more delays, Nietzsche told his publisher on 6 February 1884, due to hymn-books "und andre Teufeleien!" ("and other devilries!"; KSB 6:474). And as with parts 1 and 2, Köselitz undertook to read the proofs. Writing to Franz Overbeck on the same day, Nietzsche described "der *ganze* Zarathustra" ("the *entire* Zarathustra") as "eine Explosion von Kräften, die Jahrzehnde lang sich aufgehäuft haben: bei solchen Explosionen kann der Urheber leicht selber mit in die Luft gehen. Mir ist öfter **so** zu Muthe" ("an explosion of forces that have been building up for decades: with such explosions the creator can easily blow himself up as well. That is frequently **how** I have often felt"). If Nietzsche felt precarious about his own position, he also expressed concern about Overbeck's reaction to the conclusion of part 3, the celebration of the idea of the eternal recurrence: "[W]enn Du aus dem Finale ersehen wirst, *was* mit der ganzen Symphonie eigentlich gesagt werden soll (—

sehr artistisch und schrittweise, wie man etwa einen Thurm baut), — so wirst auch Du, mein alter treuer Freund, einen heillosen Schrecken und Schauder nicht überwinden können" (KSB 6:475; "When you see from the finale *what* the entire symphony is in fact trying to say (— very artistically and step-by-step, just as one builds, say, a tower), — then you too, my dear old, faithful friend, will not be able to suppress an awful horror and shudder"). And we find a similar concern expressed in his letter to his old university friend, Rohde, whom he had owed a letter for a couple of months: "Es ist eine Art Abgrund der Zukunft, etwas Schauerliches, namentlich in seiner Glückseligkeit. Es ist Alles drin mein Eigen, ohne Vorbild, Vergleich, Vorgänger; wer einmal darin *gelebt* hat, der kommt mit einem andern Gesichte wieder zur Welt zurück" (KSB 6:479; "It is a kind of abyss of the future, something horrifying, especially in its blissful happiness. Everything in it is my own, without any model, comparison, predecessor; whoever has once *lived* in it will return to the world with another face").

As the winter of 1884 turned into spring, and Nietzsche's impatience with his publisher resumed, very little more was said about Zarathustra in his correspondence. Although Nietzsche had repeatedly stated that, with part 3, his *Zarathustra* was now complete, his notebooks for the Summer and Autumn of 1883 were full of sketches for a fourth as well as the third part;[38] and, after all, the *Ur*-sketch of 1881, "Mittag und Ewigkeit," had envisaged four parts in total. One of the indications that Nietzsche had begun to think about writing a fourth part of *Zarathustra* can be found in his letter to Köselitz of 22 March 1884: "*nun,* nachdem ich **soweit** mein Stillschweigen gebrochen habe, bin ich zu **'mehr'** verpflichtet, zu irgend einer 'Philosophie der Zukunft' — eingerechnet 'dionysische Tänze' und 'Narren-Bücher' und anderes Teufelszeug" (KSB 6:487; "*now,* **insofar as** I have broken my silence, I am committed to **'more,'** to some kind of 'philosophy of the future' — including 'Dionysian dances' and 'fools' books,' and other devilish stuff"). Although the phrase "philosophy of the future" became part of the subtitle of *Jenseits von Gut und Böse,*[39] the "Dionysian dances" and "fools' books" sound like a hint, although no more than a hint, of what would come in *Also sprach Zarathustra,* part 4. And part 4 would be, in several respects, a very different kind of text from the three parts preceding it.

Zarathustra IV

In the *Nachlass* for Spring 1884 there is a fragment, 25 [405], which contains the following pronouncement:[40]

> Meine Aufgabe: *die Menschheit zu Entschlüssen zu drängen, die über alle Zukunft entscheiden!*

*Höchste Geduld — Vorsicht — den **Typus** solcher Menschen **zeigen**, welche sich diese Aufgabe stellen dürfen!*

(KSA 11:118)

[My task: *to urge humankind to decisions that will decide about the entire future!*

A *high degree of patience — caution — **show** the **type** of such human beings who can set themselves this task!*]

This note suggests that there was still a lurking sense that Nietzsche's "task" had not yet been fulfilled, and this was to lead him to produce a fourth installment of *Zarathustra,* which he sometimes also presented as the start of a new project, before he finally decided to begin work on a different kind of book altogether.

In the meantime, Nietzsche's exasperation with his publisher, who was now apparently facing financial difficulties, was matched by his desire not to leave Nice until he had received the first copies of part 3 of *Zarathustra.*[41] Eventually the copies arrived, on 10 April 1884,[42] and Nietzsche traveled to Venice, "*der unabhängigste Mann in Europa*" ("*the most independent man in Europe*"), as he described himself to Overbeck (30 April; KSB 6:497). He intended, he wrote, to apply to himself one of the maxims of Zarathustra: "Ich denke, Du weißt, **was** gerade in Bezug auf mich die Mahnung Zarathustras 'Werde hart!' sagen will. Mein Sinn, jedem Einzelnen Gerechtigkeit widerfahren zu lassen und im Grunde gerade das *mir* Feindseligste mit der größten Milde zu behandeln, ist *übermäßig* entwickelt und bringt Gefahr über Gefahr, nicht nur für mich, sondern für meine Aufgabe: *hier* ist Abhärtung nöthig und, der Erziehung halber, eine gelegentliche Grausamkeit" (KSB 6:497–98; "I think you know **what** exactly Zarathustra's admonition 'become hard!' means in relation to me. My way of thinking, to see that justice is done to every single person and to treat basically preceisely what is most hostile to *me* with the greatest leniency, is *excessively* developed and brings one danger after another, not just for me, but for my task: *here* toughening up is necessary and, as a matter of education, an occasional cruelty"). And his thoughts were beginning to turn back to Sils-Maria . . .

And so, on 18 July 1884, Nietzsche went back to Sils-Maria for his third visit, staying there until the end of September. "Ah diese gute Luft!" ("Ah, this good air!"), he wrote to Overbeck on the day of his return, and was moved to (mis)quote himself or, rather, Zarathustra: "Vorüber die [zögernde] Trübsal dieses/meines Frühlings! Vorüber die Bosheit meiner Schneeflocken im Juni!" (KSB 6:513; compare *Z* II 6; KSA 4:126; "Gone is the [lingering] affliction of this/my spring! Gone is the malice of my snowflakes in June!"). For all his satisfaction with parts 1, 2 and 3 of *Zarathustra* there is, however, no sense of closure to be found in his letters: "Ich stecke

222 ◆ APPENDIX: THE COMPOSITION OF ZARATHUSTRA

mitten in meinen Problem drin" ("I am still right in the middle of my problems"), he told Köselitz on 23 July, "meine Lehre, daß die Welt des Guten
und Bösen nur eine scheinbare und perspektivische Welt ist, ist eine solche
Neuerung, daß mir bisweilen dabei Hören und Sehen vergeht" (KSB 6:514;
"my doctrine, that the world of Good and Evil is only an apparent and perspectival world, is such an innovation that I sometimes lose hearing and sight
because of it"). Palpable, however, is his sense of being "away" again, and
particularly away from Basel, the site of his former university employer,
where he had visited the Overbecks earlier that year, as he told Köselitz:

> *Endlich* in Sils-Maria! Endlich Rückkehr zur — Vernunft! Inzwischen
> nämlich gieng es um mich zu unvernünftig zu (ich war wie unter
> *Kühen*); aber *daß* ich mich so lange in diesen Niederungen und
> Kuhställen aufhielt, war selber die größte Unvernunft. Wer
> Distractionen nöthig hat, wie sie *unser-Einer* hier und da nöthig hat,
> Gelegenheit zu lachen, boshafte Menschen und Bücher — der soll nur
> irgend wo anders hin gehn, aber nicht nach Basel et hoc genus omne.
> Das Spaaßhafteste, was ich erlebte war J[acob] Burckhardts
> Verlegenheit, mir etwas über den Zarathustra *sagen zu müssen:* er
> brachte nichts Anderes heraus als — "ob ich es nicht auch einmal mit
> dem *Drama* versuchen wolle." (25 July; KSB 6:515)

> [*At last* in Sils-Maria! At last a return to — reason! In the meantime
> there have been all too many stupid things going on around me (I was
> as if among *cows*); but *that* I remained so long in these lowly spheres
> and cow-stalls was itself the greatest un-reason. Whoever needs distrac-
> tions, as the likes of us need from time to time the opportunity to
> laugh, malicious books and people — he should simply go somewhere
> else, but not to Basel and to places like that. The most amusing thing I
> experienced was Jacob Burckhardt's embarrassment at *having to say*
> something to me about Zarathustra: he came out with nothing other
> than — "whether I shouldn't have a go at writing a *play*."]

During the summer of that year, Nietzsche's correspondence was less fre-
quent than usual, although the notebooks in the *Nachlass* show the usual
frenetic philosophical reflection. Correspondingly, there are fewer references
to *Zarathustra*, although the topic is by no means absent. In a letter to
Overbeck written at the beginning of August, for example, Nietzsche con-
trasted *Zarathustra* favorably with his earlier essay, "Schopenhauer als
Erzieher" ("Schopenhauer as an Educator"; KSB 6:518).[43] And in another
letter to Overbeck, this time on 18 August, Nietzsche returned to two images used previously during the composition of part 1 of *Zarathustra:* that of
alchemy — "alle meine Schicksale zu Gunsten meiner **Aufgabe** '*in Gold zu
verwandeln*'" ("'*to transform into gold*' all my destinies in favor of my
task") — and that of pregnancy: "Es gab doch wieder Stunden, wo diese

Aufgabe ganz deutlich vor mir steht, wo ein ungeheures Ganzes von Philosophie (und von Mehr als je Philosophie hieß!) sich vor meinen Blicken auseinander legt" ("There were again hours when this task stood before me quite clearly, where a monstrous entire philosophy (and more than has ever been called philosophy!) laid itself out before my eyes"). "Dies Mal," he continued, "bei dieser gefährlichsten und schwersten 'Schwangerschaft,' muß ich mir begünstigende Umstände zusammenholen und alle Sonnen mir leuchten machen, die ich noch kennen lernte" (KSB 6:520–21; "This time, with this most dangerous and most difficult 'pregnancy,' I must gather together all circumstances that favor me and make all the additional suns I have learned about illuminate me"). But Nietzsche's current project no longer involved Zarathustra who, so he implied in a letter to Köselitz of 2 September 1884, was no longer of much importance at all: "Zarathustra hat einstweilen nur den ganz persönlichen Sinn, daß es mein 'Erbauungs- und Ermuthigungs-Buch' ist — im Übrigen dunkel und verborgen und lächerlich für Jedermann" (KSB 6:525; "Zarathustra has in the meantime the entirely personal meaning of being my 'book of edification and encouragement' — it is otherwise dark and obscure and ridiculous for everyone").

From the increasingly number of theoretical, rather than dramatic, sketches in the *Nachlass*,[44] it is clear that Nietzsche was beginning to envisage a different kind of work, one that was to become *Jenseits von Gut und Böse*. Sils-Maria, "d[ie] Ursprungsstätte des Zarathustrismus" ("the place of origin of Zarathustrianism"; KSB 6:515), was no longer working its Zarathustrian magic; nor, it seems, did Nietzsche particularly want it to. Maybe, he even mused in a letter to Köselitz, the pinnacles of his writing career — *Die Geburt der Tragödie* and *Zarathustra* — had been achieved thanks to the influence of solar magnetism (20 September 1884; KSB 6:535) . . .

The end of September saw Nietzsche depart from Sils-Maria for Zurich; in October 1884 a reconciliation was effected between Nietzsche and his sister; and after a three-week visit to Menton, a town in the Italian-French Riviera, in November, Nietzsche was back in Nice again at the end of the year. Suddenly, in the notebooks for the winter of 1884–85, we find sketch after sketch relating to part 4 of *Zarathustra*, including fragments that returned to the earlier title of 1881, "Mittag und Ewigkeit."[45] After silence on the subject for several weeks, Nietzsche, upset with the lack of promotion of his work by his publisher, Schmeitzner,[46] had told his sister in mid-September that he was determined to find a new publisher — and that he now planned to have part 4 of *Zarathustra* ready by January. No explanation is offered at this point as to why Nietzsche now thought a fourth part was necessary, although we do know that it had been part of the original plan in 1881. But if silence about this new work was, at least in part, a negotiating tactic, so was silence about "dem nunmehr unvermeidlichen fünften und sechsten Theile" ("the now inevitable fifth and sixth parts") — parts that had not even formed part of the original scheme. This "inevitability," it seems, was connected with Nietzsche's desire to bring the work to a different kind of conclusion, with the death of Zarathustra — a conclusion following the logic of narrative structure, rather than the ecstatic affirmation of the idea of the eternal recurrence: "Es hilft nichts, ich muß meinem Sohne Zarathustra erst zu seinem schönen *Tode* verhelfen, er läßt mir sonst keine Ruhe" (to Elisabeth Nietzsche, circa 15 November; KSB 6:557; "It's no use, I must first help my son Zarathustra to a beautiful *death*, otherwise he will give me no peace").

The *Nachlass* contains various sketches for the death of Zarathustra, which show a development in the scenarios entertained by Nietzsche. In the first group of sketches from May-June, June-July, and Summer 1883, Zarathustra's death is initially peaceful: "Glaube es mir, Z[arathustra] starb und ist nicht mehr. Ein Stern erlosch in oedem Raum: aber sein Licht — — —" (9[15]; KSA 10:349; compare 10[17]; KSA 10:370; "Believe me, Zarathustra died and is no more. A star was extinguished in barren space: but its light — — —"). In other scenarios, everyone deserts Zarathustra and he dies of pain (see 10[45]; KSA 10:377); or he dies from a vision of the superman and the idea of the eternal recurrence (see 10[47]; KSA 10:378; compare 16[3]; KSA 10:496); or, in a scene set on the edge of a volcano, Zarathustra dies among his children (see 13[2]; KSA 10:444; compare 9[35]; KSA 10:356): "Letzte Scene am Vulkan. Volle Seligkeit. Vergessen. Vision des Weibes (oder des Kindes mit dem Spiegel) Die Jünger schauen in das tiefe Grab. (Oder *Zarathustra unter* **Kindern** an Tempelresten.) Die größte aller Todtenfeiern macht den Schluß. Goldener Sarg in den Vulkan gestürzt" (13[2]; KSA 10:444-45; "Final scene at the volcano. Complete bliss. Oblivion. Vision of the woman (or of the child with the mirror) The disciples look into the deep grave. (Or *Zarathustra among* **children** at the temple ruins.) The greatest of all memorial services forms the conclusion. The golden coffin is thrown into the volcano").[47] Other drafts envisage the introduction of a mysterious female figure called Pana (see 13[3]; KSA 10:446), who is carrying a knife (KSA 10:447).

In the second set of sketches from the Autumn of 1883, the scenarios become more violent. He dies of distress and yet of happiness (see 16[8]; KSA 10:500), or of pity for Pana's pity (see 16[38]; KSA 10:512), or he is even killed by Pana: "Zuerst wenden sich Alle von Zarathustra ab (dies *schrittweise zu schildern!*). Zarathustra entzückt, merkt nichts. Pana will ihn tödten. *Im Augenblick, wo sie den Dolch führt, versteht Zarathustra alles und stirbt am Schmerz über dieses Mitleiden.* Dies ist *deutlich zu machen!*" (16[42]; KSA 10:513; compare 20[10]; KSA 10:593; "First everyone turns away from Zarathustra (this *to be shown step by step!*). Zarathustra delighted, notices nothing. Pana wants to kill him. *In the moment when she uses the dag-*

ger, Zarathustra understands everything and dies from pain at this pity. This is *to be made very clear!*"). In other scenarios, he watches his animals fighting, and dies (see 16[45]; KSA 10:513); his followers find Zarathustra's grave and become "heirs of his soul" (see 16[53]; KSA 10:517); or, in the final sketch, at his feast everyone embraces the eternal recurrence, Zarathustra dies, and speeches of praise are offered over his corpse (see 21[3]; KSA 10:599–600).

This desire, never carried out in any published version, to see Zarathustra "killed off" is, perhaps, related in part to a possible fatigue on Nietzsche's part with his "son." In the *Nachlass* for Spring 1884, for example, we find the note, "*Entschluß.* Ich will reden, und nicht mehr Zarathustra" (25[277]; KSA 11:83; "*Decision:* I want to speak, and not Zarathustra any more"). But some of the material for part 4 had already been sketched out: this fragment, 25[148], also from Spring 1884 — "Ich mußte Zarathustra, einem *Perser,* die Ehre geben: Perser haben zuerst Geschichte im Ganzen Großen *gedacht.* Eine Abfolge von Entwicklungen, jeder präsidirt ein Prophet. Jeder Prophet hat seinen *hazar,* sein Reich von tausend Jahren" (KSA 11:53; "I had to give Zarathustra, a *Persian,* honor: the Persians first *thought* of history as a whole entirety. A sequence of developments, each presided over by a prophet. Every prophet has his *hazar,* his kingdom of a thousand years") — anticipates the lines from "Das Honig-Opfer" ("The Honey Sacrifice") in part 4: "Unser grosser Hazar, das ist unser grosses fernes Menschen-Reich, das Zarathustra-Reich von tausend Jahren" (*Z* IV 1; KSA 4:298; "our great *hazar,* our great distant human kingdom, the Zarathustra kingdom of a thousand years").

In the *Nachlass* for Winter 1884–85 we find various outlines for part 4 of *Zarathustra,* including references to "*die Versuchung Zarathustra's*" ("*the temptation of Zarathustra*"; 29[47]; KSA 11:347);[48] and: "In Zarathustra 4: der große Gedanke als *Medusenhaupt:* alle Züge der Welt werden starr, ein gefrorener Todeskampf" (31[4]; KSA 11:360; "In Zarathustra 4: the great thought as *the head of the Medusa:* all the features of the world become rigid, a frozen fight to the death");[49] and a number of outlines clearly anticipate the final version.[50] Plans for further parts of *Zarathustra,* in the meantime, included the following: "Zarathustra 5: volle Anerkennung des Menschlichen in Betreff der sichtbaren Welt — *Abweisung* der idealistischen Philosophie und Erklärung aus Sattheit, Widerwillen am Menschen. — Die 'Falschheit' in den Dingen zu erklären als Resultat *unserer* schaffenden Kraft!" (29[33]; KSB 11:345; compare 35[74] and 39[3]; KSA 11:541–42 and 620; "Zarathustra 5: complete acknowledgment of what is human in respect of the visible world — *rejection* of idealistic philosophy and explanation in terms of satiety, aversion to humankind. — The 'falseness' in things to be explained as the result of *our* creative power!"); "In Zarathustra 6 die große Synthese des Schaffenden, Liebenden, Vernichtenden" (31[3]; KSA 11:360;

"In Zarathustra 6 the great synthesis of the creator, the lover, the destroyer"); and "— so wie die niederen Menschen zu Gott aufsahen, sollten wir billigerweise einmal *zu meinem Übermenschen aufsehen*. Zarathustra 6" (31[27]; KSA 11:366; "— just as lower human beings looked up to God, so we should rightly *look up to my superman. Zarathustra 6*").

When his plans to go to Corsica fell through, Nietzsche decided to stay again in Nice for winter. It must, therefore, have been during his time in Menton and in Nice that part 4 of *Zarathustra* was written, although it is hard to be precise about the dates of composition. On 12 February 1885, however, Nietzsche told Carl von Gersdorff: "Es giebt einen vierten (letzten) Theil Zarathustra, eine Art sublimen Finale's, welches gar nicht für die Öffentlichkeit bestimmt ist" ("There is a fourth (final) part of Zarathustra, a kind of sublime finale, which is not destined at all for the public"). Adding that, in relation to the whole of Zarathustra, the word "public" sounded to him like "whorehouse" and "working girl" — a bizarrely ribald remark that made even Nietzsche append a "Pardon!" — he explained that he intended this part to be published privately, for distribution to only twenty people (KSB 7:9). The implied request to Gersdorff was for financial help with the costs of publication. So now, far from inaugurating a new global epoch, as Nietzsche had previously hoped, *Zarathustra* had become a secret project, reserved only for a few initiates — in fact, only for Nietzsche's family and friends. In a note in his *Nachlass* from the period Autumn 1884 to the beginning of 1885, Nietzsche saw Nice as the place where *Zarathustra* came to an end: "dem Engardin verdanke ich *Leben*, Zarathustra," he wrote, "Nizza verdanke ich die *Beendigung* des Zarathustra" (29[4]; KSA 11:337; "to the Engadine I am indebted for *life, Zarathustra*, [. . .] to Nice I am indebted for the *completion* of Zarathustra"). And significantly, in this later draft version in Autumn 1884 of the poem "Sils-Maria," Zarathustra now found no mention:

> Hier saß ich sehend, sehend — doch hinaus!
> Die Finger spielend im zerpflückten Strauß
> Und wenn die Thräne aus dem Lide quoll
> Schamhaft-neugierig: ach wem galt sie wohl!
>
> Da — — —
>
> Hier saß ich liebend, liebend — unbewegt,
> Dem See gleich, der — — —
> Wer diesen Spiegel-See als Zauber sieht:
> Drin eint sich Milch und Veilchen und Granit.
>
> (28[31]; KSA 11:311)

[Here I sat looking, looking — but out!
Fingers playing in the plucked bouquet
And when tears from the eyelid welled
Shameful-curious: ah, for whom were they indeed!

Then — — —

Here I sat loving, loving — fixed,
Just like the lake, which — — —
Whoever sees this mirror-lake as magic:
Therein unite milk and violet and granite.]

Other poems, drafted at this time, communicate a sense of urgency (see 28[3] and 28[21];[51] KSA 11:297–98 and 306–7, as well as 28[14]; KSA 11:304,[52] which anticipate the *Dionysos-Dithyramben*), as well as a sense of resignation (see 28[9], 28[27],[53] and 28[40];[54] KSA 11:301–2, 310 and 315).

In a letter written to Köselitz on 14 February 1885, Nietzsche wrote that "es giebt etwas Neues als *'Frucht'* dieses Winters" ("there is something new as the *'fruit'* of this winter"), but he had no publisher, and no desire to publish, and he expressed this reluctance as follows: "Die ungeheuere Albernheit, so etwas wie meinen Zarath[ustra] herauszugeben, ohne es nöthig zu haben, ist mir mit entsprechender Albernheit vergolten worden: wie es billig war" ("The tremendous silliness of publishing something such as my Zarathustra, without having to, has been repaid to me with corresponding silliness: as was to be expected"). And he described this new work as "eine 'Gotteslästerung,' gedichtet mit der Laune eines Hanswursts" (KSB 7:11–12; "a 'blasphemy,' written in the mood of a clown"). Although he had told Gersdorff that he had written a fourth and final part of *Zarathustra,* the title as it appeared in his letters to Köselitz and to Overbeck (20 February) implied, rather, the start of something new: "**Mittag und Ewigkeit**: Erster Theil: *die Versuchung Zarathustra's*" (KSB 7:14; "**Midday and Eternity**: part 1: *the Temptation of Zarathustra*"). On 14 March, however, Nietzsche told Köselitz that "der Titel, welchen ich Ihnen das letzte Mal brieflich meldete, war eine Verlegenheits-Auskunft in Hinsicht auf einen neuen Verleger" (KSB 7:21; "the title that I announced to you in my letter last time was a piece of makeshift information with a view to a new publisher"); and, when the work was finally sent off to the Leipzig publisher C. G. Naumann, it was as "den vierten und letzten Theil meines Zarathustra" ("the fourth and final part of my Zarathustra"), to be printed in 20 copies, along with an insistence on "jedweden Grad von Diskretion" ("every degree of discretion"), including the destruction of all proofs (12 March; KSB 7:19–20). Although Nietzsche told Naumann in this letter that the layout and paper should be the same as those used for part 3, he later asked for stronger paper to be used, and now wanted 40, instead of 20, copies (19 March; KSB 7:28). (Later, shortly before his collapse at the end of 1888, Nietzsche made an attempt to recall all these copies.)[55] Oddly, though, Nietzsche told Overbeck on 31 March 1885 that he still had not found a publisher (KSB 7:33–34), although by this he perhaps meant that he had had to publish part 4 privately and at his own expense (see KSB 8:21). Later, he repeated his excuse that the title "Mittag und Ewigkeit" had been "eine 'Condescendenz' an die Herrn Verleger, welche absolut keine 'vierten Theile' verlegen wollen, wenn sie nicht die drei vorher haben" (7 May 1885; KSB 7:46; "a 'concession' to the publishers, who absolutely do not want to publish 'fourth parts' when they have not previously published the earlier three").

Nietzsche's mood during this time was growing as dark as it had ever been. In a draft of a letter to his sister, he wrote: "So lange ich gesund bin, habe ich guten Humor genug, um meine *Rolle* zu spielen und mich vor aller Welt darunter zu verstecken z[um] b[eispiel] als Basler Professor. Leider bin ich sehr viel krank, und dann hasse ich die Menschen, welche ich kennen gelernt habe, unsäglich, mich eingerechnet" (KSB 7:24–25; "As long as I am healthy, I have sufficient good humor to play my *role* and to hide myself from the world behind it, e.g., as a professor from Basel. Unfortunately I am often very ill, and then I hate the people whom I have met, unutterably, including myself"). Similarly, he told Köselitz in one letter: "Ach, wenn Sie wüßten, *wie* allein ich jetzt auf der Welt bin! Und wie viel Komödie noth thut, um nicht, hier und da, aus Überdruß, irgend Jemandem in's Gesicht zu spucken!" ("Oh, if only you knew *how* alone I am now in the world! And how much comedy is necessary, in order sometimes, having had enough, not to spit into somebody's face!"). Fortunately, he added, some of the good manners of his son, Zarathustra, were still present in the mad father (30 March; KSB 7:32); and, in another: "Der Winter war ein großes Pensum der Selbst-Überwindung, und mein einziges Gebet früh und spät 'mein Herr, fahren Sie nicht aus der Haut!'" (6 April; KSB 7:35; "The winter consisted in a great task of self-overcoming, and my only prayer, early and late, was 'sir, do not let yourself be driven round the bend!'"). On 10 April, Nietzsche set off to spend two months in Venice where Köselitz (who by 13 April had finished reading the proofs of part 4) was staying. But the weather was cold, and in one of his early letters from Venice, to his mother and sister, Nietzsche begged them to send him new underwear (KSB 7:41).

At a total cost of 284 Marks 40 Pfennige, the print-run of 40 copies was completed by 7 May 1885;[56] to Köselitz, Overbeck, his sister, his mother, and von Gersdorff alike, Nietzsche had insisted, and continued to insist, they tell no-one of its existence. Unlike the publication of parts 1 to 3, the appearance of part 4 of *Zarathustra* failed to produce an upswing in Nietzsche's mood. In the same letter in which he sent Overbeck a copy, he told him: "Meine Gefahr ist in der That sehr groß, aber nicht *diese* Art Gefahr: wohl aber weiß ich mitunter nicht mehr, ob ich die Sphinx bin, die fragt, oder jener berühmte Oedipus, der gefragt wird — so daß ich für den *Abgrund zwei* Chancen habe" (7 May; KSB 7:44; "My danger is in fact very great, but not *this* kind of danger: sometimes, however, I no longer know whether I am the sphinx, who asks questions, or the famous Oedipus, who is asked them — so that I have *two* chances for the *abyss*"). Perhaps this mood can be explained in part by his sister's marriage to Bernhard Förster on 22 May (as a present, Nietzsche sent the happy couple, apparently at their request, Dürer's print "Ritter, Tod und Teufel"); perhaps the publication of the book *Kampf um Gott* by Lou von Salomé ("Im Übrigen hole sie der Teufel!" [KSB 7:46; "Besides, the devil take her!"] also contributed; and perhaps his unhappy choice of lodgings was not unrelated.[57] In terms of its position in the structure of the project, part 4 was conceived, Nietzsche told Overbeck, "als Finale" ("as a finale"), referring back to the opening of part 1: "lies nur einmal die 'Vorrede' des ersten Theils" (KSB 7:46; "just read the 'Prologue' of the first part"). In that Prologue, Zarathustra, following his failure in the market-place, decides that he needs disciples: "Gefährten brauche ich und lebendige — nicht todte Gefährten und Leichname, die ich mit mir trage, wohin ich will" (*Z* Vorrede §9; KSA 4:25; "Companions I need, living ones — not dead companions and corpses that I carry with me wherever I choose to go"). In part 4, the Higher Men seem to fulfill this need for companions and disciples; although in time they, too, will disappoint.

Furthermore, Nietzsche seemed, to a greater extent than ever previously, alienated from his creation. "Glaube ja nicht, daß mein Sohn Zarathustra *meine* Meinungen ausspricht," he told his sister: "Er ist eine meiner Vorbereitungen und Zwischen-Akte" (7 May; KSB 7:48; "Do not believe that my son Zarathustra gives voice to *my* opinions. He is one of my preparations and entr'actes"). A couple of months earlier, he had told Köselitz: "Für das, was ich noch zu sagen habe comme poète-prophète, brauche ich eine andre Form als die bisherige" (14 March; KSB 7:21; "For what I still have to say as a *poète-prophète* I need a form different from the previous one"). And so *Zarathustra* pointed forward now to other, new projects.[58]

These projects bore various names — sometimes *Der Wille zur Macht* (*The Will to Power*), which was eventually the name given to a collection of *Nachlass* fragments edited by his sister, sometimes *Umwerthung aller Werthe* (*Revaluation of All Values*), sometimes *Unschuld des Werdens* (*Innocence of Becoming*), *Der Antichrist* (*The Anti-Christ*), or *Mittag und Ewigkeit* (*Midday and Eternity*) — and were intended, to judge by Nietzsche's comments in his correspondence, to have even more apocalyptic effects than he had once hoped *Zarathustra* might. For example, of *Ecce Homo* Nietzsche wrote to Georg Brandes that "das Ganze ist das Vorspiel der *Umwerthung aller*

Werthe, das Werk, *das fertig vor mir liegt:* ich schwöre Ihnen zu, daß wir in zwei Jahren die ganze Erde in Convulsionen haben werden" (20 November 1888; KSB 8:482; "the whole thing is the prelude to the *Revaluation of All Values,* the work *that lies finished before me:* I promise you that in two years we shall have the whole earth in convulsions"), commenting to Köselitz that "es sprengt, wörtlich, die *Geschichte* der Menschheit in zwei Stücke — höchster Superlativ von *Dynamit*" (to Köselitz, 9 December 1888; KSA 8:513; "it explodes, literally, the *history* of humankind into two parts — the highest superlative of dynamite"); while of the poem "Ruhm und Ewigkeit" ("Fame and Eternity"), which came to form part of the *Dionysos-Dithyramben,* he claimed: "Ich habe gestern mein non plus ultra in die Druckerei geschickt, *Ruhm und Ewigkeit* betitelt, jenseits aller sieben Himmel gedichtet. [. . .] Man stirbt daran, wenn man's unvorbereitet liest" (to Köselitz, 30 December 1888; KSB 8:566; "Yesterday I sent my *non plus ultra* to the printer, entitled 'Fame and Eternity,' composed beyond all seven heavens. . . . One will die from it if one reads it unprepared").

But the figure of Zarathustra never disappeared entirely from Nietzsche's writings. For example, at the end of his next book, *Jenseits von Gut und Böse* — a work which, as Nietzsche told Jacob Burckhardt, says the same things as *Zarathustra,* "aber anders, sehr anders" ("but differently, very differently"; KSB 7:254) — the poem included as an aftersong, "Aus hohen Bergen" ("From High Mountains"), joins the other preliminary versions of "Sils-Maria" when it alludes to Zarathustra as follows:

> *Dies* Lied ist aus, — der Sehnsucht süsser Schrei
> Erstarb im Munde:
> Ein Zaubrer that's, der Freund zur rechten Stunde,
> Der Mittags-Freund — nein! fragt nicht, wer es sei —
> Um Mittag war's, da wurde Eins zu Zwei . . . . .
>
> Nun feiern wir, vereinten Siegs gewiss,
> Das Fest der Feste:
> Freund *Zarathustra* kam, der Gast der Gäste!
> Nun lacht die Welt, der grause Vorhang riss,
> Die Hochzeit kam für Licht und Finsterniss . . . . .
> (KSA 5:243)

> [*This* song is over, — yearning's dulcet cry
> Died in my mouth:
> A magician did it, the friend at the right time,
> The noontime friend — no! do not ask me who —
> At noon it was, when one turned into two . . . . .

> Now we celebrate, certain of joint victory,
>> The feast of feasts:
> Friend *Zarathustra* came, the guest of guests!
> Now laughs the world, the terrible drape was rent,
> The marriage came for darkness and for light . . . . .]

Then again, in *Zur Genealogie der Moral* (*On the Genealogy of Morals*, 1887), the reverse of whose original title page indicated that the work was intended to "supplement and clarify" *Jenseits*,[59] Zarathustra makes an unexpected appearance at the end of the second essay — "Aber was rede ich da? Genug! Genug! An dieser Stelle geziemt mir nur Eins, zu schweigen: ich vergriffe mich sonst an dem, was einem Jüngeren allein freisteht, einem 'Zukünftigen,' einem Stärkeren, als ich bin, — was allein *Zarathustra* freisteht, *Zarathustra dem Gottlosen* . . ." (KSA 5:337; "But what am I saying? Enough! Enough! At this point it behooves me only one thing, to be silent: otherwise I shall usurp that to which alone someone younger, a 'future one,' a stronger one than I am has a right — that to which only *Zarathustra* has a right, *Zarathustra the godless* . . .") — while he placed an aphorism from *Zarathustra* before the third essay, and invited the reader to interpret the essay as a commentary on that aphorism (KSA 5:255–56 and 339). In the foreword to *Der Fall Wagner* (*The Case of Wagner*, 1888), Nietzsche praises the self-discipline of "eine tiefe Entfremdung, Erkältung, Ernüchterung gegen alles Zeitliche, Zeitgemässe: und als höchsten Wunsch das Auge *Zarathustra's*, ein Auge, das die ganze Thatsache Mensch aus ungeheurer Ferne übersieht, — *unter* sich sieht . . ." (KSA 6:12; "a profound estrangement, cooling down, sobering up against everything timely, of the time: and as the greatest wish the eye of *Zarathustra*, an eye that looks over the whole fact of humankind from tremendous distance, — sees it *below* . . ."). And in the most compact possible condensation of Nietzsche's philosophy, the section "Wie die 'wahre Welt' endlich zur Fabel wurde" ("How the 'Real World' finally became a Fable") in *Götzen-Dämmerung* (*Twilight of the Idols*), just ten steps take us from Plato to INCIPIT ZARATHUSTRA (KSA 6:80–81). Of the many eulogies to *Zarathustra*, particularly the account of its composition, of those in *Ecce Homo* we have already made repeated mention in chapter 2, and Nietzsche's final work, the *Dionysos-Dithyramben*, represents an elaboration of the Dionysian imagery already found in *Zarathustra*,[60] as well as the final appearance on the pages of Nietzsche's philosophy of Zarathustra, at once mysterious — "Wer sind mir Vater und Mutter? / Ist nicht mir Vater Prinz Überfluss / und Mutter das stille Lachen? / Erzeugte nicht dieser Beiden Ehebund / mich Räthselthier, / mich Lichtunhold, / mich Verschwender aller Weisheit Zarathustra?" (KSA 6:407; "Who are my father and mother? / Is my father not Prince Abundance / and my mother silent laughter? Did the marriage of these two not engender / the enigmatic beast I am, / the demon of light I am, / the squanderer of wisdom I am, Zarathustra?")— and powerful— "Oh Zarathustra! . . . / *Selbstkenner!* . . . / *Selbsthenker!* . . ." (KSA 6:392; "O Zarathustra! . . . / *Self-knower!* . . . / *Self-hangman!* . . .")— and terrifying— "Wo Hass und Blitzstrahl / Eins ward, ein *Fluch* —, / auf den Bergen haust jetzt Zarathustra's Zorn, / eine Wetterwolke schleicht er seines Wegs" (KSA 6:402; "Where hate and lightning / Become one, a *curse* —, / on the mountains Zarathustra's wrath makes now its home, / a thundercloud he slinks along his path")— as well as eccentric— "Zarathustra ist kein Igel" (KSA 6:407; "Zarathustra is not a hedgehog")— and, above all, intensely moving: "Schild der Nothwendigkeit! / Höchstes Gestirn des Seins! / — das kein Wunsch erreicht, / das kein Nein befleckt, / ewiges Ja des Sein's, / ewig bin ich dein Ja: / *denn ich liebe dich, oh Ewigkeit!* — —" (KSA 6:405; "Sign of Necessity! / Highest star of Being! / — that no wish reaches, / that no denial defiles, / eternal Yes of Being, / eternally I am your Yes: / *for I love you, O eternity!* — —").

Notes

[1] Compare with Nietzsche's description in *Ecce Homo* of *Zur Genealogie der Moral* (*On the Genealogy of Morals,* 1887): "Jedes Mal ein Anfang, der irre führen *soll,* kühl, wissenschaftlich, ironisch selbst, absichtlich Vordergrund, absichtlich hinhaltend. Allmählich mehr Unruhe; vereinzeltes Wetterleuchten; sehr unangenehme Wahrheiten aus der Ferne her mit dumpfem Gebrumm laut werdend, — bis endlich ein tempo feroce erreicht ist, wo Alles mit ungeheurer Spannung vorwärts treibt. Am Schluss jedes Mal, unter vollkommen schauerlichen Detonationen, eine *neue* Wahrheit zwischen dicken Wolken sichtbar" (KSA 6:352; "Every time a beginning that is *meant* to mislead, cool, scientific, even ironic, deliberately foreground, deliberately holding off. Gradually, more unrest; sporadic lightning; very unpleasant truths in the distance with low grumbling becoming louder, — until finally a *tempo feroce* is reached, in which everything drives forward with tremendous tension. At the end, every time, amid absolutely terrifying detonations, a *new* truth becomes visible among thick clouds").

[2] Compare Goethe's *Maximen und Reflexionen,* no. 416 (HA 12:414; in English, *Johann Wolfgang von Goethe: Maxims and Reflexions,* trans. Elizabeth Stopp, ed. Peter Hutchinson [London: Penguin, 1998], 51). For further discussion, see R. H. Stephenson, *Goethe's Conception of Knowledge and Science* (Edinburgh: Edinburgh UP, 1995), 15–17.

[3] Compare with Nietzsche's letter of 1 May 1883 to the Swiss novelist Gottfried Keller (1819–90), where he promises to send him a copy of *Zarathustra:* "Seltsam! Aus einem wahren *Abgrunde* von Gefühlen, in die mich dieser Winter, der gefährlichste meines Lebens, geworfen hatte, erhob ich mich mit Einem Male und war zehn Tage lang wie unter dem hellsten Himmel und hoch auch über hohen Bergen" (KSB 6:372; "It's odd! From a real *abyss* of feelings, into which this winter, the most dan-

gerous of my whole life, had pushed me, I rose up all at once and was for ten days as if under the brightest sky and high above even the high mountains").

[4] The following sources have been used in preparing this appendix: the KSA (especially the "Chronik zu Nietzsches Leben" in vol. 15), the KSB (especially vols. 6 and 7); Curt Paul Janz, *Friedrich Nietzsche: Biographie,* 3 vols (Munich and Vienna: Hanser, 1978), vol. 2, *Die zehn Jahre des freien Philosophen;* David Farrell Krell and Donald L. Bates, *The Good European: Nietzsche's Work Sites in Word and Image* (Chicago and London: U of Chicago P, 1997); and Raymond J. Benders, Stephan Oettermann et al., *Friedrich Nietzsche: Chronik in Bildern und Texten* (Munich and Vienna: Hanser/dtv, 2000).

[5] For example, the dream in "Der Wahrsager" ("The Prophet"; KSA 4:173–74) recalls a dream experienced by Nietzsche the summer of 1877 (compare KSA 14:306) and subsequently treated in the *Nachlass* (23[197]; KSA 8:474, and 10[10]; KSA 10:368–69).

[6] In *Ueber naïve und sentimentalische Dichtung* (1796), Schiller develops the idea of art as a "second nature": "Geht man jene drey Begriffe nach den Kategorien durch, so wird man die Natur und die ihr entsprechende naive Stimmung immer in der ersten, die Kunst als Aufhebung der Natur durch den frey wirkenden Verstand immer in der zweyten, endlich das Ideal, in welchem die vollendete Kunst zur Natur zurückkehrt, in der dritten Kategorie antreffen" (NA 20:473; "If one goes through the three concepts according to the categories, then one will always find nature, and the naïve mood which corresponds to it, in the first, art as the suspension of nature through the reason working freely in the second, and finally the ideal in which a perfected art returns to nature in the third category"; Schiller, *On the Naïve and Sentimental in Literature,* trans. Helen Watanabe-O'Kelly [Manchester: Carcarnet New P, 1981], 104). See also Goethe's maxim: "Kunst: eine andere Natur, auch geheimnisvoll, aber verständlicher; denn sie entspringt aus dem Verstande" (*Maximen und Reflexionen,* no. 1105; HA 12:467; "Art: a second nature, also mysterious, but more intelligible; for it arises from the understanding").

[7] Compare with Nietzsche's letter to Erwin Rohde of December 1882: "Ich habe eine 'zweite Natur,' aber nicht um die erste zu vernichten, sondern um sie zu *ertragen.* An meiner 'ersten Natur' wäre ich längst zu Grunde gegangen — war ich beinahe zu Grunde gegangen" (KSB 6:291; "I have a 'second nature,' but not to destroy the first, rather to make it *bearable.* My 'first nature' would have destroyed me long ago — it did almost destroy me").

[8] Plato, *Symposium* 206 b (see Plato, *The Symposium,* trans. Christopher Gill (Harmondsworth: Penguin, 1999), 43. As Diotima goes on to tell Socrates, "the object of love is not beauty," but "reproduction and birth in beauty" (206 e; 44). For further discussion, see the sections "Psychical Intercourse" and "True Pregnancies and Ultimate Issues" in Graham Parkes, *Composing the Soul: Reaches of Nietzsche's Psychology* (Chicago and London: U of Chicago P, 1994), 231–47. See also *M* §552 (KSA 3:322–23) and *FW* §72 (KSA 3:430).

[9] See his letter to Franz Overbeck of 7 April 1884 (KSB 6:496); and compare his description of *Morgenröte* and *Die fröhliche Wissenschaft* as "Einleitungen und Commentare zu meinem Zarathustra" ("introductions to and commentaries on my Zarathustra") in his letter to Resa von Schirnhofer of early May 1884 (KSB 6:502).

[10] See Nietzsche's letters of 14 February 1883 to Köselitz, of 21 February 1883 to Malwida von Meysenbug, and of 27 April 1883 to Köselitz (KSB 6:329–30, 334–36 and 367).

[11] For further discussion of the motif of Zarathustra as Nietzsche's "son," and its implications for the relation between the literary figure and its author, see Janz, *Friedrich Nietzsche: Biographie*, 2:244–45.

[12] Ida Overbeck, "Erinnerungen von Frau Ida Overbeck," in Carl Albrecht Bernoulli, *Franz Overbeck und Friedrich Nietzsche: Eine Freundschaft*, 2 vols., 1:234–351; here, 336 (Jena: E. Diederichs, 1908); cited in Benders and Oettermann, *Chronik*, 540.

[13] See Lou Andreas-Salomé, *Nietzsche in seinen Werken*, ed. Thomas Pfeiffer (1894: repr. Frankfurt am Main and Leipzig: Insel, 2000).

[14] See Krell and Bates, *The Good European*, 187–89. Nietzsche added the detail that the German Emperor Frederick III visited the area when Nietzsche was there again in 1886 (see Walter Kaufmann's note in *Basic Writings of Nietzsche*, 753–54).

[15] Compare with the comment in his letter to Franz Overbeck of 18 August 1884 (KSB 6:520; see quotation later in this chapter); in the *Nachlass* for Spring-Summer 1888: "Der Goldmacher ist der einzige wahre *Wohlthäter* der Menschheit. [. . .] Denken wir einen extremen Fall: daß es etwas am meisten Gehaßtes, Verurtheiltes gäbe — und daß gerade das in Gold verwandelt werde: Das ist mein Fall . . ." (16[43]; KSA 13:501; "The gold maker is the single true *benefactor* of humanity. [. . .] Let us consider an extreme case: that there is something that is hated, condemned the most — and that precisely this is transformed into gold: this is my case . . ."); and in his letter to Georg Brandes of 23 May 1888 (KSB 8:318). For further discussion of alchemical imagery in Nietzsche's writings, see Richard Perkins, "Nietzsche's *opus alchymicum*," *Seminar* 23 (1987): 216–26; and Parkes, *Composing the Soul*, 133–34, 141, 158, 166 and 418.

[16] In terms of genre, Nietzsche described it to Overbeck as "mein Testament," "eine Dichtung und keine Aphorismen-Sammlung" (10 February 1883; KSB 6:326; "my testament," "a work of literature and not a collection of aphorisms").

[17] Nietzsche also had strict conceptions about the appearance of the book: "Nur muß ich diesmal auf zwei Äußerlichkeiten besonderen Werth legen, weil dieses Buch als eine Spitze meiner bisherigen Bücher erscheinen soll. Bei ganz gleichem Formate und Drucke bitte ich um eine schwarze Linie, welche den Text jeder Seite einfaßt: so ist es einer Dichtung würdiger. Und dann: ein *stärkeres* Velin!" (KSB 6:328; "This time I must emphasize two external aspects, because this book should appear as the pinnacle of my previous books. With the same format and type I would like to request a black line that surrounds the text on all pages: this is more worthy of a work of literature. And then: a *stronger* vellum!").

[18] "Das erinnert mich an meine letzte Thorheit, ich meine den 'Zarathustra' (Ist es jetzt deutlich zu lesen? Ich schreibe wie ein Schwein) Es passirt mir alle Paar Tage, daß ich es vergesse; ich bin neugierig, ob es *irgend einen* Werth hat — ich selber bin in diesem Winter unfähig des Urtheils und könnte mich im allergröbsten Sinne über Werth und Unwerth täuschen" (KSB 6:348; "That reminds me of my most recent folly, I mean 'Zarathustra' (can you read my writing now? I write like a pig) It happens every couple of days that I forget it; I am curious whether it has *any value at*

all — this winter I myself am incapable of judgment and could be mistaken in the grossest possible way about value and lack of value").

[19] Compare with Nietzsche's comments in his letter of 27 April 1883 to Heinrich Köselitz: "Je mehr man *mich vergißt*, um so besser hat es mein Sohn, als welcher heißt Zarathustra" (KSB 6:367; "The more people *forget me*, the better it is for my son, who is called Zarathustra"); that of 28 May 1883 to Marie Baumgartner (KSA 6:381); that of 9 July 1883 to Franz Overbeck (KSB 6:393); that of 22 May 1884 to Heinrich von Stein: "das Gesetz, das über mir ist, meine **Aufgabe**, läßt mir keine Zeit dafür [= nach Bayreuth zu gehen]. Mein Sohn Zarathustra mag Ihnen verrathen haben, *was* sich in mir bewegt; und wenn ich Alles von mir erlange, *was ich will*, so werde ich mit dem Bewußtsein sterben, daß künftige Jahrtausende auf meinen Namen ihre höchsten Gelübde thun" (KSB 6:508; "the law that is over me, my **task**, leaves me no time for going to Bayreuth. My son Zarathustra may have given away to you *what* is going on in me; and when I achieve *everything I want*, then I will die knowing that future millennia will take their highest vows on my name"; compare his letter to Malwida von Meysenbug of early June 1884: "Was ich *will*, das wird Ihnen mein Sohn Zarathustra zwar nicht sagen, aber zu *rathen* aufgeben; vielleicht ist es zu errathen" [KSB 6:509–10; "What I *want* my son Zarathustra will, it's true, not tell you, but allow you to guess; perhaps it can be guessed at"]); that of 12 July 1884 to Overbeck: "Ich habe meinen Tröster und Zusprecher bei mir — meinen Sohn Zarathustra. Wenn Du in die Ferien gehst, nimm ihn mit Dir: ich möchte, daß Du Dich auch davon überzeugtest, daß ich mit diesem Buche alles *überwunden* habe, was je in Worten gesagt worden ist, und daß dies noch nicht einmal sein größtes Verdienst ist" (KSB 6:511; "I have my comforter and encourager with me — my son Zarathustra. When you go on holiday, take it with you: I would like you too to convince yourself that with this book I have *overcome* everything that has ever been said in words, and that this is not even its greatest merit"); and that of 1 September 1884 to von Meysenbug (KSB 6:522).

[20] For further discussion, see Philip Grundlehner, *The Poetry of Friedrich Nietzsche* (New York and Oxford: Oxford UP, 1986), 120–22.

[21] See Goethe's second "Wanderers Nachtlied" ("Wanderer's Night Song," 1776), which begins: "Der du von dem Himmel bist" (HA 1:142; "Thou that from the heavens art"; Johann Wolfgang von Goethe, *Selected Poems*, ed. Christopher Middleton, Goethe Edition, 1 [Boston: Suhrkamp/Insel, 1983], 58–59).

[22] See *FW* §268 and §373 (KSA 3:268 and 625); in the poem "Sanctus Januarius" the opening four lines (quoted above from his letter to Köselitz of 6 April 1883), about which Nietzsche commented in *Ecce Homo* as follows: "Was hier 'höchste Hoffnung' heisst, wer kann darüber im Zweifel sein, der als Schluss des vierten Buchs die diamentene Schönheit der ersten Worte des Zarathustra aufglänzen sieht? — Oder der die granitnen Sätze am Ende des dritten Buchs liest, mit denen sich ein Schicksal *für alle Zeiten* zum ersten Male in Formeln fasst?" (*EH FW;* KSA 6:333; "What is here called 'highest hope,' who can have any doubt about it when he sees, as the conclusion to the fourth book, the diamond beauty of the first words of Zarathustra begin to gleam? — Or when he reads at the end of the third book the granite sentences, in which for the first time a destiny *for all time* is expressed in wording?").

[23] Compare the opening of "Vom Lesen und Schreiben" ("On Reading and Writing"): "Von allem Geschriebenen liebe ich nur Das, was Einer mit seinem Blute schreibt. Schreibe mit Blut: und du wirst erfahren, dass Blut Geist ist" (*Z* I 7; KSA 4:48; "Of all that is written I only love what someone writes with his blood. Write with blood: and you will discover that blood is spirit").

[24] The background to these remarks is formed by his disagreements with his mother and sister; the rumor, spread by Wagner, about Nietzsche's homosexuality (for further discussion, see Joachim Köhler, *Friedrich Nietzsche und Cosima Wagner: Die Schule der Unterwerfung* [Reinbek bei Hamburg: Rowohlt, 1998], 160); and the disregard for his work shown in university circles, particularly in Basel.

[25] See his letter of 10 May 1883 to Köselitz (KSB 6:375); and that of 13 May 1883 to Franziska Nietzsche (KSB 6:375).

[26] This statement stands in contradiction to his claims, repeated here in *Ecce Homo*, that part 2 of *Zarathustra*, like parts 1 and 3, was written within just ten days (*EH Z* §4; KSA 6:341). For drafts of "Das Nachtlied," see 9[53], 13[1] and 13[9]; KSA 10:363, 426 and 458.

[27] See his letters of 21 June 1883 to Franziska Nietzsche and that of early July 1883 to Elisabeth Nietzsche (KSB 6:384 and 390).

[28] See Nietzsche's letter of 1 July 1883 to Köselitz (KSB 6:388) and that of 9 July 1883 to Franz Overbeck (KSB 6:393).

[29] The "club foot" was the name Nietzsche gave to his heavy case of books (see Elisabeth Förster-Nietzsche, *Das Leben Friedrich Nietzsche's*, 2 vols. in 3 (Leipzig: C. G. Naumann, 1904), 2.2:433).

[30] See Nietzsche's comments in his letters of 26 August 1883 to Heinrich Köselitz and to Franz Overbeck (KSB 6:435–36 and 438). The article to which Nietzsche refers has not been identified (see Friedrich Nietzsche/Franz and Ida Overbeck, *Briefwechsel*, ed. Katrin Meyer and Barbara von Reibnitz (Stuttgart and Weimar: Metzler, 2000), 478).

[31] For publication details, see Benders and Oettermann, *Chronik*, 566.

[32] Compare with his remark, "Mihi ipsi scripsi" ("I wrote for myself"), after the completion of the manuscript of *Die fröhliche Wissenschaft* (letter to Paul Rée of 10 June 1882; KSB 6:202).

[33] The chapter entitled "Von alten und neuen Tafeln" ("On Old and New Tables") includes the following lines: "Ich schliesse Kreise um mich und heilige Grenzen; immer Wenigere steigen mit mir auf immer höhere Berge, — ich baue ein Gebirge aus immer heiligeren Bergen. —" (*Z* III 12 §19; KSA 4:260; "I draw circles around myself, and sacred boundaries; fewer and fewer people climb with me up ever higher mountains: I am building a mountain range out of ever more sacred mountains"; compare Krell and Bates, *The Good European*, 137 and 188).

[34] See Nietzsche's letters and postcards of late January/early February 1884 to his mother (KSB 6:468), that of 1 February 1884 to Köselitz (KSB 6:472), that of 22 February 1884 to Erwin Rohde (KSB 6:479), that of early March 1884 to Ferdinand Laban (KSB 6:482), and that of 30 March 1884 to Köselitz (KSB 6:491).

³⁵ For further discussion of this poem, see Grundlehner, *The Poetry of Friedrich Nietzsche,* 129–33. As an example of maritime imagery in *Zarathustra,* see the opening of "Vom Gesicht und Räthsel" (set on a boat, as Zarathustra travels away from the blissful islands): "Euch, den kühnen Suchern, Versuchern, und wer je sich mit listigen Segeln auf furchtbare Meere einschiffte, — / euch, den Räthsel-Trunkenen, den Zwielicht-Frohen, deren Seele mit Flöten zu jedem Irr-Schlunde gelockt wird" (*Z* III 2 §1; KSA 4:197; "To you, the bold searchers, researchers, and whoever embarks with cunning sails on terrible seas, — / to you, drunk with riddles, glad of the twilight, whose soul is lured astray with flutes to every whirlpool"). For an exploration of Nietzsche's maritime imagery in general, see Luce Irigaray, *Amante marine: de Friedrich Nietzsche* (Paris: Editions de Minuit, 1980); in English, *Marine Lover of Friedrich Nietzsche,* trans. Gillian C. Gill (New York: Columbia UP, 1991).

³⁶ Compare with Nietzsche's reported remark to Josef Paneth on 29 January 1884: "Zarathustra sei schwer zu verstehen, müsse studiert werden; es sei soviel Didaktisches darin, er sei das Resultat seiner 14jährigen Entwickelung; aus allen Irrthümern und Fehltritten habe er Nutzen gezogen" (Richard Frank Krummel, "Josef Paneth über seine Begegnung mit Nietzsche in der Zarathustra-Zeit," *Nietzsche-Studien* 17 [1988]: 478–95; here, 482; "Zarathustra is difficult to understand and must be studied; there is so much didactic material in it, it is the result of its 14 years of development; he has made use of all his errors and mistakes").

³⁷ For publication details, see Benders and Oettermann, *Chronik,* 574.

³⁸ See, for example, 15[9], 15[37], 15[44], 15[48], 16[55], 16[65–66], 16[84], 17[31], 17[41], 20[10], and 21[3]; KSA 10:481, 489, 491, 491–92, 518, 522–23, 527–28, 549, 551, and 598–600.

³⁹ The *Nachlass* from this period contains many references to plans for a work entitled "Die **ewige Wiederkunft**: *Eine Wahrsagung*" ("The **Eternal Recurrence**: *A Prophecy*"; 25[1]; KSA 11:9; compare 25[6], 25[227], 25[323]; KSA 11:10, 73 and 95), or "Weisheit und Liebe zur Weisheit: Fingerzeige zu einer Philosophie der Zukunft" ("Wisdom and Love of Wisdom: A Pointer to a Philosophy of the Future"; 25[490]; KSA 11:142; compare 25[500]; KSA 11:145).

⁴⁰ Compare with his letter to Malwida von Meysenbug of the beginning of June 1884: "Meine Aufgabe ist ungeheuer; meine Entschlossenheit aber nicht geringer. [. . .] Ich will die Menschheit zu Entschlüssen drängen, welche über die ganze menschliche Zukunft entscheiden, und es *kann* so kommen, daß einmal ganze Jahrtausende auf meinen Namen ihre höchsten Gelübde thun" (KSB 6:509–10; "My task is immense; but my determination is no less . . . I want to urge humankind to decisions that decide about the entire human future, and it *can* come about that entire millennia will come to take their highest vows on my name").

⁴¹ See Nietzsche's letter of 7 April 1884 to Franz Overbeck (KSB 6:494).

⁴² See Nietzsche's letter of 10 April 1884 to Franz Overbeck (KSB 6:496). For publication details, see Benders and Oettermann, *Chronik,* 582–83. Each copy of part 3 was priced at 3.30 Marks.

⁴³ "Ihr *Fehler* ist," Nietzsche commented in parentheses, "daß eigentlich in ihr *nicht* von Schopenhauer, sondern fast nur von mir die Rede ist — aber das wußte ich selber nicht, als ich sie machte" (KSB 6:518; "Its *mistake* is that its content is really *not*

about Schopenhauer but nearly all only about me — only I did not know that myself when I wrote it"). This remark perhaps throws light on a note in the *Nachlass* from Autumn 1883, 17[18]: "In Zarathustra 4 *kein* 'Ich'!" (KSA 10:545; "In Zarathustra 4 no 'I'!"); and compare with the passage in *Ecce Homo* where Nietzsche says of "Richard Wagner in Bayreuth" (1876): "An allen psychologisch entscheidenden Stellen ist nur von mir die Rede" (*EH GT* §4; KSA 6:314; "In all psychologically decisive passages it is really only about me").

[44] Compare with Nietzsche's remark in this same letter to Köselitz: "Ich bin überdies mit der Haupt-Aufgabe dieses Sommers, wie ich sie mir vorgestellt hatte, im Ganzen *fertig* geworden — die nächsten 6 Jahren gehören der Ausarbeitung eines Schema's an, mit welchem ich meine 'Philosophie' umrissen habe" (KSB 6:525; "Moreover, I have entirely *finished* with the main task of this summer, which I had set myself — the next 6 years will be devoted to working out the details with which I have outlined my 'philosophy'"). Earlier, in his letter to Overbeck of 7 April 1884, he had written: "Ich muß jetzt Schritt für Schritt durch eine ganze Reihe von Disciplinen hindurch, denn ich habe mich nunmehr entschlossen, die nächsten fünf Jahre zur Ausarbeitung meiner 'Philosophie' zu verwenden, für welche ich mir, durch meinen Zarathustra, eine Vorhalle gebaut habe" (KSB 6:496; "I must now work through a whole range of disciplines, for I have henceforth decided to use the next five years for working out the details of my 'philosophy,' for which, with my Zarathustra, I have built an entrance hall"). The image of the "entrance hall" recalls the title of *Die Propyläen* (*The Propylaeum* = "The Gateway"), the journal founded by Goethe in 1798 in order to propagate his aesthetic values. In his *Nachlass* for 1871 (9[85]; KSA 7:305), Nietzsche notes the passage in the "Einleitung in die 'Propyläen'" ("Introduction to the *Propylaea*") where Goethe wrote: "Der Jüngling, wenn Natur und Kunst ihn anziehen, glaubt mit einem lebhaften Streben bald in das innerste Heiligtum zu dringen; der Mann bemerkt, nach langem Umherwandeln, daß er sich noch immer in den Vorhöfen befinde" (HA 12:38; "A young man who feels attracted to nature and art expects, by striving vigorously, to gain immediate entrance to the inner sanctum. As an adult he discovers that after a long and arduous pilgrimage he is still in the vestibule"; in English, Johann Wolfgang von Goethe, *Essays on Art and Literature,* ed. John Gearey, trans. Ellen von Nardroff and Ernest H. von Nardroff, Goethe's Collected Works, vol. 3 [New York: Suhrkamp, 1986], 78). Nietzsche's statement, however, stands in apparent tension with his earlier claims that, with *Zarathustra,* his philosophy had received its final statement (letter to Carl von Gersdorff, June 1883; KSB 6:386).

[45] See 29[66], 31[30], 34[78], 34[145], 34[191], and 35[39–41]; KSA 11:352, 367–70, 443–44, 468, 485–86, and 528; and also 2[72]; KSA 12:94.

[46] For information about the later legal wranglings with Schmeitzner, see Nietzsche's letters of 4–11 December 1884 to Franziska and Elisabeth Nietzsche (KSB 6:568–69); that of 7 May 1885 to Franz Overbeck (KSB 7:46); that of mid-August 1885 to Elisabeth Förster (KSB 7:80–82); that of 7 October 1885 to Franz Overbeck (KSB 7:98–99); and his postcard of 23 October 1885 to Franziska Nietzsche (KSB 7:104).

[47] For the vision of the woman, see the disturbing sketch where Zarathustra is attacked by his animals (in 13[2]; KSA 10:446–47): "Als er aber seine Schlange gegen sich züngeln sah, da verwandelte sich langsam, langsam sein Gesicht:

widerwillig sprang ihm das Thor der Erkenntniß auf: wie ein Blitz flog es hinein in die Tiefen seines Auges und wieder wie ein Blitz: es fehlte noch ein Augenblick, und er hätte gewußt — — Als das Weib diese Verwandlung sah, schrie es auf wie aus der höchsten Noth. 'stirb Zarathustra' — / Mit seiner Linken drängte er den Adler zurück, der gegen ihn mit dem Ungestüm seiner Flügel schlug: er schrie, wie einer der zur Flucht räth; gern hätte er ihn davon getragen. Zu seiner Rechten auf dem Tische die Felsplatte" ("When, however, he saw his snake darting its tongue at him, then his face slowly, slowly altered: unwillingly the door of knowledge sprang open for him: like a bolt of lightning it flew into the depths of his eyes and again like a bolt of lightning: only one more moment was still needed, and he would have known — — When the woman saw this transformation, she cried as out of the greatest distress. 'Die, Zarathustra' — / With his left hand he pushed away the eagle, which was striking against him with the impetuousness of its wings; it cried, like someone urging escape; it would have liked to carry him away from there. To his right on the table the mountain slab").

[48] Compare 31[30] (KSA 11:367); and compare in part 4 the idea of Zarathustra's "letzte Sünde" ("last sin"; Z IV 2 and 20; KSA 4:301 and 408). When, on 8 January 1888, he sent a copy of part 4 to Georg Brandes, he called it *"Die Versuchung Zarathustra's:* Ein Zwischenspiel," describing it as "ein ineditum von mir, das zum Persönlichsten gehört, was ich vermag" (KSB 8:228; "an unpublished work by me, which is one of the most personal things I have written").

[49] Compare with fragments 29[26], 29[32], 31[2], 31[9–11], and 39[22]; KSA 11:343, 344, 359–60, 361–64, and 628.

[50] See fragments 29[23], 29[63], 31[2], 31[8–9], 31[11], 32[16], 29[24], and 31[10]; KSA 11:342, 350–51, 359–60, 361–62, 363–64, 415–16, 342–43, and 362–63.

[51] "Der Wahrheit Freier? Sahst du ihn?
  Still, starr, kalt, glatt,
  Zum Bilde geworden und zur Säule, aufgestellt
  Vor Tempeln — sprich,
  Deß gelüstet dich?
  Nein, Larven suchst du
  Und Regen-Bogen-Häute
  Wild-Katzen-Muthwillen, der durch Fenster springt,
  hinaus in allen Zufalls Wildniß!
  Nein, Urwald brauchst du,
  deinen Honig zu schlürfen,
  sündlich-gesund und schön
  gleich buntgefleckten Raubthieren"
  (KSA 11:306–7)

  ["The lover of truth? Did you see him?
  Silent, stiff, cold, smooth,
  Become as a painting and a pillar, set up
  In front of temples — say,
  Do you desire that?

No, masks are what you are looking for
And rainbow-pelts
Wild-cat-courage, that jumps through windows,
Out into the wilderness of all chance!
No, what you need is primal forest,
To savour your honey,
Sinfully healthy and beautiful
Like mottled beasts of prey"]

52   "Den Adler seht! sehnsüchtig starr
blickt er hinab in den Abgrund,
in seinen Abgrund, der sich dort
in immer tiefere Tiefen ringelt!
Plötzlich, geraden Flugs,
scharfen Zugs
stürzt er auf seine Beute.
Glaubt ihr wohl, daß es *Hunger* ist?
Eingeweiden-Armut? —
Und auch Liebe ist es nicht
— was ist ein Lamm einem Adler!
Er haß[t] die Schafe
Also stürze ich mich
abwärts, sehnsüchtig,
auf diese Lämmer-Heerden
zerreißend, blutträufend,
Hohn gegen die Gemächlichen
Wuth gegen Lämmer-Dummheit — — —"
                                    (KSA 11:304)

["Look at the eagle! fixed with yearning
he gazes into the abyss,
into his abyss, which curls downwards
Into deeper and deeper depths!
Suddenly, mid-flight
In a stroke
It attacks its prey.
Do you really think, that it is *hunger*?
Poverty of the guts? —
And nor is it love
— what does a lamb mean to an eagle!
it hate{s} the sheep
Thus I plunge
downwards, desirous,
on to this herd of sheep
ripping, dripping with blood,
Scorn for those at peace
Fury at the stupidity of lambs — — —"]

53 "[. . .] Ich liege still,
ausgestreckt,
Halbtodtem gleich, dem man die Füße wärmt
— die Käfer fürchten sich vor meinem Schweigen
— ich warte

Alles heiße ich gut
Laub und Gras, Glück, Segen und Regen"
(KSA 11:310)

[". . . I lie still,
Stretched out,
Like one half-dead, whose feet one warms
— the beetles are afraid of my silence
— I am waiting

I approve of everything
Leaves and grass, happiness, blessing and rain"]

54 "Oh die ihr spielt,
Ihr Kinder im Walde, ihr lachenden,
Flieht nicht davon — nein! schützt mich,
Versteckt das gehetzte Wild,
Bleibt, hört! Denn was mich hetzt,
seit grauem Morgen durch alle Irrniß hetzt,
sind's Jäger? Wegelagerer? sind's Gedanken?
Nicht weiß ich's noch,
doch Kinder sehen
und Kinderspiele — — —"
(KSA 11:315)

["Oh all you who are playing,
You children in the wood, you who laugh,
Don't run away — no! protect me,
Hide the hounded creature,
Stay, listen! For what is hounding me,
since the grey morning hounding me through all erroneousness,
are they hunters? highwaymen? are they thoughts?
Still I do not know,
But children look
And children's games — — —"]

55 See his letter of 9 December 1888 to Köselitz: "Jetzt eine *ernste* Sache. Lieber Freund, ich will *alle* Exemplare des *vierten* Zarathustra wieder zurückhaben, um dies ineditum gegen alle Zufälle von Leben und Tod sicher zu stellen (— ich las es dieser Tage und bin fast umgekommen vor Bewegung). Wenn ich es nach ein Paar Jahrzehnten welthistorischer Krisen — *Kriege!* — herausgeben werde, so wird es die *rechte* Zeit sein" (KSB 8:514–15; "Now for a serious matter. Dear friend, I want to have *all* copies of the fourth Zarathustra back, to protect this *ineditum* against all chances of life and death (— I have been reading it recently and have almost died of

emotion). When I issue it after a few decades of world-historical crises — *wars!* — then that will be the *right* time").

[56] For publication details, see Benders and Oettermann, *Chronik,* 610.

[57] According to an account in the Köselitz-*Nachlass,* Nietzsche had rented a room in a house belonging to a prostitute: "Teufel auch, zur Feier von Zarathustra's Fertigwerden bei einer putana veneziana wohnen, das ist toll!" (cited in *Chronik,* 610; "Damn it all! to be celebrating the completion of Zarathustra when living in the house of a Venetian prostitute, that is something!").

[58] Two — rare — examples of Nietzsche returning to the concept of Zarathustra in the notes from the *Nachlass* from Autumn 1885 to Autumn 1886 are the draft titles "*Halkyonische Zwischenreden. Zur Erholung von* 'Also sprach Zarathustra' *seinen Freunden gewidmet*" ("*Halcyon Entre'actes.* As a Relaxation after 'Thus spoke Zarathustra' dedicated to his friends"; 2[4]; KSA 12:68), and "**Die ewige Wiederkunft**. Zarathustrische Tänze und Umzüge: *Erster Theil: Gottes Todtenfest*" ("**The Eternal Recurrence**. Zarathustrian Dance and Processions: *First Part: God's Memorial Service*"; 2[129]; KSA 12:128–29).

[59] "Dem letztveröffentlichten '*Jenseits von Gut und Böse*' zur Ergänzung und Verdeutlichung beigegeben" (KSA 14:377; "A sequel to my last book '*Beyond Good and Evil,*' intended as its Supplement and Clarification").

[60] For a discussion of this Dionysian imagery, see Laurence Lampert, *Nietzsche's Teaching: An Interpretation of "Thus Spoke Zarathustra"* (New Haven and London: Yale UP, 1986), 227–34 and 242–43.

Bibliography

Abrams, M. H. "Kant and the Theology of Art." *Notre Dame English Journal,* vol. 3, no. 3 (Summer, 1981): 75–106.

———. *Natural Supernaturalism: Tradition and Revolution in Romantic Literature.* New York: Oxford UP, 1971.

Adorno, Theodor W. *Ästhetische Theorie.* Frankfurt am Main: Suhrkamp, 1970.

———. *Minima Moralia: Reflexionen aus dem beschädigten Leben.* Frankfurt am Main: Suhrkamp, 1989. Translated by E. F. N. Jephcott as *Minima Moralia: Reflections from Damaged Life* (London: Verso, 1974).

———. *Negative Dialektik.* Frankfurt am Main: Suhrkamp, 1966.

Adorno, Theodor W., and Max Horkheimer. *Dialektik der Aufklärung: Philosophische Fragmente.* Frankfurt am Main: Fischer, 1988.

Alexander, Samuel. *Beauty and Other Forms of Value.* London: Macmillan, 1933.

Allison, David B., ed. *The New Nietzsche: Contemporary Styles of Interpretation.* Cambridge, MA and London: MIT Press, 1985.

Andreas-Salomé, Lou. *Lebensrückblick.* Edited by Ernst Pfeiffer. Frankfurt am Main: Insel-Verlag, 1974.

———. *Nietzsche in seinen Werken.* Edited by Thomas Pfeiffer. Frankfurt am Main and Leipzig: Insel, 2000.

Anglet, Andreas. *Der "ewige" Augenblick: Studien zur Struktur und Funktion eines Denkbildes bei Goethe.* Cologne, Weimar, and Vienna: Böhlau, 1991.

Archilochos et al. *Archilochos, Sappho, Alkman: Three Lyric Poets of the Late Greek Bronze Age.* Translated by Guy Davenport. Berkeley, Los Angeles, London: U of California P, 1980.

Archiloque. *Fragments.* Edited by François Lasserre. Translated by André Bonnard. Paris: Les Belles lettres, 1958.

Arnheim, Rudolf. Review of E. H. Gombrich, *Art and Illusion: A Study in the Psychology of Pictorial Representations* (London: Phaidon Press, 1960). *Art Bulletin* 44 (1962): 75–79.

Ashton, Rosemary. *The German Idea: Four English Writers and the Reception of German Thought 1800–1860.* Cambridge: Cambridge UP, 1980.

Atkins, Stuart. "The Mothers, the Phorcides and the Cabiri in Goethes Faust." *Monatshefte* 45 (1953): 289–96.

Bahr, Ehrhard. *Die Ironie im Spätwerk Goethes: "Diese sehr ernsten Scherze":* *Studien zum West-östlichen Divan, zu den Wanderjahren und zu Faust II.* Berlin: Erich Schmidt Verlag, 1972.

Baudrillard, Jean. *Selected Writings.* Edited by Mark Poster. Cambridge: Polity P, 1988.

Behler, Ernst. "Nietzsche und die romantische Metapher von der Kunst als Spiel." In *Echoes and Influences of German Romanticism: Essays in Honour of Hans Eichner,* edited by Michael S. Batts, Anthony W. Riley, and Heinz Wetzel, 11–28. New York, Bern, Frankfurt am Main: Peter Lang, 1987.

Beiser, Frederick. *The Fate of Reason: German Philosophy from Kant to Fichte.* Cambridge, MA and London: Harvard UP, 1987.

Benders, Raymond J., Stephan Oettermann, Hauke Reich, Sibylle Spiegel. *Friedrich Nietzsche: Chronik in Bildern und Texten.* Munich and Vienna: Hanser/dtv, 2000.

Bennett, Benjamin. "Nietzsche's Idea of Myth: The Birth of Tragedy from the Spirit of Eighteenth-Century Aesthetics." *Publications of the Modern Languages Association* 94 (1979): 420–33.

Bennholdt-Thomsen, Anke. *Nietzsches "Also sprach Zarathustra" als literarisches Phänomen: Eine Revision.* Frankfurt am Main: Athenäum Verlag, 1974.

Berghahn, Klaus L. "Das Andere der Klassik: Von der 'Klassiker-Legende' zur jüngsten Klassik-Diskussion." *Goethe-Yearbook* 6 (1992): 1–27.

Berman, Marshall. *All That Is Solid Melts Into Air: The Experience of Modernity.* New York: Viking Penguin, 1988.

Bernoulli, Carl Albrecht. *Franz Overbeck und Friedrich Nietzsche: Eine Freundschaft.* 2 vols. Jena: E. Diederichs, 1908.

Bieling, Alexander, ed. *Gottscheds Reineke Fuchs.* Halle: Max Niemeyer, 1886.

Birrell, Frances. "'Abenteuerlich mißverstanden'? Habermas's Reception and Interpretation of Schiller." *German Life and Letters* 49 (1996): 297–310.

———. "An Investigation of the Theoretical Insights of Jürgen Habermas in Relation to the Aesthetic Writings of Friedrich Schiller." Diss., University of Strathclyde, 1997.

Bishop, Paul. *The Dionysian Self: C. G. Jung's Reception of Nietzsche.* Berlin and New York: Walter de Gruyter, 1995.

———. "Estrangement from the Deed and the Memory Thereof: Freud and Jung on the Pale Criminal in Nietzsche's *Zarathustra*." *Orbis Litterarum* 54 (1999): 424–38.

———. "An Herderian Perspective on Lacanian Psychoanalysis." *History of European Ideas* 26 (2000): 1–18.

———. "Sincerity." In *The Encyclopaedia of Literary Critics and Criticism,* edited by Chris Murray and Frank Northen Magill.

————. "Social Critique and Aesthetics in Schopenhauer." *History of European Ideas* 29 (2003): 411–35.

————. *Synchronicity and Intellectual Intuition in Kant, Swedenborg, and Jung.* Lewiston, NY, Queenston, ON, and Lampeter, Wales: Edwin Mellen, 2000.

————. "'Yonder lies the grave-island, the silent island; yonder, too, are the graves of my youth': A Commentary on Zarathustra's Grave-Song." *Orbis Litterarum* 57 (2002): 317–42.

Bishop, Paul, ed. *A Companion to Goethe's "Faust": Parts I and II.* Rochester, NY and Woodbridge, UK: Camden House, 2001.

————, ed. *Nietzsche and Antiquity: His Reaction and Response to the Classical Tradition.* Rochester, NY and Woodbridge, UK: Camden House, 2004.

Blasche, Siegfried. "'Hegelianismen im Umfeld von Nietzsches 'Geburt der Tragödie.'" *Nietzsche-Studien* 15 (1986): 59–71.

Bohrer, Karl Heinz. *Plötzlichkeit: Zum Augenblick des ästhetischen Scheins.* Frankfurt am Main: Suhrkamp, 1981.

Borchmeyer, Dieter. *Weimarer Klassik: Portrait einer Epoche.* Weinheim: Beltz Athenäum, 1994.

Bowie, Andrew. *Schelling and Modern European Philosophy: An Introduction.* London: Routledge, 1993.

Bradley, Marshall Carl. "Nietzsche's Critique of Pure Reason: With a Nietzschean Critique of Parsifal." *Neophilologus* 72 (1988): 394–403.

Bräutigam, Bernd. *Reflexion des Schönen — schöne Reflexion: Überlegungen zur Prosa ästhetischer Theorie — Hamann, Nietzsche, Adorno.* Bonn: Bouvier, 1975.

Breton, André. *Oeuvres complètes.* Edited by Marguerite Bonnet. 3 vols. Paris: Gallimard, 1988–1999.

Bruns, Friedrich. "Die Mütter in Goethes 'Faust': Versuch einer Deutung." *Monatshefte* 43 (1951): 364–89.

Bullough, Edward. *Aesthetics: Lectures and Essays.* Edited by Elizabeth M. Wilkinson. Stanford, CA: Stanford UP, 1957.

Bürger, Peter. "Zum Problem des ästhetischen Scheins in der idealistischen Ästhetik." In Willi Oelmüller, *Ästhetischer Schein,* 34–50.

Calder, William Musgrave, III. "The Lion Laughed." *Nietzsche-Studien* 14 (1985): 357–59.

Carlyle, Thomas. *Critical and Miscellaneous Essays.* 7 vols. London: Chapman and Hall, 1872.

————. *The Works in Thirty Volumes.* London: Chapman and Hall, 1841.

Cassirer, Ernst. *Freiheit und Form: Studien zur deutschen Geistesgeschichte.* Berlin: Bruno Cassirer, 1916.

————. *Goethe-Vorlesungen.* Edited by John M. Krois. Hamburg: Felix Meiner, 2003. Volume 2 of *Nachgelassene Manuskripte und Texte.* Edited by John M. Krois and Oswald Schwemmer.

Cauchi, Francesca. "Figures of *Funambule:* Nietzsche's Parable of the Rope-dancer." *Nietzsche-Studien* 23 (1994): 42–64.

Cirlot, J. E. *A Dictionary of Symbols.* Translated by Jack Sage. London: Routledge and Kegan Paul, 1967.

Clegg, Jerry S. "Nietzsche's Gods in *The Birth of Tragedy.*" *Journal of the History of Ideas* 10 (1972): 431–38.

Coleridge, Samuel Taylor. *Biographia Literaria.* Edited by John Shawcross. 2 vols. Oxford: Clarendon, 1907.

————. *The Notebooks of Samuel Taylor Coleridge.* Edited by Kathleen Coburn. 4 vols. London: Routledge and Kegan Paul, 1957.

Conrad, Joseph. *Heart of Darkness.* Harmondsworth: Penguin, 1986.

Cysarz, Herbert. "Schiller und Nietzsche," *Jahrbuch des Freien Deutschen Hochstifts* 1927: 121–50.

Danto, Arthur. *Nietzsche as Philosopher.* New York: Columbia UP, 1980.

Simpson, David, ed. *German Aestheic and Literary Criticism: Kant, Fichte, Schelling, Schopenhauer, Hegel.* Cambridge: Cambridge UP, 1984.

De Man, Paul. *The Rhetoric of Romanticism.* New York: Columbia UP, 1984.

————. "The Rhetoric of Temporality." In Charles S. Singleton, ed., *Interpretation: Theory and Practice.* Baltimore: Johns Hopkins UP, 1969. 173–209.

Decher, Friedhelm. "Nietzsches Metaphysik in der 'Geburt der Tragödie' im Verhältnis zur Philosophie Schopenhauers." *Nietzsche-Studien* 14 (1985): 110–25.

Del Caro, Adrian. "Ethical Aesthetic: Schiller and Nietzsche as Critics of the Eighteenth Century." *The Germanic Review* 55 (1980): 55–63.

————. "The Immolation of Zarathustra: A Look at 'The Fire Beacon.'" *Colloquia Germanica* 17 (1984): 251–56.

Derrida, Jacques. *La Vérité en peinture.* Paris: Flammarion, 1978; Translated by Geoff Bennington and Ian McLeod as *The Truth in Painting* (Chicago and London: U of Chicago P, 1987).

Diogenes Laertius. *Leben und Meinungen berühmter Philosophen.* Translated by Otto Apelt and Hans Günter Zekl. Hamburg: Felix Meiner, 1998.

Domin, Hilde, ed. *Doppelinterpretationen.* Frankfurt am Main: Athenäum, 1966.

Duhamel, Roland. *Nietzsches Zarathustra: Mystiker des Nihilismus; Eine Interpretation von Friedrich Nietzsches "Also sprach Zarathustra. Ein Buch für Alle und Keinen."* Würzburg: Königshausen & Neumann, 1991.

Dumont, Jean-Paul, Daniel Delattre, and Jean-Louis Poirier, eds. *Les Présocratiques*. Paris: Gallimard, 1988.

Ellis, John M. *Schiller's "Kalliasbriefe" and the Study of His Aesthetic Theory*. The Hague and Paris: Mouton, 1969.

———. *The Theory of Literary Criticism: A Logical Analysis*. Berkeley, CA: California UP, 1974.

Emerson, Ralph Waldo. *The Conduct of Life*. London: George Routledge & Sons, 1913.

———. *Selected Essays*. New York: Penguin, 1982.

Emrich, Wilhelm. *Die Symbolik von Faust II: Sinn und Vorformen*. Königstein: Athenäum, 1981.

Enders, Carl. *Faust-Studien: Müttermythos und Homunkulus-Allegorie in Goethes Faust*. Bonn: Bouvier, 1948.

Engels, Friedrich. *Deutscher Sozialismus in Versen und Prosa* [1847]. In Karl Marx/Friedrich Engels. *Werke*, 6 vols. Berlin/DDR: Dietz, 1972)

Fleischer, Margot. "Dionysos als Ding an sich: Der Anfang von Nietzsches Philosophie in der ästhetischen Metaphysik der 'Geburt der Tragödie.'" *Nietzsche-Studien* 17 (1988): 74–90.

Förster-Nietzsche, Elisabeth. *Das Leben Friedrich Nietzsche's*. 2 vols. in 3. Leipzig: C. G. Naumann, 1904.

Frederking, Arthur. "Fausts Gang zu den Müttern." *Euphorion* 18 (1911): 422–40.

Freud, Sigmund. *Gesammelte Werke: Chronologisch geordnet*. 19 vols. Frankfurt am Main: S. Fischer, 1962–1987.

Frizen, Werner. "'Von der unbefleckten Erkenntniss': Zu einem Kapitel des *Zarathustra*." *Deutsche Vierteljahrsschrift für Literaturwissenschaft und Geistesgeschichte* 58 (1984): 428–53.

Fuchs, Albert. *Goethe-Studien*. Berlin: Walter de Gruyter, 1968.

Gadamer, Hans-Georg. "Das Drama Zarathustras." *Nietzsche-Studien* 15 (1986): 1–15.

Gasser, Peter. *Rhetorische Philosophie: Leseversuche zum metaphorischen Diskurs in Nietzsches "Also sprach Zarathustra."* Bern, Berlin, Frankfurt am Main: Lang, 1993.

George, Stefan, and Karl Wolfskehl. *Das Jahrhundert Goethes*. Vol. 3 of *Deutsche Dichtung*. Berlin: Georg Bondi, 1910.

Gerhardt, Volker. *Individualität: Das Element der Welt*. Munich: Beck, 2000.

Gilbert, Katherine Everett and Kuhn, Helmut. *A History of Esthetics*. New York: Macmillan, 1939.

Gillespie, Michael Allen. *Nihilism before Nietzsche*. Chicago and London: U of Chicago P, 1995.

Girard, René. *Critiques dans un souterrain*. Paris: Grasset, 1976.

Goebbels. Joseph. *Michael: Ein deutsches Schicksal in Tagebuchblättern*. 6th edition. Munich: Verlag Franz Eber Nachfolger, 1935.

Goethe, Johann Wolfgang von. *Conversations of German Refugees/Wilhelm Meister's Journeyman Years or The Renunciants*. Edited by Jane K. Brown. Translated by Jan van Heurck/Krishna Winston. Goethe Edition, vol. 10. New York: Suhrkamp, 1989.

———. *Conversations of Goethe with Johann Peter Eckermann*. Edited by J. K. Moorhead. Translated by John Oxenford. New York: Da Capo Press, 1998.

———. *Essays on Art and Literature*. Edited by John Gearey. Translated by Ellen von Nardroff and Ernest H. von Nardroff. Goethe Edition, vol. 3. New York: Suhrkamp, 1986.

———. *Faust: A Tragedy*. Norton Critical Edition. Edited by Cyrus Hamlin. Translated by Walter Arndt. 2nd edition. New York and London: W. W. Norton, 2001.

———. *Faust: Part One*. Translated by David Luke. Oxford and New York: Oxford UP, 1987.

———. *Faust: Part Two*. Translated by David Luke. Oxford and New York: Oxford UP, 1994.

———. *From My Life: Poetry and Truth: Parts One to Three*. Edited by Thomas P. Saine and Jeffrey L. Sammons. Translated by Robert R. Heitner. Goethe Edition, vol. 4. New York: Suhrkamp, 1987.

———. *From My Life: Poetry and Truth. Part Four/Campaign in France 1792: Siege of Mainz*. Edited by Thomas P. Saine and Jeffrey L. Sammons. Translated by Robert R. Heitner/Thomas P. Saine. Goethe Edition, vol. 5. New York: Suhrkamp, 1987.

———. *Italian Journey*. Edited by Thomas P. Saine and Jeffrey L. Sammons. Translated by Robert R. Heitner. Goethe Edition, vol. 6. New York: Suhrkamp, 1989.

———. *Maxims and Reflexions*. Translated by Elizabeth Stopp. Edited by Peter Hutchinson. London: Penguin, 1998.

———. *Poems of the West and East: West-Eastern Divan — West-Östlicher Divan: Bi-Lingual Edition of the Complete Poems*. Translated by John Whaley. Bern, Berlin, Frankfurt am Main: Peter Lang, 1998.

———. *Scientific Studies*. Edited and translated by Douglas Miller. Goethe Edition, vol. 12. New York: Suhrkamp, 1988.

———. *Selected Poems*. Edited by Christopher Middleton. Goethe Edition, vol. 1. Boston: Suhrkamp/Insel, 1983.

————. *The Sorrows of Young Werther/Elective Affinities/Novella.* Edited by David E. Wellbery. Translated by Victor Lange and Judith Ryan. Goethe Edition, vol. 11. New York: Suhrkamp, 1988.

————. *Wilhelm Meister's Apprenticeship.* Edited and translated by Eric A. Blackall with Victor Lange. Goethe Edition, vol. 9. New York: Suhrkamp, 1989.

Gombrich, E. H. "The Symbol of the Veil: Psychological Reflections on Schiller's Poetry." In *Freud and the Humanities,* edited by Peregrine Horden, 75–109. London: Duckworth, 1985.

Gooding-Williams, Robert. *Zarathustra's Dionysian Modernism.* Stanford, CA: Stanford UP, 2001.

Gould, Timothy. "What Makes the Pale Criminal Pale: Nietzsche and the Image of the Deed." *Soundings: An Interdisciplinary Journal* 58 (1985): 510–36.

Graham, Ilse. "Geeinte Zwienatur: On the Structure of Goethe's Urfaust." In Magill, *Tradition and Creation,* 131–45.

Gray, Ronald. *Goethe the Alchemist: A Study of Alchemical Symbolism in Goethe's Literary and Scientific Works.* London: Cambridge UP, 1952.

Greenhalgh, Michael. *What is Classicism?* New York: Martin's P, 1990.

Greiner, Bernhard. *Friedrich Nietzsche: Versuch und Versuchung in seinen Aphorismen.* Munich: Wilhelm Fink, 1972.

Groth, H. Miles. "Nietzsche's Ontogenetic Theory of Time: The Riddle of the Laughing Shepherd." *American Imago* 37 (1980): 351–70.

————. "Nietzsche's Zarathustra: His Breakdown." *American Imago* 39 (1982): 1–20.

Grundlehner, Philip. *The Poetry of Friedrich Nietzsche.* New York and Oxford: Oxford UP, 1986.

Habermas, Jürgen. *Kultur und Kritik.* Frankfurt am Main: Suhrkamp, 1973.

————. *Legitimationsprobleme im Spätkapitalismus.* Frankfurt am Main: Suhrkamp, 1973.

————. *Der philosophische Diskurs der Moderne.* Frankfurt am Main: Suhrkamp, 1984.

————. *Theorie des kommunikativen Handelns.* 2 vols. 2nd edition. Frankfurt am Main: Suhrkamp, 1987.

Hadot, Pierre. "'The Present Alone is our Joy': The Meaning of the Present Instant in Goethe and in Ancient Philosophy." *Diogenes* 133 (1986): 60–82.

————. *Zur Idee der Naturgeheimnisse: Beim Betrachten des Widmungsblattes in den Humboldtschen 'Ideen zu einer Geographie der Pflanzen.'* Mainz: Akademie der Wissenschaften und der Literatur; Wiesbaden: Steiner, 1982, 1–33.

Hahn, Karl-Heinz. "Goethes Zeitschrift 'Über Kunst und Altertum.'" *Goethe-Jahrbuch* 92 (1975): 128–39.

Happ, Winfried. *Nietzsches "Zarathustra" als moderne Tragödie*. Frankfurt am Main, Bern, New York: Lang, 1984.

Harris, H. S. *Hegel's Development: Toward the Sunlight, 1770–1801*. Oxford: Clarendon P, 1972.

Heftrich, Eckhard. "Nietzsches Goethe." *Nietzsche-Studien* 16 (1987): 1–20.

Hegel, G. W. F. *Briefe von und an Hegel*. Edited by Johannes Hoffmeister. Vols. 27–30 of *Sämtliche Werke*. Hamburg: Felix Meiner, 1952–1960.

———. *Sämtliche Werke*. Edited by Hermann Glockner. 26 vols. Stuttgart: Fromann, 1927–1930.

———. *Vorlesungen über die Philosophie der Geschichte*. Stuttgart: Reclam, 1997.

Heidegger, Martin. *Holzwege*. Frankfurt am Main: Klostermann, 1950.

———. *Poetry, Language, Thought*. Translated by Albert Hofstadter. New York: Harper and Row, 1971.

———. *Vorträge und Aufsätze*. Pfullingen: Neske, 1954.

———. "Who is Nietzsche's Zarathustra?" Translated by Bernd Magus. In Allison, *The New Nietzsche: Contemporary Styles of Interpretation*, 64–79.

Heller, Erich. *The Artist's Journey into the Interior And Other Essays*. New York: Random House, 1968.

———. *The Importance of Nietzsche*. Chicago and London: U of Chicago P, 1988.

Hemming, Laurence Paul. "Who is Heidegger's Zarathustra?" *Literature and Theology* 12 (1998): 268–93.

Henrich, Dieter. "Der Begriff der Schönheit in Schillers Ästhetik," *Zeitschrift für philosophische Forschung* 11 (1957): 527–47.

Herder, Johann Gottfried. *Plastik*. In *Werke*, 10 vols., vol. 4, 243–326. Frankfurt am Main: Deutscher Klassiker Verlag, 1985–2000.

Higgins, Kathleen. "The Night Song's Answer." *International Studies in Philosophy* 17 (1985): 33–50.

———. "Reading *Zarathustra*." In *Reading Nietzsche*, edited by Robert C. Solomon and Kathleen M. Higgins, 132–51. New York and Oxford: Oxford UP.

———. *Nietzsche's "Zarathustra."* Philadelphia: Temple UP, 1987.

Hill, Ralph, ed. *The Symphony*. Melbourne, London, and Baltimore: Penguin, 1949.

Hinck, Walter. "Man of the Theatre," in Wilkinson, *Goethe Revisited: A Collection of Essays*, 153–69. London: John Calder, 1984.

Hoffmeister, Gerhart, ed. *A Reassessment of Weimar Classicism*. Lewiston, NY, Queenston, ON, and Lampeter, Wales: Edwin Mellen, 1996.

Holland, A. K. "Ludwig van Beethoven (1770–1827)," in Hill, *The Symphony*, 92–125.

Hollinrake, Roger. *Nietzsche, Wagner, and the Philosophy of Pessimism*. London: George Allen and Unwin, 1982.

Hörisch, Jochen. "'Ein höherer Grad von Folter': Die Weimarer Klassik im Lichte früh romantischer Kritik." In Simm, *Literarische Klassik*, 410–20.

Houlgate, Stephen. *Hegel, Nietzsche and the Criticism of Metaphysics*. Cambridge: Cambridge UP, 1986.

Huizinga, Johan. *The Waning of the Middle Ages: A Study of the Forms of Life, Thought, and Art in France and the Netherlands in the Fourteenth and Fifteenth Centuries*. Translated by F. Hopman. London: Edward Arnold, 1937.

Irigaray, Luce. *Amante marine: de Friedrich Nietzsche*. Paris: Editions de Minuit, 1980. Translated as *Marine Lover of Friedrich Nietzsche*. New York: Columbia UP, 1991.

———. *je, tu, nous: Toward a Culture of Difference*. Translated by Alison Martin. New York: Routledge, 1993.

———. *Speculum of the Other Woman*. Translated by Gillian C. Gill. Ithaca: Cornell UP, 1985.

James, William. *The Varieties of Religious Experience: A Study in Human Nature*. 1903. Reprint, Glasgow: Collins, 1960.

Jameson, Frederic. *Postmodernism or the Cultural Logic of Late Capitalism*. London: Duke UP, 1991.

Jammes, Christoph, and Helmut Schneider, eds. *Mythologie der Vernunft: Hegels "ältestes Systemprogramm des deutschen Idealismus."* Frankfurt am Main: Suhrkamp, 1984.

Jantz, Harold. *The Mothers in Faust: The Myth of Time and Creativity*. Baltimore: John Hopkins P, 1969.

Janz, Curt Paul. *Friedrich Nietzsche: Biographie,* 3 vols. Munich and Vienna: Carl Hanser, 1978.

Jay, Martin. *The Dialectical Imagination: A History of the Frankfurt School and the Institute of Social Research, 1923–1950*. Boston: Little, Brown and Company, 1973.

Jencks, Charles. *Postmodernism*. New York: Academy Editions, 1987.

Joós, Ernst. *Poetic Truth and Transvaluation in Nietzsche's "Zarathustra": A Hermeneutic Study*. Bern, Frankfurt am Main: Lang, 1987.

Joyce, James. *A Portrait of the Artist as a Young Man*. London: Jonathan Cape, 1930.

Jung, C. G. *Nietzsche's Zarathustra: Notes of the Seminar given in 1934–1939*. Edited by James Jarrett. 2 vols. London: Routledge, 1989.

Juszezak, Joseph. *L'Anthropologie de Hegel à travers la pensée moderne: Marx, Nietzsche, A. Kojève, E. Weil.* Paris: Editions Anthropos, 1977.

Kafka, Franz. *Das Urteil und andere Erzählungen.* Frankfurt am Main: Fischer, 1952.

Kant, Immanuel. *The Critique of Judgement.* Translated by James Creed Meredith. Oxford: Clarendon P, 1952.

———. *Kritik der praktischen Vernunft.* Frankfurt am Main: Insel, 1976.

———. *Kritik der Urteilskraft.* Stuttgart: Reclam, 1981.

Kaufmann, Walter. *Nietzsche: Philosopher, Psychologist, Antichrist.* Princeton, NJ: Princeton UP, 1968.

Kierkegaard, Søren. *Fear and Trembling.* Translated by Alastair Hanny. Harmondsworth: Penguin, 1985.

Klein, Joe. "Neither here nor there." *The Guardian,* 3 July 2002.

Knight, A. E. J. "Nietzsche and Goethe." *Publications of the English Goethe Society* (NS) 10 (1934): 63–78.

Koch, Franz. *Geist und Leben.* Hamburg: Hanseatische Verlagsanstalt, 1939.

Köhler, Joachim. *Friedrich Nietzsche und Cosima Wagner: Die Schule der Unterwerfung.* Reinbek bei Hamburg: Rowohlt, 1998.

———. *Zarathustras Geheimnis: Friedrich Nietzsche und seine verschlüsselte Botschaft: Eine Biographie.* Reinbek bei Hamburg: Rowohlt, 1992.

Koppe, Franz "Mimetischer Schein, imaginärer Schein, schöner Schein — und was davon bleibt." In Willi Oelmüller, *Ästhetischer Schein,* 126–30.

Kraus, Fritz. "Auf dem Wege zum Übermenschen: Friedrich Nietzsches Verhältnis zu Goethe." *Goethe-Kalendar* 32 (1939): 131–74.

Krell, David Farrell, and Donald L. Bates. *The Good European: Nietzsche's Work Sites in Word and Image.* Chicago and London: U of Chicago P, 1997.

Kriwaczek, Paul. *In Search of Zarathustra: The First Prophet and the Ideas that Changed the World.* London: Weidenfeld and Nicolson, 2002.

Krois, John M. "Urworte: Cassirer als Goethe-Interpret." In *Kulturkritik nach Ernst Cassirer,* edited by Enno Rudolph and Bernd-Olaf Küppers, 297–324. Hamburg: Felix Meiner, 1995.

———. *Cassirer: Symbolic Forms and History.* New Haven: Yale UP, 1987.

———. "Cassirer's 'Prototype and Model' of Symbolism: Its Sources and Significance." *Science in Context* 12 (1991): 531–47.

Krummel, Richard Frank. "Josef Paneth über seine Begegnung mit Nietzsche in der Zarathustra-Zeit." *Nietzsche Studien* 17 (1988): 478–95.

Kühnemund, Richard. "Faust and Zarathustra in our Time." *The Germanic Review* 15 (1940): 116–36.

Kundera, Milan. *The Unbearable Lightness of Being.* Translated by Michael Henry Heim. London and Boston: Faber and Faber, 1985.

Lampert, Laurence. *Nietzsche and Modern Times: A Study of Bacon, Descartes, and Nietzsche.* New Haven and London: Yale UP, 1993.

———. *Nietzsche's Teaching: An Interpretation of "Thus Spoke Zarathustra."* New Haven and London: Yale UP, 1986.

Lange, Victor. *The Classical Age of German Literature 1740–1815.* London: Edward Arnold, 1982.

Langer, Susanne K. *Feeling and Form: A Theory of Art Developed from Philosophy in a New Key.* London: Scribner's, 1953.

———. *Mind: An Essay on Human Feeling.* 3 vols. Baltimore: Johns Hopkins UP, 1967–1970.

———. *Philosophy in a New Key: A Study in the Symbolism of Reason, Rite, and Art.* New York: Mentor Books, 1961.

Larrett, William. "Der Dichtung Schleier: From Theology With Love to Aesthetics." In Magill, Rowley, and Smith, *Tradition and Creation: Essays in Honour of Elizabeth Mary Wilkinson,* 89–100.

Lasson, Georg. *Die Idee and das Ideal.* Leipzig: F. Meiner, 1931.

Lausberg, Heinrich. *Handbuch der literarischen Rhetorik: Eine Grundlegung der Literaturwissenschaft.* 2 vols. 2nd edition. Munich: Max Hueber, 1973.

Leader, Darian. *Stealing the Mona Lisa: What Art Stops Us from Seeing.* London: Faber and Faber, 2002.

Leavis, F. R., ed. *Mill on Bentham and Coleridge.* London: Chatto and Windus, 1950.

Lehrer, Ronald. *Nietzsche's Presence in Freud's Life and Thought: On the Origins of a Psychology of Dynamic Unconscious Mental Functioning.* Albany, NY: State U of New York P, 1995.

Lessing, G. E. *Laocoön: An Essay on the Limits of Painting and Poetry.* Translated by Edward Allen McCormick. Baltimore and London: Johns Hopkins UP, 1984.

Leue, Johannes A. E. "Goethes 'Urworte. Orphisch.'" *Acta Germanica* 2 (1967): 1–10.

Lloyd-Jones, Hugh. "Nietzsche and the Study of the Ancient World." In O'Flaherty, *Studies in Nietzsche and the Classical Tradition,* 1–15.

Lyotard, Jean-François. "Answering the Question: What is Postmodernism?" In *Innovation/Renovation: New Perspectives on the Humanities,* edited by Ihab Habib Hassan and Sally Hassan, 329–41.(Madison, WI: U of Wisconsin P, 1983).

Magill, C. P., Brian A. Rowley, and Christopher J. Smith. *Tradition and Creation: Essays in Honour of Elizabeth Mary Wilkinson* (Leeds: W. S. Maney & Son, 1978).

Mahoney, Dennis F. "Primeval Formation: Teaching *Wilhelm Meisters Lehrjahre* with the Help of Goethe's *Urworte. Orphisch.*" In *Die Goethezeit: Werke—Wirkung—Wechselbeziehungen: Eine Festschrift für Wilfried Malsch,* edited by Jeffrey L. High, 202–14. Göttingen: Verlag von Schwerin, 2001.

Maly, Kenneth. "Translating Heidegger's Works into English: The History and the Possibility." *Heidegger Studies* 16 (2000): 115–38.

Mann, Thomas. *Die Erzählungen.* Frankfurt am Main: Fischer, 1986.

Mansfeld, Jaap, ed. *Die Vorsokratiker.* 2 vols. Stuttgart: Reclam, 1983.

Marcus Aurelius. *Meditations.* Trans. Maxwell Staniforth. Harmondsworth: Penguin, 1964.

Martin, Nicholas. *Nietzsche and Schiller: Untimely Aesthetics.* Oxford: Oxford UP, 1996.

Marx, Karl. *Grundrisse der Kritik der politischen Ökonomie.* Berlin: Akademie Verlag, 1953.

———, and Friedrich Engels. *Werke.* 6 vols. Berlin/DDR: Dietz, 1972.

Mayrhofer, Manfred. "Zu einer Deutung des Zarathustra-Namens in Nietzsches Korrespondenz." In *Beiträge zur Alten Geschichte und deren Nachleben: Festschrift für Franz Altheim zum 6.10.1968,* edited by Ruth Stiehl and Hans Erich Stier, 2:369–74. Berlin: Walter de Gruyter, 1969.

Melville, Herman. *Moby Dick, or The White Whale.* Boston: Page, 1851.

Messer, August. *Erläuterungen zu Nietzsches Zarathustra.* Stuttgart: Strecker & Schröder, 1922.

Meyer, Herman. *Zarte Empirie: Studien zur Literaturgeschichte.* Stuttgart: Metzler, 1963.

Meyer, Theo. *Nietzsche und die Kunst.* Tübingen, Basel: Francke, 1993.

Mill, John Stuart. *Autobiography.* London: Oxford UP, 1971.

Miller, C. A. "Nietzsche's 'Daughters of the Desert': A Reconsideration." *Nietzsche-Studien* 2 (1973): 157–95.

Murray, Chris, and Frank Northen Magill, eds. *The Encyclopaedia of Literary Critics and Criticism.* 2 vols. London and Chicago: Fitzroy Dearborn, 1999.

Nabholz, Johannes. "A Note on the Mothers in Goethe's *Faust.*" *Symposium* 15 (1961): 198–203.

Nagel, Bert. *Kafka und die Weltliteratur: Zusammenhänge und Wechselwirkungen.* Munich: Winkler, 1983.

Nägele, Rainer. "Modernism and Postmodernism: The Margins of Articulation" *Studies in Twentieth-Century Literature* 5 (1980): 5–25.

Naumann, Barbara. *Philosophie und Poetik des Symbols: Cassirer und Goethe.* Munich: Wilhelm Fink, 1998.

Newell, Waller R. "Zarathustra's Dancing Dialectic." *Interpretation* 17 (1990): 415–32.

Nicolai, Heinz. "Die Entwicklung von Nietzsches Goethebild." *Germanisch-Romanische Monatsschrift* 21 (1933): 337–60.

Nietzsche, Friedrich. *Werke in drei Bänden.* Edited by Karl Schlechta. Munich: Hanser, 1966.

Nietzsche, Friedrich, and Franz and Ida Overbeck. *Briefwechsel.* Edited by Katrin Meyer and Barbara von Reibnitz. Stuttgart and Weimar: Metzler, 2000.

Nisbet, H. B., ed. *German Aesthetic and Literary Criticism: Winckelmann, Lessing, Hamann, Herder, Schiller, Goethe.* Cambridge: Cambridge UP, 1985.

Norton, David L. *Personal Destinies: A Philosophy of Ethical Individualism.* Princeton, NJ: Princeton UP, 1976.

Oelmüller, Willi, ed. *Ästhetischer Schein.* Paderborn, Munich, Vienna, Zurich: Ferdinand Schöningh, 1982.

O'Flaherty, James C., Timothy F. Sellner, and Robert M. Helm, eds. *Studies in Nietzsche and the Classical Tradition.* Chapel Hill, NC: U of North Carolina P, 1976.

Oppenheimer, Paul. *Rubens: A Portrait.* New York: Cooper Square Press, 2002.

Parkes, Graham. *Composing the Soul: Reaches of Nietzsche's Psychology.* Chicago and London: U of Chicago P, 1994.

Paronis, Margot. *"Also sprach Zarathustra": Die Ironie Nietzsches als Gestaltungsprinzip.* Bonn: Bouvier, 1976.

Pascal, Roy. *Kafka's Narrators: A Study of his Stories and Sketches.* Cambridge: Cambridge UP, 1982.

Paschek, Carl. *Das Goethe-Bild der Postmoderne 1975–1999 in Büchern und elektronischen Medien: Begleitschrift zur Ausstellung der Stadt- und Universitätsbibliothek zum Goethe-Jubiläum 1999.* Frankfurter Bibliotheksschriften, vol. 7. Frankfurt am Main: Vittorio Klostermann, 1999.

Pasley, Malcolm, ed. *Nietzsche: Imagery and Thought.* London: Methuen, 1978.

Perkins, Richard. "Nietzsche's *opus alchymicum.*" *Seminar* 23 (1987): 216–26.

Petsch, Robert. *Gehalt und Form: Abhandlungen zur Literaturwissenschaft und zur allgemeinen Geistesgeschichte.* Dortmund: Ruhfus, 1925.

Pfeiffer, Arthur. "Die Rollen des Zarathustra (Die Frage nach dem Ur-Zarathustra und seinen Problemen)." *Deutsches Vierteljahrsschrift für Literaturwissenschaft und Geistesgeschichte* 18 (1940): 61–111.

Pieper, Annemarie. *"Ein Seil geknüpft zwischen Mensch und Übermensch":* *Philosophische Erläuterungen zu Nietzsches erstem "Zarathustra."* Stuttgart: Klett-Cotta, 1990.

Plato. *Phaedrus and the Seventh and Eighth Letters.* Translated by Walter Hamilton. Harmondsworth: Penguin, 1973.

———. *The Republic.* Translated by Desmond Lee. 2nd edition. Harmondsworth: Penguin, 1974.

———. *The Symposium.* Translated by Christopher Gill. Harmondsworth: Penguin, 1949.

Platt, Michael. "What does Zarathustra Whisper in Life's Ear?" *Nietzsche-Studien* 17 (1988): 179–94.

Plotinus. *The Six Enneads.* Translated by Stephen Mackenna, revised by B. S. Page. 4th edition. London: Faber and Faber, 1969.

Politycki, Matthias. *Der frühe Nietzsche und die deutsche Klassik: Studien zu Problemen literarischer Wertung.* Straubing, Munich: Dornau, 1981.

Politzer, Heinz. *Franz Kafka: Parable and Paradox.* 2nd edition. Ithaca: Cornell UP, 1966.

Porter, James I. *The Invention of Dionysus: An Essay on "The Birth of Tragedy."* Stanford, CA: Stanford UP, 2000.

Portoghesi, Paolo. *Postmodern.* New York: Rizzoli, 1983.

Price, Lucien. *The Dialogues of Alfred North Whitehead.* Boston: Little, Brown & Company, 1954.

Proust, Marcel. *À la recherche du temps perdu.* 3 vols. Paris: Gallimard, 1954.

Pugh, David. Review of Nicholas Martin, *Nietzsche and Schiller. The Modern Language Review* 93 (1998): 1167–69.

Quincey, Thomas De. *Confessions of an English Opium-Eater.* Edited by Malcolm Elwin. London: Macdonald, 1956.

Raphael, Alice. *Goethe and the Philosopher's Stone.* London: Routledge & Kegan Paul, 1965.

Recki, Birgit. "'Artisten-Metaphysik' und ästhetisches Ethos: Friedrich Nietzsche über Ästhetik und Ethik." In *Falsche Gegensätze: Zeitgenössische Positionen zur philosophischen Ästhetik,* edited by Andrea Kern and Ruth Sonderegger, 262–85. Frankfurt am Main: Suhrkamp, 2002.

Reed, T. J. *The Classical Centre: Goethe and Weimar 1775–1832.* London: Croom Helm, 1980.

Rehder, Helmut. "The Reluctant Disciple: Nietzsche and Schiller." In O'Flaherty, Sellner, and Helm, eds., *Studies in Nietzsche and the Classical Tradition,* 156–64.

Reibnitz, Barbara von. *Ein Kommentar zu Friedrich Nietzsche, »Die Geburt der Tragödie aus dem Geiste der Musik« (Kap.1–12)*. Stuttgart and Weimar: Metzler, 1992.

Reiss, Hans. "Nietzsches 'Geburt der Tragödie': Eine kritische Würdigung." *Zeitschrift für deutsche Philologie* 92 (1973): 481–511.

Rethy, Robert. "The Tragic Affirmation of the 'Birth of Tragedy.'" *Nietzsche-Studien* 17 (1988): 1–44.

Rippere, Vicky. *Schiller and "Alienation,"* Bern: Peter Lang, 1981.

Ritter, Joachim, and Karlfried Gründer, eds. *Historisches Wörterbuch der Philosophie*. 9 vols. Basel: Schwabe, 1971–95.

Roberts, Julian. *German Philosophy: An Introduction*. Cambridge: Polity, 1988.

Robinson, Heidi. "Der gesellschaftsfeindliche 'innere' bzw. 'ganze Mensch': Mißdeutungen in der englischen Rezeption und Überlieferung von Schillers Kulturtheorie." *Arcadia* 15 (1980): 129–48.

———. "The Growth of a Myth: An Examination of English Responses to Schiller's Theory of Culture." Diss., University of London, 1981.

Roehr, Sabine. "Freedom and Autonomy in Schiller." *Journal of the History of Ideas* 64 (2003): 119–34.

Rose, Ernst. "Goethes 'Chorus Mysticus' als Anregung für Nietzsche und Rilke." *The Germanic Review* 17 (1942): 39–47.

Rosen, Stanley. *The Mask of Enlightenment: Nietzsche's Zarathustra*. Cambridge: Cambridge UP, 1995.

Roth, Robin Alice. "Answer to 'The Night Song's Answer.'" *International Studies in Philosophy* 17 (1985): 51–54.

Saviene, Renato. *Il Bello: Il Dionisiaco: Schiller: Nietzsche*. Florence: Olschki, 1995.

Schaper, Eva. "Friedrich Schiller: Adventures of a Kantian." *British Journal of Aesthetics* 4 (1964): 348–62.

———. "Schiller's Kant: A Chapter in the History of Creative Misunderstanding." In *Studies in Kant's Aesthetics*.

———. *Studies in Kant's Aesthetics*. Edinburgh: Edinburgh UP, 1979.

Schapiro, Meyer. "The Still Life as Personal Object — A note on Heidegger and Van Gogh." In *The Reach of Mind: Essays in Memory of Kurt Goldstein,* edited by Marianne L. Simmel, 203–9. New York: Springer, 1968.

Schiller, Friedrich. *On the Aesthetic Education of Man in a Series of Letters*. Edited and translated by Elizabeth M. Wilkinson and L. A. Willoughby. With Introduction, Commentary, and Glossary of Terms. 2nd edition. Oxford: Clarendon P, 1982.

————. *On the Naïve and Sentimental in Literature*. Translated by Helen Watanabe-O'Kelly. Manchester: Carcarnet New P, 1981.

Schlechta, Karl. "The German 'Classicist' Goethe as Reflected in Nietzsche's Works," in O'Flaherty, *Studies in Nietzsche and the Classical Tradition*, 144–55.

————. *Der junge Nietzsche und das klassische Altertum*. Mainz: Kupferberg, 1948.

Schlegel, Friedrich. *Kritische Friedrich Schlegel Ausgabe*. Edited by Ernst Behler. 19 vols. Munich, Paderborn, and Vienna: Schöningh, 1961–71.

Schopenhauer, Arthur. *Werke in fünf Bänden*, edited by Ludger Lütkehaus. Zurich: Haffmanns Verlag, 1988–99.

Schwerte, Hans. *Faust und das Faustische: Ein Kapitel deutscher Ideologie*. Stuttgart: Klett, 1962.

Shaffer, Elinor. *"Kubla Khan" and the Fall of Jerusalem*. Cambridge: Cambridge UP, 1975.

Shapiro, Gary. "How One Becomes What One Is Not." In *Nietzschean Narratives*, 142–75.

————. *Nietzschean Narratives*. Bloomington and Indianapolis: Indiana UP, 1989.

————. "The Writing on the Wall: *The Antichrist* and the Semiotics of History." In *Reading Nietzsche*, edited by Robert C. Solomon and Kathleen M. Higgins, 192–217. New York and Oxford: Oxford UP, 1988.

Sheppard, Richard. "Two Liberals: A Comparison of the Humanism of Matthew Arnold and Wilhelm von Humboldt." *German Life and Letters* 24 (1971): 219–33.

Silk, M. S., and J. P. Stern. *Nietzsche on Tragedy*. Cambridge: Cambridge UP, 1981.

Simm, Hans-Joachim, ed. *Literarische Klassik*. Frankfurt am Main: Suhrkamp, 1988.

Simmel, Georg. *Schopenhauer und Nietzsche*. Leipzig: Duncker & Humbolt, 1907. Translated as *Schopenhauer and Nietzsche* by Helmut Loiskandl, Deena Weinstein, and Michael Weinstein (Urbana and Chicago: U of Illinois P, 1991).

Simpson, David, ed. *German Aesthetic and Literary Criticism: Kant, Fichte, Schelling, Schopenhauer, Hegel*. Cambridge: Cambridge UP, 1984.

Simpson, James. *Matthew Arnold and Goethe*. Liverpool: Liverpool UP, 1979.

Siskin, Clifford. *Historicity of Romantic Discourse*. New York and London: Oxford UP, 1988.

Sloterdijk, Peter. *Der Denker auf der Bühne: Nietzsches Materialismus.* Frankfurt am Main: Suhrkamp, 1986; Translated as *Thinker on Stage: Nietzsche's Materialism* by Jamie Owen Daniel. Minneapolis: U of Minnesota P, 1989.

Smith, Philip. *Cultural Theory: An Introduction.* Oxford: Blackwell, 2001.

Solomon, Robert C. and Kathleen M. Higgins, eds. *Reading Nietzsche.* New York and Oxford: Oxford UP.

Spinoza, Benedict de. *On the Improvement of the Understanding/The Ethics/Correspondence.* Translated by R. H. M. Elwes. New York: Dover, 1955.

Sprinker, Michael. "Poetics and Music: Hopkins and Nietzsche." *Comparative Literature* 37 (1985): 334–56.

St. Augustine. *Confessions.* Translated by R. S. Pine-Coffin. Harmondsworth: Penguin, 1961.

———. *On Christian Teaching.* Translated with an introduction and notes by R. P. H. Green. Oxford: Oxford University Press, 1997.

———. *Concerning the City of God against the Pagans.* A new translation from the Latin by Henry Bettenson; with an introduction by David Knowles. Harmondsworth: Penguin, 1972.

Staiger, Emil. *Goethe.* 3 vols. Zürich: Atlantis, 1970.

Stanton, Donna C. *The Aristocrat as Art: A Study of the 'Honnête Homme' and the Dandy in Seventeenth- and Nineteenth-Century French Literature.* New York: Columbia UP, 1980.

Staten, Henry. "*The Birth of Tragedy* Reconstructed." *Studies in Romanticism* 29 (1990): 9–37.

Stausberg, Michael. *Faszination Zarathustra: Zoroaster und die europäische Religionsgeschichte der frühen Neuzeit.* 2 vols. Berlin: Walter de Gruyter, 1998.

Steinbuch, Thomas. *A Commentary on Nietzsche's* Ecce Homo. Lanham, New York, London: UP of America, 1994.

Stendhal. *De l'Amour.* Paris: Garnier-Flammarion, 1965; Translated as *Love,* by Gilbert and Suzanne Sale. Harmondsworth: Penguin, 1975.

Stephenson, R. H. "The Cultural Theory of Weimar Classicism in the Light of Coleridge's Doctrine of Aesthetic Knowledge." In *Goethe 2000: Intercultural Readings of his Work,* edited by Paul Bishop and R. H. Stephenson, 149–69. Leeds: Northern UP, 2000.

———. "The Diachronic Solidity of Goethe's *Faust.*" In Bishop, *A Companion to Goethe's "Faust": Parts I and II.*

———. *Goethe's Conception of Knowledge and Science.* Edinburgh: Edinburgh UP, 1995.

———. "Goethe's 'Sprüche in Reimen': A Reconsideration." *Publications of the English Goethe Society* 49 (1976): 102–30.

————. *Goethe's Wisdom Literature*. Bern, Frankfurt an Main and New York: Peter Lang, 1983.

————. "'Ein künstlicher Vortrag': Die symbolische Form von Goethes naturwissenschaftlichen Schriften." In *Cassirer und Goethe: Neue Aspekte einer philosophisch-literarischen Wahlverwandtschaft,* edited by Barbara Naumann and Birgit Recki. Berlin: Akademie Verlag, 2002.

————. "On the Function of a Delphic Ambiguity in Goethe's 'Urworte. Orphisch' and Kafka's 'Ein Hungerkünstler.'" *Quinquereme* 10 (1987): 165–79.

————. "The Political Import of Goethe's *Reineke Fuchs.*" In *Reynard the Fox: Cultural Metamorphoses and Social Engagement in the Beast Epic from the Middle Ages to the Present,* edited by Kenneth Varty, 191–207. 2nd edition. Oxford: Berghahn, 2003.

————. "Theorizing to Some Purpose: 'Deconstruction' in the Light of Goethe and Schiller's Aesthetics — the Case of *Die Wahlverwandtschaften.*" *The Modern Language Review* 84 (1989): 381–92.

————. "Weimar Classicism's Debt to the Scottish Enlightenment." In *Goethe and the English-Speaking World,* edited by Nicholas Boyle and John Guthrie, 61–70. Rochester, NY, and Woodbridge, UK: Camden House, 2002.

————. "'Eine zarte Differenz': Cassirer on Goethe on the Symbol." In *Symbolic Forms and Cultural Studies: Ernst Cassirer's Theory of Culture,* edited by Cyrus Hamlin and John M. Krois. New Haven: Yale UP, forthcoming.

————, and Patricia D. Zecevic. "Goethe and the Divine Feminine in the Light of the Spanish Kabbalah." *Quaderni di Lingue e Litterature Straniere* 12 (2003): 299–333.

Stern, J. P. *A Study of Nietzsche*. Cambridge: Cambridge UP, 1979.

Stern, Robert A. M. *Modern Classicism*. London: Thames and Hudson, 1988.

Stierle, Karlheinz. "Bemerkungen zur Geschichte des schönen Scheins." In Willi Oelmüller, *Ästhetischer Schein,* 208–32.

Stokes, Adrian. *Inside Out: An Essay in the Psychology and Aesthetic Appeal of Space*. Harmondsworth: Pelican, 1947.

Storr, Anthony. *The School of Genius*. London: André Deutsch, 1988.

Swales, Erika. "Johann Wolfgang von Goethe, 'Urworte. Orphisch.'" In *Landmarks in German Poetry,* edited by Peter Hutchinson, 57–71. Oxford: Lang, 2000.

Sychrava, Juliet. *Schiller to Derrida: Idealism in Aesthetics*. New York: Cambridge UP, 1989.

Tatarkiewicz, Wladyslaw. *A History of Six Ideas: An Essay in Aesthetics*. The Hague: Martinus Nijhoff, 1980.

Thatcher, David. "Eagle and Serpent in *Zarathustra*." *Nietzsche-Studien* 6 (1977): 240–60.

Trilling, Lionel. *Sincerity and Authenticity*. London: Oxford UP, 1972.

Turk, Horst. "Nietzsches 'Geburt der Tragödie' und die Rettung des Apollinischen." In *Das Subjekt der Dichtung: Festschrift für Gerhard Kaiser*, edited by Gerhard Buhr and Friedrich A. Kittler, 17–29. Würzburg: Königshausen & Neumann, 1990.

Turner, Frederick. *Natural Classicism: Essays on Literature and Science*. New York: Paragon House, 1985.

Vaget, Hans-Rudolf. *Dilettantismus und Meisterschaft: Zum Problem des Dilettantismus bei Goethe: Praxis, Theorie, Zeitkritik*. Munich: Winkler, 1971.

Van der Laan, James M. "Die Faustfigur bei Goethe und Nietzsche im Hinblick auf die Postmoderne." *Euphorion* 88 (1994): 458–67.

Veblen, Thorsten. *The Portable Veblen*. Edited by Max Lerner. New York: Viking P, 1948.

Volkmann-Schluch, K.-H. "Die Stufen der Selbstüberwindung des Lebens (Erläuterungen zum 3. Teil von Nietzsches Zarathustra)." *Nietzsche-Studien* 2 (1973): 137–56.

Von der Leyen, Friedrich. "Friedrich Nietzsche: Die Sprache des 'Zarathustra.'" *Literaturwissenschaftliches Jahrbuch* 3 (1962): 209–38.

Vosskamp, Wilhelm. "Klassik als Epoche. Zur Typologie und Funktion der Weimarer Klassik." In Simm, *Literarische Klassik*, 248–77.

———, ed. *Klassik im Vergleich: Normativität und Historizität europäischer Klassiken*. Stuttgart and Weimar: Metzler, 1993.

Wagenbach, Klaus. *Franz Kafka: Eine Biographie seiner Jugend 1883–1912*. Bern: Francke, 1958.

Wahl, Georg Moritz. "Zum Schlüssel in der Mütterszene." *Euphorion* 21 (1914): 294–97.

Waite, Geoff. *Nietzsche's Corpse: Aesthetics. Politics. Prophecy: or, The Spectacular Technoculture of Everyday Life*. Durham and London: Duke UP, 1996.

Waldeck, Marie-Luise. "Further Thoughts on the Genesis of a Key Concept in Schiller's Aesthetic Thinking." *Forum for Modern Language Studies* 12 (1976): 304–13.

———. "Shadows, Reflexions, Mirror-Images and Virtual 'Objects' in 'Die Künstler' and their Relation to Schiller's Concept of 'Schein.'" *The Modern Language Review* 58 (1963): 33–37.

Weichelt, Hans. *Zarathustra-Kommentar*. 2nd edition. Leipzig: Felix Meiner, 1922.

Wellek, René. *History of Modern Criticism: 1750–1950.* 8 vols. New Haven: Yale UP, 1955–1992.

Whitehead, Alfred North. *Adventures of Ideas.* New York: The Free P, 1961.

———. *Process and Reality: An Essay in Cosmology.* Corrected edition by David Ray Griffin and Donald W. Sherburne. New York: The Free P, 1978.

———. *Religion in the Making.* New York: Fordham UP, 1999.

Whitlock, Greg. *Returning to Sils-Maria: A Commentary to Nietzsche's "Also sprach Zarathustra."* New York, Frankfurt am Main: Lang, 1990.

Wilkinson, Elizabeth M. "'Form' and 'Content' in the Aesthetics of German Classicism." In *Stil- und Formprobleme in der Literatur: Vorträge des VII. Kongresses der Internationalen Vereinigung für moderne Sprachen und Literaturen in Heidelberg, August 1957,* edited by Paul Böckmann, 18–27. Heidelberg: C. Winter, 1959. 18–27.

———. "Schiller's Concept of *Schein* in the Light of Recent Aesthetics." *The German Quarterly* 28 (1955): 219–27.

———, ed. *Goethe Revisited: A Collection of Essays.* London: John Calder, 1984.

——— and L. A. Willoughby. "The Blind Man and the Poet: An Early Stage in Goethe's Quest for Form" [1962] In *Models of Wholeness: Some Attitudes to Language, Art and Life in the Age of Goethe,* 91–125.

———. "Missing Links or Whatever Happened to Weimar Classicism?" In *Erfahrung und Überlieferung: Festschrift for C. P. Magill,* edited by Hinrich Siefken and Alan Robinson, 57–74. Cardiff: Trivium Special Publications, 1974.

———. *Models of Wholeness: Some Attitudes to Language, Arts and Life in the Age of Goethe,* edited by Jeremy Adler, Martin Swales, and Ann Weaver. Oxford, Bern, Berlin: Peter Lang, 2002.

———. "'The Whole Man' in Schiller's Theory of Culture and Society" [1969], in *Models of Wholeness: Some Attitudes to Language, Art and Life in the Age of Goethe,* 233–68.

Williams, John R. "The Problem of the Mothers." In Bishop, *A Companion to Goethe's "Faust,"* 122–43.

Willoughby, L. A. *The Classical Age of German Literature, 1748–1805.* New York: Russell and Russell, 1966.

———. "Oscar Wilde and Goethe." In Elizabeth M. Wilkinson and L. A. Willoughby, *Models of Wholeness: Some Attitudes to Language, Art and Life in the Age of Goethe,* 195–226.

Wilson, Robert R. "Play, Transgression and Carnival: Bakhtin and Derrida on *Scriptor Ludens.*" *Mosaic* 19 (1986): 73–89.

Wissink, Jozef, *The Eternity of the World in the Thought of Thomas Aquinas and his Contemporaries.* Leiden and New York: E. J. Brill, 1990.

Wohlfart, Günter. "Wer ist Nietzsches Zarathustra?" *Nietzsche-Studien* 26 (1997): 319–30.

Wolfe, Peter. "Image and Meaning in 'Also sprach Zarathustra.'" *Modern Language Notes* 79 (1964): 546–52.

Wollheim, Richard. "Art and Illusion." *British Journal of Aesthetics* 3 (1963): 15–37.

Wood, Robert. *Placing Aesthetics: Reflections on the Philosophical Tradition.* Illinois: Ohio UP, 2000.

Woolf, Virginia. *To the Lighthouse.* Harmondsworth: Penguin, 1992.

Young, Julian. *Nietzsche's Philosophy of the Arts.* Cambridge: Cambridge UP, 1992.

Zecevic, Patricia D. *The Speaking Divine Woman: López de Úbeda's "La pícara Justina" and Goethe's "Wilhelm Meister."* Oxford: Peter Lang, 2001.

Zelle, Carsten. *Die doppelte Ästhetik der Moderne: Revisionen des Schönen von Boileau bis Nietzsche.* Stuttgart: Metzler, 1995.

Index

Baudelaire, Charles Pierre, 172
Baudrillard, Jean, 5, 163
Baumgarten, Alexander Gottlieb,
10
Baumgartner, Marie. *See*
Nietzsche, correspondence
beauty, 3, 21 n. 56, 23 n. 94, 28, 29,
30–31, 33, 99, 155, 171, 178,
184 n. 4. *See also* art; Emerson;
Goethe; Hegel; Kant; Schiller;
Weimar Classicism
and aesthetics, 107–8
as freedom, 30, 152
and nature, 92 n. 31
Platonic, 162, 167, 233 n. 8
Beethoven, Ninth Symphony, 72,
90 n. 20
Being and Becoming, 136 n. 22
Benjamin, Walter, 10, 179
Beyle, Henri. *See* Stendhal
Bible, the, 151
"binary synthesis," 2, 10, 21 n.
66, 33–34, 35, 59 n. 38, 85. *See
also* Nietzsche, and
Boethius, 95 n. 45
Boileau, 194 n. 131
Breton, André, 156
Bullough, Edward, 186 n. 25
Burckhardt, Carl, 64
Burckhardt, Jacob, 63, 205, 222.
See also Nietzsche,
correspondence
Burne-Jones, Edward, 166

Carlyle, Thomas, works by:
Life of Schiller, 165, 168
*On Heroes, Hero-Worship and
the Heroic in History,* 191 n.
94
Cassirer, Ernst:
and Goethe, 180–82
theory of symbolism, 181–82
Cassirer, Ernst, works by:
Freiheit und Form, 182

"Goethe's Intellectual
Achievement," 181
Cervantes, works by:
Don Quixote, 152
Cézanne, Paul, 5
chaos, 72, 145 n. 52, 183
child at play, symbol of. *See*
Nietzsche, imagery in writing
chorus, the, 27, 44, 46, 53 n. 11,
61 n. 44
classicism/romanticism, 6–16. *See
also* Weimar Classicism
Coleridge, Samuel Taylor, 5, 169
influence of, 165–66
and Schiller, 165, 170
Coleridge, Samuel Taylor, works
by:
Biographia Literaria, 170
*On the Constitution of Church
and State,* 165
Colli, Giorgio, and Mazzino
Montinari, 71, 76
Conrad, Joseph, works by:
Heart of Darkness, 162
creativity, 129, 191
Creuzer, Georg Friedrich, works
by: *Die Symbolik und Mythologie
der alten Völker, besonders der
Griechen,* 71
Critical Theory, 178–79
culture, 178, 183

dance, 24, 45, 85–86, 127–28
Dante, 77
Dante, works by: *Purgatory,* 11
Danto, Arthur, 16 n. 5
de Man, Paul, works by: *The
Rhetoric of Romanticism,* 6, 10
De Quincey, Thomas, works by:
Suspiria de Profundis, 170
de Staël, Madame, 7
de Staël, Madame, works by:
De l'Allemagne, 164–65
Derrida, Jacques, 163
desire, 7, 13, 76, 88

Index prepared by Andrea Bevan